THE KORAN

الْقُرْآن

SAINT GAUDENS MODERN ENGLISH VERSION

THE KORAN
القرآن

SAINT GAUDENS MODERN ENGLISH VERSION

Edited by
Kevin E. Ready

SAINT GAUDENS PRESS
Wichita, Kansas & Santa Barbara, California

See other great books available from Saint Gaudens Press
http://www.SaintGaudensPress.com

Saint Gaudens Press
Post Office Box 405
Santa Barbara, CA 93464-0405

Saint Gaudens, Saint Gaudens Press
and the Winged Liberty colophon
are trademarks of Saint Gaudens Press

This edition Copyright © 2016 Kevin E. Ready
All rights reserved.

Print edition ISBN: 978-0-943039-32-9
eBook ISBN: 978-0-943039-07-7
Library of Congress Catalog Number - 2016944132
Printed in the United States of America

In accordance with the Copyright Act of 1976 [PL 94-553; 90 Stat. 2541] and the Digital Millennium Copyright Act of 1998 (DMCA) [PL 105-304; 112 Stat. 2860], the scanning, uploading, or electronic sharing of any part of this book without the permission of the publisher constitutes unlawful piracy and theft of the author's intellectual property. If you wish to use material from this book (other than for review purposes), prior written permission must be obtained by contacting the publisher at: editorial@saintgaudenspress.com. Thank you for your support of the author's rights.

القرآن

Chapters

Editor's Note	viii
Chapter 1 — Al-Fatihah — The Opening	1
Chapter 2 — Al-Baqarah — The Cow	2
Chapter 3 — Al-Imran — The Family of Imran	20
Chapter 4 — Al-Nisa — The Women	31
Chapter 5 — Al-Ma'idah — The Dinner Table	43
Chapter 6 — Al-An'am — The Cattle	52
Chapter 7 — Al-A'raf — The Elevated Places	62
Chapter 8 — Al-Anfal — The Accessions	73
Chapter 9 — Al-Taubah — The Immunity	77
Chapter 10 — Yunus — Jonah	85
Chapter 11 — Hud — The Holy Prophet	91
Chapter 12 — Yusuf — Joseph	97
Chapter 13 — Al-Ra'd — The Thunder	103
Chapter 14 — Ibrahim — Abraham	106
Chapter 15 — Al-Hijr — The Rock	109
Chapter 16 — Al-Nahl — The Bee	112
Chapter 17 — Bani Israil — The Children of Israel	118
Chapter 18 — Al-Kahf — The Cave	124
Chapter 19 — Maryam — Mary	130
Chapter 20 — Ta Ha — Ta Ha	134
Chapter 21 — Al-Anbiya — The Prophets	139
Chapter 22 — Al-Hajj — The Pilgrimage	143
Chapter 23 — Al-Mu'minun — The Believers	148
Chapter 24 — Al-Nur — The Light	152
Chapter 25 — Al-Furqan — The Differentiation	156
Chapter 26 — Al-Shu'ara — The Poets	160
Chapter 27 — Al-Naml — The Ant	166
Chapter 28 — Al-Qasas — The Narratives	170
Chapter 29 — Al-Ankabut — The Spider	177
Chapter 30 — Al-Rum — The Romans	181
Chapter 31 — Luqman — Luqman	184
Chapter 32 — Al-Sajdah — The Adoration	186
Chapter 33 — Al-Ahzab — The Clans	188

Chapter 34 — Al-Saba — Sheba	193
Chapter 35 — Al-Fatir — The Founder	196
Chapter 36 — Ya Sin — Ya Sin	199
Chapter 37 — Al-Saffat — The Rangers	202
Chapter 38 — Saad — Saad	207
Chapter 39 — Al-Zumar — The Companions	210
Chapter 40 — Al-Mu'min — The Believer	214
Chapter 41 — Ha Mim Sajda/Fusilaat — Distinct Verses	218
Chapter 42 — Al-Shura — The Consultation	221
Chapter 43 — Al-Zhukruf — Ornaments of Gold	224
Chapter 44 — Al-Dukhan — The Smoke	228
Chapter 45 — Al-Jathiyah — The Kneeling	230
Chapter 46 — Al-Ahqaf — The Sand Dunes	232
Chapter 47 — Muhammad — Mohammed	234
Chapter 48 — Al-Fath — The Victory/Triumph	236
Chapter 49 — Al-Hujurat — The Chambers/Rooms	238
Chapter 50 — Al-Qaf — Qaf	240
Chapter 51 — Al-Dhariyat — The Scatterering Winds	242
Chapter 52 — Al-Tur — The Mountain	244
Chapter 53 — Al-Najm — The Star	246
Chapter 54 — Al-Qamar — The Moon	248
Chapter 55 — Al-Rahman — The Kind	250
Chapter 56 — Al-Waqi'ah — The Event	252
Chapter 57 — Al-Hadid — The Iron	255
Chapter 58 — Al-Mujadilah — She Who Pleaded	257
Chapter 59 — Al-Hashr — The Banishment	259
Chapter 60 — Al-Mumtahhanah — She Who is Examined	261
Chapter 61 — Al-Saff — The Ranks	263
Chapter 62 — Al-Jumu'ah — The Congregation	264
Chapter 63 — Al-Munafiqun — The Hypocrites	265
Chapter 64 — Al-Taghabun — The Mutual Deceit	266
Chapter 65 — Al-Talaq — The Divorce	267
Chapter 66 — Al- Tahrim — The Prohibition	268
Chapter 67 — Al-Mulak — The Kingdom	269
Chapter 68 — Al-Qalam — The Pen	271
Chapter 69 — Al-Haqqah — The Inevitable	273

Chapter 70 — Al-Mu'arij — The Ways of Ascent	275
Chapter 71 — Nuh — Noah	277
Chapter 72 — Al-Jinn — The Jinn	278
Chapter 73 — Al-Muzzammil — The Wrapped Up	280
Chapter 74 — Al-Mudathir — The Covered One	281
Chapter 75 — Al-Qiyamah — The Resurrection	283
Chapter 76 — Al-Dahr — Time	284
Chapter 77 — Al-Mursulat — Those Sent Forth	285
Chapter78 — Al-Naba' — The Great Event	287
Chapter 79 — Al-Nazi'at — The Draggers	289
Chapter 80 — 'Abasa — He Frowned	291
Chapter 81 — Al-Takwir — The Folded Up	292
Chapter 82 — Al-Infitar — The Rending	293
Chapter 83 — Al-Tatfif — The Measruement Cheaters	294
Chapter 84 — Al-Inshiqaq — The Tearing Apart	295
Chapter 85 — Al-Buruj — The Celestial Stations	296
Chapter 86 — Al-Tariq — The Nightly Visitor	297
Chapter 87 — Al-A'la — The Most High	298
Chapter 88 — Al-Ghashiyah — The Calamity	299
Chapter 89 — Al-Fajr — The Daybreak	300
Chapter 90 — Al-Balad — The City	301
Chapter 91 — Al-Shams — The Sun	302
Chapter 92 — Al-Lail — The Night	303
Chapter 93 — Al-Duha — The Brightness	304
Chapter 94 — Al-Inshirah — The Expansion	305
Chapter 95 — Al-Tin — The Fig	306
Chapter 96 — Al-'Alaq — The Clot	307
Chapter 97 — Al-Qadr — The Grandeur	308
Chapter 98 — Al-Bayyinah — The Clear Evidence	309
Chapter 99 — Al-Zilzal — The Quaking	310
Chapter 100 — Al-'Adiyat — The Chargers	311
Chapter 101 — Al-Qari'ah — The Calamity	312
Chapter 102 — Al-Takathur — Striving in Abundance	313
Chapter 103 — Al-'Asr — The Age	314
Chapter 104 — Al-Humazah — The Slanderer	315
Chapter 105 — Al-Fil — The Elephant	316

Chapter 106 — Al-Quraish — The Quraish Clan 317
Chapter 107 — l-Ma'un — Alms 318
Chapter 108 — Al-Kauthar — The Abundance of Good 319
Chapter 109 — Al-Kafirun — The Unbelievers 320
Chapter 110 — Al-Nasr — The Aid 321
Chapter 111 — Al-Lahab — The Flame 322
Chapter 112 — Al-Ikhlas — The Unity 323
Chapter 113 — Al-Falaq — The Dawn 324
Chapter 114 — Al-Nas — The People 325
Notes 326

Editor's Note

The purpose of this work is to provide the English speaking reader with a easily readable version of the Koran. I have always found it curious that most previous English translations of the Koran adopt a linguistic affectation of the King James Version of the Christian Bible in an attempt to give their edition an affectation of religious or biblical flavor. The archaic sixteenth-century English of King James does a disservice to the Classical Arabic original Koran when read by a modern reader. Other available versions of the Koran in English carry a stilted, imprecise English more appropriate for a Bollywood movie. The words of the Prophet Mohammed and his God should not be in the stilted voice of a Shakespearean era Anglican cleric or a inarticulate English voice. The unnecessarily confusing language of most Koranic translations leads to misunderstanding of basic concepts and difficulty in study by modern English readers. Just as modern, revised versions of the Christian Bible have become a standard for Bible study, it was felt that a more modern version of the Koran would serve Western readers. One thing we have kept from the archaic biblical English format is the capitalization of pronouns referring to God. It seems to give clarity to many massages when the deity is speaking of himself, especially in the Arabic translation, where pronouns are highly repetitive. We also use the first person plural "We" when the deity speaks of himself, since the original Arabic clearly has God speaking of himself in the plural pronoun and verb form. While it remains a tenet of the Muslim faith that study of the Koran should be in the classic Arabic, the reality is that many would-be readers of the Koran have no knowledge of Arabic and little grasp of King James' vernacular and, thus, the need for this work.

Irrespective of our intent to give a modern English voice to the Koran, it must be recognized that Classical Arabic is a lyrical, structured language, quite different from English. And, there are parts of the Koran that are best described as free-form poetry and the form, function and meaning of those passages would be lost if simply translated to prose English. In such sections of the Koran, both the short, lyrical verse and in the lengthy supplications and prayers, we have kept the structure of the original Arabic and translated the words so as to best evoke the original meaning. In other sections, such as stories, instructions, laws and histories, we have adopted a modern, prose paragraph format. We have kept the verse numbering of the original, made the numbering of verses less intrusive on the reading and less conspicuous. We have also followed the predominant method of not numbering the opening supplication in each chapter as a verse. The Surahs have been renamed as Chapters and their title is given in both Arabic and English.

Based both directly on the original Arabic and with reference to other English translations, we have attempted to give a direct meaning to the original in modern English. To this end, we have, to the extent possible, given proper names, locations and religious concepts in Western terminology, rather than in the transliterated Arabic often used for Koran translations. Primary among these is our use of "God" in reference to the Arabic "Allah." It has become somewhat standardized to refer to supreme being of the Muslims as "Allah," whereas the Christian's supreme being is denominated as "God," as though different entities are involved. It is clear that the "Allah" of Mohammed is the same as the Judeao-Christian "God" and the word for "god" in Arabic is simply "allah," so any handling of the Koran that continues the misunderstanding that the two are not the same is inappropriate. Thus, our work calls God "God," not "Allah." Likewise, Jesus, Moses, David and other persons and names are used in the form familiar to the Western reader, not the transliterated Arabic form most often used in earlier translations. For example, when Mohammed speaks of the "People of the Book" as being Muslims, Christian, Jews and Sabians, we translate Sabian as Copt, -- Saba, being the ancient Sheba, or Ehtiopia, home of the Coptic branch of Christianity.

While we try to use the appropriate English word or name for its Arabic equivalent, there are some terms that are only properly used in a transliteration of the Arabic word and for this we have tried to use standard Arabic/English transliteration, but recognized that some words are expected to be used in the commonly expected form. For example, contrary to sightings of Arabic names and places in the news media, there is no "E" or "O" in Arabic, only long and short forms of "A," "I", "U." For the voiced glottal stop consonant we use an apostrophe, for the Kaa the letter "K," and for Qaaf the letter "Q." Also; to fulfill our purpose of making this Koran useful to the Western reader, we have bowed to the common Western naming as the "Koran," rather than the philologically correct "Qur'an." Another terms we have chosen to retain in the original Arabic are "Qibla:" the direction of proper prayer, oriented toward Mecca, but in the early years of Islam, toward Jerusalem.

Kevin E. Ready, Sr.
Editor

Acknowledgements

The Editor would like to thank Professors Sayed Sa'id and Ed Mary (aka Abdul Messikh ibn Maryam), his Arabic instructors who can take the blame for setting him down this path. He would also like to thank Yusif Muhsaan, who was kind enough to render opinions and advice as needed in the course of this work.

Chapter 1 — Al-Fatihah — The Opening

In the name of God, the Kind, the Merciful.
1. All praise is due to God, the Lord of the Worlds
2. The Kind, the Merciful, the
3. Master of the Day of Judgment.
4. You do we serve and You do we seek out for assistance.
5. Keep us on the right path.
6. The path of those upon whom You have given favors. May we not be on the path of those upon whom Your displeasure is brought down, nor of those who are lost.

Chapter 2 — Al-Baqarah — The Cow

In the name of God, the Kind, the Merciful.

1. Aliph. Lam. Mim. (I am God who knows all)
2. This Book, there is no doubt of it, is a guide to those who guard against evil.
3. Those who believe in the unseen and keep up prayer and give in return that which we have given them.
4. And those who believe in that which has been revealed to you and that which was revealed before you and they are sure of the hereafter.
5. These are on a right course from their Lord and it is these who shall be successful.
6. For those who disbelieve, it makes no difference whether you warn them, or do not warn them, for they will not believe.
7. God has set a lock upon their hearts and upon their hearing and there is a covering over their eyes, and there will be a great punishment in store for them.
8. And there are some people who say, "We believe in God and the last day;" but they are not at all believers.
9. They desire to deceive God and those who believe, and they deceive only themselves, but they do not realize it.
10. There is a disease in their hearts, so God added to their disease and they shall have a painful punishment for their lies.
11. And when it is said to them, "Do not make disorder on the earth," they say, "We are but peace-makers."
12. Now certainly they themselves are the cause of disorder, but they do not recognize this.
13. And when it is said to them, "Believe as the people believe," they say, "Shall we believe as the fools believe?" Now, certainly they, themselves, are the fools, but they do not know this.
14. And when they meet those who believe, they say, "We believe;" and when they are alone with their conspirators, they say, "Certainly we are with you, we were only joking."
15. God shall pay them back for their frivolity, and He shall leave them alone in their chaos, blindly wandering on.
16. There are those who accept error instead of guidance, so their bargain shall bring no profit, nor are they the followers of the right direction.
17. Their story is like the story of one who kindled a fire but when it had illuminated all around him, God took away their light, and left them in utter darkness -- they do not see.
18. Deaf, dumb and blind, they cannot return to the path.
19. Or like the rain laden cloud in which is utter darkness and thunder and lightning; they put their fingers into their ears because of the thunder peal, for fear of death, and God surrounds the unbelievers.
20. The lightning almost takes away their sight; whenever it flashes for them they walk in the light, and when it becomes dark to them they stand still; and if God had cared to He would certainly have taken away their hearing and their sight; certainly God has power over all things.
21. Oh men! Serve your Lord Who created you and your ancestors so that you may guard against evil.
22. Who made the earth a resting place for you and the heaven a canopy and Who sends down rain from the cloud then brings forth from it fruits as subsistence for you; therefore do not set

up rivals to God while you know.

²³· And if you are in doubt as to that which We have revealed to Our servant, then take a chapter like this and call on your helpers besides God if you are truthful.

²⁴· But if you do not do ii and if you never shall do it, then be on your guard against the fire of which men and the earth shall be the fuel; which is prepared for the unbelievers.

²⁵· And convey good news to those who believe and do good deeds, that they shall have gardens in which rivers flow; whenever they shall be given a portion of the fruit thereof, they shall say, "This is what was given to us before;" and similar gifts shal be brought to them, and they shall have pure mates in the gardens, and in them, they shall abide."

²⁶· God is certainly not ashamed to give an example -- that of a mosquito or anything above that; then as for those who believe, they know that it is the truth from their Lord, and as for those who disbelieve, they say, "What is it that God means by this story: He causes many to err by it and many He leads to the right with it!" But God allows only the transgressors to be in error.

²⁷. The losers are those who break the covenant of God after its confirmation and tear apart what God has ordered to be joined, and cause disorder in the land.

²⁸· How can you deny God for you were dead and He gave you life? Once again, He will cause you to die and will again bring you to life, then you shall be brought back to Him.

²⁹. It is He Who created for you all that is in the earth, and He turned his attention to heaven, and He made them complete as seven heavens, and He knows all things.

³⁰. And when your Lord said to the angels, "I am going to place in the earth a king." They said, "What? Will You place on earth those who would cause disorder and shed blood, and we glorify you and proclaim Your holiness?" He said, "You see, I know something you do not know."

³¹. And He taught Adam the names of all things, afterward God presented these things to the angels. And then He said to the angels, "Tell me the names of those if you think are right."

³². They said, "Glory be to You! We have no knowledge but that which You have taught us. Certainly You are the Knowing, the Wise."

³³. God said, "Oh Adam! Inform the angels of the names." Then when he had informed them of the names, God said, "Did I not say to you that I certainly know the secrets in the heavens and the earth and that I know what you reveal and what you conceal?"

³⁴. And when We said to the angels, 'Be obedient to Adam' they obeyed, but Iblis did not obey. He refused and he was proud, and he was became of the unbelievers."

³⁵. And We said, "Oh Adam! Dwell in the garden with your wife and eat from it the plentiful food wherever you wish, but do not approach this one tree, for then you will be of the unjust."

³⁶. But the Satan caused both of them to fail, and caused them to depart from that state in which they were; and We said, "Get forth, some of you being the enemies of others, and there is a place for you on earth and a provision for a time."

³⁷. Then Adam learned certain words of prayer from the Lord, so He showed them mercy; and certainly God often shows mercy, He is the Merciful.

³⁸. We said, "Go away, all of you., from this place; and guidance will most assuredly come to you from Me. Then, whoever follows My guidance, they will not fear and will not grieve. ³⁹. And as to those who disbelieve in and reject My words, they shall be the inmates of the fire, in it they shall abide.

⁴⁰. Oh children of Israel! Recognize My favor which I have bestowed on you and be faithful to your covenant with Me, I will fulfill My covenant with you; and your fears should be of Me, and only me.

⁴¹. And believe in what I have revealed, verifying that which has already been given to you, and do not be the first to deny it. And do not take a small price in exchange for My words;

and your fears should be of Me, and only me.

⁴². And do not mix up the truth with the lies, nor knowingly hide the truth.

⁴³. And observe your prayers and pay gifts to the poor and bow down with those who bow down.

⁴⁴. What! Do you urge other men to be good and neglect yourself, while you read the Book. Can you not understand?

⁴⁵. And seek assistance through patience and prayer, and this is a difficult thing except for those who are humble,

⁴⁶. Do you know that you shall meet your Lord and that you shall return to Him.

⁴⁷. Oh children of Israel! think of My gifts which I have given you and that I made first amongst all the nations.

⁴⁸. And be on your guard against a day when one soul shall not serve as a substitute for another in the least, neither shall advocacy on the others behalf be allowed, nor shall any ransom be accepted for it, nor shall they be helped.

⁴⁹. And when We delivered you from Pharoah's people, who had subjected you to severe torment, killing your sons and let your women folk live. That was a great trial for you from your Lord.

⁵⁰. And when We parted the sea for you and We saved you and drowned the followers of Pharoah as you watched.

⁵¹. And when We promised Moses a period of forty nights, but in his absence you took a calf for a god and you were violators of my law.

⁵². Then We forgave you afterward and gave you an opportunity to be grateful

⁵³. And then We gave Moses the Book and the choice between right and wrong and there was a chance for you to be guided to the right.

⁵⁴. And when Moses said to his people, "Oh my people! You have indeed been unfair to yourselves by worshiping the calf for a god, therefore turn in repentance to your Creator, and kill the evil people, and that will be better for you in the eyes of your Creator. And God turned to you mercifully, for, indeed, He frequently turns to mercy, the Merciful.

⁵⁵. And when you said, "Oh Moses! we will not believe in you until we actually see God, so the thunder and lightning dazed you while you looked on.

⁵⁶. Then We raised you up after your death and you had the chance to be grateful.

⁵⁷. And We made the clouds to give you shade and We gave you delicacies and quails, "Eat of the good things that We have given you." But their rebellion did not do Us any harm, but they suffered the loss in their own souls.

⁵⁸. And when We said, "Enter this city, then eat from it a plentiful food wherever you wish, and enter the gate humbly, and seek forgiveness. We will forgive you your faults and give more to those who do good to others."

⁵⁹. But those who were unjust changed the words to other than that which had been spoken to them, so We sent upon those who were unjust a plague from heaven, because they disobeyed.

⁶⁰. And when Moses prayed for drink for his people, We said, "Strike the rock with your staff." And there gushed from it twelve springs; each tribe knew its drinking place: Eat and drink of the provisions of God and do not act corruptly and cause disorder in the land.

⁶¹. And when you said, "Oh Moses! we cannot survive on one food, therefore pray Lord on our behalf to bring forth for us out of what the earth grows, of its herbs and its cucumbers and its garlic and its lentils and its onions." He said, "Will you exchange that which is better for that which is worse? Enter a city, so you will have what you ask for. And degradation and humiliation were brought down upon them, and they became deserving of God's wrath; this was so because they did not believe the words of God and killed the prophets unjustly; this was so because they disobeyed and exceeded the limits.

⁶². Certainly those who believe in the Koran, and those who are Jewish, and the Christians, and the Copts, whoever believes in God and the Last day and does good, they shall have their reward from their Lord, and there is no fear for them, nor shall they grieve.

⁶³. And We accepted your promise made before the Mountain. Take hold of the law Torah which We have given you with firmness and bear in mind what is in it, so that you may guard against evil.

⁶⁴. Then you turned back after that; so were it not for the grace of God and His mercy on you, you would certainly have been among the losers.

⁶⁵. And certainly you have known those among you who exceeded the limits of the Sabbath, so We said to them: Be as apes, despised and hated.

⁶⁶. So We made them an example to those who witnessed it and those who came after it, and an admonition to those who guard against evil.

⁶⁷. And when Moses said to his people, "Certainly God commands you that you should sacrifice a cow;" they said, "Do you ridicule us?" He said, "I seek the protection of God from being one of the ignorant."

⁶⁸. They said, "Call on your Lord for our sake to make it plain to us what she is." Moses said, "He says, Certainly she is a cow neither advanced in age nor too young, or in between and this; therefore do what you are commanded."

⁶⁹. They said, "Call on your Lord for our sake to make it plain to us what her color is." Moses said, "He says, She is most certainly a yellow cow; her color is intensely yellow, delightful to those who see her."

⁷⁰. They said, "Call on your Lord for our sake to make it plain to us what she is, for certainly to us the cows are all alike, and if God please we shall certainly be guided correctly."

⁷¹. Moses said, "He says, Certainly she is a cow who has not been made submissive so that she should plow the land, nor does she irrigate the tilled land; she is sound, without a blemish on her." They said, "Now you have brought the truth;" so they sacrificed her, though they had not the mind to do it.

⁷². And when you killed a man, then you disagreed with respect to that, and God was to bring forth that which you were going to hide.

⁷³. So We said, "Hit the dead body with part of the Sacrificed cow," That is how God brings the dead to life, and He shows you His signs so that you may understand.

⁷⁴. Your hearts hardened after that, so that they were like rocks, Harder than the river rocks where streams flow. And certainly there are some of them which split apart so that water comes out of them, and certainly there are some of them which fall down for fear of God, and God knows what you do.

⁷⁵. Did you then hope that they would believe in you, and some of them, indeed, used to hear the Word of God, then altered the Word of God after it was made known to them, and they know this.

⁷⁶. And when they meet those who believe they say, "We believe," But, when they are alone one with another they say, "Do you talk to them of what God has disclosed to you that they may fight with you about this before your Lord? Do you not then understand?"

⁷⁷. Do they not know that God knows what they keep secret and what they make known?

⁷⁸. And there are among them illiterates who do not know the Book, but only lies, and they merely conjecture.

⁷⁹. Sorrow shall be to those who write a holy book with their hands and then say, "This is from God," so that they may sell it for a minimal price; therefore misery and sorrow to those for what their hands have written and sorrow to those for what they earn.

⁸⁰. And they say, "Fire shall not touch us except for a few days." Say, "Have you received a promise from God. Then God never breaks His promise, or do you speak against God what you do not know?"

⁸¹. Yes, whoever does evil and surrounded by his sins, these are the inmates of the fire; in it they shall abide. ⁸². But those who believe and do good works, these shall be the dwellers of Heaven; in it they shall stay.

⁸³. And remember that We made a covenant with the children of Israel, saying, "You shall not serve any but God and you shall do good to your parents, and to the next of kin and to the orphans and the needy, and you shall speak kindly to men and keep up prayer and pay the tithing to the poor. Then all except a few of you turned away and now you, too, turn aside.

⁸⁴. And remember that We made a covenant with you, saying "You shall not shed your blood and you shall not turn people out of your homes; and this you have witnessed.

⁸⁵. Yet you still slay your people and turn some from among you out of their homes, backing up each other against them unlawfully and sinfully. And if they should come to you, as captives you would ransom them -- while their very expulsion was unlawful for you. Do you then believe in a part of the Book and disbelieve in the other? What then is the reward for those among you that do this except disgrace in this current life, and on the day of resurrection they shall be reprimandd most grievously, and God is aware of what you do.

⁸⁶. These are they who prefer the life her today for the life hereafter, and their punishment will be firm and they cannot be helped.

⁸⁷. And most certainly We gave Moses the Book and We sent messengers after him one after another; and We gave Jesus, the son of Mary, clear signs and strengthened him with the holy spirit, Whenever then a messenger came to you with that which you yourselves did not desire, you were insolent and you called some liars and some you killed.

⁸⁸. And they say, "Our hearts are covered." No, God has cursed them on account of their lack of faith; so little it is that they believe.

⁸⁹. And when there came to them a Book from God verifying that which they have, and before that they used to pray for victory against those who disbelieve, but when a Prophet came to them that they did not recognize, they disbelieved him; so God's curse is on the unbelievers.

⁹⁰. Evil is that for which they have sold their souls -- that they should deny what God has revealed, out of envy that God should send down of His grace on whomsoever of His servants He pleases; so they have made themselves deserving of wrath upon wrath, and there is a disgraceful punishment for the unbelievers.

⁹¹. And when it is said to them, Believe in what God has revealed, they say, "We believe in that which was revealed to us;" and they deny what is sent down after that, while it is the truth verifying that which they already have. Say, "Why then did you kill God's Prophets before if you were indeed believers?"

⁹². And most certainly Moses came to you with clear signs, then you took the calf for a god in his absence and you were unjust.

⁹³. And when We made a covenant with you and raised the the Mount before you, saying "Hold fast to that which we have given you and be obedient." They said, "We hear and disobey." And they were absorbed the love of the calf into their hearts on account of their unbelief, then say, "Evil is that which your belief causes you to do, you if you are believers."

⁹⁴. Say, "If living with God in the hereafter is your destiny, to the exclusion of all other people, then you should wish for death, if you are truthful.

⁹⁵. And they will never wish for death it on account of what their hands have done before, and God knows the unjust.

⁹⁶. And these are most certainly the greediest of men for life, greedier than even those who set up other gods befroe God. Every one of them would love that he should be granted a life of a thousand years, but his being granted a long life will in no way protect him from the punishment, and God sees what they do.

⁹⁷. Say, "Whoever is the enemy of Gabriel -- for certainly he revealed it to your heart by God's command, verifying that which was sent before and it is guidance and good news for the believers. ⁹⁸. Whoever is the enemy of God and His angels and His apostles and Gabriel and Michael, so certainly God is the enemy of the unbelievers.

⁹⁹. And certainly We have revealed to you clear words and none disbelieves them except the disobedient.

¹⁰⁰. What! whenever they make a covenant, will some of them throw it aside? No, most of them have no faith

¹⁰¹. And when there came to them a Prophet from God verifying that which they have, some of those who were given the Book threw the Book of God behind their backs as if they knew nothing.

¹⁰². And they followed what the devils chanted of sorcery in the reign of Solomon, and Solomon was not an unbeliever, but the devils disbelieved, they taught men sorcery and that was sent down to the two angels at Babel, Harut and Marut, yet these two taught no man until they had said, "Certainly we are only a trial, therefore do not be a disbeliever." Even then men learned from these two, magic by which they might cause a separation between a man and his wife; and they cannot hurt with it anyone except with God's permission, and they learned what harmed them and did not help them, and certainly they know that he who bought it should have no share of good in the hereafter and evil was the price for which they sold their souls, if only they had known this.

¹⁰³. And if they had believed and guarded themselves against evil, reward from God would certainly have been better; if only they had known this.

¹⁰⁴. Oh you who believe! do not say Raina and say Unzurna and listen, and for the unbelievers there is a painful punishment.

¹⁰⁵. Those who disbelieve from among the followers of the Book do not approve or act as the polytheists do, so that the good should be sent down to you from your Lord, and Godspecifically chooses whom He pleases for His mercy, and God is the Lord of immense grace.

¹⁰⁶. Whatever words We abrogate or cause to be forgotten, We bring one better than it or like it. Do you not know that God has power over all things? ¹⁰⁷. Do you not know that God's is the kingdom of the heavens and the earth, and that besides God you have no guardian or helper?

¹⁰⁸. If instead you wish to put questions to your Prophet, as Moses was questioned before; and whoever adopts unbelief instead of faith, he indeed has lost the right direction of the way.

¹⁰⁹. Many of the followers of the Book wish that they could turn you back into unbelievers after you found faith, because of their own envy, even after the truth has become known to them; but pardon and forgive them, so that God should bring about His command; certainly God has power over all things.

¹¹⁰. And keep up prayer and pay the tithing for the poor and whatever good you send before for yourselves, you shall find it with God; certainly God sees what you do.

¹¹¹. And they say, "None shall enter the garden or paradise except he who is a Jew or a Christian. These are desires of their own vanity. Say, "Bring your proof if you are truthful."

¹¹². Yes! whoever submits himself entirely to God and he is the doer of good to others he has his reward from his Lord, and there is no fear for him nor shall he grieve.

¹¹³. And the Jews say, "The Christians do not follow anything good" and the Christians say,

"The Jews do not follow anything good while they recite the same Book." Even thus say those who have no knowledge, like to what they say; so God shall judge between them on the day of resurrection regarding their disagreement.

114. And who is more unjust than he who prevents men in places of worship from celebrating God's name and strives to destroy them? It is proper that they should enter therein without fear. Those who do this are disgraced in this life and shall find great punishment in the Hereafter.

115. And God's is the East and the West, therefore, wherever you turn, there is God's purpose; certainly God giftgiving is bountiful, ALL-Knowing.

116. And they say, "God has taken to himself a son. Glory be to Him." rather, whatever is in the heavens and the earth is God's; all are obedient to Him,

117. the Wonderful Originator of the heavens and the earth, and when He decides that a thing happen, He only says to it, "Be," and so there it is.

118. And those who have no knowledge say, "Why does not God speak to us or a sign come to us?" They say this as those before them said the likes of what they say; their hearts are all alike. Indeed We have made the words clear for a people who are sure.

119. Certainly We have sent you with the truth as a bearer of good news and as one who warns, and you shall not be called upon to answer for the companions of the flaming fire.

120. And the Jews will not be pleased with you, nor the Christians unless you follow their religion. Say, "Certainly God's guidance, that is the true guidance." And if you follow their desires after the knowledge that has come to you, you shall have no guardian from God, nor any helper.

121. Those to whom We have given the Book read it as it ought to be read. They believe in it; and whoever disbelieves in it, they shall be the losers.

122. Oh children of Israel, call to mind My favors which I gave to you and how I put you before the other nations.

123. And watch out for a day when no soul will substitute for another at all and neither shall any compensation be accepted from it, nor shall intercession help it, nor shall they be helped.

124. And rememberwhen his Lord tested Abraham with certain words, he fulfilled them. He said, "Certainly I will make you a Leader of men." Abraham said, "And what of my offspring?" He said,"My covenant does not include the unjust,".

125. And when We made the House a resort for men and a place of security, and: give for yourselves a place of prayer in the footsteps of Abraham. And We enjoined Abraham and Ishmael saying, "Purify My House for those who visit it and those who stay in it for devotion and those who bow down and those who prostrate themselves in prayer."

126. And when Abraham said, "My Lord, make it a secure town and provide its people with fruits, those of them as believe in God and the last day." He said, "And whoever disbelieves, I will grant him enjoyment only for a short while, then I will drive him to the punishment of the fire; and it is an evil destination.

127. And when Abraham and Ishmael raised the foundations of the House: Our Lord! accept this from us; certainly You are the Hearing, the Knowing:

128. Our Lord! and make us both submissive to You and raise from our offspring a nation obedient to You, and show us our ways of devotion and turn to us mercifully, certainly You are the One Who Often Returns to Mercy, the Merciful.

129. Our Lord! and raise up in them a Prophet from among them who shall recite to them Your words and teach them the Book and the wisdom, and purify them; certainly You are the Mighty, the Wise.

130. And he who puts aside the religion of Abraham but he who makes himself a fool, and most certainly We chose him in this world, and in the hereafter he is most certainly among

the righteous.

131. When his Lord said to him, "Be a Muslim," he said, "I submit myself to the Lord of the worlds."

132. And the same did Abraham enjoin on his sons and so did Jacob. Oh my sons! certainly God has chosen for you this faith, therefore do not die unless you are Muslims.

133. No! were you witnesses when death visited Jacob, when he said to his sons, "What will you serve after me?" They said, "We will serve your God and the God of your fathers, Abraham and Ishmael and Isaac, one God only, and to Him do we submit."

134. This is a people that have passed away; they shall have what they earned and you shall have what you earn, and you shall not be called upon to answer for what they did.

135. And they say, "Be Jews or Christians, you will be on the right course. Say, "No! we follow the religion of Abraham, the Hanif, and he was not one of the polytheists."

136. Say, "We believe in God and in that which had been revealed to us, and in that which was revealed to Abraham and Ishmael and Isaac and Jacob and the tribes, and in that which was given to Moses and Jesus, and in that which was given to the prophets from their Lord, we do not make any distinction between any of them, and to Him do we submit."

137. If then they believe as you believe in Him, they are indeed on the right path, and if they turn back, then they are departed from the great path, so God will provide for you against them, and He is the All-Hearing, the All-Knowing.

138. Receive the baptism of God, and who is better than God in baptising? and Him do we serve.

139. Say, "Do you dispute with us about God, and He is our Lord and your Lord, and we shall have our deeds and you shall have your deeds, and we are sincere to Him."

140. No! do you say that Abraham and Ishmael and Jacob and the tribes were Jews or Christians? Say, "Are you better knowing or God? And who is more unjust than he who conceals a testimony that he has from God? And God recognizes what you do."

141. This is a people that have passed away; they shall have what they earned and you shall have what you earn, and you shall not be called upon to answer for what they did.

142. The fools among the people will say, "What has turned them from their Qibla which they had?" Say, "The East and the West belong only to God; He guides whom He likes to the right path."

143. And thus We have made you an exalted people so that you may be witness to the people and that the Messenger of God may be a witness to you; and We did not announce which Qibla you would have, except that We might distinguish between him who follows the Prophet from him who turns on his heel. And this was, indeed, difficult except for those whom God has correctly guided; and God was not going to make your faith fruitless; most certainly God is Affectionate, Merciful to the people.

144. Indeed, We often see you turning of your face to heaven, so We shall certainly turn you to a Qibla of your choosing; turn then your face towards the Sacred Mosque, and wherever you are, turn your face towards it, and those who have been given the Book most certainly know that it is the truth from their Lord; and God recognizes what they do.

145. And even if you bring to those who have been given the Book every sign they would not follow your Qibla, nor can you be a follower of their Qibla, neither are they the followers of each other's Qibla, and if you follow their desires after the knowledge that has come to you, then you shall most certainly be among the unjust.

146. Thoseto whom We have given the Book recognize him as they recognize their sons, and some of them most certainly conceal the truth even though they know it is true. 147. The truth is from your Lord, therefore you should not be one of the doubters. 148. And every one has a

direction to which he should turn, therefore hasten to do good works; wherever you are, God will bring you all together; certainly God has power over all things.

149. And from whatever place you come from, turn your face towards the Sacred Mosque; and certainly it is the very truth from your Lord, and God recognizes what you do.

150. And from whatever place you come forth, turn your face towards the Sacred Mosque; and wherever you are turn your faces towards it, so that people shall have no complaint against you, except those who are unjust; so do not fear them, and fear Me, so that I may do My works on you and that you may walk on the right course.

151. We have sent to you a Prophet from among you who recites to you Our words and purifies you and teaches you the Book and the wisdom and teaches you that which you did not know. 152. Therefore remember Me, I will remember you, and be thankful to Me, and do not be ungrateful to Me.

153. Oh you who believe! seek assistance through patience and prayer; certainly God is with the patient.

154. And do not speak of those who are slain in God's way as dead; no, they are alive, but you cannot see them.

155. And We will most certainly test you with some level of fear and hunger and loss of property and lives and fruits; and good news will come to the patient,

156. Some persons, when a misfortune happens to them, say, "Certainly we are God's and to Him we shall certainly return."

157. Upon those people are blessings and mercy from their Lord, and those are the followers of the right course.

158. Certainly the mounts of Safa and Marwa are among the signs appointed by God; so whoever makes a pilgrimage to the House or pays a visit to it, there is no blame on him if he goes round them both; and whoever does good spontaneously, then certainly God is Grateful, Knowing.

159. Certainly those who conceal the clear proofs and the guidance that We revealed after We made it clear in the Book for men, these it is whom God shall curse, and all those who curse shall curse them too.

160. Except those who repent and amend and make obvious the truth, these it is to whom I turn mercifully; and I am the One Who Often Returns to Mercy, the Merciful.

161. Certainly those who disbelieve and die while they are disbelievers, on these is the curse of God and of all the angels and men;

162. Abiding in it; their punishment shall not be lightened nor shall they be given rest.

163. And your God is one God! there is no god but He; He is the Kind, the Merciful.

164. Most certainly in the creation of the heavens and the earth and the alternation of the night and the day, and the ships that run in the sea with the commerce of men, and the water that God sends down from the cloud, then gives life with it to the earth after its death and spreads in it all kinds of animals, and the changing of the winds and the clouds made subservient between the heaven and the earth, there are signs for a people who understand.

165. And there are some among men who take for themselves objects of worship besides God, whom they love as they love God, and those who believe are stronger in love for God and O, that those who are unjust had seen, when they see the punishment, that the power is wholly God's and that God is severe in requiting evil.

166. When the leaders shall renounce the followers, and they see the punishment and their ties are cut apart.

167. And those who followed shall say, "Had we had the opportunity, then we would renounce them as they have renounced us. Thus will God prove to them that their deeds will be intensely

regretful to them, and they shall not return from the fire.

168. Oh men! eat the lawful and good things out of what is in the earth, and do not follow the footsteps of the Satan; certainly he is your open enemy.

169. He only urges you to evil and indecency, and urges you to speak against God in your ignorance.

170. And when it is said to them, "Follow what God has revealed," they say, "No! we follow as our fathers did. And, because fathers had no sense at all, they too did not follow the right way.

171. And the story of those who reject faith is like the story of one who calls like a shepherd to those who hear nothing but screams and cries; deaf, dumb and blind, they have no wisdom.

172. Oh you who believe! eat of the good things that We have provided you with, and give thanks to God if Him it is that you serve.

173. He has only forbidden you flesh of dying animals, and blood, and flesh of swine, and that on which any name other than that of God has been invoked. But if one is forced by necessity, rather than desire, without exceeding the limit, no sin shall be upon him; certainly God is Forgiving, Merciful.

174. Certainly those who conceal any part of the Book that God has revealed and do it for a profit, they shall receive nothing but fire into their bellies, and God will not speak to them on the day of resurrection, nor will He purify them, and they shall have a painful punishment.

175. These are they who buy error for the right direction and punishment for forgiveness; how boldly they encounter the fire.

176. This is because God has revealed the Book as the truth; and certainly those who go against the Book create a great unrest.

177. It is not righteousness that you turn your faces towards the East and the West, but righteousness is this that one should believe in God and the last day and the angels and the Book and the prophets, and give away wealth out of love for Him to the next of kin and the orphans and the needy and the wayfarer and the beggars and for the release of the captives, and keep up prayer and are charitable. And those who keep their promise, and those patient when distressed and when afflicted and in time of conflicts. These are they who are true to themselves and these are they who guard against evil.

178. Oh you who believe! Equality of retaliation is prescribed in the case of murder, the free for the free, and the slave for the slave, and the female for the female, but if any forgiveness is made to anyone by his aggrieved brother, then grant a reasonable demand and compensate him handsomely. this is an exemption from your Lord and a mercy; so whoever exceeds the limit after this shall have a painful punishment.

179. And the law of retaliation is beneficial to your life, Oh men of understanding, that you may guard yourselves.

180. A bequest is meant for you when death approaches one of you, if he leaves behind wealth for parents and near relatives, according to custom, a duty is incumbent upon those who guard against evil. 181. Whoever then alters it after he has heard it, the sin of it then is only upon those who alter it; certainly God is Hearing, Knowing.

182. But he who suspects wrongdoing or an act of disobedience on the part of the testator, and effects an agreement between the parties, there is no blame on him. Certainly God is Forgiving, Merciful.

183. Oh you who believe! fasting is directed for you, as it was ordered for those before you, so that you may guard against evil.

184. For a certain number of days; but whoever among you is sick or on a journey, then he shall fast a like number of other days; and those who are not able to do it may effect a redemption

by feeding a poor man; so whoever does good spontaneously it is better for him; and that you fast is better for you if you know.

¹⁸⁵. The month of Ramadan is that in which the Koran was revealed, a guidance to men and clear proofs of the guidance and the distinction; therefore whoever of you is present in the month, he shall fast therein, and whoever is sick or upon a journey, then he shall fast a like number of other days; God desires ease for you, and He does not desire difficulty for you, and He desires that you should complete the number of days fasting and that you should exalt the greatness of God for His having guided you and that you may give thanks.

¹⁸⁶. And when My servants ask you concerning Me, then I am indeed close to them; I answer the prayer of the requestor when he calls on Me, so they should answer My call and believe in Me that they may walk in the right way.

¹⁸⁷. It is made lawful to you to be with your wives on the night of the fast. They are your garments and you are their garments; God knew that you secretly acted unfaithfully before, yet He has turned to you mercifully and forgave you; so now be in contact with them and seek what God has ordered for you, and eat and drink until the whiteness of the day becomes distinct from the blackness of the night at dawn, then complete the fast till night. And, do not have contact with them while you keep to the mosques; these are the limits of God, so do not go near them. Thus does God make clear His words for men that they may guard against evil.

¹⁸⁸. And do not waste your property among yourselves by falsehoos, neither seek to bribe the judges with your property, with the intent that you may take a part of the property of other men wrongfully.

¹⁸⁹. They ask you concerning the new moon. Say, "They are meant as signs to mark the times for the affairs of men, and for the pilgrimage; and it is not righteousness that you should enter the houses at their backs. There is no virtue if you enter into the houses by their rear doors and be careful of your duty to God, so that you may be successful.

¹⁹⁰. And fight on the side of God with those who fight with you, and do not exceed the limits, certainly God does not love those who exceed the limits.

¹⁹¹. And kill those who transgress wherever you find them, and drive them out from wherever they drove you out, and persecution is severer than slaughter, and do not fight with them at the Sacred Mosque unless they fight with you in it, but if they do fight you, then kill them; such is the reward of the unbelievers.

¹⁹². But if they cease their unbelieving, then certainly God is Forgiving, Merciful.

¹⁹³. And fight with them until there is no persecution, and religion should be only for God, but if they cease, then there should be no hostility except against the oppressors.

¹⁹⁴. The Sacred month for the sacred month and the law of retaliation is sacred; whoever then acts aggressively against you, inflict injury on him according to the injury he has inflicted on you and be careful of your duty to God and know that God is with those who guard against evil.

¹⁹⁵. And spend in the way of God and do not condemn yourselves to hell by your actions and do good to others; certainly God loves those who do good.

¹⁹⁶. And accomplish the pilgrimage and the visit for God, but if, you are prevented, send whatever offering you can, and do not shave your heads until the offering reaches its destination. If someone among you is sick or is mentally ill, he should make up for this by fasting or charity or sacrificing, then when you are well again, whoever profits by combining the visit with the pilgrimage should take what offering is easy to obtain; but he who cannot find any offering should fast for three days during the pilgrimage and for seven days when you return; these make ten days complete; this is for him whose family is not present in the Sacred Mosque, and be careful of your duty to God, and know that God is severe in requiting evil.

¹⁹⁷. The Hajj or pilgrimage is to be performed in the well-known months. If you decide to undertake the Hajj, you shall not speak obscenity, or have intercourse or fornicate, nor quarrel amongst one another. Whatever good you do, God knows it. And take proper provisions for the journey, but the best provision is the guarding of oneself, and be careful of your duty to Me, Oh men of understanding.

¹⁹⁸. There is no blame on you in seeking benefit from your Lord during the Hajj, so when you hasten on from Mount Arafat, then remember God near the Holy Monument, and remember Him as He has guided you, though before that you were among those in error.

¹⁹⁹. Then hurry on from the Place from which the people hurry on and ask the forgiveness of God; certainly God is Forgiving, Merciful.

²⁰⁰. When you have performed your holy rituals, then honor God as you honored your fathers, but in a greater manner than before. But there are some people who say, "Our Lord! Provide for us in the world," and they shall have no resting place.

²⁰¹. And there are some among them who say, "Our Lord! grant us good in this world and good in the hereafter, and save us from the punishment of the fire."

²⁰². They shall have their portion of what they have earned, and God is swift in judging.

²⁰³. Honor God during the designated days; then whoever hurries off in two days, there is no blame on him, and whoever remains behind, there is no blame on him, if his intentions was correct. Be careful of your duty to God, and know that you shall be gathered together to Him.

²⁰⁴. There is a type of man whose speech about the life of this world amazes you, and he calls on God to witness as to what is in his heart, yet he is the most violent of enemies.

²⁰⁵. And when he turns back, he runs along in the land in order to cause turmoil in it and destroy the crops and the livestock, and God does not love mischief-making.

²⁰⁶. And when it is said to him, guard against the punishment of God; pride carries him off to sin. So, for the likes of him hell is sufficient, and, indeed, it is the resting place of the evil.

²⁰⁷. There is a type of man who devotes his life to seek the pleasure of God; and God is Affectionate to the servants.

²⁰⁸. Oh you who believe! Submit, one and all and do not follow the footsteps of Satan; certainly he is your clear enemy.

²⁰⁹. But if you slip after clear revelation has come to you, then know that God is Mighty, Wise.

²¹⁰. Do they wait until God comes to them in the shadows of the clouds along with the angels, and the matter has already been decided; and all matters are returned to God?

²¹¹. Ask the Israelites how many a clear sign We have given them; and whoever returns to the old ways after the revelation of God has come to him, then certainly God is severe in punishing such evil.

²¹². The life of this world is attractive to those who disbelieve, and they make fun of those who believe, and those who are reverent shall be above them on the day of resurrection; and God gives His amazing abundance on those whom he wishes to receive it.

²¹³. All people are a single nation; so God raised prophets to bear good news and to warn. He revealed to them the Book with truth, in order to judge between people in the manner in which they differed; and none but the very people who were given it differed about it after clear reasons were given to them, revolting among themselves; so God has guided by His will those who believe in the truth about which they differed and God guides whom He pleases to the right path.

²¹⁴. Or do you think that you would enter Heaven while yet the state of those who have passed away before you has not come upon you; distress and harm occurred to them and they were shaken violently, so that the Prophet and those who believed with him said, "When will tGod's

aidGod come? Now certainly the aid of God is near!"

215. When they ask you as on what they should spend, say, "Whatever wealth you spend, it is for the parents and the near of kin and the orphans and the needy and the homeless, and whatever good you do, God certainly knows it."

216. You are forbidden to fight, and you should dislike it. It may be that you dislike a thing while it is good for you, and it may be that you love a thing while it is bad for you. God knows what is good for you, but you may not.

217. If they ask about fighting in the sacred month, say, "Fighting in it is a grave matter, and it keeps men from God's way and denying Him. Preventing men from going to the Sacred Mosque and turning its people out of it are even graver wrongs to God. Persecution is more grave than slaughter; Until you turn back to your religion they will continue fighting you, if possible. Whoever of you turns back from his religion, then he dies while an unbeliever -- these it is whose works shall go for nothing in this world and the hereafter, and they are the inmates of the fire; and they shall live in Hell.

218. Those who believed and those who fled their home and struggled hard in the way of God. They shall hope for the mercy of God and God is Forgiving, Merciful.

219. If they ask you about intoxicants and gambling, say, "In both of them there is a great sin and means of profit for men, and their sin is greater than their profit. If they ask you what they should spend, say, "What you can spare." God makes this clear to you, for you to study

220. On this world and the hereafter. If they ask you concerning the orphans, say, "To take care of the ophans is good, and if you share with them, they become your brethren. God can discern the ones who make turmoil from the peacemakers. If God pleases, He can certainly caused them difficulties; certainly God is Mighty, Wise.

221. And do not marry the non-believing woman until they convert, because a faithful maid is better than an idolatress woman. even if the non-believing woman is pleasing to you. Do not give believing women in marriage to idolaters until they convert, And also, a believing servant is better than an idolater, even if he should please you. These non-believers are but invitatitons to the fire, whereas God invites to Heaven and to forgiveness by His will, and makes clear His words to men, that they may be aware.

222. If they ask you about menstruation, say, "It is a discomfort; therefore keep away from the women during the menstrual discharge and do not go near them until they have become clean, Then when they have cleansed themselves, go in to them as God has commanded you; certainly God loves those who turn much to Him, and He loves those who purify themselves.

223. Your wives are a tilled soil for you, so go into your tilled soil when you like, but do some act of good beforehand yourself, and be careful of your duty to God, and know that you will meet Him, and give good news to the believers.

224. Do not use God's name as a oath, or as an obstacle to your doing good or guarding against evil or making peace between men, and God is Hearing, Knowing.

225. God will not call you to account for the thoughtlessness of your oaths your oaths, but He will call you to account for what is in your hearts, and God is Forgiving, Forbearing.

226. Those who swear that they will abstain from their wives should wait four months; and if they go back, then God is certainly Forgiving, Merciful. 227. But if they have resolved on a divorce, then God is certainly Hearing, Knowing.

228. And the divorced women should wait by themselves for three menstrual periods; for it is not lawful for them that they should conceal that God has made them pregnant. If they believe in God and the last day; and their husbands have a better right to take them back in the meanwhile if they wish for reconciliation; Divorced women have equitable rights similar

to those against them, but the men are a small bit above them, and God is Mighty, Wise.

²²⁹. Divorce is only permissible twice, after that they should stay together on fair terms or go separate with kindness. It is not lawful for a husband to take any part of what they have given their wife, unless both fear that they cannot keep within the laws of God; then if you fear that they cannot keep within the laws of God, there is not wrong for her to give up something in order to become free. These are the laws of God, so do not violate them and whoever violates the laws of God are unjust.

²³⁰. A man who irrevocably divorces a woman cannot remarry her unless she has been remarried to another man who has divorced her also. They may then remarry, if they think that they can keep within the laws of God, and these are the laws of God which He makes clear for people to know.

²³¹. And when you divorce women and they fulfill their prescribed time, then either keep them in good fellowship or set them free with liberality, and do not take them back to injure them, this would be wrong, and whoever does this, he indeed is unjust to his own soul. Do not take God's words jokingly, and remember the gifts God has given you, and that which He has revealed to you with the Book and the Wisdom, reprimanding you thereby; and be careful of your duty to God, and know that God is the Knower of all things.

²³². And when you have divorced women and they have ended their term of waiting, then do not prevent them from marrying their new husbands when they agree among themselves in a lawful manner; with this is admonished he among you who believes in God and the last day, this is more profitable and purer for you; and God knows while you do not know.

²³³. And the mothers should be allowed to breastfeed their children for two whole years, for the husband who desires to make complete the time of mothering. Their maintenance and their clothing must be borne by the father according to custom. No soul shall be forced to do that which they cannot do; nor shall a mother be made to suffer harm on account of her child, nor a father on account of his child, and a similar duty falls on the father's heir. But if both desire weaning by mutual consent and counsel, there is no blame on them, and if you wish to engage a wet-nurse for your children, there is no blame on you so long as you pay what you promised for according to custom; and be careful of your duty to God and know that God sees what you do.

²³⁴. And as for those of you who die and leave wives behind, they should keep to themselves, waiting for four months and ten days; then when they have fully completed this term, there is no blame on you and the widow may act for themselves in a lawful manner. God is aware of what you do.

²³⁵. And it is not wrong for you to speak indirectly in the asking a women for marriage or in keeping the proposal concealed within your minds; God knows that you cherish them in your heart. But do not give them a promise in secret unless you speak in a lawful manner, and do not promise marriage until it is in writing, and know that God knows what is in your minds, therefore beware of Him, and know that God is Forgiving, Forbearing.

²³⁶. It is not wrong if you divorce women before consummation or setting a dower, but make provision for them, the wealthy according to his means and the poor according to his means, a provision according to custom; this is a duty on the doers of good to others.

²³⁷. And if you divorce them before consummation, but after setting a dower, then pay to them half of the dower you have offered, unless they relinquish it or the one in whose hands the dower is held relinquishes. It is nearer to righteousness that you should relinquish; and do not neglect the giving freely the gifts between you; certainly God sees what you do.

²³⁸. Attend constantly to prayers and to the middle prayer and stand up truly obedient to God.

²³⁹. But if you are in danger, then say your prayers on foot or on horseback; and when you are secure, then remember God, since He has taught you what you did not know.

²⁴⁰. And those of you who die and leave wives behind, make a donation on behalf of your wives of maintenance for a year without turning them out, then if they themselves go away, there is no blame on you if they go about their business lawfully, and God is Mighty, Wise.

²⁴¹. Provision for the divorced woman must also be made according to custom; this is a duty on those who guard against evil.

²⁴². God thus makes clear to you His words that you may understand.

²⁴³. Have you not considered those who went forth from their homes, for fear of death, and they were thousands, then God said to them, "Die;" again He gave them life; most certainly God is Kind to people, but most people are not grateful.

²⁴⁴. And fight on behalf of God, and know that God is Hearing, Knowing.

²⁴⁵. If you give to God a nice gift, so He will multiply it to you many times, and God corrects and enhances, and you shall be returned to Him.

²⁴⁶. Have you not considered the chiefs of the children of Israel after Moses, when they said to a prophet of theirs, "Raise up for us a king, that we may fight in the way of God." He said, "Is it not likely you will not fight if fighting is forbidden for you?" They said, "And what reason have we that we should not fight in the way of God, and we have indeed been compelled to abandon our homes and our children." But when they were told to fight, they turned back, except a few of them, and God knows the unjust.

²⁴⁷. And their prophet said to them, "Certainly God has raised Saul to be a king over you." They said, "How can he hold kingship over us while we have a greater right to kingship than he, and he has not been granted an abundance of wealth?" He said, "Certainly God has chosen him in preference to you, and He has increased his knowledge and physique greatly, and God grants His kingdom to whom He pleases." God is Ample giving, Knowing.

²⁴⁸. And the prophet said to them, "The sign of his sovereignty will be that there is a tranquility in your heart from the Lord and a residue of the relics of what the children of Moses and the children of Aaron have left, the angels bearing it; most certainly there is a sign in this for those who believe."

²⁴⁹. So when Saul departed with the forces, he said, "Certainly God will try you with a river; whoever then drinks from it, he is not of me, and whoever does not taste of it, he is certainly of me, except he who takes with his hand as much of it as fills the hand; but with the exception of a few of them they drank from it." So when he had crossed it, he and those who believed with him, they said, "We have today no power against Goliath and his forces." Those who were sure that they would meet their Lord said, "How often has a small party vanquished a numerous host by God's permission, and God is with the patient."

²⁵⁰. And when they went out against Goliath and his forces they said, "Our Lord, pour down upon us patience, and make our steps firm and assist us against the unbelieving people. "

²⁵¹. So they put them to flight by God's permission. And David killed Goliath, and God gave him kingdom and wisdom, and taught him of what He pleased. And were it not for God's repelling some men with others, the earth would certainly be in a state of disorder; but God is Kind to the creatures.

²⁵². These are the words of God: We recite them to you with truth; and most certainly you are one of the apostles.

²⁵³. We have made some of these prophets greater than the others among them are they to whom God spoke. Some of them He exalted by many degrees of rank; and We gave clear miracles to Jesus son of Mary, and strengthened him with the holy spirit. And if God had pleased, those

after them would not have fought one with another after clear reasons had come to them, but they disagreed; so there were some of them who believed and others who denied; and if God had pleased they would not have fought one with another, but God brings about what He intends.

254. Oh you who believe! spend out of what We have given you before the day comes in which there is no bargaining, neither any friendship nor intercession, and the unbelievers -- they are the unjust.

255. God is He beside Whom there is no god, the Everliving, the Self-subsisting by Whom all subsist; slumber does not overtake Him nor sleep; whatever is in the heavens and whatever is in the earth is His; who is he that can intercede with Him but by His permission? He knows what is before them and what is behind them, and they cannot comprehend anything out of His knowledge except what He pleases, His knowledge extends over the heavens and the earth, and the preservation of them both tires Him not, and He is the Most High, the Great.

256. There is no compulsion in religion; truly the right way has become clearly distinct from error; therefore, whoever disbelieves in the Satan and believes in God he certainly has laid hold on the firmest handle, which shall not break off, and God is Hearing, Knowing.

257. God is the guardian of those who believe. He brings them out of the darkness into the light; and as to those who disbelieve, their guardians are Satans who take them out of the light into the darkness; they are the inmates of the fire, in it they shall abide.

258. Have you not considered him Nimrod who disputed with Abraham about his Lord, because God had given him the kingdom? When Abraham said, "My Lord is He who gives life and causes to die," he said, "I give life and cause death." Abraham said, "So certainly God causes the sun to rise from the east, then make it rise from the west;" thus he who disbelieved was confounded; and God does not guide correctly the unjust people.

259. Or the like of the one known as Uzair who passed by a town, and it had fallen down upon its roofs; he said, "When will God give it life after its death?" So God caused him to die for a hundred years, then raised him to life. He said, "How long have you waited?" He said, "I have waited a day, or a part of a day." Said He, "No! you have waited a hundred years; then look at your food and drink -- years have not passed over it; and look at your ass; and that We may make you a sign to men, and look at the bones, how We set them together, then clothed them with flesh." So when it became clear to him, he said, "I know that God has power over all things."

260. And when Abraham said, "My Lord! show me how You give life to the Dead." He said, "What! and do you not believe?" He said, "Yes, but that my heart may be at ease." He said, "Then take four of the birds, then train them to follow you, then place on every mountain a part of them, then call them, they will come to you flying." Know that God is Mighty, Wise.

261. The story of those who spend their property in the way of God is as the story of a grain growing seven ears with a hundred grains in every ear; and God multiplies for whom He pleases; and God is Ample-giving, Knowing

262. As for those who spend their property in the way of God, then do not follow up what they have spent with reproach or injury, they shall have their reward from their Lord, and they shall have no fear nor shall they grieve.

263. Kind speech and forgiveness is better than charity followed by injury. God is Self-sufficient, Forbearing.

264. Oh you who believe! do not make your charity worthless by reproach and injury, like him who spends his property to be seen of men and does not believe in God and the last day; so his story is as the story of a smooth rock with earth upon it, then a heavy rain falls upon it, so it leaves it bare; they shall not be able to gain anything of what they have earned; and God does not guide the unbelieving people.

265. And the story of those who spend their property to seek the pleasure of God and for the certainty 'of their souls is as the story of a garden on an elevated ground, upon which heavy rain falls so it brings forth its fruit twofold but if heavy rain does not fall upon it, then light rain is sufficient; and God sees what you do.

266. Does one of you like that he should have a garden of palms and vines with streams flowing beneath it; he has in it all kinds of fruits; and old age has overtaken him and he has weak offspring, when, lo! a whirlwind with fire in it smites it so it becomes blasted; thus God makes the words clear to you, that you may reflect.

267. Oh you who believe! spend benevolently of the good things that you earn and or what We have brought forth for you out of the earth, and do not aim at what is bad that you may spend in alms of it, while you would not take it yourselves unless you have its price lowered. Know that God is Self-sufficient, Praiseworthy.

268. Satan threatens you with poverty and urges you to be ungenerous, and God promises you forgiveness from Himself and abundance; and God is Ample-giving, Knowing.

269. He grants wisdom to whom He pleases, and whoever is granted wisdom, he indeed is given a great good and none but men of understanding mind.

270. And whatever alms you give or whatever vow you vow, certainly God knows it; and the unjust shall have no helpers.

271. If you give alms openly, it is well, and if you hide it and give it to the poor, it is better for you; and this will do away with some of your evil deeds; and God is aware of what you do.

272. To make them walk in the right way is not incumbent on you, but God guides aright whom He pleases; and whatever good thing you spend, it is to your own good; and you do not spend but to seek God's pleasure; and whatever good things you spend shall be paid back to you in full, and you shall not be wronged.

273. Alms are for the poor who are confined in the way of God -- they cannot go about in the land; the ignorant man thinks them to be rich on account of their abstaining from begging; you can recognise them by their mark; they do not beg from men importunately; and whatever good thing you spend, certainly God knows it.

274. As for those who spend their property by night and by day, secretly and openly, they shall have their reward from their Lord and they shall have no fear, nor shall they grieve.

275. Those who commit usury cannot arise except as one whom Satan has prostrated by his touch does rise. That is because they say, trading is only like usury; and God has allowed trading and forbidden usury. To whomsoever then the admonition has come from his Lord, then he desists, he shall have what has already passed, and his affair is in the hands of God; and whoever returns to it -- these arc the inmates of the fire; they shall abide in it.

276. God does not bless usury, and He causes charitable deeds to prosper, and God does not love any ungrateful sinner.

277. Certainly they who believe and do good deeds and keep up prayer and pay the poor-rate they shall have their reward from their Lord, and they shall have no fear, nor shall they grieve.

278. Oh you who believe! Be careful of your duty to God and relinquish what remains due from usury, if you are believers.

279. But if you do it not, then be apprised of war from God and His Prophet; and if you repent, then you shall have your capital; neither shall you make the debtor suffer loss, nor shall you be made to suffer loss.

280. And if the debtor is in dire straits, then let there be postponement until he is in ease; and that you remit it as alms is better for you, if you knew.

281. And guard yourselves against a day in which you shall be returned to God; then every soul

shall be paid back in full what it has earned, and they shall not be dealt with unjustly.

²⁸². Oh you who believe! when you deal with each other in contracting a debt for a fixed time, then write it down; and let a scribe write it down between you with fairness; and the scribe should not refuse to write as God has taught him, so he should write; and let him who owes the debt dictate, and he should be careful of his duty to God, his Lord, and not diminish anything from it; but if he who owes the debt is unsound in understanding, or weak, or if he is not able to dictate himself, let his guardian dictate with fairness; and call in to witness from among your men two witnesses; but if there are not two men, then one man and two women from among those whom you choose to be witnesses, so that if one of the two errs, the second of the two may remind the other; and the witnesses should not refuse when they are summoned; and do not be averse to writing it whether it is small or large, with the time of its falling due; this is more equitable in the sight of God and assures greater accuracy in testimony, and the closest way that you may not entertain doubts afterwards, except when it is ready merchandise which you give and take among yourselves from hand to hand, then there is no blame on you in not writing it down; and have witnesses when you barter with one another, and let no harm be done to the scribe or to the witness; and if you do it then certainly it will be a transgression in you, and be careful of your duty to God, God teaches you, and God knows all things.

²⁸³. And if you are upon a journey and you do not find a scribe, then there may be a security taken into possession; but if one of you trusts another, then he who is trusted should deliver his trust, and let him be careful of his duty to God, his Lord; and do not conceal testimony, and whoever conceals it, his heart is certainly sinful; and God knows what you do.

²⁸⁴. Whatever is in the heavens and whatever is in the earth is God's; and whether you show what is in your minds or hide it, God will call you to account according to it; then He will forgive whom He pleases and reprimand whom He pleases, and God has power over all things.

²⁸⁵. The apostle believes in what has been revealed to him from his Lord, and so do the believers; they all believe in God and His angels and His books and His apostles; We make do not differ between any of His apostles; and they say, "We hear and obey, our Lord! Your forgiveness do we crave, and to You is the eventual course.

²⁸⁶. God does not impose upon any soul a duty but to the extent of its ability; for it is the benefit of what it has earned and upon it the evil of what it has wrought: Our Lord! do not punish us if we forget or make a mistake; Our Lord! do not lay on us a burden as You laid on those before us, Our Lord do not impose upon us that which we have not the strength to bear; and pardon us and grant us protection and have mercy on us, You are our Patron, so help us against the unbelieving people.

Chapter 3 — Al-Imran — The Family of Imran

In the name of God, the Kind, the Merciful.

1. Aliph. Lam. Mim.
2. God, there is no god but He, the Everliving, the Self-subsisting by Whom all things subsist
3. He has revealed to you (Mohammed) the Book with truth, verifying that which is before it, and He revealed the Torah and the Gospel (Holy Bible) before, a guidance for mankind, and He sent the Rules of Judgment.
4. Certainly those who disbelieve the words of God they shall have a severe punishment; for God is Mighty, the Lord of retribution.
5. God -- certainly nothing is hidden from Him in the earth or in the heaven.
6. He it is Who shapes you in the wombs as He likes; there is no god but He, the Mighty, the Wise
7. He it is Who has revealed the Book to you; some of its verses are decisive, they are the basis of the Book, and others are allegorical; then as for those in whose hearts there is perversity they follow the part of it which is allegorical, seeking to mislead and seeking to give it their own interpretation. but none knows its interpretation except God, and those who are firmly rooted in knowledge say, "We believe in it, it is all from our Lord; and none do mind except those having understanding.
8. Our Lord! make not our hearts to deviate after You have guided us aright, and grant us from You mercy; certainly You are the most liberal Giver.
9. Our Lord! certainly You are the Gatherer of men on a day about which there is no doubt; certainly God will not fail His promise.
10. As for those who disbelieve, certainly neither their wealth nor their children shall avail them in the least against God, and these it is who are the fuel of the fire.
11. Like the struggle of the Pharoah's people and those before them; they rejected Our word, so God destroyed them on account of their faults; and God is severe in requiting evil.
12. Say to those who disbelieve: You shall be vanquished, and driven together to hell; and evil is the resting-place.
13. Indeed there was a sign for you in the two hosts who encountered each other; one party fighting in the way of God and the other unbelieving, whom they saw twice as many as themselves with the sight of the eye and God strengthens with His aid whom He pleases; most certainly there is a lesson in this for those who have sight.
14. The love of desires, of women and sons and hoarded treasures of gold and silver and well bred horses and cattle and tilled soil, is made to seem fair to men; this is the provision of the life of this world; and God is He with Whom is the good goal of life.
15. Say, "Shall I tell you what is better than these? For those who guard against evil are gardens with their Lord, beneath which rivers flow, to abide in them, and pure mates and God's pleasure; and God sees the servants.
16. Those who say, "Our Lord! certainly we believe, therefore forgive us our faults and save us from the punishment of the fire.
17. The patient, and the truthful, and the obedient, and those who spend benevolently and those who ask forgiveness in the morning times.
18. God bears witness that there is no god but He, and so do the angels and those possessed of knowledge, maintaining His creation with justice; there is no god but He, the Mighty, the Wise.

19. Certainly the true religion with God is Islam, and those to whom the Book had been given did not show opposition but after knowledge had come to them, out of envy among themselves; and whoever disbelieves in the words of God then certainly God will be quick in judging.

20. But if they dispute with you, say, "I have submitted myself entirely to God and so every one who follows me; and say to those who have been given the Book and the unlearned people: Do you submit yourselves? So if they submit then indeed they follow the right way; and if they turn back, then upon you is only the delivery of the message and God sees the servants.

21. Certainly as for those who disbelieve in the words of God and slay the prophets unjustly and slay those among men who enjoin justice, announce to them a painful punishment.

22. Those are they whose works shall become null in this world as well as the hereafter, and they shall have no helpers.

23. Have you not considered those Jews who are given a portion of the Book? They are invited to the Book of God that it might decide between them, then a part of them turn back and they withdraw.

24. This is because they say, "The fire shall not touch us but for a few days; and what they have created deceives them in the matter of their religion.

25. Then how will it be when We shall gather them together on a day about which there is no doubt, and every soul shall be fully paid what it has earned, and they shall not be dealt with unjustly?

26. Say, "Oh God, Master of the Kingdom! You give the kingdom to whomsoever You please and take away the kingdom from whomsoever You please, and You honor whom You please and degrade whom You please, in Your hand is the good; surety, You have power over all things.

27. You make the night to pass into the day and You make the day to pass into the night, and You bring forth the living from the dead and You bring forth the dead from the living, and You give sustenance to whom You please without measure.

28. Let not the believers take the unbelievers for friends rather than believers; and whoever does this, he shall have nothing of the guardianship of God, but you should guard yourselves against them, guarding carefully; and God makes you cautious of retribution from Himself; and to God is the eventual coming.

29. Say, "Whether you hide what is in your hearts or show it, God knows it, and He knows whatever is in the heavens and whatever is in the earth, and God has power over all things.

30. On the day that every soul shall find present what it has done of good and what it has done of evil, it shall wish that between it and that evil there were a long duration of time; and God makes you to be cautious of retribution from Himself; and God is Compassionate to the servants.

31. Say, "If you love God, then follow me, God will love you and forgive you your faults, and God is Forgiving, Merciful

32. Say, "Obey God and the Prophet; but if they turn back, then certainly God does not love the unbelievers.

33. Certainly God chose Adam and Noah and the descendants of Abraham and the descendants of Imran above the nations.

34. Offspring one of the other; and God is Hearing, Knowing.

35. When a woman of Imran said, "My Lord! certainly I vow to You what is in my womb, to be devoted to Your service; accept therefore from me, certainly You are the Hearing, the Knowing.

36. So when she brought forth, she said, "My Lord! Certainly I have brought it forth a female -- and God knew best what she brought forth -- and the male is not like the female, and I have named it Mary, and I commend her and her offspring into Your protection from the accursed Satan.

37. So her Lord accepted her with a good acceptance and made her grow up a good growing, and gave her into the charge of Zacharia; whenever Zacharia entered the sanctuary to see her, he found with her food. He said, "Oh Mary! From where does this comes to you? She said, "It is from God. Certainly God gives to whom He pleases without measure.

38. There did Zacharia pray to his Lord; he said, "My Lord! grant me from You good offspring; certainly You are the Hearer of prayer.

39. Then the angels called to him as he stood praying in the sanctuary: That God gives you the good news of Jehovah verifying a Word from God, and honorable and chaste and a prophet from among the good ones.

40. He said, "My Lord! when shall there be a son born to me, and old age
has already come upon me, and my wife is barren? He said, "even thus does God
what He pleases."

41. He said, "My Lord! appoint a sign for me. Said He: Your sign is that you should not speak to men for three days except by signs; and remember your Lord much and glorify Him in the evening and the morning.

42. And when the angels said, "Oh Mary! certainly God has chosen you and purified you and chosen you above the women of of the world.

43. Oh Mary! keep to obedience to your Lord and humble yourself, and bow down with those who bow.

44. This is of the announcements relating to the unseen which We reveal to you; and you were not with them when they make wagers to decide which of them should have Mary in his charge, and you were not with them when they contended one with another.

45. When the angels said, "Oh Mary, certainly God gives you good news with a Word from Him of one whose name is the Messiah, Jesus son of Mary, worthy of regard in this world and the hereafter and of those who are made near to God.

46. And he shall speak to the people when in the cradle and when of old age, and he shall be one of the good ones.

47. She said, "My Lord! when shall there be a son born to I me, and man has not touched me? He said, "Even so, God creates what He pleases; when He has decreed a matter, He only says to it, Be, and it is.

48. And He will teach him the Book and the wisdom and the Torah and the Gospel.

49. And make him an apostle to the children of Israel: That I have come to you with a sign from your Lord, that I determine for you out of dust like the form of a bird, then I breathe into it and it becomes a bird with God's permission and I heal the blind and the leprous, and bring the dead to life with God's permission and I inform you of what you should eat and what you should store in your houses; most certainly there is a sign in this for you, if you are believers.

50. And a verifier of that which is before me of the Torah and that I may allow you part of that which has been forbidden t you, and I have come to you with a sign from your Lord therefore be careful of your duty to God and obey me.

51. Certainly God is my Lord and your Lord, therefore serve Him; this is the right path.

52. But when Jesus perceived unbelief on their part, he said Who will be my helpers in God's way? The disciples said, "We are helpers in the way of God: We believe in God and bear witness that we are submitting ones. 53. Our Lord! we believe in what You have revealed and we follow the apostle, so write us down with those who bear witness.

54. And they planned and God also planned, and God is the best of planners.

55. And when God said, "Oh Jesus, I am going to terminate the period of your stay on earth and cause you to ascend unto Me and purify you of those who disbelieve and make those who

follow you above those who disbelieve to the day of resurrection; then to Me shall be your return, so I will decide between you concerning that in which you differed.

56. Then as to those who disbelieve, I will reprimand them with severe punishment in this world and the hereafter, and they shall have no helpers. 57. And as to those who believe and do good deeds, He will pay them fully their rewards; and God does not love the unjust.

58. This We recite to you of the words and the wise reminder.

59. Certainly the likeness of Jesus is with God as the likeness of Adam; He created him from dust, then said to him, Be, and he was.

60. This is the truth from your Lord, so do not be one of the disputers.

61. But whoever disputes with you in this matter after what has come to you of knowledge, then say, "Come let us call our sons and your sons and our women and your women and our near people and your near people, then let us be serious in prayer, and pray for the curse of God on the liars.

62. Most certainly this is the true explanation, and there is no god but God; and most certainly God -- He is the Mighty, the Wise.

63. But if they turn back, then certainly God knows the mischief-makers.

64. Say, "Oh followers of the Book! come to an equitable proposition between us and you that we shall not serve any but God and that we shall not associate anything with Him, and that some of us shall not take others for lords besides God; but if they turn back, then say, "Bear witness that we are

Muslims.

65. Oh followers of the Book! why do you dispute about Abraham, when the Torah and the Gospel were not revealed till after him; do you not then understand?

66. Behold! you are they who disputed about that of which you had knowledge; why then do you dispute about that of which you have no knowledge? And God knows while you do not know.

67. Abraham was not a Jew nor a Christian but he was an upright man, a Muslim, and he was not one of the polytheists.

68. Most certainly the nearest of people to Abraham are those who followed him and this Prophet and those who believe and God is the guardian of the believers.

69. A party of the followers of the Book desire that they should lead you astray, and they lead not astray but themselves, and they do not perceive.

70. Oh followers of the Book! Why do you disbelieve in the words of God while you witness them?

71. Oh followers of the Book! Why do you confound the truth with the falsehood and hide the truth while you know?

72. And a party of the followers of the Book say, "Avow belief in that which has been revealed to those who believe, in the first part of the day, and disbelieve at the end of it, perhaps they go back on their religion.

73. And do not believe but in him who follows your religion. Say, "Certainly the true guidance is the guidance of God -- that one may be given by Him the like of what you were given; or they would contend with you by an argument before your Lord. Say, "Certainly grace is in the hand of God, He gives it to whom He pleases; and God is Ample-giving, Knowing.

74. He specially chooses for His mercy whom He pleases; and God is the Lord of mighty grace.

75. And among the followers of the Book there are some such that if you entrust one of them with a heap of wealth, he shall pay it back to you; and among them there are some such that if you entrust one of them with a dinar he shall not pay it back to you except so long as you emain firm in demanding it; this is because they say, "There is not upon us in the matter of the unlearned people any way to reproach; and they tell a lie against God while they know.

76. Yea, whoever fulfills his promise and guards against evil -- then certainly God loves those who guard against evil.

77. As for those who take a small price for the covenant of God and their own oaths -- certainly they shall have no portion in the hereafter, and God will not speak to them, nor will He look upon them on the day of resurrection nor will He purify them, and they shall have a painful punishment.

78. Most certainly there is a party amongst those who distort the Book with their tongue that you may consider it to be a part of the Book, and they say, It is from God, while it is not from God, and they tell a lie against God while they know.

79. It is not meet for a mortal that God should give him the Book and the wisdom and prophethood, then he should say to men: Be my servants rather than God's; but rather he would say: Be worshipers of the Lord because of your teaching the Book and your reading it yourselves.

80. And neither would he enjoin you that you should take the angels and the prophets for lords; what! would he enjoin you with unbelief after you are Muslims?

81. And when God made a covenant through the prophets: Certainly what I have given you of Book and wisdom -- then an apostle comes to you verifying that which is with you, you must believe in him, and you must aid him. He said, "Do you affirm and accept My compact in this matter? They said, "We do affirm. He said, "Then bear witness, and I too am of the bearers of witness with you.

82. Whoever therefore turns back after this, these it is that are the transgressors.

83. Is it then other than God's religion that they seek to follow, and to Him submits whoever is in the heavens and the earth, willingly or unwillingly, and to Him shall they be returned.

84. Say, "We believe in God and what has been revealed to us, and what was revealed to Abraham and Ishmael and Isaac and Jacob and the tribes, and what was given to Moses and Jesus and to the prophets from their Lord; we do not make any distinction between any of them, and to Him do we submit.

85. And whoever desires a religion other than Islam, it shall not be accepted from him, and in the hereafter he shall be one of the losers. 86. How shall God guide a people who disbelieved after their believing and after they had borne witness that the Prophet was true and clear reasons had come to them; and God does not guide the unjust people.

87. As for these, their reward is that upon them is the curse of God and the angels and of men, all together.

88. Abiding in it; their punishment shall not be lightened nor shall they be respited.

89. Except those who repent after that and amend, then certainly God is Forgiving, Merciful.

90. Certainly, those who disbelieve after their believing, then increase in unbelief, their repentance shall not be accepted, and these are they that go astray.

91. Certainly, those who disbelieve and die while they are unbelievers, the earth full of gold shall not be accepted from one of them, though he should offer to ransom himself with it, these it is who shall have a painful punishment, and they shall have no helpers.

92. By no means shall you attain to righteousness until you spend benevolently out of what you love; and whatever thing you spend, God certainly knows it.

93. All food was lawful to the children of Israel except that which Israel had forbidden to himself, before the Torah was revealed. Say, "Bring then the Torah and read it, if you are truthful.

94. Then whoever fabricates a lie against God after this, these it is that are the unjust.

95. Say, "God has spoken the truth, therefore follow the religion of Abraham, the upright one; and he was not one of the polytheists."

96. Most certainly the first house appointed for men is the one at Bekka, blessed and a guidance

for the nations.

97. In it are clear signs, the standing place of Abraham, and whoever enters it shall be secure, and pilgrimage to the House is incumbent upon men for the sake of God, upon every one who is able to undertake the journey to it; and whoever disbelieves, then certainly God is Self-sufficient, above any need of the worlds.

98. Say, "Oh followers of the Book! why do you disbelieve in the words of God? And God is a witness of what you do. 99. Say, "Oh followers of the Book! Why do you hinder him who believes from the way of God? You seek to make it crooked, while you are witness, and God is not heedless of what you do."

100. Oh you who believe! if you obey a party from among those who have been given the Book, they will turn you back as unbelievers after you have believed.

101. But how can you disbelieve while it is you to whom the words of God are recited, and among you is His Prophet? And whoever holds fast to God, he indeed is guided to the right path.

102. Oh you who believe! be careful of your duty to God with the care which is due to Him, and do not die unless you are Muslims.

103. And hold fast by the covenant of God all together and do not be disunited, and remember the favor of God on you when you were enemies, then He united your hearts so by His favor you became brethren; and you were on the brink of a pit of fire, then He saved you from it, thus does God make clear to you His words that you may follow the right way. 104. And from among you there should be a party who invite to good and enjoin what is right and forbid the wrong, and these it is that shall be successful.

105. And do not be like those who became divided and disagreed after clear reasons had come to them, and these it is that shall have a grievous punishment.

106. On the day when some faces shall turn white and some faces shall turn black; then as to those whose faces turn black: Did you disbelieve after your believing? Taste therefore the punishment because you disbelieved.

107. And as to those whose faces turn white, they shall be in God's mercy; in it they shall-abide.

108. These are the words of God which We recite to you with truth, and God does not desire any injustice to the creatures.

109. And whatever is in the heavens and whatever is in the earth is God's; and to God all things return

110. You are the best of the nations raised up for the benefit of men; you enjoin what is right and forbid the wrong and believe in God; and if the followers of the Book had believed it would have been better for them; of them some are believers and most of them are transgressors.

111. They shall by no means harm you but with a slight evil; and if they fight with you they shall turn their backs to you, then shall they not be helped.

112. Abasement is made to cleave to them wherever they are found, except under a covenant with God and a covenant with men, and they have become deserving of wrath from God, and humiliation is made to cleave to them; this is because they disbelieved in the words of God and killed the prophets unjustly; this is because they disobeyed and exceeded the limits.

113. They are not all alike; of the followers of the Book there is an upright party; they recite God's words in the nighttime and they adore Him.

114. They believe in God and the last day, and they enjoin what is right and forbid the wrong and they strive with one another in hastening to good deeds, and those are among the good.

115. And whatever good they do, they shall not be denied it, and God knows those who guard against evil.

116. As for those who disbelieve, certainly neither their wealth nor their children shall avail

them in the least against God; and these are the inmates of the fire; therein they shall abide.

¹¹⁷. The likeness of what they spend in the life of this world is as the likeness of wind in which is intense cold that smites the seed produce of a people who haw done injustice to their souls and destroys it; and God is not unjust to them, but they are unjust to themselves.

¹¹⁸. Oh you who believe! do not take for intimate friends from among others than your own people; they do not fall short of inflicting loss upon you; they love what distresses you; vehement hatred has already appeared from out of their mouths, and what their hearts conceal is greater still; indeed, We have made the words clear to you, if you will understand.

¹¹⁹. Lo! you are they who will love them while they do not love you, and you believe in the Book in the whole of it; and when they meet you they say, "We believe, and when they are alone, they bite the ends of their fingers in rage against you." Say, "Die in your rage; certainly God knows what is in the hearts."

¹²⁰. If good happens to you, it grieves them, and if an evil afflicts you, they rejoice at it; and if you are patient and guard yourselves, their scheme will not injure you in any way; certainly God comprehends what they do.

¹²¹. And when you did go forth early in the morning from your family to lodge the believers in encampments for war and God is Hearing, Knowing. ¹²². When two parties from among you had determined that they should show cowardice, and God was the guardian of them both, and in God should the believers trust.

¹²³. And God did certainly assist you at Badr when you were weak; be careful of your duty to God then, that you may give thanks.

¹²⁴. When you said to the believers: Does it not suffice you that your Lord should assist you with three thousand of the angels sent down?

¹²⁵. Yea! if you remain patient and are on your guard, and they come upon you in a headlong manner, your Lord will assist you with five thousand of the havoc-making angels.

¹²⁶. And God did not make it but as good news for you, and that your hearts might be at ease thereby, and victory is only from God, the Mighty, the Wise.

¹²⁷. That He may cut off a portion from among those who disbelieve, or abase them so that they should return disappointed of attaining what they desired.

¹²⁸. You have no concern in the affair whether He turns to them mercifully or reprimands them, for certainly they are unjust.

¹²⁹. And whatever is in the heavens and whatever is in the earth is God's; He forgives whom He pleases and reprimands whom He pleases; and God is Forgiving, Merciful.

¹³⁰. Oh you who believe! do not devour usury, making it double and redouble, and be careful of your duty to God, that you may be successful.

¹³¹. And guard yourselves against the fire which has been prepared for the unbelievers.

¹³². And obey God and the Prophet, that you may be shown mercy.

¹³³. And hasten to forgiveness from your Lord; and a Garden, the extensiveness of which is as the heavens and the earth, it is prepared for those who guard against evil.

¹³⁴. Those who spend benevolently in ease as well as in straitness, and those who restrain their anger and pardon men; and God loves those who do good to others.

¹³⁵. And those who when they commit an indecency or do injustice to their souls remember God and ask forgiveness for their faults -- and who forgives the faults but God, and who do not knowingly persist in what they have done.

¹³⁶. As for these -- their reward is forgiveness from their Lord, and gardens beneath which rivers flow, to abide in them, and excellent is the reward of the laborers.

¹³⁷. Indeed there have been examples before you; therefore travel in the earth and see what was

the end of the rejecters.

¹³⁸. This is a clear statement for men, and a guidance and an admonition to those who guard against evil.

¹³⁹. And do not be infirm, and do not be grieving, and you shall have the upper hand if you are believers.

¹⁴⁰. If a wound has afflicted you at Ohud, a wound like it has also afflicted the unbelieving people; and We bring these days to men by turns, and that God may know those who believe and take witnesses from among you; and God does not love the unjust.

¹⁴¹. And that He may purge those who believe and deprive the unbelievers of blessings.

¹⁴². Do you think that you will enter the garden while God has not yet known those who strive hard from among you, and He has not known the patient. ¹⁴³. And certainly you desired death before you met it, so indeed you have seen it and you look at it

¹⁴⁴. And Muhammad is no more than an apostle; the apostles have already passed away before him; if then he dies or is killed will you turn back upon your heels? And whoever turns back upon his heels!s, he will by no means do harm
to God in the least and God will reward the grateful.

¹⁴⁵. And a soul will not die but with the permission of God the term is fixed; and whoever desires the reward of this world, I shall give him of it, and whoever desires the reward of the hereafter I shall give him of it, and I will reward the grateful.

¹⁴⁶. And how many a prophet has fought with whom were many worshipers of the Lord; so they did not become weak-hearted on account of what befell them in God's way, nor did they weaken, nor did they abase themselves; and God loves the patient.

¹⁴⁷. And their saying was no other than that they said, "Our Lord! forgive us our faults and our extravagance in our affair and make firm our feet and help us against the unbelieving people.

¹⁴⁸. So God gave them the reward of this world and better reward of the hereafter and God loves those who do good to others.

¹⁴⁹. Oh you who believe! if you obey those who disbelieve they will turn you back upon your heels, so you will turn back as losers.

¹⁵⁰. No! God is your Patron and He is the best of the helpers.

¹⁵¹. We will put terror into the hearts of those who disbelieve, because they set up with God that for which He has sent down no authority, and their home is the fire, and evil is the home of the unjust.

¹⁵². And certainly God made good to you His promise when you killed them by His permission, until when you became weak-hearted and disputed about the affair and disobeyed after He had shown you that which you loved; of you were some who desired this world and of you were some who desired the hereafter; then He turned you away from them that He might try you; and He has certainly pardoned you, and God is Kind to the believers.

¹⁵³. When you ran off precipitously and did not wait for any one, and the Prophet was calling you from your rear, so He gave you another sorrow instead of your sorrow, so that you might not grieve at what had escaped you, nor at what befell you; and God is aware of what you do.

¹⁵⁴. Then after sorrow He sent down security upon you, a calm coming upon a party of you, and there was another party whom their own souls had rendered anxious; they entertained about God thoughts of ignorance quite unjustly, saying, "We have no hand in the affair. Say, "Certainly the affair is wholly in the hands of God. They conceal within their souls what they would not reveal to you. They say, "Had we any hand in the affair, we would not have been slain here. Say, "Had you remained in your houses, those for whom slaughter was ordered would certainly have gone forth to the places where they would be slain, and that God might

test what was in your hearts and that He might purge what was in your hearts; and God knows what is in the hearts.

155. As for those of you who turned back on the day when the two armies met, only the Satan sought to cause them to make a slip on account of some deeds they had done, and certainly God has pardoned them; certainly God is Forgiving, Forbearing.

156. Oh you who believe! do not be like those who disbelieve and say of their brethren when they travel in the earth or engage in fighting: Had they been with us, they would not have died and they would not have been slain; so God makes this to be an intense regret in their hearts; and God gives life and causes
death and God sees what you do.

157. And if you are slain in the way of God or you die, certainly forgiveness from God and mercy is better than what they amass.

158. And if indeed you die or you are slain, certainly to God shall you be gathered together.

159. Thus it is due to mercy from God that you deal with them gently, and had you been rough, hard hearted, they would certainly have dispersed from around you; pardon them therefore and ask pardon for them, and take counsel with them in the affair; so when you have decided, then place your trust in God; certainly God loves those who trust.

160. If God assists you, then there is none that can overcome you, and if He abandons you, who is there then that can assist you after Him? And on God should the believers rely.

161. And it is not attributable to a prophet that he should act unfaithfully; and he who acts unfaithfully shall bring that in respect of which he has acted unfaithfully on the day of resurrection; then shall every soul be paid back fully what it has earned, and they shall not be dealt with unjustly.

162. Is then he who follows the pleasure of God like him who has made himself deserving of displeasure from God, and his home is hell; and it is an evil destination.

163. There are varying grades with God, and God sees what they do.

164. Certainly God conferred a benefit upon the believers when He raised among them a Prophet from among themselves, reciting to them His words and purifying them, and teaching them the Book and the wisdom, although before that they were certainly in great error.

165. What! when a misfortune occurred for you, and you had certainly afflicted the unbelievers with twice as much, you began to say, "Where is this from? Say, "It is from yourselves; certainly God has power over all things."

166. And what befell you on the day when the two armies met at Ohud was with God's knowledge, and that He might know the believers.

167. And that He might know the hypocrites; and it was said to them: Come, fight in God's way, or defend yourselves. They said, "If we knew fighting, we would certainly have followed you. They were on that day much nearer to unbelief than to belief. They say with their mouths what is not in their hearts, and God knows best what they conceal.

168. Those who said of their brethren while they themselves held back: Had they obeyed us, they would not have been killed. Say, "Then avert death from yourselves if you speak the truth.

169. And reckon not those who are killed in God's way as dead; no, they are alive and are provided sustenance from their Lord;

170. Rejoicing in what God has given them out of His grace and they rejoice for the sake of those who, being left behind them, have not yet joined them, that they shall have no fear, nor shall they grieve.

171. They rejoice on account of favor from God and His grace, and that God will not waste the reward of the believers.

¹⁷². As for those who responded at Ohud to the call of God and the Prophet after the wound had happened to them, those among them who do good to others and guard against evil shall have a great reward.

¹⁷³. Those to whom the people said, "Certainly men have gathered against you, therefore fear them, but this increased their faith, and they said, "God is sufficient for us and most excellent is the Protector. ¹⁷⁴. So they returned with favor from God and His grace, no evil touched them and they followed the pleasure of God; and God is the Lord of great kindness.

¹⁷⁵. It is only the Satan that causes you to fear from his friends, but do not fear them, and fear Me if you are believers.

¹⁷⁶. And let not those grieve you who fall into unbelief hastily; certainly they can do no harm to God at all; God intends that He should not give them any portion in the hereafter, and they shall have a grievous punishment.

¹⁷⁷. Certainly those who have bought unbelief at the price of faith shall do no harm at all to God, and they shall have a painful punishment.

¹⁷⁸. And let not those who disbelieve think that Our granting them respite is better for their souls; We grant them respite only that they may add to their sins; and they shall have a disgraceful punishment.

¹⁷⁹. On no account will God leave the believers in the condition which you are in until He separates the evil from the good; nor is God going to make you acquainted with the unseen, but God chooses of His apostles whom He pleases; therefore believe in God and His apostles; and if you believe and guard against evil, then you shall have a great reward.

¹⁸⁰. And let not those deem, who are wretched in giving away that which God has granted them out of His grace, that it is good for them; No, it is worse for them; they shall have that because they were miserable made to smite to their necks on the resurrection day; and God's is the heritage of the heavens and the earth; and God is aware of what you do.

¹⁸¹. God has certainly heard the saying of those who said, "Certainly God is poor and we are rich. I will record what they say, and their killing the prophets unjustly, and I will say, "Taste the punishment of burning.

¹⁸². This is for what your own hands have sent before and because God is not in the least unjust to the servants.

¹⁸³. Those are they who said, "Certainly God has enjoined us that we should not believe in any apostle until he brings us an offering which the fire consumes. Say, "Indeed, there came to you apostles before me with clear explanations and with that which you demand; why then did you kill them if you are truthful?

¹⁸⁴. But if they reject you, so indeed were rejected before you apostles who came with clear explanations and scriptures and the illuminating book.

¹⁸⁵. Every soul shall taste of death, and you shall only be paid fully your reward on the resurrection day; then whoever is removed far away from the fire and is made to enter the garden he indeed has attained the object; and the life of this world is nothing but a provision of vanities.

¹⁸⁶. You shall certainly be tried respecting your wealth and your souls, and you shall certainly hear from those who have been given the Book before you and from those who are polytheists much annoying talk; and if you are patient and guard against evil, certainly this is one of the affairs which should be determined upon.

¹⁸⁷. And when God made a covenant with those who were given the Book: You shall certainly make it known to men and you shall not hide it; but they put it behind their backs and took a small price for it; so evil is that which they buy.

¹⁸⁸. Do not think those who rejoice for what they have done and love that they should be praised

for what they have not done -- so do by no means think them to be safe from the punishment, and they shall have a painful punishment.

189. And God's is the kingdom of the heavens and the earth, and God has power over all things.

190. Most certainly in the creation of the heavens and the earth and the alternation of the night and the day there are signs for men who understand.

191. Those who remember God standing and sitting and lying on their sides and reflect on the creation of the heavens and the earth: Our Lord! You have not created this in vain! Glory be to You; save us then from the punishment of the fire:

192. Our Lord! certainly whomsoever You make enter the fire, him You have indeed brought to disgrace, and there shall be no helpers for the unjust:

193. Our Lord! certainly we have heard a preacher calling to the faith, saying, "Believe in your Lord, so we did believe; Our Lord! forgive us therefore our faults, and cover our evil deeds and make us die with the righteous. 194. Our Lord! and grant us what You have promised us by Your apostles; and do not disgrace us on the day of resurrection; certainly You dost not fail to perform the promise.

195. So their Lord accepted their prayer: That I will not waste the work of a worker among you, whether male or female, the one of you being from the other; they, therefore, who fled and were turned out of their homes and persecuted in My way and who fought and were slain, I will most certainly cover their evil deeds, and I will most certainly make them enter gardens beneath which rivers flow; a reward from God, and with God is yet better reward.

196. Let it not deceive you that those who disbelieve go to and fro in the cities fearlessly.

197. A brief enjoyment! then their home is hell, and evil is the resting-place.

198. But as to those who are careful of their duty to their Lord, they shall have gardens beneath which rivers flow, abiding in them; an entertainment from their Lord, and that which is with God is best for the righteous.

199. And most certainly of the followers of the Book there are those who believe in God and in that which has been revealed to you and in that which has been revealed to them, being lowly before God; they do not take a small price for the words of God; these it is that have their reward with their Lord; certainly God is quick in judging.

200. Oh you who believe! be patient and excel in patience and remain steadfast, and be careful of your duty to God, that you may be successful.

Chapter 4 — Al-Nisa — The Women

In the name of God, the Kind, the Merciful.

1. Oh people! be careful of your duty to your Lord, Who created you from a single being and created its mate of the same kind and spread from these two, many men and women; and be careful of your duty to God, by Whom you demand one of another your rights, and to the ties of relationship; certainly
God ever watches over you.

2. And give to the orphans their property, and do not substitute worthless things for their good ones, and do not devour their property as an addition to your own property; this is certainly a great crime.

3. And if you fear that you cannot act equitably towards orphans, then marry such women as seem good to you, two and three and four; but if you fear that you will not do justice between them, then marry only one or what your right hands possess; this is more proper, that you may not deviate from the right course.

4. And give women their dowries as a free gift, but if they of themselves be pleased to give up to you a portion of it, then eat it with enjoyment and with wholesome result.

5. And do not give away your property which God has made for you a means of support to the weak of understanding, and maintain them out of the profits of it, and clothe them and speak to them words of honest advice.

6. And test the orphans until they attain puberty; then if you find in them maturity of intellect, make over to them their property, and do not consume it extravagantly and hastily, if they do not attain full age; and whoever is rich, let him abstain altogether, and whoever is poor, let him eat reasonably; then when you give over to them their property, call witnesses in their presence; and God shall be the Decider.

7. Men shall have a portion of what the parents and the near relatives leave, and women shall have a portion of what the parents and the near relatives leave, whether there is little or much of it; a stated portion.

8. And when there are present at the division the relatives and the orphans and the needy, give them something out of it and speak to them kind words.

9. And let those fear who, should they leave behind them weakly offspring, would fear on their account, so let them be careful of their duty to God, and let them speak right words.

10. As for those who swallow the property of the orphans unjustly, certainly they only swallow fire into their bellies and they shall enter burning fire.

11. God urges you concerning your children: The male shall have the equal of the portion of two females; then if they are more than two females, they shall have two-thirds of what the deceased has left, and if there is one, she shall have the half; and as for his parents, each of them shall have the
sixth of what he has left if he has a child, but if he has no child and only his two parents inherit him, then his mother shall have the third; but if he has brothers, then his mother shall have the sixth after the payment of a bequest he may have bequeathed or a debt; your parents and your children, you do not know which of them is more useful to you; this is an ordinance from God: Certainly God is Knowing, Wise.

12. And you shall have half of what your wives leave if they have no child, but if they have a

child, then you shall have a fourth of what they leave after payment of any bequest they may have bequeathed or a debt; and they shall have the fourth of what you leave if you have no child, but if you have a child then they shall have the eighth of what you leave after payment of a bequest you may have bequeathed or a debt; and if a man or a woman leaves property to be inherited by neither parents nor offspring, and he or she has a brother or a sister, then each of them two shall have the sixth, but if they are more than that, they shall be sharers in the third after payment of any bequest that may have been bequeathed or a debt that does not harm others; this is an ordinance from God: and God is Knowing, Forbearing.

13. These are God's limits, and whoever obeys God and His Prophet, He will cause him to enter gardens beneath which rivers flow, to abide in them; and this is the great achievement.

14. And whoever disobeys God and His Prophet and goes beyond His limits, He will cause him to enter fire to abide in it, and he shall have an abasing punishment.

15. And as for those who are guilty of an indecency from among your women, call to witnesses against them four witnesses from among you; then if they bear witness confine them to the houses until death takes them away or God opens some way for them.

16. And as for the two who are guilty of indecency from among you, give them both a punishment; then if they repent and amend, turn aside from them; certainly God is Oft-returning to mercy, the Merciful.

17. Repentance with God is only for those who do evil in ignorance, then turn to God soon, so these it is to whom God turns mercifully, and God is ever Knowing, Wise.

18. And repentance is not for those who go on doing evil deeds, until when death comes to one of them, he says: Certainly now I repent; nor for those who die while they are unbelievers. These are they for whom We have prepared a painful punishment.

19. Oh you who believe! it is not lawful for you that you should take women as heritage against their will, and do not straighten them in order that you may take part of what you have given them, unless they are guilty of great indecency, and treat them kindly; then if you hate them, it may be that you dislike a thing while God has placed abundant good in it.

20. And if you wish to have one wife in place of another and you have given one of them a heap of gold, then take not from it anything; would you take it by slandering her and doing her great wrong?

21. And how can you take it when one of you has already gone in to the other and they have made with you a firm covenant?

22. And marry not woman whom your fathers married, except what has already passed; this certainly is indecent and hateful, and it is an evil way.

23. Forbidden to you are your mothers and your daughters and your sisters and your paternal aunts and your maternal aunts and brothers' daughters and sisters' daughters and your mothers that have suckled you and your foster-sisters and mothers of your wives and your step-daughters who are in your guardianship, born of your wives to whom you have gone in, but if you have not gone in to them, there is no blame on you in marrying them, and the wives of your sons who are of your own loins and that you should have two sisters together, except what has already passed; certainly God is Forgiving, Merciful.

24. And all married women except those whom your right hands possess this is God's ordinance to you, and lawful for you are all women besides those, provided that you seek them with your property, taking them in marriage not committing fornication. Then as to those whom you profit by, give them their dowries as appointed; and there is no blame on you about what you mutually agree after what is appointed; certainly God is Knowing, Wise.

25. And whoever among you has not within his power ampleness of means to marry free be-

lieving women, then he may marry of those whom your right hands possess from among your believing maidens; and God knows best your faith: you are sprung the one from the other; so marry them with the permission of their masters, and give them their dowries justly, they being chaste, not fornicating,

nor receiving paramours; and when they are taken in marriage, then if they are guilty of indecency, they shall suffer half the punishment which is inflicted upon free women. This is for him among you who fears falling into evil; and that you abstain is better for you, and God is Forgiving, Merciful.

26. God desires to explain to you, and to guide you into the ways of those before you, and to turn to you mercifully, and God is Knowing, Wise.

27. And God desires that He should turn to you mercifully, and those who follow their lusts desire that you should deviate with a great deviation.

28. God desires that He should make light your burdens, and man is created weak.

29. Oh you who believe! do not devour your property among yourselves falsely, except that it be trading by your mutual consent; and do not kill your people; certainly God is Merciful to you.

30. And whoever does this aggressively and unjustly, We will soon throw him into fire; and this is easy to God.

31. If you shun the great sins which you are forbidden, We will do away with your small sins and cause you to enter an honorable place of entering.

32. And do not covet that by which God has made some of you excel others; men shall have the benefit of what they earn and women shall have the benefit of what they earn; and ask God of His grace; certainly God knows all things.

33. And to every one We have appointed heirs of what parents and near relatives leave; and as to those with whom your rights hands have ratified agreements, give them their portion; certainly God is a witness over all things.

34. Men are the maintainers of women because God has made some of them to excel others and because they spend out of their property; the good women are therefore obedient, guarding the unseen as God has guarded; and as to those on whose part you fear desertion, reprimand them, and leave them alone in the sleeping-places and beat them; then if they obey you, do not seek a way against them; certainly God is High, Great.

35. And if you fear a breach between the two, then appoint judge from his people and a judge from her people; if they both desire agreement, God will effect harmony between them, certainly God is Knowing, Aware.

36. And serve God and do not associate any thing with Him and be good to the parents and to the near of kin and the orphans and the needy and the neighbor of your kin and the alien neighbor, and the companion in a journey and the wayfarer and those whom your right hands possess; certainly God does not love him who is proud, boastful;

37. Those who are wretched and bid people to be wretched and hide what God has given them out of His grace; and We have prepared for the unbelievers a disgraceful punishment.

38. And those who spend their property in alms to be seen of the people and do not believe in God nor in the last day; and as for him whose associate is the Satan, an evil associate is he!

39. And what harm would it have done them if they had believed in God and the last day and spent benevolently of what God had given them? And God knows them.

40. Certainly God does not do injustice to the weight of an atom, and if it is a good deed He multiplies it and gives from Himself a great reward. 41. How will it be, then, when We bring from every people a witness and bring you as a witness against these?

42. On that day will those who disbelieve and disobey the Prophet desire that the earth were

leveled with them, and they shall not hide any word from God.

⁴³. Oh you who believe! do not go near prayer when you are Intoxicated until you know well what you say, nor when you are under an obligation to perform a bath -- unless you are travelling on the road -- until you have washed yourselves; and if you are sick, or on a journey, or one of you come from the privy or you have touched the women, and you cannot find water, betake yourselves to pure earth, then wipe your faces and your hands; certainly God is Pardoning, Forgiving.

⁴⁴. Have you not considered those to whom a portion of the Book has been given? They buy error and desire that you should go astray from the way.

⁴⁵. And God knows best your enemies; and God suffices as a Guardian, and God suffices as a Helper.

⁴⁶. Of those who are Jews there are those who alter words from their places and say, "We have heard and we disobey and: Hear, may you not be made to hear! and: Raina, distorting the word with their tongues and taunting about religion; and if they had said instead: We have heard and we obey, and hearken, and Unzurna it would have been better for them and more upright; but God has cursed them on account of their unbelief, so they do not believe but a little.

⁴⁷. Oh you who have been given the Book! believe that which We have revealed, verifying what you have, before We alter faces then turn them on their backs, or curse them as We cursed the violators of the Sabbath, and the command of God shall be executed.

⁴⁸. Certainly God does not forgive that anything should be associated with Him, and forgives what is besides that to whomsoever He pleases; and whoever associates anything with God, he devises indeed a great sin.

⁴⁹. Have you not considered those who attribute purity to themselves? No, God purifies whom He pleases; and they shall not be wronged the husk of a date stone.

⁵⁰. See how they forge the lie against God, and this is sufficient as a great sin.

⁵¹. Have you not seen those to whom a portion of the Book has been given? They believe in idols and false deities and say of those who disbelieve: These are better guided in the path than those who believe.

⁵². Those are they whom God has cursed, and whomever God curses you shall not find any helper for him.

⁵³. Or have they a share in the kingdom? But then they would not give to people even the speck in the date stone.

⁵⁴. Or do they envy the people for what God has given them of His grace? But indeed We have given to Abraham's children the Book and the wisdom, and We have given them a grand kingdom.

⁵⁵. So of them is he who believes in him, and of them is he who turns away from him, and hell is sufficient to burn.

⁵⁶. As for those who disbelieve in Our words, We shall make them enter fire; so oft as their skins are thoroughly burned, We will change them for other skins, that they may taste the punishment; certainly God is Mighty, Wise.

⁵⁷. And as for those who believe and do good deeds, We will make them enter gardens beneath which rivers flow, to abide in them for ever; they shall have therein pure mates, and We shall make them enter a dense shade.

⁵⁸. Certainly God commands you to make over trusts to their owners and that when you judge between people you judge with justice; certainly God reprimands you with what is excellent; certainly God is Seeing, Hearing.

⁵⁹. Oh you who believe! obey God and obey the Prophet and those in authority from among

you; then if you quarrel about anything, refer it to God and the Prophet, if you believe in God and the last day; this is better and very good in the end.

⁶⁰. Have you not seen those who assert that they believe in what has been revealed to you and what was revealed before you? They desire to summon one another to the judgment of the Satan, though they were commanded to deny him, and the Satan desires to lead them astray into a remote error.

⁶¹. And when it is said to them: Come to what God has revealed and to the Prophet, you will see the hypocrites turning away from you with utter aversion.

⁶². But how will it be when misfortune happens to them on account of what their hands have sent before? Then they will come to you swearing by God: We did not desire anything but good and concord.

⁶³. These are they of whom God knows what is in their hearts; therefore turn aside from them and reprimand them, and speak to them effectual words concerning themselves.

⁶⁴. And We did not send any apostle but that he should be obeyed by God's permission; and had they, when they were unjust to themselves, come to you and asked forgiveness of God and the Prophet had also asked forgiveness for them, they would have found God Oft-returning to mercy, Merciful.

⁶⁵. But no! by your Lord! they do not believe in reality until they make you a judge of that which has become a matter of disagreement among them, and then do not find any straitness in their hearts as to what you have decided and submit with entire submission.

⁶⁶. And if We had prescribed for them: Lay down your lives or go forth from your homes, they would not have done it except a few of them; and if they had done what they were reprimanded, it would have certainly been better for them and best in strengthening them;

⁶⁷. And then We would certainly have given them from Ourselves a great reward.

⁶⁸. And We would certainly have guided them in the right path.

⁶⁹. And whoever obeys God and the Prophet, these are with those upon whom God has bestowed favors from among the prophets and the truthful and the martyrs and the good, and fine companions are they!

⁷⁰. This is grace from God, and sufficient is God as the Knower.

⁷¹. Oh you who believe! take your precaution, then go forth in detachments or go forth in a body.

⁷². And certainly among you is he who would certainly hang back! If then a misfortune happens to you he says: Certainly God conferred a benefit on me that I was not present with them.

⁷³. And if grace from God come to you, he would certainly cry out, as if there had not been any friendship between you and him: Would that I had been with them, then I should have attained a mighty good fortune.

⁷⁴. Therefore let those fight in the way of God, who sell this world's life for the hereafter; and whoever fights in the way of God, then be he slain or be he victorious, We shall grant him a mighty reward.

⁷⁵. And what reason have you that you should not fight in the way of God and of the weak among the men and the women and the children, of those who say, "Our Lord! cause us to go forth from this town, whose people are oppressors, and give us from You a guardian and give us from You a helper. ⁷⁶. Those who believe fight in the way of God, and those who disbelieve fight in the way of the Satan. Fight therefore against the friends of the Satan; certainly the strategy of the Satan is weak.

⁷⁷. Have you not seen those to whom it was said, "Withhold your hands, and keep up prayer and pay the poor-rate; but when fighting is prescribed for them, lo! a party of them fear men as they ought to have feared God, or even with a greater fear, and say, "Our Lord! why have You

ordered fighting for us? Why did You not grant us a delay to a near end? Say, "The provision of this world is short, and the hereafter is better for him who guards against evil; and you shall not be wronged the husk of a date stone.

78. Wherever you are, death will overtake you, though you are in lofty towers, and if a benefit comes to them, they say, "This is from God; and if a misfortune happens to them, they say, "This is from you. Say, "All is from God, but what is the matter with these people that they do not make approach to
understanding what is told them?

79. Whatever benefit comes to you Oh man!, it is from God, and whatever misfortune happens to you, it is from yourself, and We have sent you Oh Prophet!, to mankind as an apostle; and God is sufficient as a witness.

80. Whoever obeys the Prophet, he indeed obeys God, and whoever turns back, so We have not sent you as a keeper over them.

81. And they say, "Obedience. But when they go out from your presence, a party of them decide by night upon doing otherwise than what you say; and God writes down what they decide by night, therefore turn aside from them and trust in God, and God is sufficient as a protector.

82. Do they not then meditate on the Koran? And if it were from any other than God, they would have found in it many a discrepancy.

83. And when there comes to them news of security or fear they spread it abroad; and if they had referred it to the Prophet and to those in authority among them, those among them who can search out the knowledge of it would have known it, and were it not for the grace of God upon you and His mercy, you would have certainly followed the Satan save a few

84. Fight then in God's way; this is not imposed on you except In relation to yourself, and rouse the believers to ardor maybe God will restrain the fighting of those who disbelieve and God is strongest in prowess and strongest to give an exemplary punishment.

85. Whoever joins himself to another in a good cause shall have a share of it, and whoever joins himself to another in an evil cause shall have the responsibility of it, and God controls all things.

86. And when you are greeted with a greeting, greet with a better greeting than it or return it; certainly God takes account of all things.

87. God, there is no god but He -- He will most certainly gather you together on the resurrection day, there is no doubt in it; and who is more true in word than God?

88. What is the matter with you, then, that you have become two parties about the hypocrites, while God has made them return to unbelief for what they have earned? Do you wish to guide him whom God has caused to err? And whomsoever God causes to err, you shall by no means find a way for him.

89. They desire that you should disbelieve as they have disbelieved, so that you might be all alike; therefore take not from among them friends until they fly their homes in God's way; but if they turn back, then seize them and kill them wherever you find them, and take not from among them a friend or a
helper.

90. Except those who reach a people between whom and you there is an alliance, or who come to you, their hearts shrinking from fighting you or fighting their own people; and if God had pleased, He would have given them power over you, so that they should have certainly fought you; therefore if they
withdraw from you and do not fight you and offer you peace, then God has not given you a way against them.

91. You will find others who desire that they should be safe from you and secure from their

own people; as often as they are sent back to the mischief they get thrown into it headlong; therefore if they do not withdraw from you, and do not offer you peace and restrain their hands, then seize them and kill them wherever you find them; and against these We have given you a clear authority.

92. And it does not behoove a believer to kill a believer except by mistake, and whoever kills a believer by mistake, he should free a believing slave, and blood-money should be paid to his people unless they remit it as alms; but if he be from a tribe hostile to you and he is a believer, the freeing of a believing slave suffices, and if he is from a tribe between whom and you there is a convenant, the blood-money should be paid to his people along with the freeing of a believing slave; but he who cannot find a slave should fast for two months successively: a penance from God, and God is Knowing, Wise.

93. And whoever kills a believer intentionally, his punishment is hell; he shall abide in it, and God will send His wrath on him and curse him and prepare for him a painful punishment.

94. Oh you who believe! when you go to war in God's way, make investigation, and do not say to any one who offers you peace: You are not a believer. Do you seek goods of this world's life! But with God there are abundant gains; you too were such before, then God conferred a benefit on you; therefore make investigation; certainly God is aware of what you do.

95. The holders back from among the believers, not having any injury, and those who strive hard in God's way with their property and their persons are not equal; God has made the strivers with their property and their persons to excel the holders back a high degree, and to each class God has promised good; and God shall grant to the strivers above the holders back a mighty reward:

96. High degrees from Him and protection and mercy, and God is Forgiving, Merciful.

97. Certainly as for those whom the angels cause to die while they are unjust to their souls, they shall say, "In what state were you? They shall say, "We were weak in the earth. They shall say, "Was not God's earth spacious, so that you should have migrated therein? So these it is whose home is hell, and it is an evil resort

98. Except the weak from among the men and the children who have not in their power the means nor can they find a way to escape;

99. So these, it may be, God will pardon them, and God is Pardoning, Forgiving.

100. And whoever flies in God's way, he will find in the earth many a place of refuge and abundant resources, and whoever goes forth from his house flying to God and His Prophet, and then death overtakes him, his reward is indeed with God and God is Forgiving, Merciful.

101. And when you journey in the earth, there is no blame on you if you shorten the prayer, if you fear that those who disbelieve will cause you distress, certainly the unbelievers are your open enemy.

102. And when you are among them and keep up the prayer for them, let a party of them stand up with you, and let them take their arms; then when they have prostrated themselves let them go to your rear, and let another party who have not prayed come forward and pray with you, and let them take their precautions and their arms; for those who disbelieve desire that you may be careless of your arms and your luggage, so that they may then turn upon you with a sudden united attack, and there is no blame on you, if you are annoyed with rain or if you are sick, that you lay down your arms, and take your precautions; certainly God has prepared a disgraceful punishment for the unbelievers.

103. Then when you have finished the prayer, remember God standing and

sitting and reclining; but when you are secure from danger keep up prayer; certainly prayer is a timed ordinance for the believers.

104. And do not be weak hearted in pursuit of the enemy; if you suffer pain, then certainly

they too suffer pain as you suffer pain, and you hope from God what they do not hope; and God is Knowing, Wise.

105. Certainly We have revealed the Book to you with the truth that you may judge between people by means of that which God has taught you; and do not be an advocate on behalf of the treacherous.

106. And ask forgiveness of God; certainly God is Forgiving, Merciful.

107. And do not plead on behalf of those who act unfaithfully to their souls; certainly God does not love him who is treacherous, sinful;

108. They hide themselves from men and do not hide themselves from God, and He is with them when they meditate by night words which please Him not, and God encompasses what they do.

109. Behold! you are they who may plead for them in this world's life, but who will plead for them with God on the resurrection day, or who shall be their protector?

110. And whoever does evil or acts unjustly to his soul, then asks forgiveness of God, he shall find God Forgiving, Merciful.

111. And whoever commits a sin, he only commits it against his own soul; and God is Knowing, Wise.

112. And whoever commits a fault or a sin, then accuses of it one innocent, he indeed takes upon himself the burden of a defamation and a great sin.

113. And were it not for God's grace upon you and His mercy a party of them had certainly designed to bring you to hell and they do not bring anything to hell but their own souls, and they shall not harm you in any way, and God has revealed to you the Book and the wisdom, and He has taught you what you did not know, and God's grace on you is very great.

114. There is no good in most of their secret counsels except in his who urges charity or goodness or reconciliation between people; and whoever does this seeking God's pleasure, We will give him a mighty reward.

115. And whoever acts hostilely to the Prophet after that guidance has become show to him, and follows other than the way of the believers, We will turn him to that to which he has himself turned and make him enter hell; and it is an evil resort.

116. Certainly God does not forgive that anything should be associated with Him, and He forgives what is besides this to whom He pleases; and whoever associates anything with God, he indeed strays off into a remote error.

117. They do not call besides Him on anything but idols, and they do not call on anything but a rebellious Satan.

118. God has cursed him; and he said, "Most certainly I will take of Your servants an appointed portion:

119. And most certainly I will lead them astray and excite in them vain desires, and bid them so that they shall slit the ears of the cattle, and most certainly I will bid them so that they shall alter God's creation; and whoever takes the Satan for a guardian rather than God he indeed shall suffer a great loss.

120. He gives them promises and excites vain desires in them; and the Satan does not promise them but to deceive.

121. These are they whose home is hell, and they shall not find any refuge from it.

122. And as for those who believe and do good, We will make them enter into gardens beneath which rivers flow, to abide therein for ever; it is a promise of God, true indeed, and who is truer of word than God?

123. This shall not be in accordance with your vain desires nor in accordance with the vain desires of the followers of the Book; whoever does evil, he shall be avenged with it, and besides God

he will find for himself neither a guardian nor a helper.

124. And whoever does good deeds whether male or female and he or she is a believer -- these shall enter the garden, and they shall not be dealt with a jot unjustly.

125. And who has a better religion than he who submits himself entirely to God? And he is the doer of good to others and follows the faith of Abraham, the upright one, and God took Abraham as a friend.

126. And whatever is in the heavens and whatever is in the earth is God's; and God encompasses all things.

127. And they ask you a decision about women. Say, "God makes known to you His decision concerning them, and that which is recited to you in the Book concerning female orphans whom you do not give what is appointed for them while you desire to marry them, and concerning the weak among children, and that you should deal towards orphans with equity; and whatever good you do, God certainly knows it.

128. And if a woman fears ill usage or desertion on the part of her husband, there is no blame on them, if they effect a reconciliation between them, and reconciliation is better, and avarice has been made to be present in the people's minds; and if you do good to others and guard against evil, then certainly God is aware of what you do.

129. And you have it not in your power to do justice between wives, even though you may wish it, but do not be disinclined from one with total disinclination, so that you leave her as it were in suspense; and if you cause a reconciliation and guard against evil, then certainly God is Forgiving, Merciful.

130. And if they separate, God will render them both free from want out of His ampleness, and God is Ample-giving, Wise.

131. And whatever is in the heavens and whatever is in the earth is God's and certainly We enjoined those who were given the Book before you and We enjoin you too that you should be careful of your duty to God; and if you disbelieve, then certainly whatever is in the heavens and whatever is in the earth is God's and God is Self-sufficient, Praise-worthy.

132. And whatever is in the heavens and whatever is in the earth is God's, and God is sufficient as a Protector.

133. If He please, He can make you pass away, Oh people! and bring others; and God has the power to do this.

134. Whoever desires the reward of this world, then with God is the reward of this world and the hereafter; and God is Hearing, Seeing.

135. Oh you who believe! be maintainers of justice, bearers of witness of God's sake, though it may be against your own selves or your parents or near relatives; if he be rich or poor, God is nearer to them both in compassion; therefore do not follow your low desires, so you will not deviate; and if you swerve or turn aside, then certainly God is aware of what you do.

136. Oh you who believe! believe in God and His Prophet and the Book which He has revealed to His Prophet and the Book which He revealed before; and whoever disbelieves in God and His angels and His apostles and the last day, he indeed strays off into a remote error.

137. Certainly as for those who believe then disbelieve, again believe and again disbelieve, then increase in disbelief, God will not forgive them nor guide them in the right path.

138. Announce to the hypocrites that they shall have a painful punishment:

139. Those who take the unbelievers for guardians rather than believers. Do they seek honor from them? Then certainly all honor is for God.

140. And indeed He has revealed to you in the Book that when you hear God's words disbelieved in and mocked at do not sit with them until they enter into some other discourse;

certainly then you would be like them; certainly God will gather together the hypocrites and the unbelievers all in hell.

141. Those who wait for some misfortune to happen to you then If you have a victory from God they say, "Were we not with you? And if. there is a chance for the unbelievers, they say, "Did we not acquire the mastery over you and defend you from the believers? So God shall Judge between you on the day of
resurrection, and God will by no means give the unbelievers a way against the believers.

142. Certainly the hypocrites strive to deceive God, and He shall avenge their deceit to them, and when they stand up to prayer they stand up sluggishly; they do it only to be seen of men and do not remember God save a little.

143. Wavering between that and this, belonging neither to these nor to those; and whomsoever God causes to err, you shall not find a way for him.

144. Oh you who believe! do not take the unbelievers for friends rather than the believers; do you desire that you should give to God a clear proof against yourselves?

145. Certainly the hypocrites are in the lowest stage of the fire and you shall not find a helper for them.

146. Except those who repent and amend and hold fast to God and are sincere in their religion to God, these are with the believers, and God will grant the believers a mighty reward.

147. Why should God reprimand you if you are grateful and believe? And God is the Multiplier of rewards, Knowing

148. God does not love the public utterance of hurtful speech unless it be by one to whom injustice has been done; and God is Hearing, Knowing.

149. If you do good openly or do it in secret or pardon an evil then certainly God is Pardoning, Powerful.

150. Certainly those who disbelieve in God and His apostles and those who desire to make a distinction between God and His apostles and say, "We believe in some and disbelieve in others, and desire to take a course between this and that.

151. These it is that are truly unbelievers, and We have prepared for the unbelievers a disgraceful punishment.

152. And those who believe in God and His apostles and do not make a distinction between any of them -- God will grant them their rewards; and God is Forgiving, Merciful.

153. The followers of the Book ask you to bring down to them a book from heaven; so indeed they demanded of Moses a greater thing than that, for they said, "Show us God manifestly; so the lightning overtook them on account of their injustice. Then they took the calf for a god, after clear signs had come to them, but We pardoned this; and We gave to Moses clear authority.

154. And We lifted the mountain Sainai over them at the taking of the covenant and We said to them: Enter the door making obeisance; and We said to them: Do not exceed the limits of the Sabbath, and We made with them a firm covenant.

155. Therefore, for their breaking their covenant and their disbelief in the words of God and their killing the prophets wrongfully and their saying, "Our hearts are covered; no! God set a seal upon them owing to their unbelief, so they shall not believe except a few.

156. And for their unbelief and for their having uttered against Mary a grievous defamation.

157. And their saying, "Certainly we have killed the Messiah, Jesus son of Mary, the apostle of God; and they did not kill him nor did they crucify him, but it appeared to them so like Jesus and most certainly those who differ therein are only in a doubt about it; they have no knowledge respecting it, but only follow a conjecture, and they killed him not for sure.

158. No! God took him up to Himself; and God is Mighty, Wise.

159. And there is not one of the followers of the Book but most certainly believes in this before his death, and on the day of resurrection he Jesus shall be a witness against them.

160. Why for the iniquity of those who are Jews did We disallow to them the good things which had been made lawful for them and for their hindering many people from God's way.

161. And their taking usury though indeed they were forbidden it and their devouring the property of people falsely, and We have prepared for the unbelievers from among them a painful punishment.

162. But the firm in knowledge among them and the believers believe in what has been revealed to. you and what was revealed before you, and those who keep up prayers and those who give the poor-rate and the believers in God and the last day, these it is whom We will give a mighty reward.

163. Certainly We have revealed to you as We revealed to Noah, and the prophets after him, and We revealed to Abraham and Ishmael and Isaac and Jacob and the tribes, and Jesus and Ayub and Yunus and Aaron and Solomon and We gave to David

164. And We sent apostles We have mentioned to you before and apostles we have not mentioned to you; and to Moses, God addressed His Word, speaking to him:

165. We sent apostles as the givers of good news and as alarmgivers, so that people should not have a plea against God after the coming of apostles; and God is Mighty, Wise.

166. But God bears witness by what He has revealed to you that He has revealed it with His knowledge, and the angels bear witness also; and God is sufficient as a witness.

167. Certainly as for those who disbelieve and hinder men from God's way, they indeed have strayed off into a remote

168. Certainly as for those who disbelieve and act unjustly God will not forgive them nor guide them to a path

169. Except the path of hell, to abide in it for ever, and this is easy to God.

170. Oh people! certainly the Prophet has come to you with the truth from your Lord, therefore believe, it shall be good for you and If you disbelieve, then certainly whatever is in the heavens and the earth is God's; and God is Knowing, Wise.

171. Oh followers of the Book! do not exceed the limits in your religion, and do not speak lies against God, but speak the truth; the Messiah, Jesus son of Mary is only an apostle of God and His Word which He communicated to Mary and a spirit from Him; believe therefore in God and His apostles, and say not, Three. Desist, it is better for you; God is only one God; far be It from His glory that He should have a son, whatever is in the heavens and whatever is in the earth is His, and God is sufficient for a Protector.

172. The Messiah does by no means disdain that he should be a servant of God, nor do the angels who are near to Him, and whoever disdains His service and is proud, He will gather them all together to Himself.

173. Then as for those who believe and do good, He will pay them fully their rewards and give them more out of His grace; and as for those who disdain and are proud, He will reprimand them with a painful punishment. And they shall not find for themselves besides God a guardian or a helper

174. Oh people! certainly there has come to you clear proof from your Lord and We have sent to you clear light.

175. Then as for those who believe in God and hold fast by Him, He will cause them to enter into His mercy and grace and guide them to Himself on a right path.

176. They ask you for a decision of the law. Say, "God gives you a decision concerning the person who has neither parents nor offspring; if a man dies and he has no son and he has a sister, she

shall have half of what he leaves, and he shall be her heir she has no son; but if there be two sisters, they shall have two-thirds of what he leaves; and if there are brethren, men and women, then the male shall have the like of the portion of two females; God makes clear to you, so you will not err; and God knows all things.

Chapter 5 — Al-Ma'idah — The Dinner Table

In the name of God, the Kind, the Merciful.

¹. Oh you who believe! fulfill the obligations. The cattle quadrupeds are allowed to you except that which is recited to you, not violating the prohibition against game when you are entering upon the performance of the pilgrimage; certainly God orders what He desires.

². Oh you who believe! do not violate the signs appointed by God nor the sacred month, nor interfere with the offerings, nor the sacrificial animals with garlands, nor those going to the sacred house seeking the grace and pleasure of their Lord; and when you are free from the obligations of the pilgrimage, then hunt, and let not hatred of a people -- because they hindered you from the Sacred Masjid -- incite you to exceed the limits, and help one another in goodness and piety, and do not help one another in sin and aggression; and be careful of your duty to God; certainly God is severe in avenging evil.

³. Forbidden to you is that which dies of itself, and blood, and flesh of swine, and that on which any other name than that of God has been invoked, and the strangled animal and that beaten to death, and that killed by a fall and that killed by being smitten with the horn, and that which wild beasts have eaten, except what you slaughter, and what is sacrificed on stones set up for idols and that you divide by the arrows; that is a transgression. This day have those who disbelieve despaired of your religion, so fear them not, and fear Me. This day have I perfected for you your religion and completed My favor on you and chosen for you Islam as a religion; but whoever is compelled by hunger, not
inclining willfully to sin, then certainly God is Forgiving, Merciful.

⁴. They ask you as to what is allowed to them. Say, "The good things are allowed to you, and what you have taught the beasts and birds of prey, training them to hunt -- you teach them of what God has taught you -- so eat of that which they catch for you and mention the name of God over it; and be careful of your duty to God; certainly God is swift in judging.

⁵. This day all the good things are allowed to you; and the food of those who have been given the Book is lawful for you and your food is lawful for them; and the chaste from among the believing women and the chaste from among those who have been given the Book before you are lawful for you; when you have given them their dowries, taking them in marriage, not fornicating nor taking them for paramours in secret; and whoever denies faith, his work indeed is of no account, and in the hereafter he shall be one of the losers.

⁶. Oh you who believe! when you stand up to pray, wash your faces and your hands as far as the elbows, and wipe your heads and your feet to the ankles; and if you are under an obligation to perform a total ablution, then wash yourselves and if you are sick or on a journey, or one of you come from the privy, or you have touched the women, and you cannot find water, betake yourselves to pure earth and wipe your faces and your hands therewith, God does not desire to put on you any difficulty, but He wishes to purify you and that He may complete His favor on you, so that you may be grateful.

⁷. And remember the favor of God on you and His covenant with which He bound you firmly, when you said, "We have heard and we obey, and be careful of your duty to God, certainly God knows what is in the hearts.

⁸. Oh you who believe! Be upright for God, bearers of witness with justice, and let not hatred of a people incite you not to act equitably; act equitably, that is nearer to piety, and he careful

of your duty to God; certainly God is Aware of what you do.

⁹. God has promised to those who believe and do good deeds that they shall have forgiveness and a mighty reward.

¹⁰. And as for those who disbelieve and reject our words, these are the companions of the name.

¹¹. Oh you who believe! remember God's favor on you when a people had determined to stretch forth their hands towards you, but He withheld their hands from you, and be careful of your duty to God; and on God let the believers rely.

¹². And certainly God made a covenant with the children of Israel, and We raised up among them twelve chieftains; and God said, "Certainly I am with you; if you keep up prayer and pay the poor-rate and believe in My apostles and assist them and offer to God a proper gift, I will most certainly cover your evil deeds, and I will most certainly cause you to enter into gardens beneath which rivers flow, but whoever disbelieves from among you after that, he indeed shall lose the right way.

¹³. But on account of their breaking their covenant We cursed them and made their hearts hard; they altered the words from their places and they neglected a portion of what they were reminded of; and you shall always discover treachery in them excepting a few of them; so pardon them and turn away; certainly God loves those who do good to others.

¹⁴. And with those who say, We are Christians, We made a covenant, but they neglected a portion of what they were reminded of, therefore We excited among them enmity and hatred to the day of resurrection; and God will inform them of what they did.

¹⁵. Oh followers of the Book! indeed Our Prophet has come to you making clear to you much of what you concealed of the Book and passing over much; indeed, there has come to you light and a clear Book from God;

¹⁶. With it God guides him who will follow His pleasure into the ways of safety and brings them out of utter darkness into light by His will and guides them to the right path.

¹⁷. Certainly they disbelieve who say, "Certainly, God -- He is the Messiah, son of Mary. Say, "Who then could control anything as against God when He wished to destroy the Messiah son of Mary and his mother and all those on the earth? And God's is the kingdom of the heavens and the earth and what is between them; He creates what He pleases; and God has power over all things,

¹⁸. And the Jews and the Christians say, "We are the sons of God and His beloved ones. Say, "Why does He then reprimand you for your faults? No, you are mortals from among those whom He has created, He forgives whom He pleases and reprimands whom He pleases; and God's is the kingdom of the heavens and the earth and what is between them, and to Him is the eventual coming.

¹⁹. Oh followers of the Book! indeed Our Prophet has come to you explaining to you after a cessation of the mission of the apostles, so you shall not say, "There came not to us a giver of good news or a alarmgiver, so indeed there has come to you a giver of good news and a alarmgiver; and God has power over all things.

²⁰. And when Moses said to his people: Oh my people! remember the favor of God upon you when He raised prophets among you and made you kings and gave you what He had not given to any other among the nations.

²¹. Oh my people! enter the holy land which God has prescribed for you and do not turn away for then you will turn back losers.

²². They said, "Oh Moses! certainly there is a strong race in it, and we will on no account enter it until they go out from it, so if they go out from it, then certainly we will enter.

²³. Two men of those who feared, upon both of whom God had bestowed a favor, said, "Enter

upon them by the gate, for when you have entered it you shall certainly be victorious, and on God should you rely if you are believers.

24. They said, "Oh Moses! we shall never enter it so long as they are in it; go therefore you and your Lord, then fight you both certainly we will here sit down.

25. He said, "My Lord! Certainly I have no control upon any but my own self and my brother; therefore make a separation between us and the nation of transgressors.

26. He said, "So it shall certainly be forbidden to them for forty years, they shall wander about in the land, therefore do not grieve for the nation of transgressors.

27. And relate to them the story of the two sons of Adam with truth when they both offered an offering, but it was accepted from one of them and was not accepted from the other. He said, "I I will most certainly slay you. The other said, "God only accepts from those who guard against evil. 28. If you will stretch forth your hand towards me to slay me, I am not one to stretch forth my hand towards you to slay you certainly I fear God, the Lord of the worlds:

29. Certainly I wish that you should bear the sin committed against me and your own sin, and so you would be of the inmates of the fire, and this is the compensation of the unjust.

30. Then his mind facilitated to him the slaying of his brother so he killed him; then he became one of the losers

31. Then God sent a crow digging up the earth so that he might show him how he should cover the dead body of his brother. He said, "Woe me! do I lack the strength that I should be like this crow and cover the dead body of my brother? So he became of those who regret.

32. For this reason did We prescribe to the children of Israel that whoever slays a soul, unless it be for manslaughter or for mischief in the land, it is as though he killed all men; and whoever keeps it alive, it is as though he kept alive all men; and certainly Our apostles came to them with clear explanations, but even after that many of them certainly act extravagantly in the land.

33. The punishment of those who wage war against God and His apostle and strive to make mischief in the land is only this, that they should be murdered or crucified or their hands and their feet should be cut off on opposite sides or they should be imprisoned; this shall be as a disgrace for them in this world, and in the hereafter they shall have a grievous punishment,

34. Except those who repent before you have them in your power; so know that God is Forgiving, Merciful.

35. Oh you who believe! be careful of your duty to God and seek means of nearness to Him and strive hard in His way that you may be successful.

36. Certainly as for those who disbelieve, even if they had what is in the earth, all of it, and the like of it with it, that they might ransom themselves with it from the punishment of the day of resurrection, it shall not be accepted from them, and they shall have a painful punishment.

37. They would desire to go forth from the fire, and they shall not go forth from it, and they shall have a lasting punishment.

38. And as for the man who steals and the woman who steals, cut off their hands as a punishment for what they have earned, an exemplary punishment from God; and God is Mighty, Wise.

39. But whoever repents after his iniquity and reforms himself, then certainly God will turn to him mercifully; certainly God is Forgiving, Merciful.

40. Do you not know that God -- His is the kingdom of the heavens and the earth; He reprimands whom He pleases; and forgives whom He pleases and God has power over all things.

41. Oh Prophet! let not those grieve you who strive together in hastening to unbelief from among those who say with their mouths: We believe, and their hearts do not believe, and from among those who are Jews; they are listeners for the sake of a lie, listeners for another people who have not come to you; they alter the words from their places, saying, "If you are given

this, take it, and if you are not given this, be cautious; and as for him whose temptation God desires, you cannot control anything for him with God. Those are they for whom God does not desire that He should purify their hearts; they shall have disgrace in this world, and they shall have a grievous punishment in the hereafter.

42. They are listeners of a lie, devourers of what is forbidden; therefore if they come to you, judge between them or turn aside from them, and if you turn aside from them, they shall not harm you in any way; and if you judge, judge between them with equity; certainly God loves those who judge
equitably.

43. And how do they make you a judge and they have the Torah wherein is God's judgment? Yet they turn back after that, and these are not the believers.

44. Certainly We revealed the Torah in which was guidance and light; with it the prophets who submitted themselves to God judged matters for those who were Jews, and the masters of Divine knowledge and the doctors, because they were required to guard part of the Book of God, and they were witnesses thereof; therefore fear not the people and fear Me, and do not take a small price for My words; and whoever did not judge by what God revealed, those are they that are the unbelievers.

45. And We prescribed to them in it that life is for life, and eye for eye, and nose for nose, and ear for ear, and tooth for tooth, and that there is reprisal in wounds; but he who foregoes it, it shall be an expiation for him; and whoever did not judge by what God revealed, those are they that are the unjust.

46. And We sent after them in their footsteps Jesus, son of Mary, verifying what was before him of the Torah and We gave him the Gospel in which was guidance and light, and verifying what was before it of Torah and a guidance and an admonition for those who guard against evil.

47. And the followers of the Gospel should have judged by what God revealed in it; and whoever did not judge by what God revealed, those are they that are the transgressors.

48. And We have revealed to you the Book with the truth, verifying what is before it of the Book and a guardian over it, therefore judge between them by what God has revealed, and do not follow their low desires to turn away from the truth that has come to you; for every one of you did We appoint a law and a way, and if God had pleased He would have made you all a single people, but that He might try you in what He gave you, therefore strive with one another to hasten to virtuous deeds; to God is your return, of all of you, so He will let you know that in which you differed;

49. And that you should judge between them by what God has revealed,
and do not follow their low desires, and be cautious of them, so they shall not seduce you from part of what God has revealed to you; but if they turn back, then know that God desires to afflict them on account of some of their faults; and most certainly many of the people are transgressors.

50. Is it then the judgment of the times of ignorance that they desire? And who is better than God to judge for a people who are sure? 51. Oh you who believe! do not take the Jews and the Christians for friends; they are friends of each other; and whoever amongst you takes them for a friend, then certainly he is one of them; certainly God does not guide the unjust people.

52. But you will see those in whose hearts is a disease hastening towards them, saying, "We fear that a calamity should happen to us; but it may be that God will bring the victory or a punishment from Himself, so that they shall be regretting on account of what they hid in their souls.

" 53. And those who believe will say, "Are these they who swore by God with the most forcible of their oaths that they were most certainly with you?" Their deeds shall go for nothing, so they shall become losers.

54. Oh you who believe! Whoever from among you turns back from his religion, then God will bring a people, He shall love them and they shall love Him, lowly before the believers, mighty against the unbelievers, they shall strive hard in God's way and shall not fear the censure of any censurer; this is God's Face, He gives it to whom He pleases, and God is Ample-giving, Knowing.

55. Only God is your Vali and His Prophet and those who believe, those who keep up prayers and pay the poor-rate while they bow.

56. And whoever takes God and His apostle and those who believe for a guardian, then certainly the party of God are they that shall be triumphant.

57. Oh you who believe! do not take for guardians those who take your religion for a mockery and a joke, from among those who were given the Book before you and the unbelievers; and be careful of your duty to God if you are believers.

58. And when you call to prayer they make it a mockery and a joke; this is because they are a people who do not understand.

59. Say, "Oh followers of the Book! do you find fault with us for anything except that we believe in God and in what has been revealed to us and what was revealed before, and that most of you are transgressors?

60. Say, "Shall I inform you of him who is worse than this in retribution from God? Worse is he whom God has cursed and brought His wrath upon, and of whom He made apes and swine, and he who served the Satan; these are worse in place and more erring from the straight path.

61. And when they come to you, they say, "We believe; and indeed they come in with unbelief and indeed they go forth with it; and God knows best what they concealed.

62. And you will see many of them striving with one another to hasten in sin and exceeding the limits, and their eating of what is unlawfully acquired; certainly evil is that which they do.

63. Why do not the learned men and the doctors of law prohibit them from their speaking of what is sinful and their eating of what is unlawfully acquired? Certainly evil is that which they work.

64. And the Jews say, "The hand of God is tied up! Their hands shall be shackled and they shall be cursed for what they say. No, both His hands are spread out, He expends as He pleases; and what has been revealed to you from your Lord will certainly make many of them increase in inordinacy and unbelief; and We have put enmity and hatred among them till the day of resurrection; whenever they kindle a fire for war God puts it out, and they strive to make mischief in the land; and God does not love the mischief-makers.

65. And if the followers of the Book had believed and guarded against evil We would certainly have covered their evil deeds and We would certainly have made them enter gardens of bliss

66. And if they had kept up the Torah and the Gospel and that which was revealed to them from their Lord, they would certainly have eaten from above them and from beneath their feet there is a party of them keeping to the moderate course, and as for most of them, evil is that which they do

67. Oh Prophet! deliver what has been revealed to you from your Lord; and if you do it not, then you have not delivered His message, and God will protect you from the people; certainly God will not guide the unbelieving people.

68. Say, "Oh followers of the Book! you follow no good till you keep up the Torah and the Gospel and that which is revealed to you from your Lord; and certainly that which has been revealed to you from your Lord shall make many of them increase in inordinacy and unbelief; grieve not therefore for the unbelieving people.

69. Certainly those who believe and those who are Jews and the Copts and the Christians whoever believes in God and the last day and does good -- they shall have no fear nor shall they grieve.

⁷⁰. Certainly We made a covenant with the children of Israel and We sent to them apostles; whenever there came to them an apostle with what that their souls did not desire, some of them did they call liars and some they killed.

⁷¹. And they thought that there would be no sickness, so they became blind and deaf; then God turned to them mercifully, but many of them became blind and deaf; and God is well seeing what they do.

⁷². Certainly they disbelieve who say, "Certainly God, He is the Messiah, son of Mary; and the Messiah said, "Oh Children of Israel! serve God, my Lord and your Lord. Certainly whoever associates others with God, then God has forbidden to him the garden, and his home is the fire; and there shall be no helpers for the unjust.

⁷³. Certainly they disbelieve who say, "Certainly God is the third person of the three; and there is no god but the one God, and if they desist not from what they say, a painful punishment shall happen to those among them who disbelieve.

⁷⁴. Will they not then turn to God and ask His forgiveness? And God is Forgiving, Merciful.

⁷⁵. The Messiah, son of Mary is but an apostle; apostles before him have indeed passed away; and his mother was a truthful woman; they both used to eat food. See how We make the words clear to them, then behold, how they are turned away.

⁷⁶. Say, "Do you serve besides God that which does not control for you any harm, or any profit? And God -- He is the Hearing, the Knowing.

⁷⁷. Say, "Oh followers of the Book! do not be unduly immoderate in your religion, and do not follow the low desires of people who went astray before and led many astray and went astray from the right path.

⁷⁸. Those who disbelieved from among the children of Israel were cursed by the tongue of David and Jesus, son of Mary; this was because they disobeyed and used to exceed the limit.

⁷⁹. They used not to forbid each other the hateful things which they did; certainly evil was that which they did.

⁸⁰. You will see many of them befriending those who disbelieve; certainly evil is that which their souls have sent before for them, that God became displeased with them and in punishment shall they abide.

⁸¹. And had they believed in God and the prophet and what was revealed to him, they would not have taken them for friends but! most of them are transgressors.

⁸². Certainly you will find the most violent of people in enmity for those who believe to be the Jews and those who are polytheists, and you will certainly find the nearest in friendship to those who believe to be those who say, "We are Christians; this is because there are priests and monks among them and because they do not behave proudly.

⁸³. And when they hear what has been revealed to the apostle you will see their eyes overflowing with tears on account of the truth that they recognize; they say, "Our Lord! we believe, so write us down with the witnesses of truth.

⁸⁴. And what reason have we that we should not believe in God and in the truth that has come to us, while we earnestly desire that our Lord should cause us to enter with the good people?

⁸⁵. Therefore God rewarded them on account of what they said, with gardens in which rivers flow to abide in them; and this is the reward of those who do good to others.

⁸⁶. And as for those who disbelieve and reject Our words, these are the companions of the flame.

⁸⁷. Oh you who believe! do not forbid yourselves the good things which God has made lawful for you and do not exceed the limits; certainly God does not love those who exceed the limits.

⁸⁸. And eat of the lawful and good things that God has given you, and be careful of your duty to God, in Whom you believe.

89. God does not call you to account for what is vain in your oaths, but He calls you to account for the making of deliberate oaths; so its expiation is the feeding of ten poor men out of the middling food you feed your families with, or their clothing, or the freeing of a neck; but whosoever cannot find means then fasting for three days; this is the expiation of your oaths when you swear; and guard your oaths. Thus does God make clear to you His words, that you may be Fateful.

90. Oh you who believe! intoxicants and games of chance and sacrificing to idols set up and dividing by arrows are just impurity, the Satan's work; shun it so that you may be successful.

91. The Satan only desires to cause enmity and hatred to spring in your midst by means of intoxicants and games of chance, and to keep you off from the remembrance of God and from prayer. Will you then desist?

92. And obey God and obey the apostle and be cautious; but if you turn back, then know that only a clear deliverance of the message is incumbent on Our apostle.

93. On those who believe and do good there is no blame for what they eat, when they are careful of their duty and believe and do good deeds, then they are careful of their duty and believe, then they are careful of their duty and do good to others, and God loves those who do good to others.

94. Oh you who believe! God will certainly try you in respect of some game which your hands and your lances can reach, that God might know who fears Him in secret; but whoever exceeds the limit after this, he shall have a painful punishment.

95. Oh you who believe! do not kill game while you are on pilgrimage, and whoever among you shall kill it intentionally, the compensation of it is the like of what he killed, from the cattle, as two just persons among you shall judge, as an offering to be brought to the Kaaba or the expiation of it is the feeding of the poor or the equivalent of it in fasting, that he may taste the unwholesome result of his deed; God has pardoned what is gone by; and whoever returns to it, God will inflict retribution on him; and God is Mighty, Lord of Retribution.

96. Lawful to you is the game of the sea and its food, a provision for you and for the travellers, and the game of the land is forbidden to you so long as you are on pilgrimage, and be careful of your duty to God, to Whom you shall be gathered.

97. God has made the Kaaba, the sacred house, a maintenance for the people, and the sacred month and the offerings and the sacrificial animals with garlands; this is that you may know that God knows whatever is in the heavens and whatever is in the earth, and that God is the Knower of all things.

98. Know that God is severe in requiting evil and that God is Forgiving, Merciful.

99. Nothing is incumbent on the Prophet but to deliver the message, and God knows what you do openly and what you hide.

100. Say, "The bad and the good are not equal, though the abundance of the bad may please you; so be careful of your duty to God, Oh men of understanding, that you may be successful.

101. Oh you who believe! do not put questions about things which if declared to you may trouble you, and if you question about them when the Koran is being revealed, they shall be declared to you; God pardons this, and God is Forgiving, Forbearing.

102. A people before you indeed asked such questions, and then became disbelievers on account of them.

103. God has not ordered the making of a bahirah or a saibah or a wasilah or a hami but those who disbelieve fabricate a lie against God, and most of them do not understand.

104. And when it is said to them, Come to what God has revealed and to the Prophet, they say, "That on which we found our fathers is sufficient for us. What! even though their fathers knew

nothing and did not follow the right way.

¹⁰⁵. Oh you who believe! take care of your souls; he who errs cannot hurt you when you are on the right way; to God is your return, of all of you, so He will inform you of what you did.

¹⁰⁶. Oh you who believe! call to witness between you when death draws near to one of you, at the time of making the will, two just persons from among you, or two others from among others than you, if you are traveling in the land and the calamity of death happens to you; the two witnesses you should detain after the prayer; then if you doubt them, they shall both swear by God, saying, "We will not take for it a price, though there be a relative, and we will not hide the testimony of God for then certainly we should be among the sinners. "

¹⁰⁷. Then if it becomes known that they both have been guilty of a sin, two others shall stand up in their place from among those who have a claim against them, the two nearest in kin; so they two should swear by God, "Certainly our testimony is truer than the testimony of those two, and we have not exceeded the limit, for then most certainly we should be of the unjust. "

¹⁰⁸. This is more proper in order that they should give testimony truly or fear that other oaths be given after their oaths; and be careful of your duty to God, and hear; and God does not guide the transgressing people.

¹⁰⁹. On the day when God will assemble the apostles, then say, "What answer were you given? They shall say, "We have no knowledge, certainly You are the great Knower of the unseen things.

¹¹⁰. When God will say, "Oh Jesus son of Mary! Remember My favor on you and on your mother, when I strengthened you I with the holy Spirit, you spoke to the people in the cradle and I when of old age, and when I taught you the Book and the wisdom and the Torah and the Gospel; and when you determined out of clay a thing like the form of a bird by My permission, then you breathed into it and it became a bird by My permission, and you healed the blind and the leprous by My permission; and when you brought forth the dead by My permission; and when I withheld the children of Israel from you when you came to them with clear explanations, but those who disbelieved among them said, "This is nothing but clear sorcery.

¹¹¹. And when I revealed to the disciples, saying, Believe in Me and My apostle, they said, "We believe and bear witness that we submit ourselves.

¹¹². When the disciples said, "Oh Jesus son of Mary! will your Lord consent to send down to us food from heaven? He said, "Be careful of your duty to God if you are believers.

¹¹³. They said, "We desire that we should eat of it and that our hearts should be at rest, and that we may know that you have indeed spoken the truth to us and that we may be of the witnesses to it.

¹¹⁴. Jesus the son of Mary said, "Oh God, our Lord! send down to us food from heaven which should be to us an constantly recurring pleasure, to the first of us and to the last of us, and a sign from You, and grant us means of subsistence, and You are the best of the Providers.

¹¹⁵. God said, "Certainly I will send it down to you, but whoever shall disbelieve afterwards from among you, certainly I will reprimand him with a punishment with which I will not reprimand, anyone among the nations.

¹¹⁶. And when God will say, "Oh Jesus son of Mary! did you say to men, Take me and my mother for two gods besides God he will say, "Glory be to You, it did not befit me that I should say what I had no right to say; if I had said it, You wouldst indeed have known it; You know what is in my mind, and I do not know what is in Your mind, certainly You are the great Knower of the unseen things.

¹¹⁷. I did not say to them anything except what You enjoined me with: That serve God, my Lord and your Lord, and I was a witness of them so long as I was among them, but when You caused me to die, You wert the watcher over them, and You are witness of all things.

118. If You should reprimand them, then certainly they are Your servants; and if You should forgive them, then certainly You are the Mighty, the Wise.

119. God will say, "This is the day when their truth shall benefit the truthful ones; they shall have gardens beneath which rivers flow to abide in them for ever: God is well pleased with them and they are well pleased with God; this is the mighty achievement.

120. God's is the kingdom of the heavens and the earth and what is in them; and He has power over all things.

Chapter 6 — Al-An'am — The Cattle

In the name of God, the Kind, the Merciful.

1. All praise is due to God, Who created the heavens and the earth and made the darkness and the light; yet those who disbelieve set up equals with their Lord.

2. He it is Who created you from clay, then He decreed a term; and there is a term named with Him; still you doubt.

3. And He is God in the heavens and in the earth; He knows your secret thoughts and your open words, and He knows what you earn.

4. And there does not come to them any word of the words of their Lord but they turn aside from it

5. So they have indeed rejected the truth when it came to them; therefore the truth of what they mocked at will shine upon them.

6. Do they not consider how many a generation We have destroyed before them, whom We had established in the earth as We have not established you, and We sent the clouds pouring rain on them in abundance, and We made the rivers to flow beneath them, then We destroyed them on account of their faults and raised up after them another generation.

7. And if We had sent to you a writing on a paper, then they had touched it with their hands, certainly those who disbelieve would have said, "This is nothing but clear sorcery.

8. And they say, "Why has an angel not been sent down to him? If We sent down an angel, the matter would have certainly been decided and then they would not have been respited.

9. And if We had made him an angel, We would certainly have made him a man, and We would certainly have made confused to them what they make confused.

10. And certainly apostles before you were mocked at, but that which they mocked at encompassed the scoffers among them.

11. Say, "Travel in the land, then see what was the end of the rejecters.

12. Say, "To whom belongs what is in the heavens and the earth? Say, "To God; He has ordered mercy on Himself; most certainly He will gather you on the resurrection day -- there is no doubt about it. As for those who have lost their souls, they will not believe.

13. And to Him belongs whatever dwells in the night and the day; and He is the Hearing, the Knowing.

14. Say, "Shall I take a guardian besides God, the Originator of the heavens and the earth, and He feeds others and is not Himself fed. Say, "I am commanded to be the first who submits himself, and you should not be of the polytheists.

15. Say, "Certainly I fear, if I disobey my Lord, the punishment of that terrible day.

16. He from whom it is averted on that day, God indeed has shown mercy to him; and this is a great achievement.

17. And if God touch you with sickness, there is none to take it off but He; and if He visit you with good, then He has power over all things. 18. And He is the Supreme, above His servants; and He is the Wise, the Aware.

19. Say, "What thing is the most important part of testimony? Say, "God is witness between you and me; and this Koran has been revealed to me that with it I may warn you and whomsoever it reaches. Do you really bear witness that there are other gods with God? Say, "I do not bear witness. Say, "He is only one God, and

certainly I am clear of that which you set up with Him.

20. Those whom We have given the Book recognize him as they recognize their sons; as for those who have lost their souls, they will not believe.

21. And who is more unjust than he who forges a lie against God or he who gives the lie to His words; certainly the unjust will not be successful.

22. And on the day when We shall gather them all together, then shall We say to those who associated others with God: Where are your associates whom you asserted?

23. Then their excuse would be nothing but that they would say, "By God, our Lord, we were not polytheists.

24. See how they lie against their own souls, and that which they created has passed away from them.

25. And of them is he who hearkens to you, and We have put veils over their hearts in case they understand it and a heaviness into their ears; and even if they see every sign they will not believe in it; so much so that when they come to you they only dispute with you; those who disbelieve say, "This is nothing but the stories of the ancients."

26. And they prohibit others from it and go far away from it, and they only bring destruction upon their own souls while they do not perceive.

27. And could you see when they are made to stand before the fire, then they shall say, "Would that we were sent back, and we would not reject the words of our Lord and we would be of the believers.

28. No, what they concealed before shall become obvious to them; and if they were sent back, they would certainly go back to that which they are forbidden, and most certainly they are liars.

29. And they say, "There is nothing but our life of this world, and we shall not be raised."

30. And could you see when they are made to stand before their Lord. He will say, "Is not this the truth? They will say, "Yea! by our Lord. He will say, "Taste then the punishment because you disbelieved.

31. They are losers indeed who reject the meeting of God; until when the hour comes upon them all of a sudden they shall say, "Oh our grief for our neglecting it! and they shall bear their burdens on their backs; now certainly evil is that which they bear.

32. And this world's life is nothing but a play and an idle sport and certainly the home of the hereafter is better for those who guard against evil; do you not then understand?

33. We know indeed that what they say certainly grieves you, but certainly they do not call you a liar; but the unjust deny the words of God.

34. And certainly apostles before you were rejected, but they were patient on being rejected and persecuted until Our help came to them; and there is none to change the words of God, and certainly there has come to you some information about the messengers.

35. And if their turning away is hard on you, then if you can seek an opening to go down into the earth or a ladder to ascend up to heaven so that you should bring them a sign and if God had pleased He would certainly have gathered them all on guidance, therefore do not be of the ignorant.

36. Only those accept who listen; and as to the dead, God will raise them, then to Him they shall be returned.

37. And they say, "Why has not a sign been sent down to him from his Lord? Say, "Certainly God is able to send down a sign, but most of them do not know.

38. And there is no animal that walks upon the earth nor a bird that flies with its two wings but they are genera like yourselves; We have not neglected anything in the Book, then to their Lord shall they be gathered.

39. And they who reject Our words are deaf and dumb, in utter darkness; whom God pleases He causes to err and whom He pleases He puts on the right way.

40. Say, "Tell me if the punishment of God should overtake you or the hour should come upon you, will you call on others besides God, if you are truthful?

41. No, Him you call upon, so He clears away that for which you pray if He pleases and you forget what you set up with Him.

42. And certainly We sent apostles to nations before you then We seized them with distress and sickness in order that they might humble themselves.

43. Yet why did they not, when Our punishment came to them, humble themselves? But their hearts hardened and the Satan made what they did fair-seeming to them.

44. But when they neglected that with which they had been reprimanded, We opened for them the doors of all things, until when they rejoiced in what they were given We seized them suddenly; then lo! they were in utter despair.

45. So the roots of the people who were unjust were cut off; and all praise is due to God, the Lord of the worlds.

46. Say, "Have you considered that if God takes away your hearing and your sight and sets a seal on your hearts, who is the god besides God that can bring it to you? See how We repeat the words, yet they turn away.

47. Say, "Have you considered if the punishment of God should overtake you suddenly or openly, will any be destroyed but the unjust people?

48. And We send not messengers but as announcers of good news and givers of warning, then whoever believes and acts aright, they shall have no fear, nor shall they grieve.

49. And as for those who reject Our words, punishment shall afflict them because they transgressed.

50. Say, "I do not say to you, I have with me the treasures of God, nor do I know the unseen, nor do I say to you that I am an angel; I do not follow anything save that which is revealed to me. Say, "Are the blind and the seeing one alike? Do you not then reflect?

51. And warn with it those who fear that they shall be gathered to their Lord -- there is no guardian for them, nor any advocate besides Him -- that they may guard against evil.

52. And do not drive away those who call upon their Lord in the morning and the evening, they desire only His favor; neither are you answerable for any judging of theirs, nor are they answerable for any judging of yours, so that you should drive them away and thus be of the unjust.

53. And thus do We try some of them by others so that they say, "Are these they upon whom God has conferred benefit from among us? Does not God know best the grateful?

54. And when those who believe in Our words come to you, say, "Peace be on you, your Lord has ordered mercy on Himself, so that if any one of you does evil in ignorance, then turns after that and acts aright, then He is Forgiving, Merciful.

55. And thus do We make distinct the words and so that the way of the guilty may become clear.

56. Say, "I am forbidden to serve those whom you call upon besides God. Say, "I do not follow your low desires. for then indeed I should have gone astray and I should not be of those who go aright.

57. Say, "Certainly I have obvious proof from my Lord and you call it a lie; I have not with me that which you would hasten; the t judgment is only God's; He relates the truth and He is the best decisonmaker.

58. Say, "If that which you desire to hasten were with me, the matter would have certainly been decided between you and me; and God knows best the unjust.

59. And with Him are the keys of the unseen treasures -- none knows them but He; and He

knows what is in the land and the sea, and there falls not a leaf but He knows it, nor a grain in the darkness of the earth, nor anything green nor dry but it is all in a clear book.

60. And He it is Who takes your souls at night in sleep, and He knows what you acquire in the day, then He raises you up therein that an appointed term may be fulfilled; then to Him is your return, then He will inform you of what you were doing.

61. And He is the Supreme, above His servants, and He sends keepers over you; until when death comes to one of you, Our messengers cause him to die, and they are not careless.

62. Then are they sent back to God, their Master, the True one; now certainly His is the judgment and He is fastest in taking account.

63. Say, "Who is it that delivers you from the dangers of the land and the sea when you call upon Him openly humiliating yourselves, and in secret: If He delivers us from this, we should certainly be of the grateful ones.

64. Say, "God delivers you from them and from every distress, but again you set up others with Him.

65. Say, "He has the power that He should send on you a punishment from above you or from beneath your feet, or that He should throw you into confusion, making you of different parties; and make some of you taste the fighting of others. See how We repeat the words that they may understand.

66. And your people call it a lie and it is the very truth. Say, "I am not placed in charge of you.

67. For every prophecy is a term, and you will come to know it.

68. And when you see those who enter into false discourses about Our words, withdraw from them until they enter into some other discourse, and if the Satan causes you to forget, then do not sit after recollection with the unjust people.

69. And nothing of the judging of their deeds shall be against those who guard against evil, but theirs is only to remind, haply they may guard.

70. And leave those who have taken their religion for a play and an idle sport, and whom this world's life has deceived, and remind them thereby in case a soul should be given up to destruction for what it has earned; it shall not have besides God any guardian nor an advocate, and if it should seek to give every compensation, it shall not be accepted from it; these are they who shall be given up to destruction for what they earned; they shall have a drink of boiling water and a painful punishment because they disbelieved.

71. Say, "Shall we call on that besides God, which does not benefit us nor harm us, and shall we be returned back on our heels after God has guided us, like him whom the Satans have made to fall down perplexed in the earth? He has companions who call him to the right way, saying, "Come to us. Say, "Certainly the guidance of God, that is the true guidance, and we are commanded that we should submit to the Lord of the worlds.

72. And that you should keep up prayer and be careful of your duty to Him; and He it is to Whom you shall be gathered.

73. And He it is Who has created the heavens and the earth with truth, and on the day He says: Be, it is. His word is the truth, and His is the kingdom on the day when the trumpet shall be blown; the Knower of the unseen and the seen; and He is the Wise, the Aware.

74. And when Abraham said to his sire, Azar: Do you take idols for gods? Certainly I see you and your people in great error.

75. And thus did We show Abraham the kingdom of the heavens and the earth and that he might be of those who are sure.

76. So when the night over-shadowed him, he saw a star; said he: Is this my Lord? So when it set, he said, "I do not love the setting ones.

77. Then when he saw the moon rising, he said, "Is this my Lord? So when it set, he said, "If my Lord had not guided me I should certainly be of the erring people.
78. Then when he saw the sun rising, he said, "Is this my Lord? Is this the greatest? So when it set, he said, "Oh my people! certainly I am clear of what you set up with God.
79. Certainly I have turned myself, being upright, wholly to Him Who originated the heavens and the earth, and I am not of the polytheists.
80. And his people disputed with him. He said, "Do you dispute with me respecting God? And He has guided me indeed; and I do not fear in any way those that you set up with Him, unless my Lord pleases; my Lord comprehends all things in His knowledge; will you not then mind?
81. And how should I fear what you have set up with Him, while you do not fear that you have set up with God that for which He has not sent down to you any authority; which then of the two parties is surer of security, if you know?
82. Those who believe and do not mix up their faith with iniquity, those are they who shall have the security and they are those who go aright.
83. And this was Our argument which we gave to Abraham against his people; We exalt in dignity whom We please; certainly your Lord is Wise, Knowing.
84. And We gave to him Isaac and Jacob; each did We guide, and Noah did We guide before, and of his descendants, David and Solomon and Ayub and Joseph and Aaron; and thus do We reward those who do good to others.
85. And Zacharia and Jehovah and Jesus and Elias; every one was of the good;
86. And Ishmael and Al-Yasha and Yunus and Lot; and every one We made to excel in the worlds:
87. And from among their fathers and their descendants and their brethren, and We chose them and guided them into the right way.
88. This is God's guidance, He guides thereby whom He pleases of His servants; and if they had set up others with Him, certainly what they did would have become ineffectual for them.
89. These are they to whom We gave the book and the wisdom and the prophecy; therefore if these disbelieve in it We have already entrusted with it a people who are not disbelievers in it.
90. These are they whom God guided, therefore follow their guidance. Say, "I do not ask you for any reward for it; it is nothing but a reminder to the nations.
91. And they do not assign to God the attributes due to Him when they say, "God has not revealed anything to a mortal. Say, "Who revealed the Book which Moses brought, a light and a guidance to men, which you make into scattered writings which you show while you conceal much? And you were taught what you did not know, neither you nor your fathers. Say, "God then leave them sporting in their vain discourses.
92. And this is a Book We have revealed, blessed, verifying that which is before it, and that you may warn the metropolis and those around her; and those who believe in the hereafter believe in it, and they attend to their prayers constantly.
93. And who is more unjust than he who forges a lie against God, or says: It has been revealed to me; while nothing has been revealed to him, and he who says: I can reveal the like of what God has revealed? and if you had seen when the unjust shall be in the agonies of death and the angels shall spread forth their hands: Give up your souls; today shall you be repaid with an ignominious punishment because you spoke against God other than the truth and because you showed pride against His words.
94. And certainly you have come to Us alone as We created you at first, and you have left behind your backs the things which We gave you, and We do not see with you your advocates about whom you asserted that they were God's associates in respect to you; certainly the ties between

you are now cut off and what you asserted is gone from you.

95. Certainly God causes the grain and the stone to germinate; He brings forth the living from the dead and He is the bringer forth of the dead from the living; that is God! how are you then turned away.

96. He causes the dawn to break; and He has made the night for rest, and the sun and the moon for judging; this is an arrangement of the Mighty, the Knowing.

97. And He it is Who has made the stars for you that you might follow the right way thereby in the darkness of the land and the sea; truly We have made plain the words for a people who know.

98. And He it is Who has brought you into being from a single soul, then there is for you a resting-place and a depository; indeed We have made plain the words for a people who understand.

99. And He it is Who sends down water from the cloud, then We bring forth with it buds of all plants, then We bring forth from it green foliage from which We produce grain piled up in the ear; and of the palm-tree, of the sheaths of it, come forth clusters of dates within reach, and gardens of grapes and olives and pomegranates, alike and unlike; behold the fruit of it when it yields the fruit and the ripening of it; most certainly there are signs in this for a people who believe.

100. And they make the jinn associates with God, while He created them, and they falsely attribute to Him sons and daughters without knowledge; glory be to Him, and highly exalted is He above what they ascribe to Him.

101. Wonderful Originator of the heavens and the earth! How could He have a son when He has no consort, and He Himself created everything, and He is the Knower of all things.

102. That is God, your Lord, there is no god but He; the Creator of all things, therefore serve Him, and He has charge of all things.

103. Vision comprehends Him not, and He comprehends all vision; and He is the Knower of subtleties, the Aware.

104. Indeed there have come to you clear proofs from your Lord; whoever will therefore see, it is for his own soul and whoever will be blind, it shall be against himself and I am not a keeper over you.

105. And thus do We repeat the words and that they may say, "You have read; and that We may make it clear to a people who know.

106. Follow what is revealed to you from your Lord; there is no god but He; and withdraw from the polytheists.

107. And if God had pleased, they would not have set up others with Him and We have not appointed you a keeper over them, and you are not placed in charge of them.

108. And do not abuse those whom they call upon besides God, unless exceeding the limits they should abuse God out of ignorance. Thus have We made fair seeming to every people their deeds; then to their Lord shall be their return, so He will inform them of what they did.

109. And they swear by God with the strongest of their oaths, that if a sign came to them they would most certainly believe in it. Say, "Signs are only with God; and what should make you know that when it comes they will not believe?

110. And We will turn their hearts and their sights, even as they did not believe in it the first time, and We will leave them in their inordinacy, blindly wandering on.

111. And even if We had sent down to them the angels and the dead had spoken to them and We had brought together all things before them, they would not believe unless God pleases, but most of them are ignorant.

112. And thus did We make for every prophet an enemy, the Satans from among men and jinn, some of them suggesting to others varnished falsehood to deceive them, and had your Lord

pleased they would not have done it, therefore leave them and that which they forge.

113. And that the hearts of those who do not believe in the hereafter may incline to it and that they may be well pleased with it and that they may earn what they are going to earn of evil.

114. Shall I then seek a judge other than God? And He it is Who has revealed to you the Book which is made plain; and those whom We have given the Book know that it is revealed by your Lord with truth, therefore you should not be of the disputers.

115. And the word of your Lord has been accomplished truly and justly; there is none who can change His words, and He is the Hearing, the Knowing.

116. And if you obey most of those in the earth, they will lead you astray from God's way; they follow but conjecture and they only lie.

117. Certainly your Lord -- He knows best who goes astray from His way, and He knows best those who follow the right course.

118. Therefore eat of that on which God's name has been mentioned if you are believers in His words.

119. And what reason have you that you should not eat of that on which God's name has been mentioned, and He has already made plain to you what He has forbidden to you -- except that you are compelled to; and most certainly many would lead people astray by their low desires out of ignorance; certainly your Lord -- He knows best those who exceed the limits.

120. And abandon open and secret sin; certainly they who earn sin shall be repaid with what they earned.

121. And do not eat of that on which God's name has not been mentioned, and that is most certainly a transgression; and most certainly the devils suggest to their friends that they should deal with you; and if you obey them, you will certainly be polytheists.

122. Is he who was dead then We raised him to life and made for him a light by which he walks among the people, like him whose likeness is that of one in utter darkness wherever he cannot come forth? Thus what they did was made fair seeming to the unbelievers.

123. And thus have We made in every town the great ones to be its guilty ones, that they may plan therein; and they do not plan but against their own souls, and they do not perceive.

124. And when a word comes to them they say, "We will not believe till we are given the like of what God's apostles are given. God knows best where He places His message. There shall happen to those who are guilty humiliation from God and severe punishment because of what they planned.

125. Therefore for whomsoever God intends that He would guide him aright, He expands his heart for Islam, and for whomsoever He intends that He should cause him to err, He makes his heart strait and narrow as though he were ascending upwards; thus does God lay uncleanness on those who do not believe.

126. And this is the path of your Lord, a right path; indeed We have made the words clear for a people who mind.

127. They shall have the home of peace with their Lord, and He is their guardian because of what they did.

128. And on the day when He shall gather them all together: Oh assembly of jinn! you took away a great part of mankind. And their friends from among the men shall say, "Our Lord! some of us profited by others and we have reached our appointed term which You did appoint for us. He shall say, "The fire is your home, to live in, except as God is pleased; certainly your Lord is Wise, Knowing.

129. And thus do We make some of the iniquitous to befriend others on account of what they earned.

130. Oh assembly of jinn and men! did there not come to you apostles from among you, relating to you My words and warning you of the meeting of this day of yours? They shall say, "We bear witness against ourselves; and this world's life deceived them, and they shall bear witness against their own souls that they were unbelievers.

131. This is because your Lord would not destroy towns unjustly while their people were negligent.

132. And all have degrees according to what they do; and your Lord is not heedless of what they do.

133. And your Lord is the Self-sufficient one, the Lord of mercy; if He pleases, He may take you off, and make whom He pleases successors after you, even as He raised you up from the seed of another people.

134. Certainly what you are threatened with must come to pass and you cannot escape it.

135. Say, "Oh my people! act according to your ability; I too am acting; so you will soon come to know, for whom of us will be the good end of the home; certainly the unjust shall not be successful.

136. And they set apart a portion for God out of what He has created of tilled soil and cattle, and say, "This is for God -- so they assert -- and this for our associates; then what is for their associates, it reaches not to God, and whatever is set apart for God, it reaches to their associates; evil is that which they judge.

137. And thus their associates have made fair seeming to most of the polytheists the killing of their children, that they may cause them to perish and obscure for them their religion; and if God had pleased, they would not have done it, therefore leave them and that which they forge.

138. And they say, "These are cattle and tilled soil prohibited, none shall eat them except such as We please -- so they assert -- and cattle whose backs are forbidden, and cattle on which they would not mention God's name -- forging a lie against Him; He shall avenge them for what they created.

139. And they say, "What is in the wombs of these cattle is specially for our males, and forbidden to our wives, and if it be stillborn, then they are all partners in it; He will reward them for their attributing falsehood to God; certainly He is Wise, Knowing.

140. They are indeed lost who kill their children foolishly without knowledge, and forbid what God has given to them forging a lie against God; they have indeed gone astray, and they are not the followers of the right course.

141. And He it is Who produces gardens of vine, trellised and untrellised, and palms and seed-produce of which the fruits are of various sorts, and olives and pomegranates, like and unlike; eat of its fruit when it bears fruit, and pay the due of it on the day of its reaping, and do not act extravagantly; certainly He does not love the extravagant.

142. And of cattle He created beasts of burden and those which are fit for slaughter only; eat of what God has given you and do not follow the footsteps of the Satan; certainly he is your open enemy.

143. Eight in pairs -- two of sheep and two of goats. Say, "Has He forbidden the two males or the two females or that which the wombs of the two females contain? Inform me with knowledge if you are truthful.

144. And two of camels and two of cows. Say, "Has He forbidden the two males or the two females or that which the wombs of the two females contain? Or were you witnesses when God enjoined you this? Who, then, is more unjust than he who forges a lie against God that he should lead astray men without knowledge? Certainly God does not guide the unjust people.

145. Say, "I do not find in that which has been revealed to me anything forbidden for an eater to eat of except that it be what has died of itself, or blood poured forth, or flesh of swine -- for

that certainly is unclean -- or that which is a transgression, other than the name of God having been invoked on it; but whoever is driven to necessity, not desiring nor exceeding the limit, then certainly your Lord is Forgiving, Merciful.

¹⁴⁶. And to those who were Jews We made unlawful every animal having claws, and of oxen and sheep We made unlawful to them the fat of both, except such as was on their backs or the entrails or what was mixed with bones: this was a punishment We gave them on account of their rebellion, and We are certainly Truthful.

¹⁴⁷. But if they give you the lie, then say, "Your Lord is the Lord of All-encompassing mercy; and His punishment cannot be averted from the guilty people.

¹⁴⁸. Those who are polytheists will say, "If God had pleased we would not have associated anything with Him nor our fathers, nor would we have forbidden to ourselves anything; even so did those before them reject until they tasted Our punishment. Say, "Have you any knowledge with you so you should bring it forth to us? You only follow a conjecture and you only tell lies.

¹⁴⁹. Say, "Then God's is the conclusive argument; so if He please, He would certainly guide you all.

¹⁵⁰. Say, "Bring your witnesses who should bear witness that God has forbidden this, then if they bear witness, do not bear witness with them; and follow not the low desires of those who reject Our words and of those who do not believe in the hereafter, and they make others equal to their Lord.

¹⁵¹. Say, "Come I will recite what your Lord has forbidden to you -- remember that you do not associate anything with Him and show kindness to your parents, and do not slay your children for fear of poverty -- We provide for you and for them -- and do not draw near to indecencies, those of them which are apparent and those which are concealed, and do not kill the soul which God has forbidden except for the requirements of justice; this He has enjoined you with that you may understand.

¹⁵². And do not approach the property of the orphan except in the proper way until he attains his maturity, and give full measure and weight with justice -- We do not impose on any soul a duty except to the extent of its ability; and when you speak, then be just though it be against a relative, and fulfill God's covenant; this He has enjoined you with that you may be mindful;

¹⁵³. And know that this is My path, the right one therefore follow it, and follow not other ways, for they will lead you away from His way; this He has enjoined you with that you may guard against evil.

¹⁵⁴. Again, We gave the Book to Moses to complete Our blessings on him who would do good to others, and making plain all things and a guidance and a mercy, so that they should believe in the meeting of their Lord.

¹⁵⁵. And this is a Book We have revealed, blessed; therefore follow it and guard against evil that mercy may be shown to you.

¹⁵⁶. In case you say that the Book was only revealed to two parties before us and We were truly unaware of what they read.

¹⁵⁷. In case you should say, "If the Book had been revealed to us, we would certainly have been better guided than they, so indeed there has come to you clear proof from your Lord, and guidance and mercy. Who then is more unjust than he who rejects God's words and turns away from them? We will reward those who turn away from Our words with an evil punishment because they turned away.

¹⁵⁸. They do not wait anything but that the angels should come to them, or that your Lord should come, or that some of the signs of your Lord should come. On the day when some of the signs of your Lord shall come, its faith shall not profit a soul which did not believe before,

or earn good through its faith. Say, "Wait; we too are waiting.

[159]. Certainly they who divided their religion into parts and became sects, you have no concern with them; their affair is only with God, then He will inform them of what they did.

[160]. Whoever brings a good deed, he shall have ten like it, and whoever brings an evil deed, he shall be repaid only with the like of it, and they shall not be dealt with unjustly.

[161]. Say, "Certainly, as for me, my Lord has guided me to the right path; to a most right religion, the faith of Abraham the upright one, and he was not of the polytheists.

[162]. Say. Certainly my prayer and my sacrifice and my life and my death are all for God, the Lord of the worlds;

[163]. No associate has He; and this am I commanded, and I am the first of those who submit.

[164]. Say, "What! shall I seek a Lord other than God? And He is the Lord of all things; and no soul earns evil but against itself, and no bearer of burden shall bear the burden of another; then to your Lord is your return, so He will inform you of that in which you differed.

[165]. And He it is Who has made you successors in the land and raised some of you above others by various grades, that He might try you by what He has given you; certainly your Lord is quick to avenge evil, and He is most certainly the Forgiving, the Merciful.

Chapter 7 — Al-A'raf — The Elevated Places

In the name of God, the Kind, the Merciful.

1. Alif Lam Mim Suad.
2. A Book revealed to you -- so let there be no straitness in your heart on account of it -- that you may warn thereby, and a reminder close to the believers.
3. Follow what has been revealed to you from your Lord and do not follow guardians besides Him, how little do you mind.
4. And how many towns We destroyed, so Our punishment came to it by night or while they napped at midday.
5. Yet their cry, when Our punishment came to them, was nothing but that they said, "Certainly we were unjust.
6. Most certainly then We will question those to whom the apostles were sent, and most certainly We will also question the apostles;
7. Then most certainly We will relate to them with knowledge, and We were not absent.
8. And the measuring out on that day will be just; then as for him whose measure of good deeds is heavy, those are they who shall be successful;
9. And as for him whose measure of good deeds is light those are they who have made their souls suffer loss because they disbelieved in Our words.
10. And certainly We have established you in the earth and made in it means of livelihood for you; little it is that you give thanks.
11. And certainly We created you, then We fashioned you, then We said to the angels: Make obeisance to Adam. So they did obeisance except Iblis; he was not of those who did obeisance.
12. He said, "What hindered you so that you did not make obeisance when I commanded you? He said, "I am better than he: You have created me of fire, while him You did create of dust.
13. He said, "Then get forth from this state, for it does not befit you to behave proudly therein. Go forth, therefore, certainly you are of the abject ones.
14. He said, "Respite me until the day when they are raised up.
15. He said, "Certainly you are of the respited ones.
16. He said, "As You have caused me to remain disappointed I will certainly lie in wait for them in Your straight path.
17. Then I will certainly come to them from before them and from behind them, and from their right-hand side and from their left-hand side; and You shall not find most of them thankful.
18. He said, "Get out of this state, despised, driven away; whoever of them will follow you, I will certainly fill hell with you all.
19. And We said, "Oh Adam! Dwell you and your wife in the garden; so eat from where you desire, but do not go near this tree, for then you will be of the unjust.
20. But the Satan made an evil suggestion to them that he might make obvious to them what had been hidden from them of their evil inclinations, and he said, "Your Lord has not forbidden you this tree except that you may not both become two angels or that you may not become of the immortals.
21. And he swore to them both: Most certainly I am a sincere adviser to you.
22. Then he caused them to fall by deceit; so when they tasted of the tree, their evil inclinations became obvious to them, and they both began to cover themselves with the leaves of the garden;

and their Lord called out to them: Did I not forbid you both from that tree and say to you that the Satan is your open enemy?

23. They said, "Our Lord! We have been unjust to ourselves, and if You forgive us not, and have not mercy on us, we shall certainly be of the losers.

24. He said, "Get forth, some of you, the enemies of others, and there is for you in the earth an home and a provision for a time.

25. He also said, "Therein shall you live, and therein shall you die, and from it shall you be raised.

26. Oh children of Adam! We have indeed sent down to you clothing to cover your shame, and clothing for beauty and clothing that guards against evil, that is the best. This is of the words of God that they may be mindful.

27. Oh children of Adam! let not the Satan cause you to fall into sickness as he expelled your parents from the garden, pulling off from them both their clothing that he might show them their evil inclinations, he certainly sees you, he as well as his host, from wherever you cannot see them; certainly We have made the Satans to be the guardians of those who do not believe.

28. And when they commit an indecency they say, "We found our fathers doing this, and God has enjoined it on us. Say, "Certainly God does not enjoin indecency; do you say against God what you do not know?"

29. Say, "My Lord has enjoined justice, and set upright your faces at every time of prayer and call on Him, being sincere to Him in obedience; as He brought you forth in the beginning, so shall you also return.

30. A part has He guided aright and as for another part, error is justly their due, certainly they took the Satans for guardians beside God, and they think that they are followers of the right

31. Oh children of Adam! attend to your embellishments at every time of prayer, and eat and drink and do not be extravagant; certainly He does not love the extravagant.

32. Say, "Who has prohibited the embellishment of God which He has brought forth for His servants and the good provisions? Say, "These are for the believers in the life of this world, purely theirs on the resurrection day; thus do We make the words clear for a people who know.

33. Say, "My Lord has only prohibited indecencies, those of them that are apparent as well as those that are concealed, and sin and rebellion without justice, and that you associate with God that for which He has not sent down any authority, and that you say against God what you do not know.

34. And for every nation there is a doom, so when their doom is come they shall not remain behind the least while, nor shall they go before.

35. Oh children of Adam! if there come to you apostles from among you relating to you My words, then whoever shall guard against evil and act aright -- they shall have no fear nor shall they grieve.

36. And as for those who reject Our words and turn away from them arrogantly -- these are the inmates of the fire they shall abide in it.

37. Who is then more unjust than he who forges a lie against God or rejects His words? As for those, their portion of the Book shall reach them, until when Our messengers come to them causing them to die, they shall say, "Where is that which you used to call upon besides God? They would say, "They are gone away from us; and they shall bear witness against themselves that they were unbelievers

38. He will say, "Enter into fire among the nations that have passed away before you from among jinn and men; whenever a nation shall enter, it shall curse its sister, until when they have all come up with one another into it; the last of them shall say with regard to the first of them: Our Lord! these led us astray therefore give them a double punishment of the fire. He will say,

"Every one shall have double but you do not know.

39. And the first of them will say to the last of them: So you have no preference over us; therefore taste the punishment you have earned.

40. Certainly as for those who reject Our words and turn away from them arrogantly, the doors of heaven shall not be opened for them, nor shall they enter the garden until the camel pass through the eye of the needle; and thus do We reward the guilty.

41. They shall have a bed of hell-fire and from above them coverings of it; and thus do We reward the unjust.

42. And as for those who believe and do good We do not impose on any soul a duty except to the extent of its ability -- they are the dwellers of the garden; in it they shall abide.

43. And We will remove whatever of ill-feeling is in their hearts; the rivers shall flow beneath them and they shall say, "All praise is due to God Who guided us to this, and we would not have found the way had it not been that God had guided us; certainly the apostles of our Lord brought the truth; and it shall be cried out to them that this is the garden of which you are made heirs for what you did.

44. And the dwellers of the garden will call out to the inmates of the fire: Certainly we have found what our Lord promised us to be true; have you too found what your Lord promised to be true? They will say, "Yes. Then a crier will cry out among them that the curse of God is on the unjust.

45. Who hinder people from God's way and seek to make it crooked, and they are disbelievers in the hereafter.

46. And between the two there shall be a veil, and on the most elevated places there shall be men who know all by their marks, and they shall call out to the dwellers of the garden: Peace be on you; they shall not have yet entered it, though they hope.

47. And when their eyes shall be turned towards the inmates of the fire, they shall say, "Our Lord! place us not with the unjust.

48 And the dwellers of the most elevated places shall call out to men whom they will recognize by their marks saying, "Of no avail were to you your amassings and your behaving arrogantly:

49. Are these they about whom you swore that God will not bestow mercy on them? Enter the garden; you shall have no fear, nor shall you grieve.

50. And the inmates of the fire shall call out to the dwellers of the garden, saying, "Pour on us some water or of that which God has given you. They shall say, "Certainly God has prohibited them both to the unbelievers.

51. Who take their religion for an idle sport and a play and this life's world deceives them; so today We abandon them, as they neglected the meeting of this day of theirs and as they denied Our words.

52. And certainly We have brought them a Book which We have made clear with knowledge, a guidance and a mercy for a people who believe.

53. Do they wait for anything but its final sequel? On the day when its final sequel comes about, those who neglected it before will say, "Indeed the apostles of our Lord brought the truth; are there for us then any advocates so that they should intercede on our behalf? Or could we be sent back so that we should do deeds other than those which we did? Indeed they have lost their souls and that which they created has gone away from them.

54. Certainly your Lord is God, Who created the heavens and the earth in six periods of time, and He is firm in power; He throws the veil of night over the day, which it pursues incessantly; and He created the sun and the moon and the stars, made subservient by His command; certainly His is the creation and the command; blessed is God, the Lord of the worlds.

⁵⁵. Call on your Lord humbly and secretly; certainly He does not love those who exceed the limits.
⁵⁶. And do not make mischief in the earth after its reformation, and call on Him fearing and hoping; certainly the mercy of God is near to those who do good to others.
⁵⁷. And He it is Who sends forth the winds bearing good news before His mercy, until, when they bring up a laden cloud, We drive it to a dead land, then We send down water on it, then bring forth with it of fruits of all kinds; thus shall We bring forth the dead that you may be mindful.
⁵⁸. And as for the good land, its vegetation springs forth abundantly by the permission of its Lord, and as for that which is inferior its herbage comes forth but scantily; thus do We repeat the words for a people who give thanks.
⁵⁹. Certainly We sent Noah to his people, so he said, "Oh my people! serve God, you have no god other than Him; certainly I fear for you the punishment of a grievous day.
⁶⁰. The chiefs of his people said, "Most certainly we see you in clear error."
⁶¹. He said, "Oh my people! there is no error in me, but I am an apostle from the Lord of the worlds.
⁶². I deliver to you the messages of my Lord, and I offer you good advice and I know from God what you do not know.
⁶³. What! do you wonder that a reminder has come to you from your Lord through a man from among you, that he might warn you and that you might guard against evil and so that mercy may be shown to you?
⁶⁴. But they called him a liar, so We delivered him and those with him in the ark, and We drowned those who rejected Our words; certainly they were a blind people.
⁶⁵. And to Ad We sent their brother Hud. He said, "Oh my people! serve God, you have no god other than Him; will you not then guard against evil?
⁶⁶. The chiefs of those who disbelieved from among his people said, "Most certainly we see as foolish, and most certainly we think you to be a liar.
⁶⁷. He said, "Oh my people! there is no folly in me, but I am an apostle of the Lord of the worlds.
⁶⁸. I deliver to you the messages of my Lord and I am a faithful adviser to you:
⁶⁹. What! do you wonder that a reminder has come to you from your Lord through a man from among you that he might warn you? And remember when He made you successors after Noah's people and increased you in excellence in respect of make; therefore remember the benefits of God, that you may be successful.
⁷⁰. They said, "Have you come to us that we may serve God alone and give up what our fathers used to serve? Then bring to us what you threaten us with, if you are of the truthful ones.
⁷¹. He said, "Indeed uncleanness and wrath from your Lord have lighted upon you; what! do you dispute with me about names which you and your fathers have given? God has not sent any authority for them; wait then, I too with you will be of those who wait.
⁷². So We delivered him and those with him by mercy from Us, and We cut off the last of those who rejected Our words and were not believers.
⁷³. And to Samood We sent their brother Salih. He said, "⁰ my people! serve God, you have no god other than Him; clear proof indeed has come to you from your Lord; this is as God's she-camel for you -- a sign, therefore leave her alone to pasture on God's earth, and do not touch her with any harm, otherwise painful punishment will overtake you.
⁷⁴. And remember when He made you successors after Ad and settled you in the land -- you make mansions on its plains and hew out houses in the mountains -- remember therefore God's benefits and do not act corruptly in the land, making mischief.
⁷⁵. The chief of those who behaved proudly among his people said to those who were considered weak, to those who believed from among them: Do you know that Salih is sent by his Lord?

They said, "Certainly we are believers in what he has been sent with

⁷⁶. Those who were haughty said, "Certainly we are deniers of what you believe in.

⁷⁷. So they killed the she-camel and revolted against their Lord's commandment, and they said, "Oh Salih! bring us what you threatened us with, if you are one of the apostles.

⁷⁸. Then the earthquake overtook them, so they became motionless corpses in their home.

⁷⁹. Then he turned away from them and said, "Oh my people I did certainly deliver to you the message of my Lord, and I gave you good advice, but you do not love those who give good advice.

⁸⁰. And We sent Lot when he said to his people: What! do you commit an indecency which any one in the world has not done before you?

⁸¹. Most certainly you come to males in lust besides females; No you are an extravagant people.

⁸². And the answer of his people was no other than that they said, "Turn them out of your town, certainly they are a people who seek to purify themselves.

⁸³. So We delivered him and his followers, except his wife; she was of those who remained behind.

⁸⁴. And We rained upon them a rain; consider then what was the end of the guilty.

⁸⁵. And to Madyan We sent their brother Shu'aib. He said, "⁰ my people! serve God, you have no god other than Him; clear proof indeed has come to you from your Lord, therefore give full measure and weight and do not diminish to men their things, and do not make mischief in the land after its reform; this is better for you if you are believers:

⁸⁶. And do not lie in wait in every path, threatening and turning away from God's way him who believes in Him and seeking to make it crooked; and remember when you were few then He multiplied you, and consider what was the end of the mischief-makers.

⁸⁷. And if there is a party of you who believe in that with which am sent, and another party who do not believe, then wait patiently until God judges between us; and He is the best Judge.

⁸⁸. The chiefs, those who were proud from among his people said, "We will most certainly turn you out, Oh Shu'aib, and also; those who believe with you, from our town, or you shall come back to our faith. He said, "What! though we dislike it?

⁸⁹. Indeed we shall have created a lie against God If we go back to your religion after God has delivered us from It, and it befits us not that we should go back to it, except if God our Lord please: Our Lord comprehends all things :n His knowledge; in God do we trust: Our Lord! decide between us and our people with truth; and You are the best of decision maker.

⁹⁰. And the chiefs of those who disbelieved from among his people said, "If you follow Shu'aib, you shall then most certainly be losers

⁹¹. Then the earthquake overtook them, so they became motionless bodies
in their home.

⁹². Those who called Shu'aib a liar were as though they had never dwelt therein; those who called Shu'aib a liar, they were the losers.

⁹³. So he turned away from them and said, "Oh my people! certainly I delivered to you the messages of my Lord and I gave you good advice; how shall I then be sorry for an unbelieving people?

⁹⁴. And We did not send a prophet in a town but We overtook its people with distress and sickness in order that they might humble themselves.

⁹⁵. Then We gave them good in the place of evil until they became many and said, "Distress and happiness did indeed happen to our fathers. Then We took them by surprise while they did not perceive.

⁹⁶. And if the people of the towns had believed and guarded against evil We would certainly have opened up for them blessings from the heaven and the earth, but they rejected, so We overtook them for what they had earned.

⁹⁷. What! do the people of the towns then feel secure from Our punishment coming to them by night while they sleep?

⁹⁸. What! do the people of the towns feel secure from Our punishment coming to them in the morning while they play?

⁹⁹. What! do they then feel secure from God's plan? But none feels secure from God's plan except the people who shall perish.

¹⁰⁰. Is it not clear to those who inherit the earth after its former residents that if We please We would afflict them on account of their faults and set a seal on their hearts so they would not hear.

¹⁰¹. These towns -- We relate to you some of their stories, and certainly their apostles came to them with clear explanations, but they would not believe in what they rejected at first; thus does God set a seal over the hearts of the unbelievers

¹⁰². And We did not find in most of them any faithfulness to covenant, and We found most of them to be certainly transgressors.

¹⁰³. Then we raised after them Moses with Our words to Pharoah and his chiefs, but they disbelieved in them; consider then what was the end of the mischief makers.

¹⁰⁴. And Moses said, "Oh Pharoah! certainly I am an apostle from the Lord of the worlds:

¹⁰⁵. I am worthy of not saying anything about God except the truth: I have come to you indeed with clear proof from your Lord, therefore send with me the children of Israel

¹⁰⁶. He said, "If you have come with a sign, then bring it, if you are of the truthful ones.

¹⁰⁷. So he threw his rod, then lo! it was a clear serpent.

¹⁰⁸. And he drew forth his hand, and lo! it was white to the beholders.

¹⁰⁹. The chiefs of Pharoah's people said, "most certainly this is an magician possessed of knowledge:

¹¹⁰. He intends to turn you out of your land. What counsel do you then give?

¹¹¹. They said, "Put him off and his brother, and send collectors into the cities:

¹¹². That they may bring to you every magician possessed of knowledge.

¹¹³. And the magicians came to Pharoah and said, "We must certainly have a reward if we are the prevailing ones.

¹¹⁴. He said, "Yes, and you shall certainly be of those who are near to me.

¹¹⁵. They said, "Oh Moses! will you strike, or shall we be the first to strike?

¹¹⁶. He said, "Strike. So when they strike, they deceived the people's eyes and frightened them, and they produced a mighty sorcery.

¹¹⁷. And We revealed to Moses, saying, "thrust your rod; then it devoured the lies they told.

¹¹⁸. So the truth was established, and what they did became null.

¹¹⁹. Thus they were vanquished there, and they went back abased.

¹²⁰. And the magicians were thrown down, prostrating themselves.

¹²¹. They said, "We believe in the Lord of the worlds,

¹²². The Lord of Moses and Aaron.

¹²³. Pharoah said, "Do you believe in Him before I have given you permission? Certainly this is a plot which you have secretly devised in this city, that you may turn out of it its people, but you shall know:

¹²⁴. I will certainly cut off your hands and your feet on opposite sides, then will I crucify you all together.

¹²⁵. They said, "Certainly to our Lord shall we return:

¹²⁶. And you do not take revenge on us except because we have believed in the words of our Lord when they came to us! Our Lord: Pour out upon us patience and cause us to die in submission.

¹²⁷. And the chiefs of Pharoah's people said, "Do you leave Moses and his people to make

mischief in the land and to abandon you and your gods? He said, "We will slay their sons and spare their women, and certainly we are masters over them.

¹²⁸. Moses said to his people: Ask help from God and be patient; certainly the land is God's; He causes such of His servants to inherit it as He pleases, and the end is for those who guard against evil.

¹²⁹. They said, "We have been persecuted before you came to us and since you have come to us. He said, "It may be that your Lord will destroy your enemy and make you rulers in the land, then He will see how you act.

¹³⁰. And certainly We overtook Pharoah's people with droughts and diminution of fruits that they may be mindful.

¹³¹. But when good occurred for them they said, "This is due to us; and when evil afflicted them, they attributed it to the ill-luck of Moses and those with him; certainly their evil fortune is only from God but most of them do not know.

¹³². And they said, "Whatever sign you may bring to us to charm us with it -- we will not believe in you.

¹³³. Therefore We sent upon them widespread death, and the locusts and the lice and the frog and the blood, clear signs; but they behaved arrogantly and they were a guilty people.

¹³⁴. And when the plague fell upon them, they said, "Oh Moses! pray for us to your Lord as He has promised with you, if you remove the plague from us, we will certainly believe in you and we will certainly send away with you the children of Israel.

¹³⁵. But when We removed the plague from them till a term which they should attain lo! they broke the promise.

¹³⁶. Therefore We inflicted retribution on them and drowned them in the sea because they rejected Our signs and were heedless of them.

¹³⁷. And We made the people who were deemed weak to inherit the eastern lands and the western ones which We had blessed; and the good word of your Lord was fulfilled in the children of Israel because they bore up sufferings patiently; and We utterly destroyed what Pharoah and his people had wrought and what they built.

¹³⁸. And We made the children of Israel to pass the sea; then they came upon a people who kept to the worship of their idols They said, "Oh Moses! make for us a god as they have their gods He said, "Certainly you are a people acting ignorantly:

¹³⁹. As to these, certainly that about which they are shall be brought to nothing and that which they do is vain.

¹⁴⁰. He said, "What! shall I seek for you a god other than God while He has made you excel above all created things?

¹⁴¹. And when We delivered you from Pharoah's people who subjected you to severe torment, killing your sons and sparing your women, and in this there was a great trial from your Lord.

¹⁴². And We appointed with Moses a time of thirty nights and completed them with ten more, so the appointed time of his Lord was complete forty nights, and Moses said to his brother Aaron: Take my place among my people, and act well and do not follow the way of the mischief-makers.

¹⁴³. And when Moses came at Our appointed time and his Lord spoke to him, he said, "My Lord! show me Yourself, so that I may look upon You. He said, "You cannot bear to see Me but look at the mountain, if it remains firm in its place, then will you see Me; but when his Lord manifested His glory to the mountain He made it crumble and Moses fell down in a swoon; then when he recovered, he said, "Glory be to You, I turn to You, and I am the first of the believers.

¹⁴⁴. He said, "Oh Moses! certainly I have chosen you above the people with My messages and

with My words, therefore take hold of what I give to you and be of the grateful ones.

¹⁴⁵. And We ordered for him in the tablets admonition of every kind and clear explanation of all things; so take hold of them with firmness and order your people to take hold of what is best thereof; I will show you the home of the transgressors.

¹⁴⁶. I will turn away from My words those who are unjustly proud in the earth; and if they see every sign they will not believe in It; and if they see the way of rectitude they do not take It for a way, and if they see the way of error. they take it for a way; this is because they rejected Our words and were heedless of them.

¹⁴⁷. And as to those who reject Our words and the meeting of the hereafter, their deeds are null. Shall they be rewarded except for what they have done?

¹⁴⁸. And Moses's people made of their ornaments a calf after him, a mere body, which gave a mooing sound. What! could they not see that it did not speak to them nor guide them in the way? They took it for worship and they were unjust.

¹⁴⁹. And when they repented and saw that they had gone astray, they said, "If our Lord show not mercy to us and forgive us we shall certainly be of the losers.

¹⁵⁰. And when Moses returned to his people, wrathful and in violent grief, he said, "Evil is it that you have done after me; did you turn away from the bidding of your Lord? And he threw down the tablets and seized his brother by the head, dragging him towards him. He said, "Son of my mother! certainly the people reckoned me weak and had almost slain me, therefore make not the enemies to rejoice over me and count me not among the unjust people.

¹⁵¹. He said, "My Lord! forgive me and my brother and cause us to enter into Your mercy, and You are the most Merciful of the merciful ones.

¹⁵². As for those who took the calf for a god, certainly wrath from their Lord and disgrace in this world's life shall overtake them, and thus We will repay the devisers of lies.

¹⁵³. And as to those who do evil deeds, then repent after that and believe, your Lord after that is most certainly Forgiving, Merciful.

¹⁵⁴. And when Moses's anger calmed down he took up the tablets, and in the writing thereof was guidance and mercy for those who fear for the sake of their Lord.

¹⁵⁵. And Moses chose out of his people seventy men for Our appointment; so when the earthquake overtook them, he said, "My Lord! if You had pleased, You had destroyed them before and myself too; will You destroy us for what the fools among us have done? It is nothing but Your trial, You make err with it whom You please and guide whom You please: You are our Guardian, therefore forgive us and have mercy on us, and You are the best of the forgivers.

¹⁵⁶. And ordain for us good in this world's life and in the hereafter, for certainly we turn to You. He said, "As for My punishment, I will afflict with it whom I please, and My mercy encompasses all things; so I will ordain it specially for those who guard against evil and pay the poor-rate, and those who believe in Our words.

¹⁵⁷. Those who follow the Prophet-Prophet, the Ummi, whom they find written down with them in the Torah and the Gospel who urges them good and forbids them evil, and makes lawful to them the good things and makes unlawful to them impure things, and removes from them their burden and the shackles which were upon them; so as for those who believe in him and honor him and help him, and follow the light which has been sent down with him, these it is that are the successful.

¹⁵⁸. Say, "Oh people! certainly I am the Prophet of God to you all, of Him Whose is the kingdom of the heavens and the earth there is no god but He; He brings to life and causes to die therefore believe in God and His apostle, the Ummi Prophet who believes in God and His words, and follow him so that you may walk in the right way.

¹⁵⁹. And of Moses's people was a party who guided people with the truth, and thereby did they do justice.

¹⁶⁰. And We divided them into twelve tribes, as nations; and We revealed to Moses when his people asked him for water: Strike the rock with your staff, so outnowed from it twelve springs; each tribe knew its drinking place; and We made the clouds to give shade over them and We sent to them manna and quails: Eat of the good things We have given you. And they did not do Us any harm, but they did injustice to their own souls.

¹⁶¹. And when it was said to them: Reside in this town and eat from it wherever you wish, and say, Put down from us our heavy burdens: and enter the gate making obeisance, We will forgive you your wrongs: We will give more to those who do good to others.

¹⁶². But those who were unjust among them changed it for a saying other than that which had been spoken to them; so We sent upon them a pestilence from heaven because they were unjust.

¹⁶³. And ask them about the town which stood by the sea; when they exceeded the limits of the Sabbath, when their fish came to them on the day of their Sabbath, appearing on the surface of the water, and on the day on which they did not keep the Sabbath they did not come to them; thus did We try them because they transgressed.

¹⁶⁴. And when a party of them said, "Why do you reprimand a with a severe punishment? They said, "To be free from blame before your Lord, and that haply they may guard against evil.

¹⁶⁵. So when they neglected what they had been reminded of, We delivered those who forbade evil and We overtook those who were unjust with an evil punishment because they transgressed.

¹⁶⁶. Therefore when they revoltingly persisted in what they had been forbidden, We said to them, "Be like apes, despised and hated."

¹⁶⁷. And when your Lord announced that He would certainly send against them to the day of resurrection those who would subject them to severe torment; most certainly your Lord is quick to avenge evil and most certainly He is Forgiving, Merciful.

¹⁶⁸. And We cut them up on the earth into parties, some of them being righteous and others of them falling short of that, and We tried them with blessings and misfortunes that they might turn.

¹⁶⁹. Then there came after them an evil posterity who inherited the Book, taking only the frail good of this low life and saying, "It will be forgiven us." And if a similiar good came to them, they would take it, too. Was not a promise taken from them in the Book that they would not speak anything about God but the truth, and they have read what is in it; and the home of the hereafter is better for those who guard against evil. Do you not then understand?

¹⁷⁰. And as for those who hold fast by the Book and keep up prayer, certainly We do not waste the reward of the right doers.

¹⁷¹. And when We shook the mountain over them as if it were a covering overhead, and they thought that it was going to fall down upon them: Take hold of what We have given you with firmness, and be mindful of what is in it, so that you may guard against evil.

¹⁷². And when your Lord brought forth from the children of Adam, from their backs, their descendants, and made them bear witness against their own souls: Am I not your Lord? They said, "Yes! we bear witness. In case you should say on the day of resurrection: Certainly we were heedless of this."

¹⁷³. Or you should say, "Only our fathers associated others with God before, and we were an offspring after them: Will You then destroy us for what the vain doers did?"

¹⁷⁴. And thus do We make clear the words, and that haply they might return.

¹⁷⁵. And recite to them the narrative of him to whom We give Our words, but he withdraws himself from them, so the Satan overtakes him, so he is of those who go astray.

176. And if We had pleased, We would certainly have exalted him thereby; but he clung to the earth and followed his low desire, so his story is as the story of the dog; if you attack him he lolls out his tongue; and if you leave him alone he lolls out his tongue; this is the story of the people who reject Our words; therefore relate the narrative that they may reflect.

177. Evil is the likeness of the people who reject Our words and are unjust to their own souls.

178. Whomsoever God guides, he is the one who follows the right way; and whomsoever He causes to err, these are the losers.

179. And certainly We have created for hell many of the jinn and the men; they have hearts with which they do not understand, and they have eyes with which they do not see, and they have ears with which they do not hear; they are as cattle, no, they are in worse errors; these are the heedless ones.

180. And God's are the best names, therefore call on Him thereby, and avoid those who violate the sanctity of His names; they shall be repaid for what they have done.

181. And of those whom We have created are a people who guide with the truth and thereby they do justice.

182. And as to those who reject Our words, We draw them near to destruction by degrees from wherever they know not.

183. And I grant them respite; certainly My scheme is effective.

184. Do they not reflect that their companion has not unsoundness in mind; he is only a plain alarmgiver.

185. Do they not consider the kingdom of the heavens and the earth and whatever things God has created, and that may be their doom shall have drawn near; what announcement would they then believe in after this?

186. Whomsoever God causes to err, there is no guide for him; and He leaves them alone in their inordinacy, blindly wandering on.

187. They ask you about the hour, when will be its taking place? Say, "The knowledge of it is only with my Lord; none but He shall show it at its time; it will be momentous in the heavens and the earth; it will not come on you but of a sudden. " They ask you as if you were solicitous about it. Say, "Its knowledge is only with God, but most people do not know. "

188. Say, I do not control any benefit or harm for my own soul except as God please; and had I known the unseen I would have had much of good and no evil would have touched me; I am nothing but a alarmgiver and the giver of good news to a people who believe.

189. He it is Who created you from a single being, and of the same kind did He make his mate, that he might incline to her; so when he covers her she bears a light burden, then moves about with it; but when it grows heavy, they both call upon God, their Lord: If You give us a good one, we shall certainly be of the grateful ones.

190. But when He gives them a good one, they set up with Him associates in what He has given them; but high is God above what they associate with Him.

191. What! they associate with Him that which does not create any thing, while they are themselves created!

192. And they have no power to give them help, nor can they help themselves.

193. And if you invite them to guidance, they will not follow you; it is the same to you whether you invite them or you are silent.

194. Certainly those whom you call on besides God are in a state of subjugation like yourselves; therefore call on them, then let them answer you if you are truthful.

195. Have they feet with which they walk, or have they hands with which they hold, or have they eyes with which they see, or have they ears with which they hear? Say, "Call your associates,

then struggle to prevail against me and give me no rest.

¹⁹⁶. "Certainly my guardian is God, Who revealed the Book, and He befriends the good."

¹⁹⁷. And those whom you call upon besides Him are not able to help you, nor can they help themselves.

¹⁹⁸. And if you invite them to guidance, they do not hear; and you see them looking towards you, yet they do not see.

¹⁹⁹. Take to forgiveness and enjoin good and turn aside from the ignorant.

²⁰⁰. And if a false imputation from the Satan afflict you, seek refuge in God; certainly He is Hearing, Knowing.

²⁰¹. Certainly those who guard against evil, when a visitation from the Satan afflicts them, they become mindful, then lo! they see.

²⁰². And their brethren increase them in error, then they cease not.

²⁰³. And when you bring them not a revelation they say, "Why do you not forge it? Say, "I only follow what is revealed to me from my Lord; these are clear proofs from your Lord and a guidance and a mercy for a people who believe.

²⁰⁴. And when the Koran is recited, then listen to it and remain silent, that mercy may be shown to you.

²⁰⁵. And remember your Lord within yourself humbly and fearing and in a voice not loud in the morning and the evening and do not be of the heedless ones.

²⁰⁶. Certainly those who are with your Lord are not too proud to serve Him, and they declare His glory and throw themselves down in humility before Him.

Chapter 8 — Al-Anfal — The Accessions

In the name of God the Kind, the Merciful.

1. They ask you about the windfalls. Say, "The windfalls are for God and the Prophet. So be careful of your duty to God and set aright matters of your difference, and obey God and His Prophet if you are believers.
2. Those only are believers whose hearts become full of fear when God is mentioned, and when His words are recited to them they increase them in faith, and in their Lord do they trust.
3. Those who keep up prayer and spend benevolently out of what We have given them.
4. These are the believers in truth; they shall have from their Lord exalted grades and forgiveness and an honorable sustenance.
5. Even as your Lord caused you to go forth from your house with the truth, though a party of the believers were certainly averse;
6. They disputed with you about the truth after it had become clear, and they went forth as if they were being driven to death while they saw it.
7. And when God promised you one of the two parties that it shall be yours and you loved that the one not armed should he yours and God desired to show the truth of what was true by His words and to cut off the root of the unbelievers.
8. That He may show the truth of what was true and show the falsehood of what was false, though the guilty disliked.
9. When you sought aid from your Lord, so He answered you: I will assist you with a thousand of the angels following one another.
10. And God only gave it as a good news and that your hearts might be at ease thereby; and victory is only from God; certainly God is Mighty, Wise.
11. When He caused calm to fall on you as a security from Him and sent down upon you water from the cloud that He might thereby purify you, and take away from you the uncleanness of the Satan, and that He might fortify your hearts and steady your footsteps thereby.
12. When your Lord revealed to the angels: I am with you, therefore make firm those who believe. I will put terror into the hearts of those who disbelieve. Therefore strike off their heads and strike off every fingertip of them.
13. This is because they acted adversely to God and His Prophet; and whoever acts adversely to God and His Prophet -- then certainly God is severe in requiting evil.
14. This -- taste it, and know that for the unbelievers is the punishment of fire.
15. Oh you who believe! when you meet those who disbelieve marching for war, then turn not your backs to them.
16. And whoever shall turn his back to them on that day -- unless he turn aside for the sake of fighting or withdraws to a company -- then he, indeed, becomes deserving of God's wrath, and his home is hell; and an evil destination shall it be.
17. So you did not slay them, but it was God Who killed them, and you did not smite when you smote the enemy, but it was God Who smote, and that He might confer upon the believers a good gift from Himself; certainly God is Hearing, Knowing.
18. This, and that God is the weakener of the struggle of the unbelievers.
19. If you demanded a judgment, the judgment has then indeed come to you; and if you desist, it will be better for you; and if you turn back to fight, We too shall turn back, and your forces

shall avail you nothing, though they may be many, and know that God is with the believers.

20. Oh you who believe! obey God and His Prophet and do not turn back from Him while you hear.

21. And do not be like those who said, We hear, and they did not obey.

22. Certainly the most vile of animals, in God's sight, are the deaf, the dumb, who do not understand.

23. And if God had known any good in them He would have made them hear, and if He makes them hear they would turn back while they withdraw.

24. Oh you who believe! answer the call of God and His Prophet when he calls you to that which gives you life; and know that God intervenes between man and his heart, and that to Him you shall be gathered.

25. And fear an sickness which may not smite those of you in particular who are unjust; and know that God is severe in requiting evil.

26. And remember when you were few, deemed weak in the land, fearing that people might carry you off by force, but He sheltered you and strengthened you with His aid and gave you of the good things that you may give thanks.

27. Oh you who believe! do not be unfaithful to God and the Prophet, nor be unfaithful to your trusts while you know.

28. And know that your property and your children are a temptation, and that God is He with Whom there is a mighty reward.

29. Oh you who believe! If you are careful of your duty to God, He will grant you a distinction and do away with your evils and forgive you; and God is the Lord of mighty grace.

30. And when those who disbelieved devised plans against you that they might confine you or slay you or drive you away; and they devised plans and God too had arranged a plan; and God is the best of planners.

31. And when Our words are recited to them, they say, "We have heard indeed; if we pleased we could say the like of it; this is nothing but the stories of the ancients.

32. And when they said, "Oh God! if this is the truth from You, then rain upon us stones from heaven or inflict on us a painful punishment.

33. But God was not going to reprimand them while you were among them, nor is God going to reprimand them while yet they ask for forgiveness.

34. And what excuse have they that God should not reprimand them while they hinder men from the Sacred Mosque and they are not fit to be guardians of it; its guardians are only those who guard against evil, but most of them do not know.

35. And their prayer before the House is nothing but whistling and
clapping of hands; taste then the punishment, for you disbelieved.

36. Certainly those who disbelieve spend their wealth to hinder people from the way of God; so they shall spend it, then it shall be to them an intense regret, then they shall be overcome; and those who disbelieve shall be driven together to hell.

37. That God might separate the impure from the good, and put the impure, some of it upon the other, and pile it up together, then throw it into hell; these it is that are the losers.

38. Say to those who disbelieve, if they desist, that which is past shall be forgiven to them; and if they return, then what happened to the ancients has already passed.

39. And fight with them until there is no more persecution and religion should be only for God; but if they desist, then certainly God sees what they do.

40. And if they turn back, then know that God is your Patron; most excellent is the Patron and most excellent the Helper.

⁴¹. And know that whatever thing you gain, a fifth of it is for God and for the Prophet and for the near of kin and the orphans and the needy and the wayfarer, if you believe in God and in that which We revealed to Our servant, on the day of distinction, the day on which the two parties met; and God has power over all things.

⁴². When you were on the nearer side of the valley and they were on the farthest side, while the caravan was below you; and if you had mutually made an appointment, you would certainly have broken away from the appointment, but -- in order that God might cause to be done, so that he who would perish might perish by clear proof, and he who would live might live by clear proof; and most certainly God is Hearing, Knowing;

⁴³. When God showed them to you in your dream as few; and if He had shown them to you as many you would certainly have become weak-hearted and you would have disputed about the matter, but God saved you; certainly He is the Knower of what is in the hearts.

⁴⁴. And when He showed them to you, when you met, as few in your eyes and He made you to appear little in their eyes, in order that God might bring about a matter which was to be done, and to God are all affairs returned.

⁴⁵. Oh you who believe! when you meet a party, then be firm, and remember God much, that you may be successful.

⁴⁶. And obey God and His Prophet and do not quarrel for then you will be weak in hearts and your power will depart, and be patient; certainly God is with the patient.

⁴⁷. And do not be like those who came forth from their homes in great exultation and to be seen of men, and who turn away from the way of God, and God comprehends what they do.

⁴⁸. And when the Satan made their works fair seeming to them, and said, "No one can overcome you this day, and certainly I am your protector: but when the two parties came in sight of each other he turned upon his heels, and said, "Certainly I am clear of you, certainly I see what you do not see, certainly I fear God; and God is severe in requiting evil.

⁴⁹. When the hypocrites and those in whose hearts was disease said, "Their religion has deceived them; and whoever trusts in God, then certainly God is Mighty, Wise.

⁵⁰. And had you seen when the angels will cause to die those who disbelieve, smiting their faces and their backs, and saying, "Taste the punishment of burning.

⁵¹. This is for what your own hands have sent on before, and because God is not in the least unjust to the servants;

⁵². In the manner of the people of Pharoah and those before them; they disbelieved in God's words, therefore God destroyed them on account of their faults; certainly God is strong, severe in requiting evil.

⁵³. This is because God has never changed a favor which He has conferred upon a people until they change their own condition; and because God is All-hearing, All-knowing;

⁵⁴. In the manner of the people of Pharoah and those before them; they rejected the words of their Lord, therefore We destroyed them on account of their faults and We drowned Pharoah's people, and they were all unjust.

⁵⁵. Certainly the most vile of animals in God's sight are those who disbelieve, then they would not believe.

⁵⁶. Those with whom you make an agreement, then they break their agreement every time and they do not guard against punishment.

⁵⁷. Therefore if you overtake them in fighting, then scatter by making an example of them those who are in their rear, that they may be mindful.

⁵⁸. And if you fear treachery on the part of a people, then throw back to them on terms of equality; certainly God does not love the treacherous.

⁵⁹. And let not those who disbelieve think that they shall come in first; certainly they will not escape.

⁶⁰. And prepare against them what force you can and horses tied at the frontier, to frighten thereby the enemy of God and your enemy and others besides them, whom you do not know but God knows them; and whatever thing you will spend in God's way, it will be paid back to you fully and you shall not be dealt with unjustly.

⁶¹. And if they incline to peace, then incline to it and trust in God; certainly He is the All-hearing, the All-knowing.

⁶². And if they intend to deceive you -- then certainly God is sufficient for you; He it is Who strengthened you with His help and with the believers

⁶³. And united their hearts; had you spent all that is in the earth, you could not have united their hearts, but God united them; certainly He is Mighty, Wise.

⁶⁴. Oh Prophet! God is sufficient for you and for such of the believers as follow you.

⁶⁵. Oh Prophet! urge the believers to war; if there are twenty patient ones of you they shall overcome two hundred, and if there are a hundred of you they shall overcome a thousand of those who disbelieve, because they are a people who do not understand.

⁶⁶. For the present God has made light your burden, and He knows that there is weakness in you; so if there are a hundred patient ones of you they shall overcome two hundred, and if there are a thousand they shall overcome two thousand by God's permission, and God is with the patient.

⁶⁷. It is not fit for a prophet that he should take captives unless he has fought and triumphed in the land; you desire the frail goods of this world, while God desires for you the hereafter; and God is Mighty, Wise.

⁶⁸. Were it not for an ordinance from God that had already gone forth, certainly there would have happened to you a great punishment for what you had taken to.

⁶⁹. Eat then of the lawful and good things which you have acquired in war, and be careful of your duty to God; certainly God is Forgiving, Merciful.

⁷⁰. Oh Prophet! say to those of the captives who are in your hands: If God knows anything good in your hearts, He will give to you better than that which has been taken away from you and will forgive you, and God is Forgiving, Merciful.

⁷¹. And if they intend to act unfaithfully towards you, so indeed they acted unfaithfully towards God before, but He gave you mastery over them; and God is Knowing, Wise.

⁷². Certainly those who believed and fled their homes and struggled hard in God's way with their property and their souls, and those who gave shelter and helped -- these are guardians of each other; and as for those who believed and did not fly, not yours is their guardianship until they fly; and if they seek aid from you in the matter of religion, aid is incumbent on you except against a people between whom and you there is a treaty, and God sees what you do.

⁷³. And as for those who disbelieve, some of them are the guardians of others; if you will not do it, there will be in the land persecution and great mischief.

⁷⁴. And as for those who believed and fled and struggled hard in God's way, and those who gave shelter and helped, these are the believers truly; they shall have forgiveness and honorable provision.

⁷⁵. And as for those who believed afterwards and fled and struggled hard along with you, they are of you; and the possessors of relationships are nearer to each other in the ordinance of God; certainly God knows all things.

Chapter 9 — Al-Taubah — The Immunity

¹. This is a declaration of immunity by God and His Prophet towards those of the idolaters with whom you made an agreement.
². So go about in the land for four months and know that you cannot weaken God and that God will bring disgrace to the unbelievers.
³. And an announcement from God and His Prophet to the people on the day of the greater pilgrimage that God and His Prophet are free from liability to the idolaters; therefore if you repent, it will be better for you, and if you turn back, then know that you will not weaken God; and announce painful punishment to those who disbelieve.
⁴. Except those of the idolaters with whom you made an agreement, then they have not failed you in anything and have not backed up any one against you, so fulfill their agreement to the end of their term; certainly God loves those who are careful of their duty.
⁵. So when the sacred months have passed away, then slay the idolaters wherever you find them, and take them captives and besiege them and lie in wait for them in every ambush, then if they repent and keep up prayer and pay the poor-rate, leave their way free to them; certainly God is Forgiving, Merciful.
⁶. And if one of the idolaters seek protection from you, grant him protection till he hears the word of God, then make him attain his place of safety; this is because they are a people who do not know.
⁷. How can there be an agreement for the idolaters with God and with His Prophet; except those with whom you made an agreement at the Sacred Mosque? So as long as they are true to you, be true to them; certainly God loves those who are careful of their duty.
⁸. How can it be! while if they prevail against you, they would not pay regard in your case to ties of relationship, nor those of covenant; they please you with their mouths while their hearts do not consent; and most of them are transgressors.
⁹. They have taken a small price for the words of God, so they turn away from His way; certainly evil is it that they do.
¹⁰. They do not pay regard to ties of relationship nor those of covenant in the case of a believer; and these are they who go beyond the limits.
¹¹. But if they repent and keep up prayer and pay the poor-rate, they are your brethren in faith; and We make the words clear for a people who know.
¹². And if they break their oaths after their agreement and openly revile your religion, then fight the leaders of unbelief -- certainly their oaths are nothing -- so that they may desist.
¹³. What! will you not fight a people who broke their oaths and aimed at the expulsion of the Prophet, and they attacked you first; do you fear them? But God is most deserving that you should fear Him, if you are believers.
¹⁴. Fight them, God will punish them by your hands and bring them to disgrace, and assist you against them and heal the hearts of a believing people.
¹⁵. And remove the rage of their hearts; and God turns mercifully to whom He pleases, and God is Knowing, Wise.
¹⁶. What! do you think that you will be left alone while God has not yet known those of you who have struggled hard and have not taken any one as an adherent besides God and His Prophet and the believers; and God is aware of what you do.

17. The idolaters have no right to visit the mosques of God while bearing witness to unbelief against themselves, these it is whose doings are null, and in the fire shall they abide.
18. Only he shall visit the mosques of God who believes in God and the latter day, and keeps up prayer and pays the poor-rate and fears none but God; so as for these, it may be that they are of the followers of the right course.
19. What! do you make one who undertakes the giving of drink to the pilgrims and the guarding of the Sacred Mosque like him who believes in God and the latter day and strives hard in God's way? They are not equal with God; and God does not guide the unjust people.
20. Those who believed and fled their homes, and strove hard in God's way with their property and their souls, are much higher in rank with God; and those are they who are the achievers of their objects.
21. Their Lord gives them good news of mercy from Himself and His good pleasure and gardens, wherein lasting blessings shall be theirs;
22. Abiding therein for ever; certainly God has a Mighty reward with Him.
23. Oh you who believe! do not take your fathers and your brothers for guardians if they love unbelief more than belief; and whoever of you takes them for a guardian, these it is that are the unjust.
24. Say, "If your fathers and your sons and your brethren and your mates and your kinsfolk and property which you have acquired, and the slackness of trade which you fear and dwellings which you like, are dearer to you than God and His Prophet and striving in His way, then wait till God brings about His command: and God does not guide the transgressing people.
25. Certainly God helped you in many battlefields and on the day of Hunain, when your great numbers made you vain, but they availed you nothing and the earth became strait to you notwithstanding its spaciousness, then you turned back retreating.
26. Then God sent down His tranquillity upon His Prophet and upon the believers, and sent down hosts which you did not see, and reprimandd those who disbelieved, and that is the reward of the unbelievers.
27. Then will God after this turn mercifully to whom He pleases, and God is Forgiving, Merciful.
28. Oh you who believe! the idolaters are nothing but unclean, so they shall not approach the Sacred Mosque after this year; and if you fear poverty then God will enrich you out of His grace if He please; certainly God is Knowing Wise.
29. Fight those who do not believe in God, nor in the latter day, nor do they prohibit what God and His Prophet have prohibited, nor follow the religion of truth, out of those who have been given the Book, until they pay the tax in acknowledgment of superiority and they are in a state of subjection.
30. And the Jews say, "Uzair is the son of God; and the Christians say, "The Messiah is the son of God; these are the words of their mouths; they imitate the saying of those who disbelieved before; may God destroy them; how they are turned away!
31. They have taken their doctors of law and their monks for lords besides God, and also the Messiah son of Mary and they were enjoined that they should serve one God only, there is no god but He; far from His glory be what they set up with Him.
32. They desire to put out the light of God with their mouths, and God will not consent save to perfect His light, though the unbelievers are averse.
33. He it is Who sent His Prophet with guidance and the religion of truth, that He might cause it to prevail over all religions, though the polytheists may be averse.
34. Oh you who believe! most certainly many of the doctors of law and the monks pervert the works of men, and turn them from God's way; and as for those who hoard up gold and silver

and do not spend it in God's way, announce to them a painful punishment,

35. On the day when it shall be heated in the fire of hell, then their foreheads and their sides and their backs shall be branded with it; this is what you hoarded up for yourselves, therefore taste what you hoarded.

36. Certainly the number of months with God is twelve months in God's ordinance since the day when He created the heavens and the earth, of these four being sacred; that is the right judging; therefore do not be unjust to yourselves regarding them, and fight the polytheists all together as they fight you all together; and know that God is with those who guard against evil.

37. Postponing of the sacred month is only an addition in unbelief, wherewith those who disbelieve are led astray, violating it one year and keeping it sacred another, that they may agree in the number of months that God has made sacred, and thus violate what God has made sacred; the evil of their doings is made fairseeming to them; and God does not guide the unbelieving people.

38. Oh you who believe! What excuse have you that when it is said to you: Go forth in God's way, you should incline heavily to earth; are you contented with this world's life instead of the hereafter? But the provision of this world's life compared with the hereafter is but little.

39. If you do not go forth, He will reprimand you with a painful punishment and bring in your place a people other than you, and you will do Him no harm; and God has power over all things. 40. If you will not aid him, God certainly aided him when those who disbelieved expelled him, he being the second of the two, when they were both in the cave, when he said to his companion: Grieve not, certainly God is with us. So God sent down His tranquillity upon him and strengthened him with hosts which you did not see, and made lowest the word of those who disbelieved; and the word of God, that is the highest; and God is Mighty, Wise.

41. Go forth light and heavy, and strive hard in God's way with your property and your persons; this is better for you, if you know.

42. Had it been a near advantage and a short journey, they would certainly have followed you, but the tedious journey was too long for them; and they swear by God: If we had been able, we would certainly have gone forth with you; they cause their own souls to perish, and God knows that they are most certainly

43. God pardon you! Why did you give them leave until those who spoke the truth had become greatto you and you had known the liars?

44. They do not ask leave of you who believe in God and the latter day to stay away from striving hard with their property and their persons, and God knows those who guard against evil.

45. They only ask leave of you who do not believe in God and the latter day and their hearts are in doubt, so in their doubt do they waver.

46. And if they had intended to go forth, they would certainly have provided equipment for it, but God did not like their going forth, so He withheld them, and it was said to them: Hold back with those who hold back.

47. Had they gone forth with you, they would not have added to you anything except corruption, and they would certainly have hurried about among you seeking to sow dissension among you, and among you there are those who hearken for their sake; and God knows the unjust.

48. Certainly they sought to sow dissension before, and they meditated
plots against you until the truth came, and God's commandment prevailed although they were averse from it.

49. And among them there is he who says: Allow me and do not try me. Certainly into trial have they already tumbled down, and most certainly hell encompasses the unbelievers.

50. If good happens to you, it grieves them, and if hardship afflicts you, they say, "Indeed we

had taken care of our affair before; and they turn back and are glad.

⁵¹. Say, "Nothing will afflict us save what God has ordered for us; He is our Patron; and on God let the believers rely.

⁵². Say, "Do you await for us but one of two most excellent things? And we await for you that God will afflict you with punishment from Himself or by our hands. So wait; we too will wait with you.

⁵³. Say, "Spend willingly or unwillingly, it shall not be accepted from you; certainly you are a transgressing people.

⁵⁴. And nothing hinders their spendings being accepted from them, except that they disbelieve in God and in His Prophet and they do not come to prayer but while they are sluggish, and they do not spend but while they are unwilling.

⁵⁵. Let not then their property and their children excite your admiration; God only wishes to reprimand them with these in this world's life and that their souls may depart while they are unbelievers.

⁵⁶. And they swear by God that they are most certainly of you, and they are not of you, but they are a people who are afraid of you.

⁵⁷. If they could find a refuge or cave or a place to enter into, they would certainly have turned thereto, running away in all haste.

⁵⁸. And of them there are those who blame you with respect to the alms; so if they are given from it they are pleased, and if they are not given from it, lo! they are full of rage.

⁵⁹. And if they were content with what God and His Prophet gave them, and had said, "God is sufficient for us; God will soon give us more out of His grace and His Prophet too; certainly to God do we make our petition.

⁶⁰. Alms are only for the poor and the needy, and the officials appointed over them, and those whose hearts are made to incline to truth and the ransoming of captives and those in debts and in the way of God and the wayfarer; an ordinance from God; and God is knowing, Wise.

⁶¹. And there are some of them who molest the Prophet and say, "He is one who believes every thing that he hears; say, "A hearer of good for you who believes in God and believes the faithful and a mercy for those of you who believe; and as for those who molest the Prophet of God, they shall have a painful punishment.

⁶². They swear to you by God that they might please you and, God, as well as His Prophet, has a greater right that they should please Him, if they are believers.

⁶³. Do they not know that whoever acts in opposition to God and His Prophet, he shall certainly have the fire of hell to abide in it? That is the grievous abasement.

⁶⁴. The hypocrites fear that a chapter should be sent down to them telling them plainly of what is in their hearts. Say, "Go on mocking, certainly God will bring forth what you fear.

⁶⁵. And if you should question them, they would certainly say, "We were only idly discoursing and sporting. Say, "Was it at God and His words and His Prophet that you mocked?"

⁶⁶. Do not make excuses; you have denied indeed after you had believed; if We pardon a party of you, We will reprimand another party because they are guilty.

⁶⁷. The hypocritical men and the hypocritical women are all alike; they enjoin evil and forbid good and withhold their hands; they have abandoned God, so He has abandoned them; certainly the hypocrites are the transgressors.

⁶⁸. God has promised the hypocritical men and the hypocritical women and the unbelievers the fire of hell to abide therein; it is enough for them; and God has cursed them and they shall have lasting punishment.

⁶⁹. Like those before you; they were stronger than you in power and more abundant in wealth

and children, so they enjoyed their portion; thus have you enjoyed your portion as those before you enjoyed their portion; and you entered into vain discourses like the vain discourses in which entered those before you. These are they whose works are null in this world and the hereafter, and these are they who are the losers.

70. Has not the news of those before them come to them; of the people of Noah and Ad and Samood, and the people of Abraham and the dwellers of Madyan and the overthrown cities; their apostles came to them with clear explanations; so it was not God Who should do them injustice, but they were unjust to themselves.

71. And as for the believing men and the believing women, they are guardians of each other; they enjoin good and forbid evil and keep up prayer and pay the poor-rate, and obey God and His Prophet; as for these, God will show mercy to them; certainly God is Mighty, Wise.

72. God has promised to the believing men and the believing women gardens, beneath which rivers flow, to abide in them, and fine dwellings in gardens of perpetual home; and best of all is God's pleasure; that is the grand achievement.

73. Oh Prophet! strive hard against the unbelievers and the hypocrites and be unyielding to them; and their home is hell, and evil is the destination.

74. They swear by God that they did not speak, and certainly they did speak, the word of unbelief, and disbelieved after their Islam, and they had determined upon what they have not been able to effect, and they did not find fault except because God and His Prophet enriched them out of His grace; therefore if they repent, it will be good for them; and if they turn back, God will reprimand them with a painful punishment in this world and the hereafter, and they shall not have in the land any guardian or a helper.

75. And there are those of them who made a covenant with God: If He give us out of His grace, we will certainly give alms and we will certainly be of the good.

76. But when He gave them out of His grace, they became miserable from it and they turned back and they withdrew.

77. So He causaed hypocrisy as a consequence in their hearts till the day when they shall meet Him because they failed to perform towards God what they had promised Him and because they told lies.

78. Do they not know that God knows their hidden thoughts and their secret counsels, and that God is the great Knower of the unseen things?

79. They who taunt those of the faithful who give their alms freely, and those who give to the extent of their earnings and scoff at them; God will pay them back their scoffing, and they shall have a painful punishment.

80. Ask forgiveness for them or do not ask forgiveness for them; even if you ask forgiveness for them seventy times, God will not forgive them; this is because they disbelieve in God and His Prophet, and God does not guide the transgressing people.

81. Those who were left behind were glad on account of their sitting behind God's Prophet and they were averse from striving in God's way with their property and their persons, and said, "Do not go forth in the heat. Say, "The fire of hell is much severe in heat. Would that they understood it.

82. Therefore they shall laugh little and weep much as a repayment for what they earned.

83. Therefore if God brings you back to a party of them and then they ask your permission to go forth, say, "By no means shall you ever go forth with me and by no means shall you fight an enemy with me; certainly you chose to sit the first time, therefore sit now with those who remain behind.

84. And never offer prayer for any one of them who dies and do not stand by his grave; certainly

they disbelieve in God and His Prophet and they shall die in transgression.

85. And let not their property and their children excite your admiration; God only wishes to reprimand them with these in this world and that their souls may depart while they are unbelievers

86. And whenever a chapter is revealed, saying, "Believe in God and strive hard along with His Prophet, those having ampleness of means ask permission of you and say, "Leave us behind, that we may be with those who sit.

87. They preferred to be with those who remained behind, and a seal is set on their hearts so they do not understand.

88. But the Prophet and those who believe with him strive hard with their property and their persons; and these it is who shall have the good things and these it is who shall be successful.

89. God has prepared for them gardens beneath which rivers flow, to abide in them; that is the great achievement.

90. And the defaulters from among the dwellers of the desert came that permission may be given to them and they sat at home who lied to God and His Prophet; a painful punishment shall afflict those of them who disbelieved.

91. It shall be no crime in the weak, nor in the sick, nor in those who do not find what they should spend to stay behind, so long as they are sincere to God and His Prophet; there is no way to blame against the doers of good; and God is Forgiving, Merciful;

92. Nor in those who when they came to you that you might carry them, you said, "I cannot find that on which to carry you; they went back while their eyes overflowed with tears on account of grief for not finding that which they should spend.

93. The way to blame is only against those who ask permission of you though they are rich; they have chosen to be with those who remained behind, and God has set a seal upon their hearts so they do not know.

94. They will excuse themselves to you when you go back to them. Say, "Urge no excuse, by no means will we believe you; indeed God has informed us of matters relating to you; and now God and His Prophet will see what you have done, then you shall be brought back to the Knower of the unseen and the seen, then He will inform you of what you did.

95. They will swear to you by God when you return to them so that you may turn aside from them; so do turn aside from them; certainly they are unclean and their home is hell; a repayment for what they earned.

96. They will swear to you that you may be pleased with them; but if you are pleased with them, yet certainly God is not pleased with the transgressing people.

97. The dwellers of the desert are very hard in unbelief and hypocrisy, and more disposed not to know the limits of what God has revealed to His Prophet; and God is Knowing, Wise.

98. And of the dwellers of the desert are those who take what they spend to be a fine, and they wait those who have caused calamities to you; on them will be the evil calamity; and God is Hearing, Knowing.

99. And of the dwellers of the desert are those who believe in God and the latter day and take what they spend to be means of the nearness of God and the Prophet's prayers; certainly it shall be means of nearness for them; God will make them enter into His mercy; certainly God is Forgiving, Merciful.

100. And as for the foremost, the first of the Muhajirs and the Ansars, and those who followed them in goodness, God is well pleased with them and they are well pleased with Him, and He has prepared for them gardens beneath which rivers flow, to abide in them for ever; that is the mighty achievement.

101. And from among those who are round about you of the dwellers of the desert there are

hypocrites, and from among the people of Medina also; they are stubborn in hypocrisy; you do not know them; We know them; We will reprimand them twice then shall they be turned back to a grievous punishment

102. And others have confessed their faults, they have combined a good deed and an evil one; may be God will turn to them mercifully; certainly God is Forgiving, Merciful.

103. Take alms out of their property, you would cleanse them and purify them thereby, and pray for them; certainly your prayer is a relief to them; and God is Hearing, Knowing.

104. Do they not know that God accepts repentance from His servants and takes the alms, and that God is the Oft-returning to mercy, the Merciful?

105. And say, "Work; so God will see your work and so will His Prophet and the believers; and you shall be brought back to the Knower of the unseen and the seen, then He will inform you of what you did. 106. And others are made to await God's command, whether He reprimand them or whether He turn to them mercifully, and God is Knowing, Wise.

107. And those who built a place of worship to cause harm and for unbelief and to cause disunion among the believers and an ambush to him who made war against God and His Prophet before; and they will certainly swear: We did not desire anything but good; and God bears witness that they are most certainly liars.

108. Never stand in it; certainly a masjid founded on piety from the very first day is more deserving that you should stand in it; in it are men who love that they should be purified; and God loves those who purify themselves.

109. Is he, therefore, better who lays his foundation on fear of God and His good pleasure, or he who lays his foundation on the edge of a cracking hollowed bank, so it broke down with him into the fire of hell; and God does not guide the unjust people.

110. The building which they have built will ever continue to be a source of disquiet in their hearts, except that their hearts get cut into pieces; and God is Knowing, Wise.

111. Certainly God has bought of the believers their persons and their property for this, that they shall have the garden; they fight in God's way, so they slay and are slain; a promise which is binding on Him in the Torah and the Gospel and the Koran; and who is more faithful to his covenant than God? Rejoice therefore in the pledge which you have made; and that is the mighty achievement.

112. They who turn to God, who serve Him, who praise Him, who fast, who bow down, who prostrate themselves, who enjoin what is good and forbid what is evil, and who keep the limits of God; and give good news to the believers.

113. It is not fit for the Prophet and those who believe that they should ask forgiveness for the polytheists, even though they should be near relatives, after it has become clear to them that they are inmates of the flaming fire.

114. And Abraham asking forgiveness for his sire was only owing to a promise which he had made to him; but when it became clear to him that he was an enemy of God, he declared himself to be clear of him; most certainly Abraham was very tender-hearted forbearing.

115. It is not attributable to God that He should lead a people astray after He has guided them; He even makes clear to them what they should guard against; certainly God knows all things.

116. Certainly God's is the kingdom of the heavens and the earth; He brings to life and causes to die; and there is not for you besides God any Guardian or Helper.

117. Certainly God has turned mercifully to the Prophet and those who fled their homes and the helpers who followed him in the hour of straitness after the hearts of a part of them were about to deviate, then He turned to them mercifully; certainly to them He is Compassionate, Merciful.

118. And to the three who were left behind, until the earth became strait to them notwithstanding its spaciousness and their souls were also straightened to them; and they knew it for certain that there was no refuge from God but in Him; then He turned to them mercifully that they might turn to Him; certainly God frequently-returns to mercy, the Merciful.

119. Oh you who believe! be careful of your duty to God and be with the true ones.

120. The people of Medina and the dwellers of the desert around them did not support the Prophet of God, nor should they desire anything for themselves in preference to him; this is because there afflicts them not thirst or fatigue or hunger in God's way, nor do they tread a path which enrages the unbelievers, nor do they attain from the enemy what they attain, but a good work is written down to them on account of it; certainly God does not waste the reward of the doers of good;

121. Nor do they spend anything that may be spent, small or great, nor do they traverse a valley, but it is written down to their credit, that God may reward them with the best of what they have done.

122. And it does not occur to the believers that they should go forth all together; why should not some of them go forth that they might apply themselves to obtain understanding in religion, and that they may warn their people when they come back to them that they should be cautious?

123. Oh you who believe! fight those of the unbelievers who are near to you and let them find in you hardness; and know that God is with those who guard against evil.

124. And whenever a chapter is revealed, there are some of them who say, "Which of you has it strengthened in faith? Then as for those who believe, it strengthens them in faith and they rejoice.

125. And as for those in whose hearts is a disease, it adds uncleanness to their uncleanness and they die while they are unbelievers.

126. Do they not see that they are tried once or twice in every year, yet they do not turn to God nor do they mind.

127. And whenever a chapter is revealed, they cast glances at one another: Does any one see you? Then they turn away: God has turned away their hearts because they are a people who do not understand.

128. Certainly a Prophet has come to you from among yourselves; grievous to him is your falling into distress, excessively solicitous respecting you; to the believers he is compassionate,

129. But if they turn back, say, "God is sufficient for me, there is no god but He; on Him do I rely, and He is the Lord of mighty power.

Chapter 10 — Yunus — Jonah

In the name of God, the Kind, the Merciful.

1. Alif Lam Ra. These are the verses of the wise Book.
2. What! is it a wonder to the people that We revealed to a man from among themselves, saying, "Warn the people and give good news to those who believe that theirs is a firm foundation with their Lord. The unbelievers say, "This is most certainly a great magician."
3. Certainly your Lord is God, Who created the heavens and the earth in six days, and He is firm in power, regulating all htings, there is no interediary except with His permission; this is God, your Lord, therefore serve Him; will you not then pay attention?
4. He is your path, for all of you; the promise of God made in truth; certainly He begins the creation in the first instance, then He reproduces it, that He may with justice repay those who believe and do good; and as for those who disbelieve, they shall have a drink of hot water and painful punishment because they disbelieved.
5. He it is Who made the sun a shining brightness and the moon a light, and ordered for it mansions that you might know the computation of years and the judging. God did not create it but with truth; He makes the great signs for a people who
6. Most certainly in the variation of the night and the day, and what God has created in the heavens and the earth, there are signs for a people who guard against evil.
7. Certainly those who do not hope in Our meeting and are pleased with this world's life and are content with it, and those who are heedless of Our words:
8. As for those, their home is the fire because of what they have earned.
9. Certainly, for those who believe and do good, their Lord will guide them by their faith; there shall flow around them rivers in gardens of bliss.
10. Their cry in it shall be: Glory to You, Oh God! and their greeting in it shall be: Peace; and the last of their cry shall be: Praise be to God, the Lord of the worlds.
11. And if God should hasten the evil to men as they desire the hastening on of good, their doom should certainly have been decreed for them; but We leave those alone who hope not for Our meeting in their inordinacy, blindly wandering on.
12. And when sickness touches a man, he calls on Us, whether lying on his side or sitting or standing; but when We remove his sickness from him, he passes on as though he had never called on Us on account of an sickness that touched him; thus that which they do is made fair-seeming to the extravagant.
13. And certainly We did destroy generations before you when they were unjust, and their apostles had come to them with clear explanations, and they would not believe; thus do We repay the guilty people.
14. Then We made you successors in the land after them so that We may see how you act.
15. And when Our clear words are recited to them, those who hope not for Our meeting say, "Bring a Koran other than this or change it. Say, "It does not seem to me that I should change it by myself; I follow nothing but what is revealed to me; certainly I fear, if I disobey my Lord, the punishment of a mighty day.
16. Say, "If God had desired otherwise I would not have recited it to you, nor would He have taught it to you; indeed I have lived a lifetime among you before it; do you not then understand?
17. Who is then more unjust than who forges a lie against God or who gives the lie to His

words? Certainly the guilty shall not be successful.

18. And they serve beside God what can neither harm them nor profit them, and they say, "These are our advocates with God. Say, "Do you presume to inform God of what He knows not in the heavens and the earth? Glory be to Him, and supremely exalted is He above what they set up with Him.

19. And people are nothing but a single nation, so they disagree; and had not a word already gone forth from your Lord, the matter would have certainly been decided between them in respect of that concerning which they disagree.

20. And they say, "Why is not a sign sent to him from his Lord? Say, "The unseen is only for God; therefore wait -- certainly I too, with you am of those who wait.

21. And when We make people taste of mercy after a sickness touches them, lo ! they devise plans against Our word. Say, "God is quicker to plan; certainly Our messengers write down what you plan.

22. He it is Who makes you travel by land and sea; until when you are in the ships, and they sail on with them in a pleasant breeze, and they rejoice, a violent wind overtakes them and the billows surge in on them from all sides, and they become certain that they are encompassed about, they pray to God, being sincere to Him in obedience: If You dost deliver us from this, we will most certainly be of the grateful ones.

23. But when He delivers them, lo! they are unjustly rebellious in the earth. Oh men! your rebellion is against your own souls -- provision only of this world's life -- then to Us shall be your return, so We will inform you of what you did.

24. The likeness of this world's life is only as water which We send down from the cloud, then the herbage of the earth of which men and cattle eat grows luxuriantly thereby, until when the earth puts on its golden raiment and it becomes garnished, and its people think that they have power over it, Our command comes to it, by night or by day, so We render it as reaped seed; produce, as though it had not been in existence yesterday; thus do We make clear the words for a people who reflect.

25. And God invites to the home of peace and guides whom He pleases into the right path.

26. For those who do good is good reward and more than this; and blackness or embarassment shall not cover their faces; these are the dwellers of the garden; in it they shall abide.

27. And as for those who have earned evil, the punishment of an evil is the like of it, and abasement shall come upon them -- they shall have none to protect them from God -- as if their faces had been covered with slices of the dense darkness of night; these are the inmates of the fire; in it they shall
abide.

28. And on the day when We will gather them all together, then We will say to those who associated others with God: Keep where you are, you and your associates; then We shall separate them widely one from another and their associates would say, "It was not us that you served:

29. Therefore God is sufficient as a witness between us and you that we were quite unaware of your serving us.

30. There shall every soul become acquainted with what it sent before, and they shall be brought back to God, their true Patron, and what they devised shall escape from them.

31. Say, "Who gives you sustenance from the heaven and the earth? Or Who controls the hearing and the sight? And Who brings forth the living from the dead, and brings forth the dead from the living? And Who regulates the affairs? Then they will say, "God. Say then: Will you not then guard against evil?

32. This then is God, your true Lord; and what is there after the truth but error; how are you

then turned back?

33. Thus does the word of your Lord prove true against those who transgress that they do not believe.

34. Say, "Is there any one among your associates who can bring into existence the creation in the first instance, then reproduce it? Say, "God brings the creation into existence, then He reproduces it; how are you then turned away?

35. Say, "Is there any of your associates who leads to the truth? Say, "God leads to the truth. Is He then Who leads to the truth more worthy to be followed, or he who himself does not go correctly unless he is guided? What then is the matter with you; how do you judge?

36. And most of them do not follow anything but conjecture; certainly conjecture will not persist against the truth; certainly God is cognizant of what they do.

37. And this Koran is not something that could be made by any other than God, but it is a verification of that which jas gone before and a clear explanation of the book, ot cannot be doubted, from the Lord of the worlds.

38. Or do they say, "He has created it? Say, "Then bring a chapter like this and invite whom you can besides God, if you are truthful.

39. No, they reject that of which they have no comprehensive knowledge, and the final sequel of it has not yet come to them; even thus did those before them reject the truth; see then what was the end of the unjust.

40. And of them is he who believes in it, and of them is he who does not believe in it, and your Lord knows best the mischief-makers.

41. And if they call you a liar, say, "My work is for me and your work for you; you are clear of what I do and I am clear of what you do.

42. And there are those of them who hear you, but can you make the deaf to hear though they will not understand?

43. And there are those of them who look at you, but can you show the way to the blind though they will not see?

44. Certainly God does not do any injustice to men, but men are unjust to themselves.

45. And on the day when He will gather them as though they had not stayed but an hour of the day, they will know each other. They will perish indeed who called the meeting with God to be a lie, and they are not followers of the right direction.

46. And if We show you something of what We threaten them with, or cause you to die, yet to Us is their return, and God is the bearer of witness to what they do.

47. And every nation had an apostle; so when their apostle came, the matter was decided between them with justice and they shall not be dealt with unjustly.

48. And they say, "When will this threat come about, if you are truthful?

49. Say, "I do not control for myself any harm, or any benefit except what God pleases; every nation has a term; when their term comes, they shall not then remain behind for an hour, nor can they go before their time.

50. Say, "Tell me if His punishment overtakes you by night or by day! what then is there of it that the guilty would hasten on?

51. And when it comes to pass, will you believe in it? What! now you believe, and already you wished to have it hastened on.

52. Then it shall be said to those who were unjust: Taste abiding punishment; you are not avenged except for what you earned.

53. And they ask you: Is that true? Say, "Aye! by my Lord! it is most certainly the truth, and you will not escape.

⁵⁴. And if every soul that has done injustice had all that is in the earth, it would offer it for ransom, and they will greatly regret when they see the punishment and the matter shall be decided between them with justice and they shall not be dealt with unjustly.

⁵⁵. Now certainly God's is what is in the heavens and the earth; now certainly God's promise is true, but most of them do not know.

⁵⁶. He gives life and causes death, and to Him you shall be brought back.

⁵⁷. Oh men! there has come to you indeed an admonition from your Lord and a healing for what is in the hearts and a guidance and a mercy for the believers.

⁵⁸. Say, "In the grace of God and in His mercy -- in that they should rejoice; it is better than that which they gather.

⁵⁹. Say, "Tell me what God has sent down for you of sustenance, then you make a part of it unlawful and a part lawful. Say, "Has God commanded you, or do you forge a lie against God?

⁶⁰. And what will be the thought of those who forge lies against God on the day of resurrection? Most certainly God is the Lord of grace towards men, but most of them do not give thanks.

⁶¹. And you are not engaged in any affair, nor do you recite concerning it any portion of the Koran, nor do you do any work but We are witnesses over you when you enter into it, and there does not lie concealed from your Lord the weight of an atom in the earth or in the heaven, nor any thing

less than that nor greater, but it is in a clear book.

⁶². Now certainly the friends of God -- they shall have no fear nor shall they grieve.

⁶³. Those who believe and guarded against evil:

⁶⁴. They shall have good news in this world's life and in the hereafter; there is no changing the words of God; that is the mighty achievement.

⁶⁵. And let not their speech grieve you; certainly might is wholly God's; He is the Hearing, the Knowing.

⁶⁶. Now, certainly, whatever is in the heavens and whatever is in the earth is God's; and they do not really follow any associates, who call on others besides God; they do not follow anything but conjectures, and they only lie.

⁶⁷. He it is Who made for you the night so that you might then rest, and the day giving light; most certainly there are signs in it for a people who would hear.

⁶⁸. They say, "God has taken a son to Himself! Glory be to Him: He is the Self-sufficient: His is what is in the heavens and what is in the earth; you have no authority for this; do you say against God what you do not know?

⁶⁹. Say, "Those who forge a lie against God shall not be successful. ⁷⁰. It is only a provision in this world, then to Us shall be their return; then We shall make them taste severe punishment because they disbelieved.

⁷¹. And recite to them the story of Noah when he said to his people: Oh my people! if my stay and my reminding you by the words of God is hard on you -- yet on God do I rely -- then resolve upon your affair and gather your associates, then let not your affair remain dubious to you, then have it executed against me and give me no respite:

⁷². But if you turn back, I did not ask for any reward from you; my reward is only with God, and I am commanded that I should be of those who submit.

⁷³. But they rejected him, so We delivered him and those with him in the

ark, and We made them rulers and drowned those who rejected Our words; see then what was the end of the people warned.

⁷⁴. Then did We raise up after him apostles to their people, so they came to them with clear explanations, but they would not believe in what they had rejected before; thus it is that We

set seals upon the hearts of those who exceed the limits.

75. Then did We send up after them Moses and Aaron to Pharoah and his chiefs with Our signs, but they showed pride and they were a guilty people.

76. So when the truth came to them from Us they said, "This is most certainly clear sorcery!

77. Moses said, "Do you say this of the truth when it has come to you? Is it magic? And the magicians are not successful.

78. They said, "Have you come to us to turn us away from what we found our fathers upon, and that greatness in the land should be for you two? And we are not going to believe in you.

79. And Pharoah said, "Bring to me every skillful magician.

80. And when the magicians came, Moses said to them: Cast down what you have to cast.

81. So when they cast down, Moses said to them: What you have brought is deception; certainly God will make it nothing; certainly God does not make the work of mischief-makers to thrive. 82. And God will show the truth to be the truth by His words, though the guilty may be averse to it.

83. But none believed in Moses except the offspring of his people, on account of the fear of Pharoah and their chiefs, in case he should persecute them; and most certainly Pharoah was lofty in the land; and most certainly he was of the extravagant.

84. And Moses said, "Oh my people! if you believe in God, then rely on Him alone if you submit to God.

85. So they said, "On God we rely: Oh our Lord! make us not subject to the persecution of the unjust people:

86. And do You deliver us by Your mercy from the unbelieving people.

87. And We revealed to Moses and his brother, saying, "Take for your people houses to abide in Egypt and make your houses places of worship and keep up prayer and give good news to the believers.

88. And Moses said, "Our Lord! certainly You have given to Pharoah and his chiefs finery and riches in this world's life, to this end, our Lord, that they lead people astray from Your way: Our Lord! destroy their riches and harden their hearts so that they believe not until they see the painful punishment.

89. He said, "The prayer of you both has indeed been accepted, therefore continue in the right way and do not follow the path of those who do not know.

90. And We made the children of Israel to pass through the sea, then Pharoah and his hosts followed them for oppression and tyranny; until when drowning overtook him, he said, "I believe that there is no god but He in Whom the children of Israel believe and I am of those who submit.

91. What! now! and indeed you disobeyed before and you were of the mischief-makers.

92. But We will this day deliver you with your body that you may be a sign to those after you, and most certainly the majority of the people are heedless to Our words.

93. And certainly We lodged the children of Israel in a fine home and We provided them with good things; but they did not disagree until the knowledge had come to them; certainly your Lord will judge between them on the resurrection day concerning that in which they disagreed.

94. But if you are in doubt as to what We have revealed to you, ask those who read the Book before you; certainly the truth has come to you from your Lord, therefore you should not be of the disputers.

95. And you should not be of those who reject the words of God, for then you should be one of the losers.

96. Certainly those against whom the word of your Lord has proved true will not believe,

⁹⁷. Though every sign should come to them, until they witness the painful punishment.

⁹⁸. And why was there not a town which should believe so that their belief should have profited them but the people of Yunus? When they believed, We removed from them the punishment of disgrace in this world's life and We gave them provision till a time.

⁹⁹. And if your Lord had pleased, certainly all those who are in the earth would have believed, all of them; will you then force men till they become believers?

¹⁰⁰. And it is not for a soul to believe except by God's permission;
and He casts uncleanness on those who will not understand.

¹⁰¹. Say, "Consider what is it that is in the heavens and the earth; and
signs and alarmgivers do not avail a people who would not believe.

¹⁰². What do they wait for then but the like of the days of those who
passed away before them? Say, "Wait then; certainly I too am with you of those who wait.

¹⁰³. Then We deliver Our apostles and those who believe -- even so
now, it is binding on Us that We deliver the believers.

¹⁰⁴. Say, "Oh people! if you are in doubt as to my religion, then know
that I do not serve those whom you serve besides God but I do serve God,
Who will cause you to die, and I am commanded that I should be of the believers.

¹⁰⁵. And that you should keep your course towards the religion
uprightly; and you should not be of the polytheists.

¹⁰⁶. And do not call besides God on that which can neither benefit you
nor harm you, for if you do then certainly you will in that case be of the unjust.

¹⁰⁷. And if God should afflict you with harm, then there is none to
remove it but He; and if He intends good to you there is none to repel His
grace; He brings it to whom He pleases of His servants; and He is the Forgiving,
the Merciful.

¹⁰⁸. Say, "Oh people! indeed there has come to you the truth from your
Lord, therefore whoever goes aright, he goes aright only for the good of his own
soul, and whoever goes astray, he goes astray only to the detriment of it, and I
am not a custodian over you.

¹⁰⁹. And follow what is revealed to you and be patient till God should
give judgment, and He is the greatest judge.

set seals upon the hearts of those who exceed the limits.

75. Then did We send up after them Moses and Aaron to Pharoah and his chiefs with Our signs, but they showed pride and they were a guilty people.
76. So when the truth came to them from Us they said, "This is most certainly clear sorcery!
77. Moses said, "Do you say this of the truth when it has come to you? Is it magic? And the magicians are not successful."
78. They said, "Have you come to us to turn us away from what we found our fathers upon, and that greatness in the land should be for you two? And we are not going to believe in you.
79. And Pharoah said, "Bring to me every skillful magician.
80. And when the magicians came, Moses said to them: Cast down what you have to cast.
81. So when they cast down, Moses said to them: What you have brought is deception; certainly God will make it nothing; certainly God does not make the work of mischief-makers to thrive. 82. And God will show the truth to be the truth by His words, though the guilty may be averse to it.
83. But none believed in Moses except the offspring of his people, on account of the fear of Pharoah and their chiefs, in case he should persecute them; and most certainly Pharoah was lofty in the land; and most certainly he was of the extravagant.
84. And Moses said, "Oh my people! if you believe in God, then rely on Him alone if you submit to God.
85. So they said, "On God we rely: Oh our Lord! make us not subject to the persecution of the unjust people:
86. And do You deliver us by Your mercy from the unbelieving people.
87. And We revealed to Moses and his brother, saying, "Take for your people houses to abide in Egypt and make your houses places of worship and keep up prayer and give good news to the believers.
88. And Moses said, "Our Lord! certainly You have given to Pharoah and his chiefs finery and riches in this world's life, to this end, our Lord, that they lead people astray from Your way: Our Lord! destroy their riches and harden their hearts so that they believe not until they see the painful punishment.
89. He said, "The prayer of you both has indeed been accepted, therefore continue in the right way and do not follow the path of those who do not know.
90. And We made the children of Israel to pass through the sea, then Pharoah and his hosts followed them for oppression and tyranny; until when drowning overtook him, he said, "I believe that there is no god but He in Whom the children of Israel believe and I am of those who submit.
91. What! now! and indeed you disobeyed before and you were of the mischief-makers.
92. But We will this day deliver you with your body that you may be a sign to those after you, and most certainly the majority of the people are heedless to Our words.
93. And certainly We lodged the children of Israel in a fine home and We provided them with good things; but they did not disagree until the knowledge had come to them; certainly your Lord will judge between them on the resurrection day concerning that in which they disagreed.
94. But if you are in doubt as to what We have revealed to you, ask those who read the Book before you; certainly the truth has come to you from your Lord, therefore you should not be of the disputers.
95. And you should not be of those who reject the words of God, for then you should be one of the losers.
96. Certainly those against whom the word of your Lord has proved true will not believe,

⁹⁷. Though every sign should come to them, until they witness the painful punishment.

⁹⁸. And why was there not a town which should believe so that their belief should have profited them but the people of Yunus? When they believed, We removed from them the punishment of disgrace in this world's life and We gave them provision till a time.

⁹⁹. And if your Lord had pleased, certainly all those who are in the earth would have believed, all of them; will you then force men till they become believers?

¹⁰⁰. And it is not for a soul to believe except by God's permission; and He casts uncleanness on those who will not understand.

¹⁰¹. Say, "Consider what is it that is in the heavens and the earth; and signs and alarmgivers do not avail a people who would not believe.

¹⁰². What do they wait for then but the like of the days of those who passed away before them? Say, "Wait then; certainly I too am with you of those who wait.

¹⁰³. Then We deliver Our apostles and those who believe -- even so now, it is binding on Us that We deliver the believers.

¹⁰⁴. Say, "Oh people! if you are in doubt as to my religion, then know that I do not serve those whom you serve besides God but I do serve God, Who will cause you to die, and I am commanded that I should be of the believers.

¹⁰⁵. And that you should keep your course towards the religion uprightly; and you should not be of the polytheists.

¹⁰⁶. And do not call besides God on that which can neither benefit you nor harm you, for if you do then certainly you will in that case be of the unjust.

¹⁰⁷. And if God should afflict you with harm, then there is none to remove it but He; and if He intends good to you there is none to repel His grace; He brings it to whom He pleases of His servants; and He is the Forgiving, the Merciful.

¹⁰⁸. Say, "Oh people! indeed there has come to you the truth from your Lord, therefore whoever goes aright, he goes aright only for the good of his own soul, and whoever goes astray, he goes astray only to the detriment of it, and I am not a custodian over you.

¹⁰⁹. And follow what is revealed to you and be patient till God should give judgment, and He is the greatest judge.

Chapter 11 — Hud — The Holy Prophet

In the name of God, the Kind, the Merciful.

1. Alif Lam Ra This is a Book, whose verses are made decisive, then are they made plain, from the Wise, All-aware:
2. That you shall not serve any but God; certainly I am a alarmgiver for you from Him and a giver of good news,
3. And you that ask forgiveness of your Lord, then turn to Him; He will provide you with proper provisions at the appointed time and will give His grace to every one who shows kindness, and if you turn back, then certainly I fear that you will find the punishment on that great day.
4. To God is your return, and He has power over all things.
5. Now certainly they fold up their hearts that they may conceal their enmity from Him; now certainly, when they use their garments as a covering, He knows what they conceal and what they make public; certainly He knows what is in the hearts.
6. And there is no animal in the earth but on God is the sustenance of it, and He knows its resting place and its depository all things are in a great book.
7. And He it is Who created the heavens and the earth in six periods -- and His dominion extends on the water -- that He might to you, which of you is best in action, and if you say, certainly you shall be raised up after death, those who disbelieve would certainly say, "This is nothing but clear magic.
8. And if We hold back from them the punishment until a stated period of time, they will certainly say, "What prevents it? Now certainly on the day when it will come to them, it shall not be averted from them and that which they scoffed at shall beset them.
9. And if We make man taste mercy from Us, then take it off from him, most certainly he is despairing, ungrateful.
10. And if We make him taste a favor after distress has afflicted him, he will certainly say, "The evils are gone away from me. Most certainly he is exulting, boasting;
11. Except those who are patient and do good, they shall have forgiveness and a great reward.
12. Then, it may be that you will give up part of what is revealed to you and your heart will become straightened by it because they say, "Why has not a treasure been sent down upon him or an angel come with him? You are only a alarmgiver; and God is custodian over all things.
13. Or, do they say, "He has made it. Say, "Then bring ten created chapters like it and call upon whom you can besides God, if you are truthful.
14. But if they do not answer you, then know that it is revealed by God's knowledge and that there is no god but He; will you then submit?
15. Whoever desires this world's life and its finery, We will pay them in full their deeds therein, and they shall not be made to. suffer loss in respect of them.
16. These are they for whom there is nothing but fire in the hereafter, and what they wrought in it shall go for nothing, and vain is what they do.
17. Is then he who has clear proof from his Lord, and a witness from Him recites it and before it is the Book of Moses, a guide and a mercy? These believe in it; and whoever else disbelieves it, certainly it is the truth from your Lord, but most men do not believe.
18. And who is more unjust than he who forges a lie against God? These shall be brought before their Lord, and the witnesses shall say, "These are they who lied against their Lord. Now

certainly the curse of God is on the unjust.

19. Who turn away from the path of God and desire to make it crooked; and they are disbelievers in the hereafter.

20. These shall not escape in the earth, nor shall they have any guardians besides God; the punishment shall be doubled for them, they could not bear to hear and they did not see.

21. These are they who have lost their souls, and what they created is gone from them.

22. Truly in the hereafter they shall be the biggest losers.

23. Certainly as to those who believe and do good and humble themselves to their Lord, these are the dwellers of the garden, in it they will abide.

24. The likeness of the two parties is as the blind and the deaf and the seeing and the hearing: are they equal in condition? Will you not then mind?

25. And certainly We sent Noah to his people: Certainly I am a plain alarmgiver for you:

26. That you shall not serve any but God, certainly I fear for you the punishment of a painful day.

27. But the chiefs of those who disbelieved from among his people said, "We do not consider you but a mortal like ourselves, and we do not see any have followed you but those who are the meanest of us at first thought and we do not see in you any excellence over us; no, we deem you liars.

28. He said, "Oh my people! tell me if I have with me clear proof from my Lord, and He has granted me mercy from Himself and it has been made obscure to you; shall we constrain you to accept it while you are averse from it?

29. And, Oh my people! I ask you not for wealth in return for it; my reward is only with God and I am not going to drive away those who believe; certainly they shall meet their Lord, but I consider you a people who are ignorant:

30. And, Oh my people! who will help me against God if I drive them away? Will you not then mind?

31. And I do not say to you that I have the treasures of God and I do not know the unseen, nor do I say that I am an angel, nor do I say about those whom your eyes hold in mean estimation that God will never grant them any good -- God knows best what is in their souls -- for then most certainly I should be of the unjust.

32. They said, "Oh Noah! indeed you have disputed with us and lengthened dispute with us, therefore bring to us what you threaten us with, if you are of the truthful ones.

33. He said, "God only will bring it to you if He please, and you will not escape:

34. And if I intend to give you good advice, my advice will not profit you if God intended that He should leave you to go astray; He is your Lord, and to Him shall you be returned.

35. Or do they say, "He has created it? Say, "If I have created it, on me is my guilt, and I am clear of that of which you are guilty.

36. And it was revealed to Noah: That none of your people will believe except those who have already believed, therefore do not grieve at what they do:

37. And make the ark before Our eyes and according to Our revelation, and do not speak to Me in respect of those who are unjust; certainly they shall be drowned.

38. And he began to make the ark; and whenever the chiefs from among his people passed by him they laughed at him. He said, "If you laugh at us, certainly we too laugh at you as you laugh at us.

39. So shall you know who it is on whom will come a punishment which will disgrace him, and on whom will lasting punishment come down.

40. Until when Our command came and water came forth from the valley, We said, "Carry in it two of all things, a pair, and your own family -- except those against whom the word has

already gone forth, and those who believe. And there believed not with him but a few.

41. And he said, "Embark in it, in the name of God be its sailing and its anchoring; most certainly my Lord is Forgiving, Merciful.

42. And it moved on with them amid waves like mountains; and Noah called out to his son, and he was distant: Oh my son! embark with us and do not be with the unbelievers.

43. He said, "I will take refuge in a mountain that shall protect me from the water. Noah said, "There is no protector today from God's punishment but He Who has mercy; and a wave intervened between them, so he was drowned.

44. And it was said, "Oh earth, swallow down your water, and Oh cloud, clear away; and the water was made to abate and the affair was decided, and the ark rested on the Judi, and it was said, "Away with the unjust people.

45. And Noah cried out to his Lord and said, "My Lord! certainly my son is of my family, and Your promise is certainly true, and You are the most just of the judges. 46. He said, "Oh Noah! certainly he is not of your family; certainly he is the doer of other than good deeds, therefore ask not of Me that of which you have no knowledge; certainly I reprimand you in case you may be of the ignorant

47. He said, "My Lord! I seek refuge in You from asking You that of which I have no knowledge; and if You should not forgive me and have mercy on me, I should be of the losers.

48. It was said, "Oh Noah! descend with peace from Us and blessings on you and on the people from among those who are with you, and there shall be nations whom We will afford provisions, then a painful punishment from Us shall afflict them.

49. These are announcements relating to the unseen which We reveal to you, you did not know them -- neither you nor your people -- before this; therefore be patient; certainly the end is for those who guard against evil.

50. And to Ad We sent their brother Hud. He said, "Oh my people! serve God, you have no god other than He; you are nothing but forgers of lies.

51. Oh my people! I do not ask of you any reward for it; my reward is only with Him Who created me; do you not then understand?

52. And, Oh my people! ask forgiveness of your Lord, then turn to Him; He will send on you clouds pouring down abundance of rain and add strength to your strength, and do not turn back guilty.

53. They said, "Oh Hud! you have not brought to us any clear argument and we are not going to desert our gods for your word, and we are not believers in you:

54. We cannot say anything except that some of our gods have smitten you with evil. He said, "Certainly I call God to witness, and do you bear witness too, that I am clear of what you associate with God.

55. Besides Him, therefore scheme against me all together; then give me no rest:

56. Certainly I rely on God, my Lord and your Lord; there is no living creature but He holds it by its forelock; certainly my Lord is on the right path.

57. But if you turn back, then indeed I have delivered to you the message with which I have been sent to you, and my Lord will bring another people in your place, and you cannot do Him any harm; certainly my Lord is the Preserver of all things.

58. And when Our decree came to pass, We delivered Hud and those who believed with him with mercy from Us, and We delivered them from strict punishment.

59. And this was Ad; they denied the words of their Lord, and disobeyed His apostles and followed the bidding of every insolent opposer of truth.

60. And they were overtaken by curse in this world and on the resurrection day; now certainly

Ad disbelieved in their Lord; now certainly, away with Ad, the people of Hud.

61. And to Samood We sent their brother Salih. He said, "Oh my people! serve God, you have no god other than He; He brought you into being from the earth, and made you dwell in it, therefore ask forgiveness of Him, then turn to Him; certainly my Lord is Nigh, Answering.

62. They said, "Oh Salih! certainly you were one amongst us in whom great expectations were placed before this; do you now forbid us from worshiping what our fathers worshiped? And as to that which you call us to, most certainly we are in disquieting doubt.

63. He said, "Oh my people! tell me if I have clear proof from my Lord and He has granted to me mercy from Himself -- who will then help me against God if I disobey Him? Therefore you do not add to me other than loss:

64. And, Oh my people! this will be as God's she-camel for you, a sign; therefore leave her to pasture on God's earth and do not touch her with evil, for then a near punishment will overtake you.

65. But they killed her, so he said, "Enjoy yourselves in your home for three days, that is a promise not to be belied.

66. So when Our decree came to pass, We delivered Salih and those who believed with him by mercy from Us, and We saved them from the disgrace of that day; certainly your Lord is the Strong, the Mighty.

67. And the rumbling overtook those who were unjust, so they became motionless corpses in their homes,

68. As though they had never dwelt in them; now certainly did Samood disbelieve in their Lord; now certainly, away with Samood.

69. And certainly Our messengers came to Abraham with good news. They said, "Peace. Peace, said he, and he made no delay in bringing a roasted calf.

70. But when he saw that their hands were not extended towards it, he deemed them strange and conceived fear of them. . They said, "Fear not, certainly we are sent to Lot's people.

71. And his wife was standing by, so she laughed, then We gave her the good news of Isaac and after Isaac of a son's son Jacob.

72. She said, "Oh wonder! shall I bear a son when I am an extremely old woman and this my husband an extremely old man? Most certainly this is a wonderful thing.

73. They said, "Do you wonder at God's bidding? The mercy of God and His blessings are on you, Oh people of the house, certainly He is Praised, Glorious.

74. So when fear had gone away from Abraham and good news came to him, he began to plead with Us for Lot's people.

75. Most certainly Abraham was forbearing, tender-hearted, oft-returning to God:

76. Oh Abraham! leave off this, certainly the decree of your Lord has come to pass, and certainly there must come to them a punishment that cannot be averted.

77. And when Our messengers came to Lot, he was grieved for them, and he lacked strength to protect them, and said, "This is a hard day.

78. And his people came to him, as if rushed on towards him, and already they did evil deeds. He said, "Oh my people! these are my daughters -- they are purer for you, so guard against the punishment of God and do not disgrace me with regard to my guests; is there not among you one right-minded man?

79. They said, "Certainly you know that we have no claim on your daughters, and most certainly you know what we desire.

80. He said, "Ah! that I had power to suppress you, rather I shall have recourse to a strong support.

81. They said, "Oh Lot! we are the messengers of your Lord; they shall by no means reach you;

so remove your followers in a part of the night -- and let none of you turn back -- except your wife, for certainly whatsoever happens to them shall happen to her; certainly their appointed time is the morning; is not the morning near?

82. So when Our decree came to pass, We turned them upside down and rained down upon them stones, as had been decreed, one after another.

83. Marked for punishment with your Lord and it is not far off from the unjust.

84. And to Madyan We sent their brother Shu'aib. He said, "Oh my people! serve God, you have no god other than He, and do not give short measure and weight: certainly I see you in prosperity and certainly I fear for you the punishment of an all-encompassing day.

85. And, Oh my people! give full measure and weight fairly, and do not defraud men of their things, and do not act corruptly in the land, making mischief:

86. What remains with God is better for you if you are believers, and I am not a keeper over you.

87. They said, "Oh Shu'aib! does your prayer enjoin you that we should abandon what our fathers worshiped or that we should not do what we please with regard to our property? Forsooth you are the forbearing, the right-directing one.

88. He said, "Oh my people! have you considered if I have a clear proof from my Lord and He has given me proper nourishment from Himself, and I do not desire that in opposition to you I should take for myself that which I forbid you: I desire nothing but reform so far as I am able, and only God may direct my affairs to the right path; on Him I rely and to Him I turn:

89. And, Oh my people! let not opposition to me make you guilty so that there may happen you that which happened the people of Noah, or the people of Hud, or the people of Salih, nor are the people of Lot in the past;

90. And ask forgiveness of your Lord, then turn to Him; certainly my Lord is Merciful, Loving-kind.

91. They said, "Oh Shu'aib! we do not understand much of what you say and most certainly we see you to be weak among us, and were it not for your family we would certainly stone you, and you are not mighty against us.

92. He said, "Oh my people! is my family more respected by you than God? And you neglect Him and cast him over your shoulder; certainly my Lord encompasses all that you do:

93. And, Oh my people! act according to your ability, I too am acting; you will come to know soon who it is upon whom will rest the punishment that will disgrace him and who it is that is a liar, and watch, certainly I too am watching along with you.

94. And when Our decree came to pass We delivered Shu'aib, and those with him who believed were shown mercy by Us, and the rumbling overtook those who were unjust so they became motionless corpses in their homes,

95. As though they had never dwelt in them; now certainly hell overtook Madyan as had perished Samood.

96. And certainly We sent Moses with Our words and a clear authority,

97. To Pharoah and his chiefs, but they followed the bidding of Pharoah, and Pharoah's bidding was ill advised.

98. He shall lead his people on the resurrection day, and bring them down to the fire; and the place to which they are brought shall be evil.

99. And they are overtaken by curse in this world, and on the resurrection day, the gift they shall be given is evil.

100. This is an account of the fate of the towns which We tell you of; some of them still stood and others were mown down.

101. And We did not do them injustice, but they were unjust to themselves, so their gods whom

they called upon besides God did not assist them when the decree of your Lord came to pass; they caused to their own ruin.

¹⁰². And such is the punishment of your Lord when He punishes the towns that are unjust; certainly His punishment is painful, severe.

¹⁰³. Most certainly there is a sign in this for those who fear the punishment of the hereafter; this is a day on which the people shall be gathered together and this is a day that shall be witnessed.

¹⁰⁴. And We do not delay it but have set an appointed time.

¹⁰⁵. On the day when it shall come, no soul shall speak except with His permission, then some will be unhappy and others happy.

¹⁰⁶. So as to those who are unhappy, they shall be in the fire; and they shall be sighing and groaning in the fire:

¹⁰⁷. Abiding therein so long as the heavens and the earth endure, except as your Lord please; certainly your Lord mightily carries out his own intentions.

¹⁰⁸. And as to those who are made happy, they shall be in the garden, abiding in it as long as the heavens and the earth endure, as your Lord may please; this gift shall never be cut off.

¹⁰⁹. Therefore do not doubt what these people worship; they do not worship but as their fathers worshiped before; and most certainly We will pay them back in full, their gift undiminished.

¹¹⁰. And certainly We gave the book to Moses, but it was opposed; and did not word go forth from your Lord, the matter would certainly have been decided between them; and certainly they have uncomfortable doubts about it.

¹¹¹. And your Lord will most certainly pay back to all their deeds in full; certainly He is aware of what they do.

¹¹². Continue then in the right way as you are commanded, as do those who have turned to God with you, and do not be immoderate Oh men!, certainly He sees what you do.

¹¹³. And do not side with those who are unjust, or the fire might touch you, and you have no guardians besides God, and you shall not be helped.

¹¹⁴. And keep up prayer in the two parts of the day and in the first hours of the night; certainly good deeds take away evil deeds. This is a reminder to the mindful.

¹¹⁵. And be patient, for certainly God does not waste the reward of the righteous people.

¹¹⁶. But why did not the generations before you posses understanding, who should have forbidden the making of mischief in the earth, except a few of those whom We delivered from among them? And those who were unjust failed enjoy the plentifulness, and they were guilty.

¹¹⁷. And it did not seem to your Lord to have destroyed the towns tyrannously, while their people acted well.

¹¹⁸. And if your Lord had pleased He would certainly have made people a single nation, and they shall continue to differ.

¹¹⁹. Except those on whom your Lord has mercy; and for this did He create them; and the word of your Lord is fulfilled: Certainly I will fill hell with the jinn and the men, all together.

¹²⁰. And all we relate to you of the accounts of the apostles is to strengthen your heart therewith; and in this has come to you the truth and an admonition, and a reminder to the believers.

¹²¹. And say to those who do not believe: Act according to your state; certainly we too are acting.

¹²². And wait; certainly we are waiting also.

¹²³. And God's is the unseen in the heavens and the earth, and to Him is returned the whole of the affair; therefore serve Him and rely on Him, and your Lord is not heedless of what you do.

Chapter 12 — Yusuf — Joseph

In the name of God, the Kind, the Merciful.

1. Alif Lam Ra. These are the verses of the Book that makes things manifest.
2. Certainly We have revealed it -- an Arabic Koran -- that you may understand.
3. We narrate to you the best of narratives, by Our revealing to you this Koran, though before this you were certainly one of those who did not know.
4. When Joseph said to his father: Oh my father! certainly I saw eleven stars and the sun and the moon -- I saw them making obeisance to me.
5. He said, "Oh my son! do not relate your vision to your brothers, in case they devise a plan against you; certainly the Satan is an open enemy to man.
6. And thus will your Lord choose you and teach you the interpretation of sayings and make His favor complete to you and to the children of Jacob, as He made it complete before to your fathers, Abraham and Isaac; certainly your Lord is Knowing, Wise.
7. Certainly in Joseph and his brothers there are signs for the inquirers.
8. When they said, "Certainly Joseph and his brother are dearer to our father than we, though we are a stronger company; most certainly our father is in great error:
9. Slay Joseph or cast him forth into some land, so that your father's regard may be exclusively for you, and after that you may be a righteous people.
10. A speaker from among them said, "Do not slay Joseph, and cast him down into the bottom of the pit if you must do it, so that some of the travellers may pick him up.
11. They said, "Oh our father! what reason have you that you do not trust in us with respect to Joseph? And most certainly we are his sincere well-wishers: 12. Send him with us tomorrow that he may enjoy himself and sport, and certainly we will guard him well.
13. He said, "Certainly it grieves me that you should take him off, and I fear should the wolf devour him while you are heedless of him.
14. They said, "Certainly if the wolf should devour him notwithstanding that we are a strong company, we should then certainly be losers.
15. So when they had gone off with him and agreed that they should put him down at the bottom of the pit, and We revealed to him: You will most certainly inform them of this their affair while they do not perceive.
16. And they came to their father at nightfall, weeping.
17. They said, "Oh our father! certainly we went off racing and left Joseph by our goods, so the wolf devoured him, and you will not believe us though we are truthful.
18. And they brought his shirt with false blood upon it. He said, "No, your souls have made the matter light for you, but patience is good and God is He Whose help is sought for against what you describe.
19. And there came travellers and they sent their water-drawer and he let down his bucket. He said, "Oh good news! this is a youth; and they concealed him as an article of merchandise, and God knew what they did.
20. And they sold him for a small price, a few pieces of silver, and they showed no concern for him.
21. And the Egyptian who bought him said to his wife: Give him an honorable home, maybe he will be useful to us, or we may adopt him as a son. And thus did We establish Joseph in the land and that We might teach him the interpretation of sayings; and God is the master of His

affair, but most people do not know.

²². And when he had attained his maturity, We gave him wisdom and knowledge: and thus do We reward those who do good.

²³. And she in whose house he was sought to make himself yield to her, and she made fast the doors and said, "Come forward. He said, "I seek God's refuge, certainly my Lord made good my home: Certainly the unjust do not prosper.

²⁴. And certainly she made for him, and he would have made for her, were it not that he had seen the great evidence of his Lord; thus it was that We might turn away from him evil and indecency, certainly he was one of Our sincere servants.

²⁵. And they both hastened to the door, and she rent his shirt from behind and they met her husband at the door. She said, "What is the punishment of him who intends evil to your wife except imprisonment or a painful punishment?

²⁶. He said, "She sought to make me yield to her; and a witness of her own family bore witness: If his shirt is rent from front, she speaks the truth and he is one of the liars:

²⁷. And if his shirt is rent from behind, she tells a lie and he is one of the truthful.

²⁸. So when he saw his shirt rent from behind, he said, "Certainly it is a guile of you women; certainly your guile is great:

²⁹. Oh Joseph! turn aside from this; and Oh my wife! ask forgiveness for your fault, certainly you are one of the wrong-doers.

³⁰. And women in the city said, "The chief's wife asks her slave to yield himself to her, certainly he has affected her deeply with his love; most certainly we see her in great error.

³¹. So when she heard of their sly talk she sent for them and prepared for them a feast, and gave each of them a knife, and said to Joseph: Come forth to them. So when they saw him, they deemed him great, and cut their hands in amazement, and said, "Remote is God from imperfection; this is not a mortal; this is but a noble angel.

³². She said, "This is he with respect to whom you blamed me, and certainly I sought his yielding himself to me, but he abstained, and if he does not do what I bid him, he shall certainly be imprisoned, and he shall certainly be of those who are in a state of embarrassment.

³³. He said, "My Lord! the prison house is dearer to me than that to which they invite me; and if You turn not away their device from me, I will yearn towards them and become one of the ignorant.

³⁴. Thereupon his Lord accepted his prayer and turned away their guile from him; certainly He is the Hearing, the Knowing.

³⁵. Then it occurred to them after they had seen the signs that they should imprison him till a time.

³⁶. And two youths entered the prison with him. One of them said, "I saw myself pressing wine. And the other said, "I saw myself carrying bread on my head, of which birds ate. Inform us of its interpretation; certainly we see you to be of the doers of good.

³⁷. He said, "There shall not come to you the food with which you are fed, but I will inform you both of its interpretation before it comes to you; this is of what my Lord has taught me; certainly I have abandoned the religion of a people who do not believe in God, and they are deniers of the hereafter:

³⁸. And I follow the religion of my fathers, Abraham and Isaac and Jacob; it does not seem to us that we should compare with God; this is by God's grace upon us and on mankind, but most people do not give thanks:

³⁹. Oh my two friends of the prison! are various lords better or God the One, the Supreme?

⁴⁰. You do not serve any other than Him but names which you have named, you and your fathers;

God has not sent down any authority for them; judgment is only God's; He has commanded that you shall not serve any but Him; this is the right religion, but most people do not know this:

41. Oh my two friends in the prison! as for one of you, he shall cause his lord to drink wine; and as for the other, he shall be crucified, so that the birds shall eat from his head, the matter which you inquired about is decreed.

42. And he said to him whom he knew would be delivered of the two: Remind your lord of me; but the Satan caused him to forget to mention it to his lord, so he remained in the prison a few years.

43. And the king said, "Certainly I see seven fat cattle which seven lean ones devoured; and seven green ears and seven others dry: Oh chiefs! explain to me my dream, if you can interpret the dream.

44. They said, "Confused dreams, and we do not know anything about the interpretation of dreams.

45. And of the two prisoners he who released and who he remembered after a long time said, "I will inform you of the dream's interpretation, so let me go:

46. Joseph! Oh truthful one! explain to us seven fat cattle which seven lean ones devoured, and seven green ears and seven others dry, so that I may return to the people let them know.

47. He said, "You shall sow for seven years continuously, then what you reap, but leave on the ear a little of which you eat.

48. Then there shall come after that seven years of hardship which shall eat away all that you have earlier stored for them, except a little of what you shall have preserved:

49. Then there will come after that a year in which people shall have rain and in which they shall press grapes.

50. And the king said, "Bring him to me. So when the messenger came to him, he said, "Go back to your lord and ask him, what is the case of the women who cut their hands; certainly my Lord knows their guile.

51. He said, "How was your affair when you sought Joseph to yield himself to you? They said, "Remote is God from imperfection, we knew of no evil on his part. The chief's wife said, "Now has the truth become established: I sought him to yield himself to me, and he is most certainly of the truthful ones.

52. This is so he can know that I have not been secretly unfaithful to him and that God does not guide the actions of the unfaithful.

53. And I do not declare myself free, most certainly man's self is unable to command him to do evil, except such as my Lord has had mercy on, certainly my Lord is Forgiving, Merciful.

54. And the king said, "Bring him to me, I will decide about him for myself. So when he had spoken with him, he said, "Certainly you are in our presence today an honorable, a faithful man.

55. He said, "Place me in authority over the treasures of the land, certainly I am a good keeper, and knowledgeable.

56. And thus did We give to Joseph power in the land -- he had mastery over wherever he liked; We send down Our mercy upon whom We please, and We do not waste the reward of those who do good.

57. And certainly the reward of the hereafter is much better for those who believe and guard against evil.

58. And Joseph's brothers came and went in to him, and he knew them, while they did not recognize him.

59. And when he furnished them with their provision, he said, "Bring to me a brother of yours from your father; do you not see that I give full measure and that I am the best of hosts?

60. But if you do not bring him to me, you shall have no measure of corn from me, nor shall you come near me.
61. They said, "We will strive to make his father yield in respect of him, and we are sure to do it."
62. And he said to his servants: Put their money into their bags that they may recognize it when they go back to their family, so that they may come back.
63. So when they returned to their father, they said, "Oh our father, the measure is withheld from us, therefore send with us our brother, so that we may get the measure, and we will most certainly guard him."
64. He said, "I cannot trust in you with respect to him, except as I trusted in you with respect to his brother before; but God is the best Keeper, and He is the most Merciful of the merciful ones."
65. And when they opened their goods, they found their money returned to them. They said, "Oh our father! what more can we desire? This is our property returned to us, and we will bring corn for our family and guard our brother, and will have in addition the measure of a camel load; this is an easy measure."
66. He said, "I will by no means send him with you until you give me a firm covenant in God's name that you will most certainly bring him back to me, unless you are completely surrounded." And when they gave him their covenant, he said, "God is the One in Whom trust is placed as regards what we say."
67. And he said, "Oh my sons ! do not all enter by one gate and enter by different gates and I cannot help you against God; judgment is only God's; on Him do I rely, and on Him let those who are reliant rely."
68. And when they had entered as their father had bidden them, it did not help them at all against God, but it was only a desire in the soul of Jacob which he satisfied; and certainly he was possessed of knowledge because We had given him knowledge, but most people do not know.
69. And when they went in to Joseph. he lodged his brother with himself, saying, "I am your brother, therefore grieve not at what they do."
70. So when he furnished them with their provisions, someone placed the drinking cup in his brother's bag. Then a crier cried out: Oh caravan! you are most certainly thieves.
71. They said while they were facing them: What is it that you miss?
72. They said, "We miss the king's drinking cup, and he who shall bring it shall have a camel-load and I am responsible for it."
73. They said, "By God! you know for certain that we have not come to make mischief in the land, and we are not thieves."
74. They said, "But what shall be the requital of this, if you are liars?"
75. They said, "The requital of this is that the person in whose bag it is found shall himself be held for the satisfaction thereof; thus do we punish the wrongdoers."
76. So he began with their sacks before the sack of his brother, then he brought it out from his brother's sack. Thus did We plan for the sake of Joseph; it was not lawful that he should take his brother under the king's law unless God pleased; We raise the degrees of whomsoever We please, and above every one possessed of knowledge is the All-knowing one.
77. They said, "If he steal, a brother of his did indeed steal before; but Joseph kept it secret in his heart and did not disclose it to them. He said, "You are in an evil condition and God knows best what you state.
78. They said, "Oh chief! he has a father, a very old man, therefore retain one of us in his stead; certainly we see you to be of the doers of good."
79. He said, "God protect us that we should seize other than him with whom we found our property, for then most certainly we would be unjust.

80. Then when they despaired of him, they retired, conferring privately together. The oldest of them said, "Do you not know that your father took from you a covenant in God's name, and how you fell short of your duty with respect to Joseph before? Therefore I will by no means depart from this land until my father permits me or God decides for me, and He is the greatest judge:
81. Go back to your father and say, "Oh our father! certainly your son committed theft, and we do not bear witness except to what we have known, and we could not keep watch over the unseen:
82. And inquire in the town in which we were and the caravan with which we proceeded, and most certainly we are truthful.
83. He Jacob said, "No, your souls have made a matter light for you, so patience is good; maybe God will bring them all together to me; certainly He is the Knowing, the Wise.
84. And he turned away from them, and said, "Oh my sorrow for Joseph! and his eyes became white on account of the grief, and he was a repressor of grief.
85. They said, "By God! you will not cease to remember Joseph until you are a prey to constant disease or until you are of those who perish.
86. He said, "I only complain of my grief and sorrow to God, and I know from God what you do not know.
87. Oh my sons! Go and inquire respecting Joseph and his brother, and despair not of God's mercy; certainly none despairs of God's mercy except the unbelieving people.
88. So when they came in to him, they said, "Oh chief! distress has afflicted us and our family and we have brought scanty money, so give us full measure and be charitable to us; certainly God rewards the charitable.
89. He said, "Do you know how you treated Joseph and his brother when you were ignorant?
90. They said, "Are you indeed Joseph? He said, "I am Joseph and this is my brother; God has indeed been kind to us; certainly he who guards against evil and is patient is rewarded for certainly God does not waste the reward of those who do good.
91. They said, "By God! now has God certainly chosen you over us, and we were certainly sinners.
92. He said, "There shall be no reproof against you this day; God may forgive you, and He is the most Merciful of the merciful.
93. Take this my shirt and cast it on my father's face, he will again be able to see, and come to me with all your families.
94. And when the caravan had departed, their father said, "Most certainly I perceive the greatness of Joseph, unless you pronounce me to be weak in judgment.
95. They said, "By God, you are most certainly in your old error.
96. So when the bearer of good news came he cast it on his face, so forthwith he regained his sight. He said, "Did I not say to you that I know from God what you do not know?
97. They said, "Oh our father! ask forgiveness of our faults for us, certainly we were sinners.
98. He said, "I will ask for you forgiveness from my Lord; certainly He is the Forgiving, the Merciful.
99. Then when they came in to Joseph, he took his parents to lodge with him and said, "Enter safe into Egypt, if God please.
100. And he raised his parents upon the throne and they fell down in prostration before him, and he said, "Oh my father! this is the significance of my vision of old; my Lord has indeed made it to be true; and He was indeed kind to me when He brought me forth from the prison and brought you from the desert after the Satan had sown dissensions between me and my brothers, certainly my Lord is benignant to whom He pleases; certainly He is the Knowing, the Wise.
101. My Lord! You have given me of the kingdom and taught me of the interpretation of sayings: Originator of the heavens and the earth! You are my guardian in this world and the hereafter;

make me die a muslim and join me with the good.

¹⁰². This is of the announcements relating to the unseen which We reveal to you, and you were not with them when they resolved upon their affair, and they were devising plans.

¹⁰³. And most men will not believe though you desire it eagerly.

¹⁰⁴. And you do not ask them for a reward for this; it is nothing but a reminder for all mankind.

¹⁰⁵. And how many a sign in the heavens and the earth which they pass by, yet they turn aside from it.

¹⁰⁶. And most of them do not believe in God without associating others with Him.

¹⁰⁷. Do they then feel secure that there may come to them an extensive punishment from God or that the hour may come to them suddenly while they do not perceive?

¹⁰⁸. Say, "This is my way: I call to God, I and those who follow me being certain, and glory be to God, and I am not one of the polytheists.

¹⁰⁹. And We have not sent before you but men from among the people of the towns, to whom We sent revelations. Have they not then traveled in the land and seen what was the end of those before them? And certainly the home of the hereafter is best for those who guard against evil; do you not then understand?

¹¹⁰. Until when the apostles despaired and the people became sure that they were indeed told a lie, Our help came to them and whom We pleased was delivered; and Our punishment is not averted from the guilty people.

¹¹¹. In their histories there is certainly a lesson for men of understanding. It is not a narrative which could be created, but a verification of what is before it and a distinct explanation of all things and a guide and a mercy to a people who believe.

Chapter 13 — Al-Ra'd — The Thunder

In the name of God, the Kind, the Merciful.

1. Alif Lam Mim Ra. These are the verses of the Book; and that which is revealed to you from your Lord is the truth, but most people do not believe.
2. God is He Who raised the heavens without any pillars that you see, and He is firm in power and He made the sun and the moon subservient to you; each one pursues its course to an appointed time; He regulates the affair, making clear the signs that you may be certain of meeting your Lord.
3. And He it is Who spread the earth and made in it firm mountains and rivers, and of all fruits He has made in it two kinds; He makes the night cover the day; most certainly there are signs in this for a people who reflect.
4. And in the earth there are tracts side by side and gardens of grapes and corn and palm trees having one root and others having distinct roots -- they are watered with one water, and We make some of them excel others in fruit; most certainly there are signs in this for a people who understand.
5. And if you would wonder, then wondrous is their saying, "What! when we are dust, shall we then certainly be in a new creation? These are they who disbelieve in their Lord, and these have chains on their necks, and they are the inmates of the fire; in it they shall abide.
6. And they ask you to hasten on the evil before the good, and indeed there have been exemplary punishments before them; and most certainly your Lord is the Lord of forgiveness to people, notwithstanding their injustice; and most certainly your Lord is severe in requiting evil.
7. And those who disbelieve say, "Why has not a sign been sent down upon him from his Lord? You are only a alarmgiver and there is a guide for every people.
8. God knows what every female bears, and that of which the wombs fall short of completion and that in which they increase; and there is a measure with Him of everything.
9. The knower of the unseen and the seen, the Great, the Most High.
10. Alike to Him among you is he who conceals his words and he who speaks them openly, and he who hides himself by night and who goes forth by day.
11. For his sake there are angels following one another, before him and behind him, who guard him by God's commandment; certainly God does not change the condition of a people until they change their own condition; and when God intends evil to a people, there is no averting it, and besides Him they have no protector.
12. He it is Who shows you the lightning causing fear and hope and Who brings up the heavy cloud.
13. And the thunder declares His glory with His praise, and the angels too for awe of Him; and He sends the thunderbolts and smites with them whom He pleases, yet they dispute concerning God, and He is mighty in prowess.
14. To Him is due the true prayer; and those whom they pray to besides God give them no answer, but they are like one who stretches forth his two hands towards water that it may reach his mouth, but it will not reach it; and the prayer of the unbelievers is only in error.
15. And whoever is in the heavens and the earth makes obeisance to God only, willingly and unwillingly, and their shadows too at morn and eve.
16. Say, "Who is the Lord of the heavens and the earth? -- Say, "God. Say, "Do you take then

besides Him guardians who do not control any profit or harm for themselves? Say, "Are the blind and the seeing alike? Or can the darkness and the light be equal? Or have they set up with God associates who have created creation like His, so that what is created became confused to them? Say, "God is the Creator of all things, and He is the One, the Supreme.

17. He sends down water from the cloud, then watercourses flow with water according to their measure, and the torrent bears along the swelling foam, and from what they melt in the fire for the sake of making ornaments or apparatus arises a scum like it; thus does God compare truth and falsehood; then as for the scum, it passes away as a worthless thing; and as for that which profits the people, it tarries in the earth; thus does God set forth parables.

18. For those who respond to their Lord is good; and as for those who do not respond to Him, had they all that is in the earth and the like thereof with it they would certainly offer it for a ransom. As for those, an evil judging shall be theirs and their home is hell, and evil is the resting-place.

19. Is he then who knows that what has been revealed to you from your Lord is the truth like him who is blind? Only those possessed of understanding will mind,

20. Those who fulfil the promise of God and do not break the covenant,

21. And those who join that which God has bidden to be joined and have awe of their Lord and fear the evil judging.

22. And those who are constant, seeking the pleasure of their Lord, and keep up prayer and spend benevolently out of what We have given them secretly and openly and repel evil with good; as for those, they shall have the happy issue of the home

23. The gardens of perpetual home which they will enter along with those who do good from among their parents and their spouses and their offspring; and the angels will enter in upon them from every gate:

24. Peace be on you because you were constant, how excellent, is then, the issue of the home.

25. And those who break the covenant of God after its confirmation and cut asunder that which God has ordered to be joined and make mischief in the land; as for those, upon them shall be curse and they shall have the evil issue of the home.

26. God amplifies and straightens the means of subsistence for whom He pleases; and they rejoice in this world's life, and this world's life is nothing compared with the hereafter but a temporary enjoyment.

27. And those who disbelieve say, "Why is not a sign sent down upon him by his Lord? Say, "Certainly God makes him who will go astray, and guides to Himself those who turn to Him.

28. Those who believe and whose hearts are calmed by the memory of God; now certainly with memory of God's their hearts are calmed.

29. As for those who believe and do good, a good final state shall be theirs and a proper return.

30. And thus We have sent you among a nation before which other nations have passed away, that you might recite to them what We have revealed to you and still they deny the Kind God. Say, "He is my Lord, there is no god but He; on Him do I rely and to Him is my return.

31. And even if there were a Koran with which the mountains were made to pass away, or the earth were travelled over with it, or the dead were made to speak thereby; no! the commandment is wholly God's, Have not yet those who believe known that if God please He would certainly guide all the people? And as for those who disbelieve, there will not cease to afflict them because of what they do a repelling calamity, or it will alight close by their homes, until the promise of God comes about; certainly God will not fail in His promise.

32. And apostles before you were certainly mocked at, but I gave respite to those who disbelieved, then I destroyed them; how then was My requital of

evil?

33. Is He then Who watches every soul as to what it earns? And yet they give associates to God! Say, "Give them a name; no, do you mean to inform Him of what He does not know in the earth, or do you affirm this by an outward saying? Rather, their plans are made to appear fair-seeming to those who disbelieve, and they are kept back from the path; and whom God makes err, he shall have no guide.

34. They shall have punishment in this world's life, and the punishment of the hereafter is certainly more grievous, and they shall have no protector against God.

35. A likeness of the garden which the righteous are promised; there now beneath it rivers, its food and shades are perpetual; this is the requital of those who guarded against evil, and the requital of the unbelievers is the fire.

36. And those to whom We have given the Book rejoice in that which has been revealed to you, and of the confederates are some who deny a part of it. Say, "I am only commanded that I should serve God and not compare anything with Him, to Him do I invite you and to Him is my return.

37. And thus have We revealed it, a true judgment in Arabic, and if you follow their low desires after what has come to you of knowledge, you shall not have against God any guardian or a protector.

38. And certainly We sent apostles before you and gave them wives and children, and it is not in the power of an apostle to bring a sign except by God's permission; for every term there is an appointment.

39. God makes to pass away and establishes what He pleases, and with Him is the basis of the Book.

40. And We will either let you see part of what We threaten them with or cause you to die, for only the delivery of the message is incumbent on you, while calling them to account is Our business.

41. Do they not see that We are bringing destruction upon the land by curtailing it of its sides? And God pronounces a doom -- there is no repeller of His decree, and He is swift to take account.

42. And those before them did indeed make plans, but all planning is God's; He knows what every soul earns, and the unbelievers shall come to know for whom is the better issue of the home.

43. And those who disbelieve say, "You are not a messenger. Say, "God is sufficient as a witness between me and you and whoever has knowledge of the Book.

Chapter 14 — Ibrahim — Abraham

In the name of God, the Kind, the Merciful.

1. Alif Lam Ra. This is a Book which We have revealed to you that you may bring forth men, by their Lord's permission from utter darkness into light -- to the way of the Mighty, the Praised One,

2. Of God, Whose is whatever is in the heavens and whatever Is in the earth; and woe to the unbelievers on account of the severe punishment,

3. To those who love this world's life more than the hereafter, and turn away from God's path and desire to make it crooked; these are in a great error.

4. And We did not send any apostle but with the language of his people, so that he might explain to them clearly; then God makes whom He pleases err and He guides whom He pleases and He is the Mighty, the Wise.

5. And certainly We sent Moses with Our words, saying, "Bring forth your people from utter darkness into light and remind them of the days of God; most certainly there are signs in this for every patient, grateful one.

6. And when Moses said to his people: Call to mind God's favor to you when He delivered you from Pharoah's people, who subjected you to severe torment, and killed your sons and spared your women; and in this there was a great trial from your Lord.

7. And when your Lord made it known: If you are grateful, I would certainly give to you more, and if you are ungrateful, My punishment is truly severe.

8. And Moses said, "If you are ungrateful, you and those on earth all together, most certainly God is Self-sufficient, Praised;

9. Has not the account reached you of those before you, of the people of Noah and Ad and Samood, and those after them? None knows them but God. Their apostles come to them with clear explanations, but they thrust their hands into their mouths and said, "Certainly we deny that with which you are sent, and most certainly we are in serious doubt as to that to which you invite us.

10. Their apostles said, "Is there doubt about God, the Maker of the heavens and the earth? He invites you to forgive you your faults and to respite you till an appointed term. They said, "You are nothing but mortals like us; you wish to turn us away from what our fathers used to worship; bring us therefore some clear authority.

11. Their apostles said to them: We are nothing but mortals like yourselves, but God bestows His favors on whom He pleases of His servants, and it is not for us that we should bring you an authority except by God's permission; and on God should the believers rely.

12. And what reason have we that we should not rely on God? And He has indeed guided us in our ways; and certainly we would bear with patience your persecution of us; and on God should the reliant rely.

13. And those who disbelieved said to their apostles: We will most certainly drive you forth from our land, or else you shall come back into our religion. So their Lord revealed to them: Most certainly We will destroy the unjust.

14. And most certainly We will settle you in the land after them; this is for him who fears standing in My presence and who fears My threat.

15. And they asked for judgment and every insolent opposer was disappointed:

¹⁶. Hell is before him and he shall be given to drink of festering water:

¹⁷. He will drink it little by little and will not be able to swallow it agreeably, and death will come to him from every quarter, but he shall not die; and there shall be vehement punishment before him.

¹⁸. The story of those who disbelieve in their Lord: their actions are like ashes on which the wind blows hard on a stormy day; they shall not have power over any thing out of what they have earned; this is the great error.

¹⁹. Do you not see that God created the heavens and the earth with truth? If He please He will take you off and bring a new creation,

²⁰. And this is not difficult for God.

²¹. And they shall all come forth before God, then the weak shall say to those who were proud: Certainly we were your followers, can you therefore avert from us any part of the punishment of God? They would say, "If God had guided us, we too would have guided you; it is the same to us whether we are impatient now or patient, there is no place for us to fly to.

²². And the Satan shall say after the affair is decided: Certainly God promised you the promise of truth, and I gave you promises, then failed to keep them to you, and I had no authority over you, except that I called you and you obeyed me, therefore do not blame me but blame yourselves: I cannot be your aider now nor can you be my aiders; certainly I disbelieved in your associating me with God before; certainly it is the unjust that shall have the painful punishment.

²³. And those who believe and do good are made to enter gardens, beneath which rivers flow, to abide in them by their Lord's permission; their greeting therein is, Peace.

²⁴. Have you not considered how God sets forth a story of a good word being like a good tree, whose root is firm and whose branches are in heaven,

²⁵. Yielding its fruit in every season by the permission of its Lord? And God sets forth parables for men that they may be mindful.

²⁶. And the story of an evil word is as an evil tree pulled up from the earth's surface; it has no stability.

²⁷. God confirms those who believe with the sure word in this world's life and in the hereafter, and God causes the unjust to go astray, and God does what He pleases.

²⁸. Have you not seen those who have changed God's favor for ungratefulness and made their people to alight into the home of hell

²⁹. Into hell? They shall enter into it and an evil place it is to settle in.

³⁰. And they set up equals with God that they may lead people astray from His path. Say, "Enjoy yourselves, for certainly your return is to the fire.

³¹. Say to My servants who believe that they should keep up prayer and spend out of what We have given them secretly and openly before the coming of the day in which there shall be no bartering nor mutual befriending.

³². God is He Who created the heavens and the earth and sent down water from the clouds, then brought forth with it fruits as a sustenance for you, and He has made the ships subservient to you, that they might run their course in the sea by His command, and He has made the rivers subservient to you.

³³. And He has made subservient to you the sun and the moon pursuing their courses, and He has made subservient to you the night and the day.

³⁴. And He gives you of all that you ask Him; and if you count God's favors, you will not be able to number them; most certainly man is very unjust, very ungrateful.

³⁵. And when Abraham said, "My Lord! make this city secure, and save me and my sons from worshiping idols:

36. My Lord! certainly they have led many men astray; then whoever follows me, he is certainly of me, and whoever disobeys me, You certainly arc Forgiving, Merciful:

37. Oh our Lord! certainly I have settled a part of my offspring in a valley unproductive of fruit near Your Sacred House, our Lord! that they may keep up prayer; therefore make the hearts of some people yearn towards them and provide them with fruits; haply they may be grateful:

38. Oh our Lord! Certainly You know what we hide and what we make public, and nothing in the earth nor any thing in heaven is hidden from God:

39. Praise be to God, Who has given me in old age Ishmael and Isaac; most certainly my Lord is the Hearer of prayer:

40. My Lord! make me keep up prayer and those of my chilren too, Oh our Lord, and accept my prayer:

41. Oh our Lord! grant me protection and my parents and the believers on the day when the judging shall come to pass!

42. And do not think God to be heedless of what the unjust do; He only respites them to a day on which the eyes shall be fixedly open,

43. Hastening forward, their heads upraised, their eyes not reverting to them and their hearts vacant.

44. And warn people of the day when the punishment shall come to them, then those who were unjust will say, "Oh our Lord! respite us to a near term, so we shall respond to Your call and follow the apostles. What! did you not swear before that there will be no passing away for you!

45. And you dwell in the homes of those who were unjust to themselves, and it is clear to you how We dealt with them and We have made them examples to you.

46. And they have indeed planned their plan, but their plan is with God, though their plan was such that the mountains should pass away thereby.

47. Therefore do not think God to be one failing in His promise to His apostles; certainly God is Mighty, the Lord of Retribution.

48. On the day when the earth shall be changed into a different earth, and the heavens as well, and they shall come forth before God, the One, the Supreme.

49. And you will see the guilty on that day linked together in chains.

50. Their shirts made of pitch and the fire covering their faces

51. That God may avenge each soul according to what it has earned; certainly God is swift in judging.

52. This is a sufficient exposition for the people and that they may be warned thereby, and that they may know that He is One God and that those possessed of understanding may mind.

Chapter 15 — Al-Hijr — The Rock

In the name of God, the Kind, the Merciful.

1. Alif Lam Ra. These are the verses of the Book and of a Koran that makes things clear.
2. Often will those who disbelieve wish that they had been Muslims.
3. Leave them that they may eat and enjoy themselves and that hope may entice them, for they will soon know.
4. And never have We destroyed a town except with fair warning and at its proper time.
5. No people can hasten on their doom nor can they postpone it.
6. And they say, "Oh you to whom the Reminder has been revealed! you are most certainly insane"
7. Why do you not bring to us the angels if you are of the truthful ones?
8. We do not send the angels but with truth, and then they would not be respited.
9. Certainly We have revealed the Reminder and We will most certainly be its guardian.
10. And certainly We sent apostles before you among the nations of yore.
11. And there never came an apostle to them but they mocked him.
12. Thus do We make it to enter into the hearts of the guilty;
13. They do not believe in it, and indeed the example of the former people has already passed.
14. And even if We open to them a gateway of heaven, so that they ascend into it all the while,
15. They would certainly say, "Only our eyes have been covered over, rather we are an enchanted people.
16. And certainly We have made strongholds in the heaven and We have made it fair seeming to the beholders.
17. And We guard it against every accursed Satan,
18. But he who steals a hearing, so there follows him a visible flame. 19. And the earth -- We have spread it forth and made in it firm mountains and caused to grow in it of every suitable thing.
20. And We have made in it means of subsistence for you and for him for whom you are not the suppliers.
21. And there is not a thing but with Us are the treasures of it, and We do not send it down but in a known measure.
22. And We send the winds fertilizing, then send down water from the cloud so We give it to you to drink of, nor is it you who store it up.
23. And most certainly We bring to life and cause to die and We are the heirs.
24. And certainly We know those of you who have gone before and We certainly know those who shall come later.
25. And certainly your Lord will gather them together; certainly He is Wise, Knowing.
26. And certainly We created man of clay that gives forth sound, of black mud fashioned in shape.
27. And the jinn We created before, of intensely hot fire.
28. And when your Lord said to the angels: Certainly I am going to create a mortal of the essence of black mud fashioned in shape.
29. So when I have made him complete and breathed into him of My spirit, fall down making obeisance to him.
30. So the angels made obeisance, all of them together,
31. But Iblis did it not; he refused to be with those who made obeisance.

32. He said, "Oh Iblis! what excuse have you that you are not with those who make obeisance?
33. He said, "I am not such that I should make obeisance to a mortal whom You have created of the essence of black mud fashioned in shape.
34. He said, "Then get out of it, for certainly you are driven away:
35. And certainly on you is curse until the day of judgment.
36. He said, "My Lord! then respite me till the time when they are raised.
37. He said, "So certainly you are of the respited ones
38. Till the period of the time made known.
39. He said, "My Lord! because You have made life evil to me, I will certainly make evil fair-seeming to them on earth, and I will certainly cause them all to deviate
40. Except Your servants from among them, the devoted ones.
41. He said, "This is a right way with Me:
42. Certainly. as regards My servants, you have no authority ,over them except those who follow you of the deviators.
43. And certainly Hell is the promised place of them all:
44. It has seven gates; for every gate there shall be a separate party of them.
45. Certainly those who guard against evil shall be in the midst of gardens and fountains:
46. Enter them in peace, secure.
47. And We will root out whatever of bitterness is in their hearts -- they shall be as brethren, on raised couches, face to face.
48. Toil shall not afflict them in it, nor shall they be ever ejected from it.
49. Inform My servants that I am the Forgiving, the Merciful,
50. And that My punishment -- that is the painful punishment.
51. And inform them of the guests of Abraham:
52. When they entered upon him, they said, Peace. He said, "Certainly we are afraid of you.
53. They said, "Do not be afraid, certainly we give you the good news of a boy, possessing knowledge.
54. He said, "Do you give me good news of a son when old age has come upon me? -- Of what then do you give me good news!
55. . They said, "We give you good news with truth, therefore do not be of the despairing.
56. He said, "And who despairs of the mercy of his Lord but the erring ones?
57. He said, "What is your business then, Oh messengers?
58. They said, "Certainly we are sent towards a guilty people,
59. Except Lot's followers: We will most certainly deliver them all,
60. Except his wife; We ordered that she shall certainly be of those who remain behind.
61. So when the messengers came to Lot's followers,
62. He said, "Certainly you are an unknown people.
63. They said, "No, we have come to you with that about which they disputed.
64. And we have come to you with the truth, and we are most certainly truthful.
65. Therefore go forth with your followers in a part of the night and yourself follow their rear, and let not any one of you turn round, and go forth whither you are commanded.
66. And We revealed to him this decree, that the roots of these shall be cut off in the morning.
67. And the people of the town came rejoicing.
68. He said, "Certainly these are my guests, therefore do not disgrace me,
69. And guard against the punishment of God and do not put me to shame.
70. They said, "Have we not forbidden you from other people?
71. He said, "These are my daughters, if you will do anything.

72. By your life! they were blindly wandering on in their intoxication.
73. So the rumbling overtook them while entering upon the time of sunrise;
74. Thus did We turn it upside down, and rained down upon them stones of what had been decreed.
75. Certainly in this are signs for those who examine.
76. And certainly it is on a road that still abides.
77. Most certainly there is a sign in this for the believers.
78. And the dwellers of the thicket also were most certainly unjust.
79. So We inflicted retribution on them, and they are both, indeed, on an open road still pursued.
80. And the dwellers of the Rock certainly rejected the messengers;
81. And We gave them Our words, but they turned aside from them;
82. And they hewed houses in the mountains in security.
83. So the rumbling overtook them in the morning;
84. And what they earned did not avail them.
85. And We did not create the heavens and the earth and what is between them two but in truth; and the hour is most certainly coming, so turn away with kindly forgiveness.
86. Certainly your Lord is the Creator of all things, the Knowing.
87. And certainly We have given you seven of the oft-repeated verses and the grand Koran.
88. Do not strain your eyes after what We have given certain classes of them to enjoy, and do not grieve for them, and make yourself gentle to the believers.
89. And say, "Certainly I am the plain alarmgiver.
90. Like as We sent down on the dividers
91. Those who made the Koran into shreds.
92. So, by your Lord, We would most certainly question them all,
93. As to what they did.
94. Therefore declare openly what you are bidden and turn aside from the polytheists.
95. Certainly We will suffice you against the scoffers
96. Those who set up another god with God; so they shall soon know.
97. And certainly We know that your heart straightens at what they say;
98. Therefore celebrate the praise of your Lord, and be of those who make obeisance.
99. And serve your Lord until there comes to you that which is certain.

Chapter 16 — Al-Nahl — The Bee

In the name of God, the Kind, the Merciful.

1. God's commandment has come, therefore do not desire to hasten it; glory be to Him, and highly exalted be He above what they compare with Him.
2. He sends down the angels with the inspiration by His commandment on whom He pleases of His servants, saying, "Give the warning that there is no god but Me, therefore be careful of your duty to Me.
3. He created the heavens and the earth with the truth, highly exalted be He above what they compare with Him.
4. He created man from a small seed and lo! he is an open contender.
5. And He created the cattle for you; you have in them warm clothing and many advantages, and of them do you eat.
6. And there is beauty in them for you when you drive them back to home, and when you send them forth to pasture.
7. And they carry your heavy loads to regions which you could not reach but with distress of the souls; most certainly your Lord is Compassionate, Merciful.
8. And He made horses and mules and asses that you might ride upon them and as an ornament; and He creates what you do not know.
9. And upon God it rests to show the right way, and there are some deviating ways; and if He please He would certainly guide you all aright.
10. He it is Who sends down water from the cloud for you; it gives drink, and by it grow the trees upon which you pasture.
11. He causes to grow for you thereby herbage, and the olives, and the palm trees, and the grapes, and of all the fruits; most certainly there is a sign in this for a people who reflect.
12. And He has made subservient for you the night and the day and the sun and the moon, and the stars are made subservient by His commandment; most certainly there are signs in this for a people who ponder;
13. And what He has created in the earth of varied hues most certainly there is a sign in this for a people who are mindful.
14. And He it is Who has made the sea subservient that you may eat fresh flesh from it and bring forth from it ornaments which you wear, and you see the ships cleaving through it, and that you might seek of His bounty and that you may give thanks.
15. And He has cast great mountains in the earth in case it might be shaken with you, and rivers and roads that you may go aright,
16. And landmarks; and by the stars they find the right way.
17. Is He then Who creates like him who does not create? Do you not then mind?
18. And if you would count God's favors, you will not be able to number them; most certainly God is Forgiving, Merciful.
19. And God knows what you conceal and what you do openly.
20. And those whom they call on besides God have not created anything while they are themselves created;
21. Dead are they, not living, and they know not when they shall be raised.
22. Your God is one God; so as for those who do not believe in the hereafter, their hearts are

ignorant and they are proud.

23. Truly God knows what they hide and what they manifest; certainly He does not love the proud.

24. And when it is said to them, what is it that your Lord has revealed? They say, "Stories of the ancients;

25. That they may bear their burdens entirely on the day of resurrection and also of the burdens of those whom they lead astray without knowledge; now certainly evil is what they bear.

26. Those before them did indeed devise plans, but God demolished their building from the foundations, so the roof fell down on them from above them, and the punishment came to them from wherever they did not perceive.

27. Then on the resurrection day He will bring them to disgrace and say, "Where are the associates you gave Me, for whose sake you became hostile? Those who are given the knowledge will say, "Certainly the disgrace and the evil are this day upon the unbelievers:

28. Those whom the angels cause to die while they are unjust to themselves. Then would they offer submission: We used not to do any evil. Aye! certainly God knows what you did.

29. Therefore enter the gates of hell, to abide therein; so certainly evil is the dwelling place of the proud.

30. And it is said to those who guard against evil: What is it that your Lord has revealed? They say, Good. For those who do good in this world is good, and certainly the home of the hereafter is better; and certainly most excellent is the home of those who guard against evil;

31. The gardens of perpetuity, they shall enter them, rivers flowing beneath them; they shall have in them what they please. Thus does God reward those who guard against evil,

32. Those whom the angels cause to die in a good state, saying, "Peace be on you: enter the garden for what you did.

33. They do not wait for anything but that the angels should come to them or that the commandment of your Lord should come to pass. Thus did those before them; and God was not unjust to them, but they were unjust to themselves.

34. So the evil consequences of what they did shall afflict them and that which they mocked shall encompass them.

35. And they who give associates to God say, "If God had pleased, we would not have served any besides God, neither we nor our fathers, nor would we have prohibited anything without order from Him. Thus did those before them; is then any incumbent upon the apostles except a simple delivery of the message?

36. And certainly We raised in every nation an apostle saying, "Serve God and shun the Satan. So there were some of them whom God guided and there were others against whom error was due; therefore travel in the land, then see what was the end of the rejecters.

37. If you desire for their guidance, yet certainly God does not guide him who leads astray, nor shall they have any helpers.

38. And they swear by God with the most energetic of their oaths: God will not raise up him who dies. Yea! it is a promise binding on Him, quite true, but most people do not know;

39. So that He might make cleart to them that about which they differ, and that those who disbelieve might know that they were liars.

40. Our word for a thing when We intend it, is only that We say to it, Be, and it is.

41. And those who fly for God's sake after they are oppressed, We will most certainly give them a good home in the world, and the reward of the hereafter is certainly much greater, did they but know;

42. Those who are patient and on their Lord do they rely.

43. And We did not send before you any but men to whom We sent revelation -- so ask the followers of the Reminder if you do not know --
44. With clear explanations and scriptures; and We have revealed to you the Reminder that you may make clear to men what has been revealed to them, and that haply they may reflect.
45. Do they then who plan evil deeds feel secure of this that God will not cause the earth to swallow them or that punishment may not overtake them from wherever they do not perceive?
46. Or that He may not seize them in the course of their journeys, then shall they not escape;
47. Or that He may not seize them by causing them to suffer gradual loss, for your Lord is most certainly Compassionate, Merciful.
48. Do they not consider every thing that God has created? Its very shadows return from right and left, making obeisance to God while they are in utter abasement.
49. And whatever creature that is in the heavens and that is in the earth makes obeisance to God only, and the angels too and they do not show pride.
50. They fear their Lord above them and do what they are commanded.
51. And God has said, "Take not two gods, He is only one God; so of Me alone should you be afraid.
52. And whatever is in the heavens and the earth is His, and to Him should obedience be rendered constantly; will you then guard against other than the punishment of God?
53. And whatever favor is bestowed on you it is from God; then when evil afflicts you, to Him do you cry for aid.
54. Yet when He removes the evil from you, lo ! a party of you compare others with their Lord;
55. So that they be ungrateful for what We have given them; then enjoy yourselves; for soon will you know
56. And they set apart for what they do not know a portion of what We have given them. By God, you shall most certainly be questioned about that which you created.
57. And they ascribe daughters to God, glory be to Him; and for themselves they would have what they desire.
58. And when a daughter is announced to one of them his face becomes black and he is full of wrath.
59. He hides himself from the people because of the evil of that which is announced to him. Shall he keep it with disgrace or bury it alive in the dust? Now certainly evil is what they judge.
60. For those who do not believe in the hereafter is an evil attribute, and God's is the highest attribute; and He is the Mighty, the Wise.
61. And if God had destroyed men for their iniquity, He would not leave on the earth a single creature, but He respites them till an appointed time; so when their doom will come they shall not be able to delay it an hour nor can they bring it on before its time.
62. And they ascribe to God what they themselves hate and their tongues relate the lie that they shall have the good; there is no avoiding it that for them is the fire and that they shall be sent before.
63. By God, most certainly We sent apostles to nations before you, but the Satan made their deeds fair-seeming to them, so he is their guardian today, and they shall have a painful punishment.
64. And We have not revealed to you the Book except that you may make clear to them that about which they differ, ind as a guidance and a mercy for a people who believe.
65. And God has sent down water from the cloud and therewith given life to the earth after its death; most certainly there is a sign in this for a people who would listen.
66. And most certainly there is a lesson for you in the cattle; We give you to drink of what is in their bellies -- from in between the feces and the blood -- pure milk, easy and agreeable to

swallow for those who drink.

⁶⁷. And of the fruits of the palms and the grapes -- you obtain from them intoxication and good provisions; most certainly there is a sign in this for a people who contemplate it.

⁶⁸. And your Lord revealed to the bee saying, "Make hives in the mountains and in the trees and in what they build:

⁶⁹. Then eat of all the fruits and walk in the ways of your Lord submissively. There comes forth from within it a beverage of many colours, in which there is healing for men; most certainly there is a sign in this for a people who reflect.

⁷⁰. And God has created you, then He causes you to die, and of you is he who is brought back to the worst part of life, so that after having knowledge he does not know anything; certainly God is Knowing, Powerful.

⁷¹. And God has made some of you excel others in the means of subsistence, so those who are made to excel do not give away their sustenance to those whom their right hands possess so that they should be equal therein; is it then the favor of God which they deny?

⁷². And God has made wives for you from among yourselves, and has given you sons and grandchildren from your wives, and has given you of the good things; is it then in the falsehood that they believe while it is in the favor of God that they disbelieve?

⁷³. And they serve besides God that which does not control for them any sustenance at all from the heavens and the earth, nor have they any power. ⁷⁴. Therefore do not give likenesses to God; certainly God knows and you do not know.

⁷⁵. God sets forth a story: consider a slave, the property of another, who has no power over anything, and one whom We have granted from Ourselves proper nourishment so he spends from it secretly and openly; are the two alike? All praise is due to God! No, most of them do not know.

⁷⁶. And God sets forth a story of two men; one of them is dumb, not able to do anything, and he is a burden to his master; wherever he sends him, he brings no good; can he be held equal with him who urges what is just, and he himself is on the right path?

⁷⁷. And God's is the unseen of the heavens and the earth; and the matter of the hour is but as the twinkling of an eye or it is higher still; certainly God has power over all things.

⁷⁸. And God has brought you forth from the wombs of your mothers -- you did not know anything -- and He gave you hearing and sight and hearts that you may give thanks.

⁷⁹. Do they not see the birds, constrained in the middle of the sky? None withholds them but God; most certainly there are signs in this for a people who believe.

⁸⁰. And God has given you a place to abide in your houses, and He has given you tents of the skins of cattle which you find light to carry on the day of your march and on the day of your halting, and of their wool and their fur and their hair He has given you household stuff and a provision for a time.

⁸¹. And God has made for you of what He has created shelters, and He has given you in the mountains places of retreat, and He has given you garments to preserve you from the heat and coats of mail to preserve you in your fighting; even thus does He complete His favor upon you, that haply you may submit.

⁸². But if they turn back, then on you devolves only the clear deliverance of the message.

⁸³. They recognize the favor of God, yet they deny it, and most of them are ungrateful.

⁸⁴. And on the day when We will raise up a witness out of every nation, then shall no permission be given to those who E disbelieve, nor shall they be made to solicit favor.

⁸⁵. And when those who are unjust shall see the punishment, it shall not be lightened for them, nor shall they be respited. .

⁸⁶. And when those who compare others with God shall see their associate-gods, they shall say, "Our Lord, these are our associate-gods on whom we called besides You. But they will give them back the reply: Most certainly you are liars.

⁸⁷. And they shall tender submission to God on that day; and what they used to forge shall depart from them.

⁸⁸. As for those who disbelieve and turn away from God's way, We will add punishment to their punishment because they made mischief.

⁸⁹. And on the day when We will raise up in every people a witness against them from among themselves, and bring you as a witness against these -- and We have revealed the Book to you explaining clearly everything, and a guidance and mercy and good news for those who submit.

⁹⁰. Certainly God urges the doing of justice and the doing of good to others and the giving to the kindred, and He forbids indecency and evil and rebellion; He reprimands you that you may be mindful.

⁹¹. And fulfill the covenant of God when you have made a covenant, and
do not break the oaths after making them fast, and you have indeed made God a surety for you; certainly God I . knows what you do.

⁹². And do not be like her who unravels her yarn, disintegrating it into pieces after she has spun it strongly. You make your oaths to be means of deceit between you because one nation is more numerous than another nation. God only tries you by this; and He will most certainly make clear to you on the resurrection day that about which you differed.

⁹³. And if God please He would certainly make you a single nation, but He causes to err whom He pleases and guides whom He pleases; and most certainly you will be questioned as to what you did.

⁹⁴. And do not make your oaths a means of deceit between you, in case a foot should slip after its stability and you should taste evil because you turned away from God's way and grievous punishment be your lot.

⁹⁵. And do not take a small price in exchange for God's covenant; certainly what is with God is better for you, did you but know.

⁹⁶. What is with you passes away and what is with God is enduring; and We will most certainly give to those who are patient their reward for the best of what they did.

⁹⁷. Whoever does good whether male or female and he is a believer, We will most certainly make him live a happy life, and We will most certainly give them their reward for the best of what they did.

⁹⁸. So when you recite the Koran, seek refuge with God from the accursed Satan,

⁹⁹. Certainly he has no authority over those who believe and rely on their Lord.

¹⁰⁰. His authority is only over those who befriend him and those who associate others with Him.

¹⁰¹. And when We change one word for another word, and God knows best what He reveals, they say, "You are only a forger. No, most of them do not know.

¹⁰². Say, "The Holy spirit has revealed it from your Lord with the truth, that it may establish those who believe and as a guidance and good news for those who submit.

¹⁰³. And certainly We know that they say, "Only a mortal teaches him. The tongue of him whom they reproach is barbarous, and this is clear Arabic tongue.

¹⁰⁴. As for those who do not believe in God's words, certainly God will not guide them, and they shall have a painful punishment.

¹⁰⁵. Only they forge the lie who do not believe in God's words, and these are the liars.

¹⁰⁶. He who disbelieves in God after his having believed, not he who is compelled while his heart is calmed on account of faith, but he who opens his heart to disbelief -- on these is the

wrath of God, and they shall have a grievous punishment.

107. This is because they love this world's life more than the hereafter, and because God does not guide the unbelieving people.

108. These are they on whose hearts and their hearing and their eyes God has set a seal, and these are the heedless ones.

109. No doubt that in the hereafter they will be the losers.

110. Yet certainly your Lord, with respect to those who fly after they are persecuted, then they struggle hard and are patient, most certainly your Lord after that is Forgiving, Merciful.

111. Remember the day when every soul shall come, pleading for itself and every soul shall be paid in full what it has done, and they shall not be dealt with unjustly.

112. And God sets forth a story: Consider a town safe and secure to which its means of subsistence come in abundance from every quarter; but it became ungrateful to God's favors, therefore God made it to taste the utmost degree of hunger and fear because of what they wrought.

113. And certainly there came to them a Prophet from among them, but they rejected him, so the punishment overtook them while they were unjust.

114. Therefore eat of what God has given you, lawful and good things, and give thanks for God's favor if Him do you serve.

115. He has only forbidden you what dies of itself and blood and flesh of swine and that over which any other name than that of God has been invoked, but whoever is driven to necessity, not desiring nor exceeding the limit, then certainly God is Forgiving, Merciful.

116. And, for what your tongues describe, do not utter the lie, saying This is lawful and this is unlawful, in order to forge a lie against God; certainly those who forge the lie against God shall not prosper.

117. A little enjoyment and they shall have a painful punishment.

118. And for those who were Jews We prohibited what We have related to you already, and We did them no injustice, but they were unjust to themselves.

119. Yet certainly your Lord, with respect to those who do an evil in ignorance, then turn after that and make amends, most certainly your Lord after that is Forgiving, Merciful.

120. Certainly Abraham was an exemplar, obedient to God, upright, and he was not of the polytheists.

121. Grateful for His favors; He chose him and guided him on the right path.

122. And We gave him good in this world, and in the next he will most certainly be among the good.

123. Then We revealed to you: Follow the faith of Abraham, the upright one, and he was not of the polytheists.

124. The Sabbath was ordered only for those who differed about it, and most certainly your Lord will judge between them on the resurrection day concerning that about which they differed.

125. Call to the way of your Lord with wisdom and proper appeal, and have arguments with them in the best manner; certainly your Lord knows best those who stray from His path, and He knows best those who follow the right way.

126. And if you take your turn, then retaliate with the like of that with which you were afflicted; but if you are patient, it will certainly be best for those who are patient.

127. And be patient and your patience is not but by the assistance of God, and grieve not for them, and do not distress yourself at what they plan.

128. Certainly God is with those who guard against evil and those who do good to others.

Chapter 17 — Bani Israil — The Children of Israel

In the name of God, the Kind, the Merciful.

1. Glory be to Him Who made His servant to go on a night from the Sacred Mosque to the remote mosque of which We have blessed the precincts, so that We may show to him some of Our signs; certainly He is the Hearing, the Seeing.

2. And We gave Moses the Book and made it a guidance to the children of Israel, saying, "Do not take a protector besides Me;

3. The offspring of those whom We bore with Noah; certainly he was a grateful servant.

4. And We had made known to the children of Israel in the Book: Most certainly you will make mischief in the land twice, and most certainly you will behave insolently with great insolence.

5. So when the promise for the first of the two came, We sent over you Our servants, of mighty prowess, so they went to and fro among the houses, and it was a promise to be accomplished.

6. Then We gave you back the turn to prevail against them, and aided you with wealth and children and made you a numerous band.

7. If you do good, you will do good for your own souls, and if you do evil, it shall be for them. So when the second promise came We raised another people that they may bring you to grief and that they may enter the mosque as they entered it the first time, and that they might destroy whatever they gained ascendancy over with utter destruction.

8. It may be that your Lord will have mercy on you, and if you again return to disobedience We too will return to punishment, and We have made hell a prison for the unbelievers.

9. Certainly this Koran guides to that which is most upright and gives good news to the believers who do good that they shall have a great reward.

10. And that as for those who do not believe in the hereafter, We have prepared for them a painful punishment.

11. And man prays for evil as he ought to pray for good, and man is ever hasty.

12. And We have made the night and the day two signs, then We have made the sign of the night to pass away and We have made the sign of the day manifest, so that you may seek grace from your Lord, and that you might know the numbering of years and the judging; and We have explained everything with distinctness.

13. And We have made every man's actions to cling to his neck, and We will bring forth to him on the resurrection day a book which he will find wide open:

14. Read your book; your own self is sufficient as a reckoner against you this day.

15. Whoever goes aright, for his own soul does he go aright; and whoever goes astray, to its detriment only does he go astray: nor can the bearer of a burden bear the burden of another, nor do We reprimand until We raise an apostle.

16. And when We wish to destroy a town, We send Our commandment to the people of it who lead easy lives, but they transgress therein; thus the word proves true against it, so We destroy it with utter destruction.

17. And how many of the generations did We destroy after Noah! and your Lord is sufficient as Knowing and Seeing with regard to His servants' faults.

18. Whoever desires this present life, We hasten to him therein what We please for whomsoever We desire, then We assign to him the hell; he shall enter it despised, driven away.

¹⁹. And whoever desires the hereafter and strives for it as he ought to strive and he is a believer; as for these, their striving shall certainly be accepted.

²⁰. All do We aid -- these as well as those -- out of the bounty of your Lord, and the bounty of your Lord is not confined.

²¹. See how We have made some of them to excel others, and certainly the hereafter is much superior in respect of excellence.

²². Do not associate with God any other god, in case you may sit down despised, neglected.

²³. And your Lord has commanded that you shall not serve any but Him, and goodness to your parents. If either or both of them reach old age with you, say not to them so much as "Ugh" nor chide them, and speak to them a generous word.

²⁴. And make yourself submissively gentle to them with compassion, and say, "Oh my Lord! have compassion on them, as they brought me up when I was little."

²⁵. Your Lord knows best what is in your minds; if you are good, then He is certainly Forgiving to those who turn to Him frequently.

²⁶. And give to the near of kin his due and to the needy and the wayfarer, and do not squander wastefully.

²⁷. Certainly the squanderers are the fellows of the Satans and the Satan is ever ungrateful to his Lord.

²⁸. And if you turn away from them to seek mercy from your Lord, which you hope for, speak to them a gentle word.

²⁹. And do not make your hand to be shackled to your neck nor stretch it forth to the utmost limit of its stretching forth, in which case you should afterwards sit down blamed, stripped off.

³⁰. Certainly your Lord makes plentiful the means of subsistence for whom He pleases and He straightens them; certainly He is ever Aware of, Seeing, His servants.

³¹. And do not kill your children for fear of poverty; We give them sustenance and yourselves too; certainly to kill them is a great wrong.

³². And stay clear of fornication; certainly it is an indecency and an evil way.

³³. And do not kill any one whom God has forbidden, except for a just cause, and whoever is slain unjustly, We have indeed given to his heir authority, so let him not exceed the just limits in slaying; certainly he is aided.

³⁴. And draw not near to the property of the orphan except in a proper way till he attains his maturity and fulfill the promise; certainly every promise shall be questioned about.

³⁵. And give full measure when you measure out, and weigh with a true balance; this is fair and better in the end.

³⁶. And follow not that of which you have not the knowledge; certainly the hearing and the sight and the heart, all of these, shall be questioned about that.

³⁷. And do not go about in the land exultingly, for you cannot cut through the earth nor reach the mountains in height.

³⁸. All this -- the evil of it -- is hateful in the sight of your Lord.

³⁹. This is of what your Lord has revealed to you of wisdom, and do not associate any other god with God unless you should be thrown into hell, blamed, cast away.

⁴⁰. What! has then your Lord preferred to give you sons, and for Himself taken daughters from among the angels? Most certainly you utter a grievous saying.

⁴¹. And certainly We have repeated warnings in this Koran that they may be mindful, but it does not add save to their aversion.

⁴². Say, "If there were with Him gods as they say, then certainly they would have been able to

seek a way to the Lord of power.

⁴³. Glory be to Him and exalted be He in high exaltation above what they say.

⁴⁴. The seven heavens declare His glory and the earth too, and those who are in them; and there is not a single thing but glorifies Him with His praise, but you do not understand their glorification; certainly He is Forbearing, Forgiving.

⁴⁵. And when you recite the Koran, We place between you and those who do not believe in the hereafter a hidden barrier;

⁴⁶. And We have placed coverings on their hearts and a heaviness in their ears should they not they understand it, and when you mention your Lord alone in the Koran they turn their backs in aversion.

⁴⁷. We know best what they hear when they listen to you, and when they take counsel secretly, when the unjust say, "You follow only a crazy man.

⁴⁸. See what they liken you to! So they have gone astray and cannot find the way.

⁴⁹. And they say, "What! when we shall have become bones and decayed particles, shall we then certainly be raised up, being a new creation?

⁵⁰. Say, "Become stones or iron,

⁵¹. Or some other creature of those which are too hard to receive life in your minds! But they will say, "Who will return us? Say, "Who created you at first. Still they will shake their heads at you and say, "When will it be? Say, "Maybe it has drawn near.

⁵². On the day when He will call you forth, then shall you obey Him, giving Him praise, and you will think that you tarried but a little while.

⁵³. And say to My servants that they speak that which is best; certainly the Satan sows dissensions among them; certainly the Satan is an open enemy to man.

⁵⁴. Your Lord knows you best; He will have mercy on you if He pleases, or He will reprimand you if He pleases; and We have not sent you as being in charge of them.

⁵⁵. And your Lord knows best those who are in the heavens and the earth; and certainly We have made some of the prophets to excel others, and to David We gave a scripture.

⁵⁶. Say, "Call on those whom you assert besides Him, and see if they can control the removal of distress from you nor can they control its transfer to others.

⁵⁷. Those whom they call upon, themselves seek the means of access to their Lord -- whoever of them is nearest -- and they hope for His mercy and fear His punishment; certainly the punishment of your Lord is a thing to be cautious of.

⁵⁸. And there is not a town but We will destroy it before the day of resurrection or reprimand it with a severe punishment; this is written in the Divine ordinance.

⁵⁹. And nothing could have hindered Us that We should send signs except that the ancients rejected them; and We gave to Samood the she-camel -- a great sign -- but on her account they did injustice, and We do not send signs but to make men fear.

⁶⁰. And when We said to you: Certainly your Lord encompasses men; and We did not make the vision which We showed you but a trial for men and the cursed tree in the Koran as well; and We cause them to fear, but it only adds to their great inordinacy.

⁶¹. And when We said to the angels: Make obeisance to Adam; they made obeisance, but Iblis did it not. He said, "Shall I make obeisance to him whom You have created of dust?

⁶². He said, "Tell me, is this he whom You have honored above me? If You should respite me to the day of resurrection, I will most certainly cause his progeny to perish except a few.

⁶³. He said, "Be gone! for whoever of them will follow you, then certainly hell is your payment, a full punishment:

⁶⁴. And beguile whomsoever of them you can with your voice, and collect against them your

forces riding and on foot, and share with them in wealth and children, and hold out promises to them; and the Satan makes not promises to them but to deceive:

65. Certainly as for My servants, you have no authority over them; and your Lord is sufficient as a Protector.

66. Your Lord is He Who speeds the ships for you in the sea that you may seek of His grace; certainly He is ever Merciful to you.

67. And when distress afflicts you in the sea, away go those whom you call on except He; but when He brings you safe to the land, you turn aside; and man is ever ungrateful.

68. What! Do you then feel secure that He will not cause a tract of land to engulf you or send on you a tornado? Then you shall not find a protector for yourselves.

69. Or, do you feel secure that He will not take you back into it another time, then send on you a fierce gale and thus drown you on account of your ungratefulness? Then you shall not find any aider against Us in the matter.

70. And certainly We have honored the children of Adam, and We carry them in the land and the sea, and We have given them of the good things, and We have made them to excel by an appropriate excellence over most of those whom We have created.

71. Remember the day when We will call every people with their Imam; then whoever is given his book in his right hand, these shall read their book; and they shall not be dealt with a whit unjustly.

72. And whoever is blind in this, he shall also be blind in the hereafter; and more erring from the way.

73. And certainly they had purposed to turn you away from that which We have revealed to you, that you should forge against Us other than that, and then they would certainly have taken you for a friend.

74. And had it not been that We had already established you, you would certainly have been near to incline to them a little;

75. In that case We would certainly have made you to taste a double punishment in this life and a double punishment after death, then you would not have found any helper against Us.

76. And certainly they purposed to unsettle you from the land that they might expel you from it, and in that case they will not tarry behind you but a little.

77. This is Our course with regard to those of Our apostles whom We sent before you, and you shall not find a change in Our course.

78. Keep up prayer from the declining of the sun till the darkness of the night and the morning recitation; certainly the morning recitation is witnessed.

79. And during a part of the night, pray Tahajjud beyond what is incumbent on you; maybe your Lord will raise you to a position of great glory.

80. And say, "My Lord! Cause me to enter properly, and cause me to go forth properly, and grant me from near You power to assist me.

81. And say, "The truth has come and the falsehood has vanished; certainly falsehood is a vanishing thing.

82. And We reveal of the Koran that which is a healing and a mercy to the believers, and it adds only to the hell of the unjust.

83. And when We bestow favor on man, he turns aside and behaves proudly, and when evil afflicts him, he is despairing.

84. Say, "Every one acts according to his manner; but your Lord knows best who is best guided in the path.

85. And they ask you about the soul. Say, "The soul is one of the commands of my Lord, and

you are not given any knowledge except a little.

⁸⁶. And if We please, We should certainly take away that which We have revealed to you, then you would not find for it any protector against Us.

⁸⁷. But on account of mercy from your Lord -- certainly His grace to you is abundant.

⁸⁸. Say, "If men and jinn should combine together to bring the like of this Koran, they could not bring the like of it, though some of them were aiders of others.

⁸⁹. And certainly We have explained for men in this Koran every kind of similitude, but most men do not consent to anything except denial.

⁹⁰. And they say, "We will by no means believe in you until you cause a fountain to gush forth from the earth for us.

⁹¹. Or you should have a garden of palms and grapes in the midst of which you should cause rivers to flow forth, gushing out.

⁹². Or you should cause the heaven to come down upon us in pieces as you think, or bring God and the angels face to face with us.

⁹³. Or you should have a house of gold, or you should ascend into heaven, and we will not believe in your ascending until you bring down to us a book which we may read. Say, "Glory be to my Lord; am I nothing except a mortal apostle?

⁹⁴. And nothing prevented people from believing when the guidance came to them except that they said, "What! has God raised up a mortal to be an apostle?

⁹⁵. Say, "Had there been in the earth angels walking about as settlers, We would certainly have sent down to them from the heaven an angel as an apostle.

⁹⁶. Say, "God suffices as a witness between me and you; certainly He is Aware of His servants, Seeing.

⁹⁷. And whomsoever God guides, he is the follower of the right way, and whomsoever He causes to err, you shall not find for him guardians besides Him; and We will gather them together on the day of resurrection on their faces, blind and dumb and deaf; their home is hell; whenever it becomes allayed We will add to their burning.

⁹⁸. This is their retribution because they disbelieved in Our words and said What! when we shall have become bones and decayed particles, shall we then indeed be raised up into a new creation?

⁹⁹. Do they not consider that God, Who created the heavens and the earth, is able to create their like, and He has appointed for them a doom about which there is no doubt? But the unjust do not consent to anything except denial.

¹⁰⁰. Say, "If you control the treasures of the mercy of my Lord, then you would withhold them from fear of spending, and man is wretched.

¹⁰¹. And certainly We gave Moses nine clear signs; so ask the children of
Israel. When he came to them, Pharoah said to him: Most certainly I deem you, Oh Moses, to be a man deprived of reason.

¹⁰². He said, "Truly you know that none but the Lord of the heavens and
the earth has sent down these as clear proof and most certainly I believe you, Oh Pharoah, to be given over to hell.

¹⁰³. So he desired to destroy them out of the earth, but We drowned him
and those with him all together;

¹⁰⁴. And We said to the Israelites after him: Dwell in the land: and
when the promise of the next life shall come to pass, we will bring you both together in judgment.

¹⁰⁵. And with truth have We revealed it, and with truth did it come; and We have not sent you but as the giver of good news and as a alarmgiver.

¹⁰⁶. And it is a Koran which We have revealed in portions so that you may read it to the people by slow degrees, and We have revealed it, revealing in portions.

¹⁰⁷. Say, "Believe in it or believe not; certainly those who are given the knowledge before it fall down on their faces, making obeisance when it is recited to them.

¹⁰⁸. And they say, "Glory be to our Lord! most certainly the promise of our Lord was to be fulfilled.

¹⁰⁹. And they fall down on their faces weeping, and it adds to their humility.

¹¹⁰. Say, "Call upon God or call upon, the Kind God; whichever you call upon, He has the best names; and do not utter your prayer with a very raised voice nor be silent with regard to it, and seek a way between these.

¹¹¹. And say, "All praise is due to God, Who has not taken a son and Who has not a partner in the kingdom, and Who has not a helper to save Him from disgrace; and proclaim His greatness magnifying Him.

Chapter 18 — Al-Kahf — The Cave

In the name of God, the Kind, the Merciful.

¹. All praise is due to God, Who revealed the Book to His servant and did not make in it any crookedness.

². Rightly directing, that he might give warning of severe punishment from Him and give good news to the believers who do good that they shall have a proper reward,

³. Staying in it for ever;

⁴. And warn those who say, "God has taken a son.

⁵. They have no knowledge of it, nor had their fathers; a grievous word it is that comes out of their mouths; they speak nothing but a lie.

⁶. Then maybe you will kill yourself with grief, sorrowing after them, if they do not believe in this announcement.

⁷. Certainly We have made whatever is on the earth an embellishment for it, so that We may try them as to which of them is best in works.

⁸. And most certainly We will make what is on it bare ground without herbage.

⁹. Or, do you think that the Fellows of the Cave and the Inscription were of Our wonderful signs?

¹⁰. When the youths sought refuge in the cave, they said, "Our Lord! grant us mercy from You, and provide for us a right course in our affair.

¹¹. So We prevented them from hearing in the cave for a number of years.

¹². Then We raised them up that We might know which of the two parties was best able to compute the time for which they remained.

¹³. We relate to you their story with the truth; certainly they were youths who believed in their Lord and We increased them in guidance.

¹⁴. And We strengthened their hearts with patience, when they stood up and said, "Our Lord is the Lord of the heavens and the earth; we will by no means call upon any god besides Him, for then indeed we should have said an extravagant thing.

¹⁵. These our people have taken gods besides Him; why do they not produce any clear authority in their support? Who is then more unjust than he who forges a lie against God?

¹⁶. And when you abandon them and what they worship save God, take your refuge in the cave; your Lord will extend to you largely of His mercy and provide for you a profitable course in your affair.

¹⁷. And you might see the sun when it rose, decline from their cave towards the right hand, and when it set, leave them behind on the left while they were in a wide space thereof. This is of the signs of God; whomsoever God guides, he is the rightly guided one, and whomsoever He causes to err, you shall not find for him any friend to lead him aright.

¹⁸. And you might think them awake while they were asleep and We turned them about to the right and to the left, while their dog lay outstretching its paws at the entrance; if you looked at them you would certainly turn back from them in flight, and you would certainly be filled with awe because of them.

¹⁹. And thus did We rouse them that they might question each other. A speaker among them said, "How long have you tarried? They said, "We have tarried for a day or a part of a day. Others said, "Your Lord knows best how long you have tarried. Now send one of you with this silver coin of yours to the city, then let him see which of them has purest food, so let him

bring you provision from it, and let him behave with gentleness, and by no means make your case known to any one:

20. For certainly if they prevail against you they would stone you to death or force you back to their religion, and then you will never succeed.

21. And thus did We make men to get knowledge of them that they might know that God's promise is true and that as for the hour there is no doubt about it. When they disputed among themselves about their affair and said, "Erect an edifice over them -- their Lord knows them best. Those who prevailed in their affair said, "We will certainly raise a masjid over them.

22. Some say, "They are three, the fourth of them being their dog; and others say, "Five, the sixth of them being their dog, making conjectures at what is unknown; and others yet say, "Seven, and the eighth of them is their dog. Say, "My Lord knows best their number, none knows them but a few; therefore contend not in the matter of them but with an outward contention, and do not question concerning them any of them.

23. And do not say of anything: Certainly I will do it tomorrow, 24. Unless God pleases; and remember your Lord when you forget and say, "Maybe my Lord will guide me to a nearer course to the right than this.

25. And they remained in their cave three hundred years and some add another nine.

26. Say, "God knows best how long they remained; to Him are known the unseen things of the heavens and the earth; how clear His sight and how clear His hearing! There is none to be a guardian for them besides Him, and He does not make any one His associate in His Judgment.

27. And recite what has been revealed to you of the Book of your Lord, there is none who can alter His words; and you shall not find any refuge besides Him.

28. And withhold yourself with those who call on their Lord morning and evening desiring His goodwill, and let not your eyes pass from them, desiring the beauties of this world's life; and do not follow him whose heart We have made unmindful to Our remembrance, and he follows his low desires and his case is one in which due bounds are exceeded.

29. And say, "The truth is from your Lord, so let him who please believe, and let him who please disbelieve; Certainly We have prepared for the iniquitous a fire, the curtains of which shall encompass them about; and if they cry for water, they shall be given water like molten brass which will scald their faces; evil the drink and ill the resting-place.

30. Certainly as for those who believe and do good, We do not waste the reward of him who does a good work.

31. These it is for whom are gardens of perpetuity beneath which rivers flow, ornaments shall be given to them therein of bracelets of gold, and they shall wear green robes of fine silk and thick silk brocade interwoven with gold, reclining therein on raised couches; excellent the repayment and fine the resting place.

32. And set forth to them a story of two men; for one of them We made two gardens of grape vines, and We surrounded them both with palms, and in the midst of them We made cornfields.

33. . Both these gardens yielded their fruits, and nothing failed thereof, and We caused a river to gush forth in their midst,

34. And he possessed much wealth; so he said to his companion, while he disputed with him: I have greater wealth than you, and am mightier in followers.

35. And he entered his garden while he was unjust to himself. He said, "I do not think that this will ever perish

36. And I do not think the hour will come, and even if I am returned to my Lord I will most certainly find a returning place better than this.

37. His companion said to him while disputing with him: Do you disbelieve in Him Who

created you from dust, then from a small seed, then He made you a perfect man?

38. But as for me, He, God, is my Lord, and I do not associate anyone with my Lord.

39. And why did you not say when you entered your garden: It is as God has pleased, there is no power save in God? If you consider me to be inferior to you in wealth and children,

40. Then maybe my Lord will give me what is better than your garden, and send on it a thunderbolt from heaven so that it shall become even ground without plant,

41. Or its waters should sink down into the ground so that you are unable to find it.

42. And his wealth was destroyed; so he began to wring his hands for what he had spent on it, while it lay, having fallen down upon its roofs, and he said, "Ah me! would that I had not associated anyone with my Lord.

43. And he had no host to help him besides God nor could he defend himself.

44. Here is protection only God's, the True One; He is best in the giving of reward and best in requiting.

45. And set forth to them story of the life of this world: like water which We send down from the cloud so the herbage of the earth becomes tangled on account of it, then it becomes dry broken into pieces which the winds scatter; and God is the holder of power over all things.

46. Wealth and children are an adornment of the life of this world; and the ever-abiding, the good works, are better with your Lord in reward and better in expectation.

47. And the day on which We will cause the mountains to pass away and you will see the earth a leveled plain and We will gather them and leave not any one of them behind.

48. And they shall be brought before your Lord, standing in ranks: Now certainly you have come to Us as We created you at first. No, you thought that We had not appointed to you a time of the fulfillment of the promise.

49. And the Book shall be placed, then you will see the guilty fearing from what is in it, and they will say, "Ah! woe to us! what a book is this! it does not omit a small one nor a great one, but numbers them all; and what they had done they shall find present there; and your Lord does not deal unjustly
with anyone.

50. And when We said to the angels: Make obeisance to Adam; they made obeisance but Iblis did it not. He was of the jinn, so he transgressed the commandment of his Lord. What! would you then take him and his offspring for friends rather than Me, and they are your enemies? Evil is this change for the
unjust.

51. I did not make them witnesses of the creation of the heavens and the earth, nor of the creation of their own souls; nor could I take those who lead others astray for aiders.

52. And on the day when He shall say, "Call on those whom you considered to be My associates. So they shall call on them, but they shall not answer them, and We will cause a separation between them.

53. And the guilty shall see the fire, then they shall know that they are going to fall into it, and they shall not find a place to which to turn away from it.

54. And certainly We have explained in this Koran every kind of example, and man is most of all given to contention.

55. And nothing prevents men from believing when the guidance comes to them, and from asking forgiveness of their Lord, except that what happened to the ancients should overtake them, or that the punishment should come face to face with them.

56. And We do not send apostles but as givers of good news and warning, and those who disbelieve make a false contention that they may render null thereby the truth, and they take My

words and that with which they are warned for a mockery.

57. And who is more unjust than he who is reminded of the words of his Lord, then he turns away from them and forgets what his two hands have sent before? Certainly We have placed veils over their hearts so that they should not understand it and a heaviness in their ears; and if you call them to the guidance, they will not ever follow the right course in that case.

58. And your Lord is Forgiving, the Lord of Mercy; were He to punish them for what they earn, He would certainly have hastened the punishment for them; but for them there is an appointed time from which they shall not find a refuge.

59. And as for these towns, We destroyed them when they acted unjustly, and We have appointed a time for their destruction.

60. And when Moses said to his servant: I will not cease until I reach the junction of the two rivers or I will go on for years.

61. So when they had reached the junction of the two rivers they forgot their fish, and it took its way into the sea, going away.

62. But when they had gone farther, he said to his servant: Bring to us our morning meal, certainly we have met with fatigue from this our journey.

63. He said, "Did you see when we took refuge on the rock then I forgot the fish, and nothing made me forget to speak of it but the Satan, and it took its way into the river; what a wonder!

64. He said, "This is what we sought for; so they returned retracing their footsteps.

65. Then they found one from among Our servants whom We had granted mercy from Us and whom We had taught knowledge from Ourselves.

66. Moses said to him: Shall I follow you on condition that you should teach me right knowledge of what you have been taught?

67. He said, "Certainly you cannot have patience with me

68. And how can you have patience in that of which you have not got a comprehensive knowledge?

69. He said, "If God pleases, you will find me patient and I shall not disobey you in any matter.

70. He said, "If you would follow me, then do not question me about any thing until I myself speak to you about it

71. So they went their way until when they embarked in the boat he made a hole in it. Moses said, "Have you made a hole in it to drown its inmates? Certainly you have done a grievous thing.

72. He said, "Did I not say that you will not be able to have patience with me?

73. He said, "Blame me not for what I forgot, and do not constrain me to a difficult thing in my affair.

74. So they went on until, when they met a boy, he killed him. Moses said, "Have you slain an innocent person otherwise than for manslaughter? Certainly you have done an evil thing.

75. He said, "Did I not say to you that you will not be able to have patience with me?

76. He said, "If I ask you about anything after this, keep me not in your company; indeed you shall have then found an excuse in my case.

77. So they went on until when they came to the people of a town, they asked them for food, but they refused to entertain them as guests. Then they found in it a wall which was on the point of falling, so he put it into a right state. Moses said, "If you had pleased, you might certainly have taken compensation for it.

78. He said, "This shall be separation between me and you; now I will inform you of the significance of that with which you could not have patience.

79. As for the boat, it belonged to some poor men who worked on the river and I wished that I should damage it, and there was behind them a king who seized every boat by force.

⁸⁰. And as for the boy, his parents were believers and we feared that he might show disobedience and ingratitude to come upon them:

⁸¹. So we desired that their Lord might give them in his place one better than him in purity and nearer to having compassion.

⁸². And as for the wall, it belonged to two orphan boys in the city, and there was beneath it a treasure belonging to them, and their father was a righteous man; so your Lord desired that they should attain their maturity and take out their treasure, a mercy from your Lord, and I did not do it of my own accord. This is the significance of that with which you could not have patience.

⁸³. And they ask you about Zulqarnain. Say, "I will recite to you an account of him.

⁸⁴. Certainly We established him in the land and granted him means of access to every thing.

⁸⁵. So he followed a course.

⁸⁶. Until when he reached the place where the sun set, he found it going down into a black sea, and found by it a people. We said, "Oh Zulqarnain! either give them a punishment or do them a benefit.

⁸⁷. He said, "As to him who is injust, we will reprimand him, then shall he be returned to his Lord, and He will reprimand him with an exemplary punishment: And as for him who believes and does good, he shall have proper reward, and We will speak to him an easy word of Our command.

⁸⁹. Then he followed another course.

⁹⁰. Until when he reached the land of the rising of the sun, he found it rising on a people to whom We had given no shelter from It;

⁹¹. Even so! and We had a full knowledge of what he had.

⁹². Then he followed another course.

⁹³. Until when he reached a place between the two mountains, he found on that side of them a people who could hardly understand a word.

⁹⁴. They said, "Oh Zulqarnain! certainly Gog and Magog make mischief in the land. Shall we then pay you a tribute on condition that you should raise a barrier between us and them

⁹⁵. He said, "That in which my Lord has established me is better, therefore you only help me with workers, I will make a fortified barrier between you and them;

⁹⁶. Bring me blocks of iron; until when he had filled up the space between the two mountain sides, he said, "Blow, until when he had made it as fire, he said, "Bring me molten brass which I may pour over it.

⁹⁷. So they were not able to scale it nor could they make a hole in it. ⁹⁸. He said, "This is a mercy from my Lord, but when the promise of my Lord comes to pass He will make it level with the ground, and the promise of my Lord is ever true.

⁹⁹. And on that day We will leave a part of them in conflict with another part, and the trumpet will be blown, so We will gather them all together;

¹⁰⁰. And We will bring forth hell, exposed to view, on that day before the unbelievers.

¹⁰¹. They whose eyes were under a cover from My reminder and they could not even hear.

¹⁰². What! do then those who disbelieve think that they can take My servants to be guardians besides Me? Certainly We have prepared hell for the entertainment of the unbelievers.

¹⁰³. Say, "Shall We inform you of the greatest losers in their deeds?

¹⁰⁴. These are they whose labor is lost in this world's life and they think that they are well versed in skill of the work of hands.

¹⁰⁵. These are they who disbelieve in the words of their Lord and His meeting, so their deeds become null, and therefore We will not set up a balance for them on the day of resurrection.

¹⁰⁶. Thus it is that their punishment is hell, because they disbelieved and held My words and

My apostles in mockery.

¹⁰⁷. Certainly as for those who believe and do good deeds, their place of entertainment shall be the gardens of paradise,

¹⁰⁸. Abiding therein; they shall not desire removal from them.

¹⁰⁹. Say, "If the sea were ink for the words of my Lord, the sea would certainly be consumed before the words of my Lord are exhausted, though We were to bring the like of that sea to add

¹¹⁰. Say, "I am only a mortal like you; it is revealed to me that your god is one God, therefore whoever hopes to meet his Lord, he should do good deeds, and not join any one in the service of his Lord.

Chapter 19 — Maryam — Mary

In the name of God, the Kind, the Merciful.

¹. Kaf Ha Ya Ain Sad.
². A mention of the mercy of your Lord to His servant Zacharia.
³. When he called upon his Lord in a low voice,
⁴. He said, "My Lord! certainly my bones are weakened and my head flares with hoariness, and, my Lord! I have never been unsuccessful in my prayer to You:
⁵. And certainly I fear my cousins after me, and my wife is barren, therefore grant me from Yourself an heir,
⁶. Who should inherit me and inherit from the children of Jacob, and make him, my Lord, one in whom You are well pleased.
⁷. Oh Zacharia! certainly We give you good news of a boy whose name shall be Jehovah: We have not made before anyone his equal.
⁸. He said, "Oh my Lord! when shall I have a son, and my wife is barren, and I myself have reached indeed the extreme degree of old age?
⁹. He said, "So shall it be, your Lord says: It is easy to Me, and indeed I created you before, when you were nothing.
¹⁰. He said, "My Lord! give me a sign. He said, "Your sign is that you will not be able to speak to the people three nights while in sound health.
¹¹. So he went forth to his people from his place of worship, then he made known to them that they should glorify God morning and evening.
¹². Oh Jehovah! take hold of the Book with strength, and We granted him wisdom while yet a child
¹³. And tenderness from Us and purity, and he was one who guarded against evil,
¹⁴. And dutiful to his parents, and he was not insolent, disobedient.
¹⁵. And peace on him on the day he was born, and on the day he dies, and on the day he is raised to life
¹⁶. And mention Mary in the Book when she drew aside from her family to an eastern place;
¹⁷. So she took a veil to screen herself from them; then We sent to her Our spirit, and there appeared to her a well-made man.
¹⁸. She said, "Certainly I fly for refuge from you to the Kind God, if you are one guarding against evil.
¹⁹. He said, "I am only a messenger of your Lord: That I will give you a pure boy.
²⁰. She said, "When shall I have a boy and no mortal has yet touched me, nor have I been sinful?
²¹. He said, "Even so; your Lord says: It is easy to Me: and that We may make him a sign to men and a mercy from Us, and it is a matter which has been decreed.
²². So she conceived him; then withdrew herself with him to a remote place.
²³. And the throes of childbirth compelled her to betake herself to the trunk of a palm tree. She said, "Oh, would that I had died before this, and had been a thing quite forgotten!
²⁴. Then the child called out to her from beneath her: Grieve not, certainly your Lord has made a stream to flow beneath you;
²⁵. And shake towards you the trunk of the palmtree, it will drop on you fresh ripe dates:
²⁶. So eat and drink and refresh the eye. Then if you see any mortal, say, "Certainly I have

vowed a fast to the Kind God, so I shall not speak to any man today.

27. And she came to her people with him, carrying him with her. They said, "Oh Mary! certainly you have done a strange thing.

28. Oh sister of Aaron! your father was not a bad man, nor, was your mother an unchaste woman.

29. But she pointed to him. They said, "How should we speak to one who was a child in the cradle?

30. He said, "Certainly I am a servant of God; He has given me the Book and made me a prophet;

31. And He has made me blessed wherever I may be, and He has enjoined on me prayer and poor-rate so long as I live;

32. And dutiful to my mother, and He has not made me insolent, unblessed;

33. And peace on me on the day I was born, and on the day I die, and on the day I am raised to life.

34. Such is Jesus, son of Mary; this is the saying of truth about which they dispute.

35. It does not seem to God that He should take to Himself a ! son, glory to be Him; when He has decreed a matter He only says to it "Be," and it is.

36. And certainly God is my Lord and your Lord, therefore serve Him; this is the right path.

37. But parties from among them disagreed with each other, so woe to those who disbelieve, because of presence on a great

38. How clearly shall they hear and how clearly shall they see on the day when they come to Us; but the unjust this day are in great error.

39. And warn them of the day of intense regret, when the matter shall have been decided; and they are now in negligence and they do not believe.

40. Certainly We inherit the earth and all those who are on it, and to Us they shall be returned.

41. And mention Abraham in the Book; certainly he was a truthful man, a prophet.

42. When he said to his father; Oh my father! why do you worship what neither hears nor sees, nor does it avail you in the least:

43. Oh my father! truly the knowledge has come to me which has not come to you, therefore follow me, I will guide you on a right path:

44. Oh my father! serve not the Satan, certainly the Satan is disobedient to the Kind God:

45. Oh my father! certainly I fear that a punishment from the Kind God should afflict you so that you should be a friend of the Satan.

46. He said, "Do you dislike my gods, Oh Abraham? If you do not desist I will certainly revile you, and leave me for a time.

47. He said, "Peace be on you, I will pray to my Lord to forgive you; certainly He is ever Affectionate to me:

48. And I will withdraw from you and what you call on besides God, and I will call upon my Lord; may be I shall not remain unblessed in calling upon my Lord.

49. So when he withdrew from them and what they worshiped besides God, We gave to him Isaac and Jacob, and each one of them We made a prophet.

50. And We granted to them of Our mercy, and We left behind them a truthful mention of eminence for them.

51. And mention Moses in the Book; certainly he was one purified, and he was an apostle, a prophet.

52. And We called to him from the blessed side of the mountain, and We made him draw near, holding communion with Us.

53. And We gave to him out of Our mercy his brother Aaron a prophet.

54. And mention Ishmael in the Book; certainly he was truthful in his promise, and he was an

apostle, a prophet.

55. And he enjoined on his family prayer and almsgiving, and was one in whom his Lord was well pleased.

56. And mention Idris in the Book; certainly he was a truthful man, a prophet,

57. And We raised him high in Heaven.

58. These are they on whom God bestowed favors, from among the prophets of the seed of Adam, and of those whom We carried with Noah, and of the seed of Abraham and Israel, and of those whom We guided and chose; when the words of the Kind God were recited to them, they fell down making homage and weeping.

59. But there came after them an evil generation, who neglected prayers and followed and sensual desires, so they win meet hell,

60. Except such as repent and believe and do good, these shall enter the garden, and they shall not be dealt with unjustly in any way:

61. The gardens of perpetuity which the Kind God has promised to His servants while unseen; certainly His promise shall come to pass.

62. They shall not hear therein any vain discourse, but only: Peace, and they shall have their sustenance therein morning and evening.

63. This is the garden which We cause those of Our servants to inherit who guard against evil.

64. And we do not descend but by the command of your Lord; to Him belongs whatever is before us and whatever is behind us and whatever is between these, and your Lord is not forgetful.

65. The Lord of the heavens and the earth and what is between them, so serve Him and be patient in His service. Do you know any one equal to Him?

66. And says man: What! when I am dead shall I truly be brought forth alive?

67. Does not man remember that We created him before, when he was nothing?

68. So by your Lord! We will most certainly gather them together and the Satans, then shall We certainly cause them to be present round hell on their knees.

69. Then We will most certainly draw forth from every sect of them him who is most exorbitantly rebellious against the Kind God.

70. Again We do certainly know best those who deserve most to be burned therein.

71. And there is not one of you but shall come to it; this is an unavoidable decree of your Lord.

72. And We will deliver those who guarded against evil, and We will leave the unjust therein on their knees.

73. And when Our clear words are recited to them, those who disbelieve say to those who believe: Which of the two parties is best in abiding and best in assembly?

74. And how many of the generations have We destroyed before them who were better in respect of goods and outward appearance!

75. Say, "As for him who remains in error, the Kind God will certainly prolong his length of days, until they see what they were threatened with, either the punishment or the hour; then they shall know who is in more evil plight and weaker in forces

76. And God increases in guidance those who go aright; and ever-abiding good works are with your Lord best in compensation and best in yielding fruit.

77. Have you, then, seen him who disbelieves in Our words and says: I shall certainly be given wealth and children?

78. Has he gained knowledge of the unseen, or made a covenant with the Kind God?

79. By no means! We write down what he says, and We will lengthen to him the length of the punishment

80. And We will inherit of him what he says, and he shall come to Us alone.

81. And they have taken gods besides God, that they should be to them a source of strength;
82. By no means! They shall soon deny their worshiping them, and they shall be adversaries to them.
83. Do you not see that We have sent the Satans against the unbelievers, inciting them by incitement?
84. Therefore do not be in haste against them, We only number out to them a number of days.
85. The day on which We will gather those who guard against evil to the Kind God to receive honors
86. And We will drive the guilty to hell thirsty
87. They shall not control intercession, save he who has made a covenant with the Kind God.
88. And they say, "The Kind God has taken to Himself a son.
89. Certainly you have made an abominable assertion
90. The heavens may almost be rent thereat, and the earth cleave asunder, and the mountains fall down in pieces,
91. That they ascribe a son to the Kind God.
92. And it is not worthy of the Kind God that He should take to Himself a son.
93. There is no one in the heavens and the earth but will come to the Kind God as a servant.
94. Certainly He has a comprehensive knowledge of them and He has numbered them a comprehensive numbering.
95. And every one of them will come to Him on the day of resurrection alone.
96. Certainly as for those who believe and do good deeds for t them will God bring about love.
97. So We have only made it easy in your tongue that you may give good news thereby to those who guard against evil and warn thereby a vehemently contentious people.
98. And how many a generation have We destroyed before them! Do you see any one of them or hear a sound of them?

Chapter 20 — Ta Ha — Ta Ha

In the name of God, the Kind, the Merciful.

1. Ta Ha.
2. We have not revealed the Koran to you that you may be unsuccessful.
3. No, it is a reminder to him who fears:
4. A revelation from Him Who created the earth and the high heavens.
5. The Kind God is firm in power.
6. His is what is in the heavens and what is in the earth and what is between them two and what is beneath the ground.
7. And if you utter the saying aloud, then certainly He knows the secret, and what is yet more hidden.
8. God -- there is no god but He; His are the very best names.
9. And has the story of Moses come to you?
10. When he saw fire, he said to his family: Stop, for certainly I see a fire, haply I may bring to you therefrom a live coal or find a guidance at the fire.
11. So when he came to it, a voice was uttered, "Oh Moses. 12. Certainly I am your Lord, therefore put off your shoes; certainly you are in the sacred valley, Tuwa, 13. And I have chosen you, so listen to what is revealed: 14. Certainly I am God, there is no god but 1, therefore serve Me and keep up prayer for My remembrance: 15. Certainly the hour is coming -- I am about to make it clear -- so that every soul may be rewarded as it strives: 16. Therefore let not him who believes not in it and follows his low desires turn you away from it so that you should perish; 17. And what is this in your right hand, Oh Moses!"
18. He said, "This is my staff: I recline on it and I beat the leaves with it to make them fall upon my sheep, and I have other uses for it."
19. He said, "Cast it down, "Oh Moses!"
20. So he cast it down; and lo! it was a serpent running.
21. He said, "Take hold of it and fear not; We will restore it to its former state "
22. And press your hand to your side, it shall come out white without evil: another sign:
23. That We may show you of Our greater signs
24. Go to Pharoah, certainly he has exceeded all limits.
25. He said, "Oh my Lord! Expand my heart for me, 26. And make my affair easy to me, 27. And loose the knot from my tongue, 28. That they may understand my word; 29. And give to me an aider from my family: 30. Aaron, my brother, 31. Strengthen my back by him, 32. And associate him with me in my affair, 33. So that we should glorify You much, 34. And remember You oft. 35. Certainly, You are seeing us."
36. He said, "You are indeed granted your petition, Oh Moses
37. And certainly We bestowed on you a favor at another time;
38. When We revealed to your mother what was revealed;
39. Saying, "Put him into a chest, then cast it down into the river, then the river shall throw him on the shore; there shall take him up one who is an enemy to Me and enemy to him, and I cast down upon you love from Me, and that you might be brought up before My eyes;
40. When your sister went and said, "Shall I direct you to one who will take charge of him? So We brought you back to your mother, that her eye might be cooled and she should not

grieve and you killed a man, then We delivered you from the grief, and We tried you with a severe trying. Then you stayed for years among the people of Madyan; then you came hither as ordered, Oh Moses.

41. And I have chosen you for Myself"

42. "Go you and your brother with My words and do not be careless in remembering Me; 43. Go both to Pharoah, certainly he has become inordinate; 44. Then speak to him a gentle word haply he may mind or fear.

45. Both said, "Oh our Lord! Certainly we fear that he may hurry to do evil to us or that he may become inordinate.

46. He said, "Fear not, certainly I am with you both: I do hear and see.

47. So go you both to him and say, "Certainly we are two apostles of your Lord; therefore send the children of Israel with us and do not torment them! Indeed we have brought to you a word from your Lord, and peace is on him who follows the guidance;

48. Certainly it has been revealed to us that the punishment will certainly come upon him who rejects and turns back.

49. Pharoah said, "And who is your Lord, Oh Moses?

50. He said, "Our Lord is He Who gave to everything its creation, then guided it to its goal.

51. He said, "Then what is the state of the former generations?

52. He said, "The knowledge thereof is with my Lord in a book, my Lord errs not, nor does He forget;

53. Who made the earth for you an expanse and made for you therein paths and sent down water from the cloud; then thereby We have brought forth many species of various herbs.

54. Eat and pasture your cattle; most certainly there are signs in this for those endowed with understanding.

55. From it We created you and into it We shall send you back and from it will We raise you a second time.

56. And truly We showed him Our signs, all of them, but he rejected and refused.

57. Said he, "Have you come to us that you should turn us out of our land by your magic, Oh Moses?

58. So we too will produce before you magic like it, therefore make between us and you an appointment, which we should not break, neither we nor you, in a central place.

59. Moses said, "Your appointment is the day of the Festival and let the people be gathered together in the early forenoon."

60. So Pharoah turned his back and settled his plan, then came.

61. Moses said to them, "Woe to you! do not forge a lie against God, on case He would destroy you with a punishment, and he who forges a lie certainly fails to attain his desire."

62. So they disputed with one another about their affair and kept the discourse secret.

63. They said, "These are most certainly two magicians who wish to turn you out from your land by their magic and to take away your best traditions.

64. Therefore settle your plan, then come standing in ranks and he will prosper indeed this day who overcomes.

65. They said, "Oh Moses! will you cast, or shall we be the first who cast down?

66. He said, "No! cast down. then lo! their cords and their rods -- it was imaged to him on account of their magic as if they were running.

67. So Moses conceived in his mind a fear.

68. We said, "Fear not, certainly you shall be the uppermost,

69. And cast down what is in your right hand; it shall devour what they have wrought; they

have wrought only the plan of a magician, and the magician shall not be successful wheresoever he may come from.

70. And the magicians were cast down making obeisance; they said, "We believe in the Lord of Aaron and Moses."

71. Pharoah said, "You believe in him before I give you leave; most certainly he is the chief of you who taught you sorcery, therefore I will certainly cut off your hands and your feet on opposite sides, and I will certainly crucify you on the trunks of the palm trees, and certainly you will come to know which of us is the more severe and the more abiding in chastising.

72. They said, "We do not prefer you to what has come to us of clear explanations and to He Who made us, therefore decide what you are going to decide; you can only decide about this world's life.

73. Certainly we believe in our Lord that He may forgive us our sins and the magic to which you compelled us; and God is better and more abiding.

74. Whoever comes to his Lord being guilty, for him is certainly hell; he shall not die therein, nor shall he live.

75. And whoever comes to Him a believer and he has done good deeds indeed, these it is who shall have the high ranks,

76. The gardens of perpetuity, beneath which rivers flow, to abide therein; and this is the reward of him who has purified himself.

77. And certainly We revealed to Moses, saying, "Travel by night with My servants, then make for them a dry path in the sea, not fearing to be overtaken, nor being afraid.

78. And Pharoah followed them with his armies, so there came upon them of the sea that which came upon them.

79. And Pharoah led astray his people and he did not guide them aright.

80. Oh children of Israel! indeed We delivered you from your enemy, and We made a covenant with you on the blessed side of the mountain, and We sent to you the manna and the quails.

81. Eat of the good things We have given you for sustenance, and do not be inordinate with respect to them, so that My wrath should be due to you, and to whomsoever My wrath is due be shall perish indeed.

82. And most certainly I am most Forgiving to him who repents and believes and does good, then continues to follow the right direction.

83. And what caused you to hasten from your people, Oh Moses?

84. He said, "They are here because of me and I hurried to You, my Lord, so that You might be pleased.

85. He said, "So certainly We have tried your people after you, and the Samiri has led them astray.

86. So Moses returned to his people wrathful, sorrowing. Said he, "Oh my people! did not your Lord give you a fine promise: did then the time seem long to you, or did you wish that displeasure from your Lord should be due to you, so that you broke your promise to me?"

87. They said, "We did not break our promise to you of our own accord, but we were made to bear the burdens of the ornaments of the people, then we made a casting of them, and thus did the Samiri suggest."

88. So he brought forth for them a calf, a mere body, which had a mooing sound, so they said, "This is your god and the god of Moses," but he forgot.

89. What! could they not see that it did not return to them a reply, and that it did not control any harm or benefit for them?

90. And certainly Aaron had said to them before, "Oh my people! you are only tried by it, and certainly your Lord is the Kind God, therefore follow me and obey my order."

91. They said, "We will by no means cease to keep to its worship until Moses returns to us.
92. Moses said, "Oh Aaron! what prevented you, when you saw them going astray,
93. So that you did not follow me? Did you then disobey my order?
94. He said, "Oh son of my mother! seize me not by my beard nor by my head; certainly I was afraid that you should say, "You have caused a division among the children of Israel and not waited for my word.
95. He said, "What was then your object, Oh Samiri?
96. He said, "I saw Gabriel what they did not see, so I took a handful of the dust from the footsteps of the messenger, then I threw it in the casting; thus did my soul commend to me
97. He said, "Begone then, certainly for you it will be in this life to say, Touch me not; and certainly there is a threat for you, which shall not be made to fail to you, and look at your god to whose worship you kept so long; we will certainly burn it, then we will certainly scatter it a wide scattering in the sea.
98. Your God is only God, there is no god but He; He comprehends all things in His knowledge.
99. Thus do We relate to you some of the news of what has gone before; and indeed We have given to you a Reminder from Ourselves.
100. Whoever turns aside from it, he shall certainly bear a burden on the day of resurrection
101. Abiding in this state, and evil will it be for them to bear on the day of resurrection;
102. On the day when the trumpet shall be blown, and We will gather the guilty, blue-eyed, on that day
103. They shall consult together secretly: You did tarry but ten centuries.
104. We know best what they say, when the fairest of them in course would say, "You tarried but a day.
105. And they ask you about the mountains. Say, "My Lord will carry them away from the roots.
106. Then leave it a plain, smooth level
107. You shall not see therein any crookedness or unevenness.
108. On that day they shall follow the inviter, there is no crookedness in him, and the voices shall be low before the Kind God so that you shall not hear anything but a soft sound.
109. On that day shall no intercession avail except of him whom the Kind God allows and whose word He is pleased with.
110. He knows what is before them and what is behind them, while they do not comprehend it in knowledge.
111. And the faces shall be humbled before the Living, the Self-subsistent God, and he who bears iniquity is indeed a failure.
112. And whoever does good works and he is a believer, he shall have no fear of injustice nor of the withholding of his due.
113. And thus have We sent it down an Arabic Koran, and have distinctly set forth therein of threats that they may guard against evil or that it may produce a reminder for them.
114. Supremely exalted is therefore God, the King, the Truth, and do not make haste with the Koran before its revelation is made complete to you and say, "Oh my Lord ! increase me in knowledge.
115. And certainly We gave a commandment to Adam before, but he forgot; and We did not find in him any determination.
116. And when We said to the angels: Make obeisance to Adam, they made obeisance, but Iblis did it not; he refused.
117. So We said, "Oh Adam! This is an enemy to you and to your wife; therefore let him not drive you both forth from the garden so that you should be unhappy;

118. Certainly it is ordered for you that you shall not be hungry therein nor bare of clothing;

119. And that you shall not be thirsty therein nor shall you feel the heat of the sun.

120. But the Satan made an evil suggestion to him; he said, "Oh Adam! Shall I guide you to the tree of immortality and a kingdom which decays not?

121. Then they both ate of it, so their evil inclinations became clear to them, and they both began to cover themselves with leaves of the garden, and Adam disobeyed his Lord, so his life became evil to him.

122. Then his Lord chose him, so He turned to him and guided him.

123. He said, "Get forth you two therefrom, all of you, one of you is enemy to another. So there will certainly come to you guidance from Me, then whoever follows My guidance, he shall not go astray nor be unhappy;

124. And whoever turns away from My reminder, his shall be a straightened life, and We will raise him on the day of resurrection, blind.

125. He shall say, "My Lord! why have You raised me blind and I was made to see, indeed?

126. He will say, "Even so, Our words came to you but you neglected them; even thus shall you be abandoned this day.

127. And thus do We repay him who is extravagant and does not believe in the words of his Lord, and certainly the punishment of the hereafter is severer and more

128. Does it not then direct them aright how many of the generations In whose dwelling-places they go about We destroyed before them? Most certainly there are signs in this for those endowed with understanding.

129. And had there not been a word that had already gone forth from your Lord and an appointed term, it would certainly have been made to cleave to them.

130. Bear then patiently what they say, and glorify your Lord by the praising of Him before the rising of the sun and before its setting, and during hours of the night do also glorify Him and during parts of the day, that you may be well pleased

131. And do not stretch your eyes after that with which We have provided different classes of them, of the splendor of this world's life, that We may thereby try them; and the sustenance given by your Lord is better and more abiding.

132. And enjoin prayer on your followers, and steadily adhere to it; We do not ask you for subsistence; We do give you subsistence, and the good end is for guarding against evil.

133. And they say, "Why does he not bring to us a sign from his Lord? Has not there come to them a clear evidence of what is in the previous books?

134. And had We destroyed them with punishment before this, they would certainly have said, "Oh our Lord! why did You not send us an apostle, for then we would have followed Your words before we met disgrace and shame.

135. Say, "Every one of us is awaiting, therefore do await: So you will come to know who is the follower of the even path and who goes aright.

Chapter 21 — Al-Anbiya — The Prophets

In the name of God, the Kind, the Merciful.

1. Their judging has drawn near to men, and in heedlessness are they turning aside.
2. There comes not to them a new reminder from their Lord but they hear it while they sport,
3. Their hearts trifling; and those who are unjust counsel together in secret: He is nothing but a mortal like yourselves; what! will you then yield to sorcery while you see?
4. He said, "My Lord knows what is spoken in the heaven and the earth, and He is the Hearing, the Knowing."
5. "No!" say they, "Medleys of dreams; no! he has created it; no! he is a poet; so let him bring to us a sign as the former prophets were sent with."
6. There did not believe before them any town which We destroyed, will they then believe? 7. And We did not send before you any but men to whom We sent revelation, so ask the followers of the reminder if you do not 8. And We did not make them bodies not eating the food, and they were not to abide forever. 9. Then We made Our promise good to them, so We delivered them and those whom We pleased, and We destroyed the ex 10. Certainly We have revealed to you a Book in which is your good remembrance; what! do you not then understand?"
11. "And how many a town which was iniquitous did We demolish, and We raised up after it another people!
12. So when they felt Our punishment, lo! they began to fly
13. Do not fly now and come back to what you were made to lead easy lives in and to your dwellings, haply you will be questioned.
14. They said, "Oh woe to us! certainly we were unjust.
15. And this ceased not to be their cry till We made them cut
16. And We did not create the heaven and the earth and what is between them for sport.
17. Had We wished to make a diversion, We would have made it from before Ourselves: by no means would We do it.
18. No! We cast the truth against the falsehood, so that it breaks its head, and lo! it vanishes; and woe to you for what you describe;
19. And whoever is in the heavens and the earth is His; and those who are with Him are not proud to serve Him, nor do they grow weary.
20. They glorify Him by night and day; they are never languid.
21. Or have they taken gods from the earth who raise the dead.
22. If there had been in them any gods except God, they would both have certainly been in a state of disorder; therefore glory be to God, the Lord of the dominion, above what they attribute to Him.
23. He cannot be questioned concerning what He does and they shall be questioned.
24. Or, have they taken gods besides Him? Say, "Bring your proof; this is the reminder of those with me and the reminder of those before me. No! most of them do not know the truth, so they turn aside.
25. And We did not send before you any apostle but We revealed to him that there is no god but Me, therefore serve Me.
26. And they say, "The Kind God has taken to Himself a ! son. Glory be to Him. No! they are honored servants

27. They do not precede Him in speech and only according to His commandment do they act.

28. He knows what is before them and what is behind them, and they do not intercede except for him whom He approves and for fear of Him they tremble.

29. And whoever of them should say, "Certainly I am a god besides Him, such a one do We punish with hell; thus do, We punish the unjust.

30. Do not those who disbelieve see that the heavens and the earth were closed up, but We have opened them; and We have made of water everything living, will they not then believe?

31. And We have made great mountains in the earth so that it might be trembled by them, and We have made in it wide ways that they may follow a right direction.

32. And We have made the heaven a guarded canopy and yet they turn aside from its signs.

33. And He it is Who created the night and the day and the sun and the moon; all orbs travel along swiftly in their celestial spheres.

34. And We did not ordain abiding for any mortal before you. What! Then if you die, will they abide?

35. Every soul must taste of death and We try you by evil and good by way of probation; and to Us you shall be brought back.

36. And when those who disbelieve see you, they do not take you but for one to be scoffed at: Is this he who speaks of your gods? And they are deniers at the mention of the Kind God.

37. Man is created of haste; now will I show to you My signs, therefore do not ask Me to hasten them on.

38. And they say, "When will this threat come to pass if you are truthful?

39. Had those who disbelieve but known of the time when they shall not be able to ward off the fire from their faces nor from their backs, nor shall they be helped.

40. No, it shall come on them all of a sudden and cause them to become confounded, so they shall not have the power to avert it, nor shall they be respited.

41. And certainly apostles before you were scoffed at, then thaose who scoffed were now scoffed thamselves.

42. Say, "Who guards you by night and by day from the Kind God? No, they turn aside at the mention of their Lord.

43. Or, have they gods who can defend them against Us? They shall not be able to assist themselves, nor shall they be defended from Us.

44. No, We gave provision to these and their fathers until life was prolonged to them. Do they not then see that We are visiting the land, curtailing it of its sides? Shall they then prevail?

45. Say, "I warn you only by revelation; and the deaf do not hear the call whenever they are warned.

46. And if a blast of the punishment of your Lord were to touch them, they will certainly say, "Oh woe to us! certainly we were unjust.

47. And We will set up a just balance on the day of resurrection, so no soul shall be dealt with unjustly in the least; and though there be the weight of a grain of mustard seed, yet will We bring it, and sufficient are We to take account.

48. And certainly We gave to Moses and Aaron the Furqan and a light and a reminder for those who would guard against evil.

49. For those who fear their Lord in secret and they are fearful of the hour.

50. And this is a blessed Reminder which We have revealed; will you then deny it?

51. And certainly We gave to Abraham his rectitude before, and We knew him fully well.

52. When he said to his father and his people: What are these images to whose worship you cleave?

⁵³. They said, "We found our fathers worshiping them.
⁵⁴. He said, "Certainly you have been, both you and your fathers, in great error.
⁵⁵. They said, "Have you brought to us the truth, or are you one of the triflers?
⁵⁶. He said, "No! your Lord is the Lord of the heavens and the earth, Who brought them into existence, and I am of those who bear witness to this:
⁵⁷. And, by God! I will certainly do something against your idols after you go away, turning back.
⁵⁸. So he broke them into pieces, except the chief of them, that haply they may return to it.
⁵⁹. They said, "Who has done this to our gods? Most certainly he is one of the unjust.
⁶⁰. They said, "We heard a youth called Abraham speak of them.
⁶¹. Said they: Then bring him before the eyes of the people, perhaps they may bear witness.
⁶². They said, "Have you done this to our gods, Oh Abraham?
⁶³. He said, "Certainly some doer has done it; the chief of them is this, therefore ask them, if they can speak.
⁶⁴. Then they turned to themselves and said, "Certainly you yourselves are the unjust;
⁶⁵. Then they were made to hang down their heads: Certainly you know that they do not speak.
⁶⁶. He said, "What! do you then serve besides God what brings you not any benefit at all, nor does it harm you?
⁶⁷. Fie on you and on what you serve besides God; what! do you not then understand?
⁶⁸. They said, "Burn him and help your gods, if you are going to do anything.
⁶⁹. We said, "Oh fire! be a comfort and peace to Abraham;
⁷⁰. And they desired a war on him, but We made them the greatest losers.
⁷¹. And We delivered him as well as Lot removing them to the land which We had blessed for all people.
⁷². And We gave him Isaac and Jacob, a son's son, and We made them all good.
⁷³. And We made them Imams who guided people by Our command, and We revealed to them the doing of good and the keeping up of prayer and the giving of the alms, and they did serve Us alone;
⁷⁴. And as for Lot, We gave him wisdom and knowledge, and We delivered him from the town which wrought abominations; certainly they were an evil people, transgressors;
⁷⁵. And We took him into Our mercy; certainly he was of the good.
⁷⁶. And Noah, when he cried aforetime, so We answered him, and delivered him and his followers from the great calamity.
⁷⁷. And We helped him against the people who rejected Our words; certainly they were an evil people, so We drowned them all.
⁷⁸. And David and Solomon when they gave judgment concerning the field when the people's sheep pastured therein by night, and We were bearers of witness to their judgment.
⁷⁹. So We made Solomon to understand it; and to each one We gave wisdom and knowledge; and We made the mountains, and the birds to celebrate Our praise with David; and We were the doers.
⁸⁰. And We taught him the making of coats of mail for you, that they might protect you in your wars; will you then be grateful?
⁸¹. And We made subservient to Solomon the wind blowing violent, pursuing its course by his command to the land which We had blessed, and We are knower of ail things.
⁸². And of the rebellious people there were those who dived for him and did other work besides that, and We kept guard over them;
⁸³. And Ayub, when he cried to his Lord, saying, "Harm has afflicted me, and You are the most Merciful of the merciful.

84. Therefore We responded to him and took off what harm he had, and We gave him his family and the like of them with them: a mercy from Us and a reminder to the worshipers.
85. And Ishmael and Idris and Zulkifl; all were of the patient ones;
86. And We caused them to enter into Our mercy, certainly they were of the good ones.
87. And Yunus, when he went away in wrath, so he thought that We would not correct him, so he called out among afflictions: There is no god but You, glory be to You; certainly I am of those who make themselves to suffer loss.
88. So We responded to him and delivered him from the grief and thus do We deliver the believers.
89. And Zacharia, when he cried to his Lord: Oh my Lord leave me not alone; and You are the best of inheritors.
90. So We responded to him and gave him Jehovah and made his wife fit for him; certainly they used to hasten, one with another In deeds of goodness and to call upon Us, hoping and fearing and they were humble before Us.
91. And she who guarded her chastity, so We breathed into her of Our inspiration and made her and her son a sign for the nations.
92. Certainly this Islam is your religion, one religion only, and I am your Lord, therefore serve Me.
93. And they broke their religion into sects between them: to Us shall all come back.
94. Therefore whoever shall do of good deeds and he is a believer, there shall be no denying of his exertion, and certainly We will write It down for him.
95. And it is binding on a town which We destroy that they shall not return.
96. Even when Gog and Magog are let loose and they shall break forth from every elevated place.
97. And the true promise shall draw near, then lo! the eyes of those who disbelieved shall be fixedly open: Oh woe to us! certainly we were in a state of heedlessness as to this; no, we were unjust.
98. Certainly you and what you worship besides God are the firewood of hell; to it you shall come.
99. Had these been gods, they would not have come to it and all shall abide therein.
100. For them therein shall be groaning and therein they shall not hear.
101. Certainly as for those for whom the good has already gone forth from Us, they shall be kept far off from it;
102. They will not hear its faintest sound, and they shall abide in that which their souls long for.
103. The great fearful event shall not grieve them, and the angels shall meet them: This is your day which you were promised.
104. On the day when We will roll up heaven like the rolling up of the scroll for writings, as We originated the first creation, so We shall reproduce it; a promise binding on Us; certainly We will bring it about.
105. And certainly We wrote in the Book after the reminder that as for the land, My righteous servants shall inherit it.
106. Most certainly in this is a message to a people who serve
107. And We have hot sent you but as a mercy to the worlds.
108. Say, "It is only revealed to me that your God is one God; will you then submit?
109. But if they turn back, say, "I have given you warning in fairness and I do not know whether what you are threatened with is near or far:
110. Certainly He knows what is spoken openly and He knows what you hide:
111. And I do not know if this may be a trial for you and a provision till a time.
112. He said, "Oh my Lord! judge You with truth; and our Lord is the Kind God, Whose help is sought against what you ascribe to Him.

Chapter 22 — Al-Hajj — The Pilgrimage

In the name of God, the Kind, the Merciful.

¹. Oh people! guard against the punishment from your Lord; certainly the violence of the hour is a grievous thing.

². On the day when you shall see it, every woman giving suck shall quit in confusion what she suckled, and every pregnant woman shall lay down her burden, and you shall see men intoxicated, and they shall not be intoxicated but the punishment of God will be severe.

³. And among men there is he who disputes about God without knowledge and follows every rebellious Satan;

⁴. Against him it is written down that whoever takes him for a friend, he shall lead him astray and conduct him to the punishment of the burning fire.

⁵. Oh people! if you are in doubt about the raising, then certainly We created you from dust, then from a small seed, then from a clot, then from a lump of flesh, complete in make and incomplete, that We may make clear to you; and We cause what We please to stay in the wombs till an appointed time, then We bring you forth as babies, then that you may attain your maturity; and of you is he who is caused to die, and of you is he who is brought back to the worst part of life, so that after having knowledge he does not know anything; and you see the earth sterile land, but when We send down on it the water, it stirs and swells and brings forth of every kind a beautiful herbage.

⁶. This is because God is the Truth and because He gives life to the dead and because He has power over all things

⁷. And because the hour is coming, there is no doubt about it; and because God shall raise up those who are in the graves.

⁸. And among men there is he who disputes about God without knowledge and without guidance and without an illuminating book,

⁹. Turning away arrogantly that he may lead others astray from the way of God; for him is disgrace in this world, and on the day of resurrection We will make him taste the punishment of burning:

¹⁰. This is due to what your two hands have sent before, and because God is not in the least unjust to the servants.

¹¹. And among men is he who serves God standing on the verge, so that if good happens to him he is satisfied therewith, but if a trial afflict him he turns back headlong; he loses this world as well as the hereafter; that is a great loss.

¹². He calls besides God upon that which does not harm him and that which does not profit him, that is the great straying.

¹³. He calls upon him whose harm is nearer than his profit; evil certainly is the guardian and evil certainly is the associate.

¹⁴. Certainly God will cause those who believe and do good deeds to enter gardens beneath which rivers flow, certainly God does what He pleases.

¹⁵. Whoever thinks that God will not assist him in this life and the hereafter, let him stretch a rope to the ceiling, then let him cut it off, then let him see if his struggle will take away that at which he is enraged.

¹⁶. And thus have We revealed it, being clear explanations, and because God guides whom

He intends.

17. Certainly those who believe and those who are Jews and the Sabeans and the Christians and the Magians and those who associate others with God -- certainly God will decide between them on the day of resurrection; certainly God is a witness over all things.

18. Do you not see that God is He, Whom obeys whoever is in the heavens and whoever is in the earth, and the sun and the moon and the stars, and the mountains and the trees, and the animals and many of the people; and many there are against whom punishment has become necessary; and whomsoever God abases, there is none who can make him honorable; certainly God does what He pleases.

19. These are two adversaries who dispute about their Lord; then as to those who disbelieve, for them are cut out garments of fire, boiling water shall be poured over their heads.

20. With it shall be melted what is in their bellies and their skins as well.

21. And for them are whips of iron.

22. Whenever they will desire to go forth from it, from grief, they shall be turned back into it, and taste the punishment of burning.

23. Certainly God will make those who believe and do good deeds enter gardens beneath which rivers flow; they shall be adorned therein with bracelets of gold and with pearls, and their garments therein shall be of silk.

24. And they are guided to proper words and they are guided into the path of the Praised One.

25. Certainly as for those who disbelieve, and hinder men from God's way and from the Sacred Mosque which We have made equally for all men, for the dweller therein and for the visitor, and whoever shall incline therein to wrong unjustly, We will make him taste of a painful punishment.

26. And when We assigned to Abraham the place of the House, saying, "Do not associate anything with Me, and purify My House for those who make the circuit and stand to pray and bow and prostrate themselves.

27. And proclaim among men the Pilgrimage: they will come to you on foot and on every lean camel, coming from every remote path,

28. That they may witness advantages for them and mention the name of God during stated days over what He has given them of the cattle quadrupeds, then eat of them and feed the distressed one, the needy.

29. Then let them accomplish their needful acts of shaving and cleansing, and let them fulfil their vows and let them go round the Ancient House.

30. That shall be so; and whoever respects the sacred ordinances of God, it is better for him with his Lord; and the cattle are made lawful for you, except that which is recited to you, therefore avoid the uncleanness of the idols and avoid false words,

31. Being upright for God, not comparing anything with Him and whoever compares others with God, it is as though he had fallen from on high, then the birds snatch him away or the wind carries him off to a far-distant place.

32. That shall be so; and whoever respects the signs of God, this certainly is the outcome of the piety of hearts.

33. You have advantages in them till a fixed time, then their place of sacrifice is the Ancient House.

34. And to every nation We appointed acts of devotion that they may mention the name of God on what He has given them of the cattle quadrupeds; so your God is One God, therefore to Him should you submit, and give good news to the humble,

35. To those whose hearts tremble when God is mentioned, and those who are patient under that which afflicts them, and those who keep up prayer, and spend benevolently out of what We have given them.

36. And as for the camels, We have made them of the signs of the religion of God for you; for you therein is much good; therefore mention the name of God on them as they stand in a row, then when they fall down eat of them and feed the poor man who is contented and the beggar; thus have We made them subservient to you, that you may be grateful.

37. There does not reach God their flesh nor their blood, but to Him is acceptable the guarding against evil on your part; thus has He made them subservient to you, that you may magnify God because He has guided you aright; and give good news to those who do good to others.

38. Certainly God will defend those who believe; certainly God does not love any one who is unfaithful, ungrateful.

39. Permission to fight is given to those upon whom war is made because they are oppressed, and most certainly God is well able to assist them;

40. Those who have been expelled from their homes without a just cause except that they say, "Our Lord is God. And had there not been God's repelling some people by others, certainly there would have been pulled down cloisters and churches and synagogues and mosques in which God's name is much remembered; and certainly God will help him who helps His cause; most certainly God is Strong, Mighty.

41. Those who, should We establish them in the land, will keep up prayer and pay the poor-rate and enjoin good and forbid evil; and God's is the end of affairs.

42. And if they reject you, then already before you did the people of Noah and Ad and Samood reject prophets.

43. And the people of Abraham and the people of Lot,

44. As well as those of Madyan and Moses too was rejected, but I gave respite to the unbelievers, then did I overtake them, so how severe was My disapproval.

45. So how many a town did We destroy while it was unjust, so it was fallen down upon its roofs, and how many a deserted well and palace raised high.

46. Have they not travelled in the land so that they should have hearts with which to understand, or ears with which to hear? For certainly it is not the eyes that are blind, but blind are the hearts which are in the breasts.

47. And they ask you to hasten on the punishment, and God will by no means fail in His promise, and certainly a day with your Lord is as a thousand years of what you number.

48. And how many a town to which I gave respite while it was unjust, then I overtook it, and to Me is the return.

49. Say, "Oh people! I am only a plain alarmgiver to you.

50. Then as for those who believe and do good, they shall have forgiveness and an honorable sustenance.

51. And as for those who strive to oppose Our words, they shall be the inmates of the flaming fire.

52. And We did not send before you any apostle or prophet, but when he desired, the Satan made a suggestion respecting his desire; but God annuls that which the Satan casts, then does God establish His words, and God is Knowing, Wise,

53. So that He may make what the Satan casts a trial for those in whose hearts is disease and those whose hearts are hard; and most certainly the unjust are in a great opposition,

54. And that those who have been given the knowledge may know that it is the truth from your Lord, so they may believe in it and their hearts may be lowly before it; and most certainly God is the Guide of those who believe into a right path.

55. And those who disbelieve shall not cease to be in doubt concerning it until the hour overtakes them suddenly, or there comes on them the punishment of a destructive day.

56. The kingdom on that day shall be God's; He will judge between them; so those who believe

and do good will be in gardens of bliss.

57. And as for those who disbelieve in and reject Our words, these it is who shall have a disgraceful punishment.

58. And as for those who fly in God's way and are then slain or die, God will most certainly grant them a fine provisions, and most certainly God is the best Giver of sustenance.

59. He will certainly cause them to enter a place of entrance which they shall be well pleased with, and most certainly God is Knowing, Forbearing.

60. That shall be so; and he who retaliates with the like of that with which he has been afflicted and he has been oppressed, God will most certainly aid him; most certainly God is Pardoning, Forgiving.

61. That is because God causes the night to enter into the day and causes the day to enter into the night, and because God is Hearing, Seeing.

62. That is because God is the Truth, and that what they call upon besides Him -- that is the falsehood, and because God is the High, the Great.

63. Do you not see that God sends down water from the cloud so the earth becomes green? Certainly God is Benignant, Aware.

64. His is whatsoever is in the heavens and whatsoever is in the earth; and most certainly God is the Self-sufficient, the Praised.

65. Do you not see that God has made subservient to you whatsoever is in the earth and the ships running in the sea by His command? And He withholds the heaven from falling on the earth except with His permission; most certainly God is Compassionate, Merciful to men.

66. And He it is Who has brought you to life, then He will cause you to die, then bring you to life again; most certainly man is ungrateful.

67. To every nation We appointed acts of devotion which they observe, therefore they should not dispute with you about the matter and call to your Lord; most certainly you are on a right way.

68. And if they contend with you, say, "God knows best what you do.

69. God will judge between you on the day of resurrection respecting that in which you differ.

70. Do you not know that God knows what is in the heaven and the earth? Certainly this is in a book; certainly this is easy to God.

71. And they serve besides God that for which He has not sent any authority, and that of which they have no knowledge; and for the unjust there shall be no helper.

72. And when Our clear words are recited to them you will find denial on the faces of those who disbelieve; they almost spring upon those who recite to them Our words. Say, "Shall I inform you of what is worse than this? The fire; God has promised it to those who disbelieve; and how evil the resort!

73. Oh people! a story is set forth, therefore listen to it: certainly those whom you call upon besides God cannot create fly, though they should all gather for it, and should the fly snatch away anything from them, they could not take it back from i weak are the invoker and the invoked.

74. They have not estimated God with the estimation that i due to Him; most certainly God is Strong, Mighty.

75. God chooses messengers from among the angels and from among the men; certainly God is Hearing, Seeing.

76. He knows what is before them and what is behind them and to God are all affairs turned back.

77. Oh you who believe! bow down and prostrate yourselves and serve your Lord, and do good that you may succeed.

78. And strive hard in the way of God, such a striving a is due to Him; He has chosen you and has not laid upon you an hardship in religion; the faith of your father Abraham; He named you

Muslims before and in this, that the Prophet may be a bearer of witness to you, and you may be bearers of witness to the people; therefore keep up prayer and pay the poor-rate and hold fast by God; He is your Guardian; how excellent the Guardian and how excellent the Helper!

Chapter 23 — Al-Mu'minun — The Believers

In the name of God, the Kind, the Merciful.

1. Successful indeed are the believers,
2. Who are humble in their prayers,
3. And who keep apart from that which is vain, 4. And who are charitable, 5. And who guard their private parts,
6. Except before their mates or those whom their right hands possess, for they certainly are not to be blamed,
7. But whoever seeks to go beyond that, these are they that exceed the limits;
8. And those who are keepers of their trusts and their covenant,
9. And those who keep a guard on their prayers;
10. These are they who are the heirs,
11. Who shall inherit the Paradise; they shall abide therein.
12. And certainly We created man of an extract of clay,
13. Then We made him a small seed in a firm resting-place,
14. Then We made the seed a clot, then We made the clot a lump of flesh, then We made in the lump of flesh bones, then We clothed the bones with flesh, then We caused it to grow into another creation, so blessed be God, the best of the creators.
15. Then after that you will most certainly die.
16. Then certainly on the day of resurrection you shall be raised.
17. And certainly We made above you seven heavens; and never are We heedless of creation.
18. And We send down water from the cloud according to a measure, then We cause it to settle in the earth, and most certainly We are able to carry it away.
19. Then We cause to grow thereby gardens of palm trees and grapes for you; you have in them many fruits and from them do you eat;
20. And a tree that grows out of Mount Sinai which produces oil and a condiment for those who eat.
21. And most certainly there is a lesson for you in the cattle: We make you to drink of what is in their bellies, and you have in them many advantages and of them you eat,
22. And on them and on the ships you are borne.
23. And certainly We sent Noah to his people, and he said, "Oh my people! serve God, you have no god other than Him; will you not then guard against evil?"
24. And the chiefs of those who disbelieved from among his people said, "He is nothing but a mortal like yourselves who desires that he may have superiority over you, and if God had pleased, He could certainly have sent down angels. We have not heard of this among our fathers of yore:
25. He is only a madman, so bear with him for a time.
26. He said, "Oh my Lord! help me against their calling me a liar."
27. So We revealed to him, saying, "Make the ark before Our eyes and according to Our revelation; and when Our command is given and the valley overflows, take into it of every kind a pair, two, and your followers, except those among them against whom the word has gone forth, and do not speak to Me in respect of those who are unjust; certainly they shall be drowned.

28. And when you are firmly seated, you and those with you, in the ark, say, "All praise is due to God who delivered us from the unjust people:
29. And say, "Oh my Lord! cause me to disembark a blessed alighting, and You are the best to cause to alight.
30. Most certainly there are signs in this, and most certainly We are ever testing men.
31. Then We raised up after them another generation.
32. So We sent among them an apostle from among them, saying, "Serve God, you have no god other than Him; will you not then guard against evil?
33. And the chiefs of his people who disbelieved and called the meeting of the hereafter a lie, and whom We had given plenty to enjoy in this world's life, said, "This is nothing but a mortal like yourselves, eating of what you eat from and drinking of what you drink.
34. And if you obey a mortal like yourselves, then most certainly you will be losers:
35. What! does he threaten you that when you are dead and become dust and bones that you shall then be brought forth?
36. Far, far is that which you are threatened with.
37. There is nothing but our life in this world; we die and we live and we shall not be raised again.
38. He is nothing but a man who has created a lie against God, and we are not going to believe in him.
39. He said, "Oh my Lord! help me against their calling me a liar.
40. He said, "In a little while they will most certainly be repenting.
41. So the punishment overtook them in justice, and We made them as rubbish; so away with the unjust people.
42. Then We raised after them other generations.
43. No people can hasten on their doom nor can they postpone it.
44. Then We sent Our apostles one after another; whenever there came to a people their apostle, they called him a liar, so We made some of them follow others and We made them stories; so away with a people who do not believe!
45. Then We sent Moses and his brother Aaron, with Our words
and a clear authority,
46. To Pharoah and his chiefs, but they behaved arrogantly and they were an insolent people.
47. And they said, "What! shall we believe in two mortals like ourselves while their people serve us?
48. So they rejected them and became of those who were destroyed.
49. And certainly We gave Moses the Book that they may follow a right direction.
50. And We made the son of Mary and his mother a sign, and We gave them a shelter on a lofty ground having meadows and springs.
51. Oh apostles! eat of the good things and do good; certainly I know what you do.
52. And certainly this your religion is one religion and I am your Lord, therefore be careful of your duty to Me.
53. But they cut off their religion among themselves into sects, each part rejoicing in that which is with them.
54. Therefore leave them in their overwhelming ignorance till
55. Do they think that by what We aid them with of wealth and children,
56. We are hastening to them of good things? No, they do not perceive.
57. Certainly they who from fear of their Lord are cautious,
58. And those who believe in the words of their Lord,
59. And those who do not compare anything with their Lord,
60. And those who give what they give. in alms while their hearts are full of fear that to their

Lord they must return,

61. These hasten to good things and they are foremost in attaining them.

62. And We do not lay on any soul a burden except to the extent of its ability, and with Us is a book which speaks the truth, and they shall not be dealt with unjustly.

63. No, their hearts are in overwhelming ignorance with respect to it and they have besides this other deeds which they do.

64. Until when We overtake those who lead easy lives among them with punishment, lo! they cry for succor.

65. Cry not for succor this day; certainly you shall not be given help from Us.

66. My words were indeed recited to you, but you used to turn back on your heels,

67. In arrogance; talking nonsense about the Koran, and left him like one telling fables by night.

68. Is it then that they do not ponder over what is said, or is it that there has come to them that which did not come to their fathers of old?

69. Or is it that they have not recognized their Prophet, so that they deny him?

70. Or do they say, "There is madness in him? No! he has brought them the truth, and most of them are averse from the truth.

71. And should the truth follow their low desires, certainly the heavens and the earth and all those who are therein would have perished. No! We have brought to them their reminder, but from their reminder they turn aside.

72. Or is it that you ask them for compensation? But the repayment of your Lord is best, and He is the best of those who provide sustenance.

73. And most certainly you invite them to a right way.

74. And most certainly those who do not believe in the hereafter are deviating from the way.

75. And if We show mercy to them and remove the distress they have, they would persist in their inordinacy, blindly wandering on.

76. And already We overtook them with punishment, but they were not submissive to their Lord, nor do they humble themselves.

77. Until when We open upon them a door of severe punishment, lo! they are in despair at it.

78. And He it is Who made for you the ears and the eyes and the hearts; little is it that you give thanks.

79. And He it is Who multiplied you in the earth, and to Him you shall be gathered.

80. And He it is Who gives life and causes death, and in His control is the alternation of the night and the day; do you not then understand?

81. No, they say the like of what the ancients said, "

82. They say, "What! When we are dead and become dust and bones, shall we then be raised?

83. Certainly we are promised this, and so were our fathers aforetime; this is nnothing but stories of those of old.

84. Say, "Whose is the earth, and whoever is therein, if you know?

85. They will say, "God's. Say, "Will you not then mind?

86. Say, "Who is the Lord of the seven heavens and the Lord of the mighty dominion?

87. They will say, "This is God's. Say, "Will you not then guard against evil?

88. Say, "Who is it in Whose hand is the kingdom of all things and Who gives succor, but against Him Succor is not given, if you do but know?

89. They will say, "This is God's. Say, "From where are you then deceived?

90. No! We have brought to them the truth, and most certainly they are liars.

91. Never did God take to Himself a son, and never was there with him any other god -- in that case would each god have certainly taken away what he created, and some of them would

certainly have overpowered others; glory be to God above what they describe!

92. The Knower of the unseen and the seen, so may He be exalted above what they associate with Him.

93. Say, "Oh my Lord! if You should make me see what they are threatened with:

94. My Lord! then place me not with the unjust.

95. And most certainly We are well able to make you see what We threaten them with.

96. Repel evil by what is best; We know best what they describe.

97. And say, "Oh my Lord! I seek refuge in You from the evil suggestions of the Satans;

98. And I seek refuge in You! Oh my Lord! from their presence.

99. Until when death overtakes one of them, he says: Send me back, my Lord, send me back;

100. Haply I may do good in that which I have left. By no means! it is a mere word that he speaks; and before them is a barrier until the day they are raised.

101. So when the trumpet is blown, there shall be no ties of relationship between them on that day, nor shall they ask of each other.

102. Then as for him whose good deeds are preponderant, these are the successful.

103. And as for him whose good deeds are light, these are they who shall have lost their souls, abiding in hell

104. The fire shall scorch their faces, and they therein shall be in severe sickness.

105. Were not My words recited to you? But you used to reject them.

106. They shall say, "Oh our Lord! our adversity overcame us and we were an erring people:

107. Oh our Lord! Take us out of it; then if we return to evil certainly we shall be unjust.

108. He shall say, "Go away into it and speak not to Me;

109. Certainly there was a party of My servants who said, "Oh OUI . Lord! we believe, so do You forgive us and have mercy on us, and You are the best of the Merciful ones.

110. But you took them for a mockery until they made you forget My remembrance and you used to laugh at them.

111. Certainly I have rewarded them this day because they were patient, that they are the achievers.

112. He will say, "How many years did you tarry in the earth?

113. They will say, "We tarried a day or part of a day, but ask those who keep account.

114. He will say, "You did tarry but a little -- had you but known it:

115. What! did you then think that We had created you in vain and that you shall not be returned to Us?

116. So exalted be God, the True King; no god is there but He, the Lord of the honorable dominion.

117. And whoever invokes with God another god -- he has no proof of this -- his judging is only with his Lord; certainly the unbelievers shall not be successful.

118. And say, "Oh my Lord! forgive and have mercy, and You are the best of the Merciful ones.

Chapter 24 — Al-Nur — The Light

In the name of God, the Kind, the Merciful.

1. This is a chapter which We have revealed and made obligatory and in which We have revealed clear words that you may be mindful.
2. As for the fornicatress and the fornicator, flog each of them, giving a hundred stripes, and let not pity for them detain you in the matter of obedience to God, if you believe in God and the last day, and let a party of believers witness their punishment.
3. The fornicator shall not marry any but a fornicatress or idolatress, and as for the fornicatress, none shall marry her but a fornicator or an idolater; and it is forbidden to the believers.
4. And those who accuse free women then do not bring four witnesses, flog them, giving eighty stripes, and do not admit any evidence from them ever; and these it is that are the transgressors,
5. Except those who repent after this and act aright, for certainly God is Forgiving, Merciful.
6. And as for those who accuse their wives and have no witnesses except themselves, the evidence of one of these should be taken four times, bearing God to witness that he is most certainly of the truthful ones.
7. And the fifth time that the curse of God be on him if he is one of the liars.
8. And it shall avert the punishment from her if she testify four times, bearing God to witness that he is most certainly one of the liars;
9. And the fifth time that the wrath of God be on her if he is one of the truthful.
10. And were it not for God's grace upon you and His mercy -- and that God is Oft-returning to mercy, Wise!
11. Certainly they who concocted the lie are a party from among you. Do not regard it an evil to you; no, it is good for you. Every man of them shall have what he has earned of sin; and as for him who took upon himself the main part thereof, he shall have a grievous punishment.
12. Why did not the believing men and the believing women, when you heard it, think well of their own people, and say, "This is an evident falsehood?
13. Why did they not bring four witnesses of it? But as they have not brought witnesses they are liars before God.
14. And were it not for God's grace upon you and His mercy in this world and the hereafter, a grievous punishment would certainly have touched you on account of the discourse which you entered into.
15. When you received it with your tongues and spoke with your mouths what you had no knowledge of, and you deemed it an easy matter while with God it was grievous.
16. And why did you not, when you heard it, say, "It does not seem to us that we should talk of it; glory be to You! this is a great defamation?
17. God reprimands you that you should not return to the like of it ever again if you are believers.
18. And God makes clear to you the words; and God is Knowing, Wise.
19. Certainly as for those who love that scandal should circulate respecting those who believe, they shall have a grievous punishment in this world and the hereafter; and God knows, while you do not know.
20. And were it not for God's grace on you and His mercy, and that God is Compassionate, Merciful.
21. Oh you who believe! do not follow the footsteps of the Satan, and whoever follows the

footsteps of the Satan, then certainly he bids the doing of indecency and evil; and were it not for God's grace upon you and His mercy, not one of you would have ever been pure, but God purifies whom He pleases;
and God is Hearing, Knowing.

22. And let not those of you who possess grace and abundance swear against giving to the near of kin and the poor and those who have fled in God's way, and they should pardon and turn away. Do you not love that God should forgive you? And God is Forgiving, Merciful.

23. Certainly those who accuse chaste believing women, unaware of the evil, are cursed in this world and the hereafter, and they shall have a grievous punishment.

24. On the day when their tongues and their hands and their feet shall bear witness against them as to what they did.

25. On that day God will pay back to them in full their just reward, and they shall know that God is the evident Truth.

26. Bad women . are for bad men and bad men are for bad women. Good women are for good men and good men are for good women

27. Oh you who believe! Do not enter houses other than your own houses until you have asked permission and saluted their inhabitants; this is better for you, that you may be mindful.

28. But if you do not find any one therein, then do not enter them until permission is given to you; and if it is said to you: Go back, then go back; this is purer for you; and God is Cognizant of what you do.

29. It is no sin in you that you enter uninhabited houses wherein you have your necessaries; and God knows what you do openly and what you hide.

30. Say to the believing men that they cast down their looks and guard their private parts; that is purer for them; certainly God is Aware of what they do.

31. And say to the believing women that they cast down their looks and guard their private parts and do not display their ornaments except what appears thereof, and let them wear their head-coverings over their bosoms, and not display their ornaments except to their husbands or their fathers, or the fathers of their husbands, or their sons, or the sons of their husbands, or their brothers, or their brothers' sons, or their sisters' sons, or their women, or those whom their right hands possess, or the male servants not having need of women, or the children who have not attained knowledge of what is hidden of women; and let them not strike their feet so that what they hide of their ornaments may be known; and turn to God all of you, Oh believers! so that you may be successful.

32. And marry those among you who are single and those who are fit among your male slaves and your female slaves; if they are needy, God will make them free from want out of His grace; and God is Ample-giving, Knowing.

33. And let those who do not find the means to marry keep chaste until God makes them free from want out of His grace. And as for those who ask for a writing from among those whom your right hands possess, give them the writing if you know any good in them, and give them of the wealth of God which He has given you; and do not compel your slave girls to prostitution, when they desire to keep chaste, in order to seek the frail good of this world's life; and whoever compels them, then certainly after their compulsion God is Forgiving, Merciful.

34. And certainly We have sent to you clear words and a description of those who have passed away before you, and an admonition to those who guard against evil.

35. God is the light of the heavens and the earth; a likeness of His light is as a niche in which is a lamp, the lamp is in a glass, and the glass is as it were a brightly shining star, lit from a blessed olive-tree, neither eastern nor western, the oil whereof almost gives light though fire

touch it not -- light upon light -- God guides to His light whom He pleases, and God sets forth parables for men, and God is Cognizant of all things.

36. In houses which God has permitted to be exalted and that His name may be remembered in them; there glorify Him therein in the mornings and the evenings,

37. Men whom neither merchandise nor selling diverts from the remembrance of God and the keeping up of prayer and the giving of poor-rate; they fear a day in which the hearts and eyes shall turn about;

38. That God may give them the best reward of what they have done, and give them more out of His grace; and God gives sustenance to whom He pleases without measure.

39. And as for those who disbelieve, their deeds are like the mirage in a desert, which the thirsty man deems to be water; until when he comes to it he finds it to be nothing, and there he finds God, so He pays back to him his judging in full; and God is quick in judging;

40. Or like utter darkness in the deep sea: there covers it a wave above which is another wave, above which is a cloud, layers of utter darkness one above another; when he holds out his hand, he is almost unable to see it; and to whomsoever God does not give light, he has no light.

41. Do you not see that God is He Whom do glorify all those who are in the heavens and the earth, and the very birds with expanded wings? He knows the prayer of each one and its glorification, and God is Cognizant of what they do.

42. And God's is the kingdom of the heavens and the earth, and to God is the eventual coming.

43. Do you not see that God drives along the clouds, then gathers them together, then piles them up, so that you see the rain coming forth from their midst? And He sends down of the clouds that are like mountains wherein is hail, afflicting therewith whom He pleases and turning it away from whom He pleases; the flash of His lightning almost takes away the sight.

44. God turns over the night and the day; most certainly there is a lesson in this for those who have sight.

45. And God has created from water every living creature: so of them is that which walks upon its belly, and of them is that which walks upon two feet, and of them is that which walks upon four; God creates what He pleases; certainly God has power over all things.

46. Certainly We have revealed clear words, and God guides whom He pleases to the right way.

47. And they say, "We believe in God and in the apostle and we obey; then a party of them turn back after this, and these are not believers.

48. And when they are called to God and His Prophet that he may judge between them, lo! a party of them turn aside.

49. And if the truth be on their side, they come to him quickly, obedient.

50. Is there in their hearts a disease, or are they in doubt, or do they fear that God and His Prophet will act wrongfully towards them? No! they themselves are the unjust.

51. The response of the believers, when they are invited to God and His Prophet that he may judge between them, is only to say, "We hear and we obey; and these it is that are the successful.

52. And he who obeys God and His Prophet, and fears God, and is careful of his duty to Him, these it is that are the achievers.

53. And they swear by God with the most energetic of their oaths that if you command them they would certainly go forth. Say, "Swear not; reasonable obedience is desired; certainly God is aware of what you do.

54. Say, "Obey God and obey the Prophet; but if you turn back, then on him rests that which is imposed on him and on you rests that which is imposed on you; and if you obey him, you are on the right way; and nothing rests on the Prophet but clear delivering of the message.

55. God has promised to those of you who believe and do good that He will most certainly

make them rulers in the earth as He made rulers those before them, and that He will most certainly establish for them their religion which He has chosen for them, and that He will most certainly, after their fear, give them security in exchange; they shall serve Me, not comparing anything with Me; and whoever is ungrateful after this, these it is who are the transgressors.

56. And keep up prayer and pay the poor-rate and obey the Prophet, so that mercy may be shown to you.

57. Think not that those who disbelieve shall escape in the earth, and their home is the fire; and certainly evil is the resort!

58. Oh you who believe! let those whom your right hands possess and those of you who have not attained to puberty ask permission of you three times; before the morning prayer, and when you put off your clothes at midday in summer, and after the prayer of the nightfall; these are three times of privacy for you; neither is it a sin for you nor for them besides these, some of you must go round about waiting upon others; thus does God make clear to you the words, and God is Knowing, Wise.

59. And when the children among you have attained to puberty, let them seek permission as those before them sought permission; thus does God make clear to you His words, and God is knowing, Wise.

60. And as for women advanced in years who do not hope for a marriage, it is no sin for them if they put off their clothes without displaying their ornaments; and if they restrain themselves it is better for them; and God is Hearing, Knowing.

61. There is no blame on the blind man, nor is there blame on the lame, nor is there blame on the sick, nor on yourselves that you eat from your houses, or your fathers' houses or your mothers' houses, or your brothers' houses, or your sisters' houses, or your paternal uncles' houses, or your paternal aunts' houses, or your maternal uncles' houses, or your maternal aunts' houses, or what you possess the keys of, or your friends' houses. It is no sin in you that you eat together or separately. So when you enter houses, greet your people with a salutation from God, blessed and worthy; thus does God make clear to you the words that you may understand.

62. Only those are believers who believe in God and His Prophet, and when they are with him on a momentous affair they go not away until they have asked his permission; certainly they who ask your permission are they who believe in God and His Prophet; so when they ask your permission for some affair of theirs, give permission to whom you please of them and ask forgiveness for them from God; certainly God is Forgiving, Merciful.

63. Do not hold the Prophet's calling you among you to be like your calling one to the other; God indeed knows those who steal away from among you, concealing themselves; therefore let those beware who go against his order unles a trial is inflicted upon them or there they are given a painful punishment.

64. Now certainly God's is whatever is in the heavens and the earth; He knows indeed that to which you are conforming yourselves; and on the day on which they are returned to Him He will inform them of what they did; and God is Cognizant of all things.

Chapter 25 — Al-Furqan — The Differentiation

In the name of God, the Kind, the Merciful.

1. Blessed is He Who has made a distinction of His servant that he may warn the nations;
2. He, Whose is the kingdom of the heavens and the earth, and Who did not take to Himself a son, and Who has no associate in the kingdom, and Who created everything, then ordered for it a plan.
3. And they have taken besides Him gods, who do not create anything while they are themselves created, and they control not for themselves any harm or profit, and they control not death nor life, nor raising the dead to life.
4. And those who disbelieve say, "This is nothing but a lie which he has created, and other people have helped him with it; so indeed they have done injustice and uttered a falsehood."
5. And they say, "The stories of the ancients -- he has got them written -- so these are read out to him morning and evening."
6. Say, "He has revealed it Who knows the secret in the heavens and the earth; certainly He is ever Forgiving, Merciful."
7. And they say, "What is the matter with this Prophet that he eats food and goes about in the markets; why has not an angel been sent down to him, so that he should have been a alarmgiver with him?
8. Or why is not a treasure sent down to him, or he is made to have a garden from which he should eat? And the unjust say, "You do not follow any but a man deprived of reason.
9. See what likenesses do they apply to you, so they have gone astray, therefore they shall not be able to find a way.
10. Blessed is He Who, if He please, will give you what is better than this, gardens beneath which rivers flow, and He will give you palaces.
11. But they reject the hour, and We have prepared a burning fire for him who rejects the hour.
12. When it shall come into their sight from a distant place, they shall hear its vehement raging and roaring.
13. And when they are cast into a narrow place in it, bound, they shall there call out for destruction.
14. Call not this day for one destruction, but call for destructions many.
15. Say, "Is this better or the abiding garden which those who guard against evil are promised? That shall be a reward and a resort for them.
16. They shall have therein what they desire abiding in it; it is a promise which it is proper to be prayed for from your Lord.
17. And on the day when He shall gather them, and whatever they served besides God, He shall say, "Was it you who led astray these My servants, or did they themselves go astray from the path?
18. They shall say, "Glory be to You; it did not seemto us that we should take any guardians besides You, but You caused them and their fathers to enjoy until they abandoned the reminder, and they were a people in hell,
19. So they shall indeed give you the lie in what you say, then you shall not be able to ward off or help, and whoever among you is unjust, We will make him feel a great punishment.
20. And We have not sent before you any messengers but they most certainly ate food and went about in the markets; and We have made some of you a trial for others; will you bear patiently?

And your Lord is ever Seeing.

21. And those who do not hope for Our meeting, say, "Why have angels not been sent down upon us, or why do we not see our Lord? Now certainly they are too proud of themselves and have revolted in a great revolt.

22. On the day when they shall see the angels, there shall be no joy on that day for the guilty, and they shall say, "It is a forbidden thing totally prohibited.

23. And We will proceed to what they have done of deeds, so We shall render them as scattered floating dust.

24. The dwellers of the garden shall on that day be in a better abiding-place and a better resting-place.

25. And on the day when the heaven shall burst asunder with the clouds, and the angels shall be sent down descending in ranks.

26. The kingdom on that day shall rightly belong to the Kind God, and a hard day shall it be for the unbelievers.

27. And the day when the unjust one shall bite his hands saying, "O! would that I had taken a way with the Prophet

28. Oh woe is me! would that I had not taken such a one for a friend !

29. Certainly he led me astray from the reminder after it had come to me; and the Satan fails to aid man.

30. And the Prophet cried out: Oh my Lord! certainly my people have treated this Koran as a abandoned thing.

31. And thus have We made for every prophet an enemy from among the sinners and sufficient is your Lord as a Guide and a Helper.

32. And those who disbelieve say, "Why has not the Koran been revealed to him all at once? Thus, that We may strengthen your heart by it and We have arranged it well in arranging.

33. And they shall not bring to you any argument, but We have brought to you one with truth and best in significance.

34. As for those who shall be gathered upon their faces to hell, they are in a worse plight and straying farther away from the path.

35. And certainly We gave Moses the Book and We appointed with him his brother Aaron an aider.

36. Then We said, "Go you both to the people who rejected Our words; so We destroyed them with utter destruction.

37. And the people of Noah, when they rejected the apostles, We drowned them, and made them a sign for men, and We have prepared a painful punishment for the unjust;

38. And Ad and Samood and the dwellers of the Rass and many generations between them.

39. And to every one We gave examples and every one did We destroy with utter destruction.

40. And certainly they have often passed by the town on which was rained an evil rain; did they not then see it? No! they did not hope to be raised again.

41. And when they see you, they do not take you for anything but a mockery: Is this he whom God has raised to be an apostle?

42. He had almost led us astray from our gods had we not adhered to them patiently! And they will know, when they see the punishment, who is straying farther off from the path.

43. Have you seen him who takes his low desires for his god? Will you then be a protector over him?

44. Or do you think that most of them do hear or understand? They are nothing but as cattle;

no, they are straying farther off from the path.

45. Have you not considered the work of your Lord, how He extends the shade? And if He had pleased He would certainly have made it stationary; then We have made the sun an indication of it.

46. Then We take it to Ourselves, taking little by little.

47. And He it is Who made the night a covering for you, and the sleep a rest, and He made the day to rise up again.

48. And He it is Who sends the winds as good news before His mercy; and We send down pure water from the cloud,

49. That We may give life thereby to a dead land and give it for drink, out of what We have created, to cattle and many people.

50. And certainly We have repeated this to them that they may be mindful, but the greater number of men do not consent to anything except denial.

51. And if We had pleased We would certainly have raised a alarmgiver in every town.

52. So do not follow the unbelievers, and strive against them a mighty striving with it.

53. And it is He Who has made two seas to flow freely, the one sweet that subdues thirst by its sweetness, and the other salt that burns by its saltness; and between the two He has made a barrier and inviolable obstruction.

54. And He it is Who has created man from the water, then He has made for him blood relationship and marriage relationship, and your Lord is powerful.

55. And they serve besides God that which neither profits them nor causes them harm; and the unbeliever is a partisan against his Lord.

56. And We have not sent you but as a giver of good news and as a alarmgiver.

57. Say, "I do not ask you anything in return except that he who will, may take the way to his Lord.

58. And rely on the Ever-living Who dies not, and celebrate His praise; and Sufficient is He as being aware of the faults of His servants,

59. Who created the heavens and the earth and what is between them in six days, and He is firmly established on the throne of authority; the Kind God, so be aware and be respectful.

60. And when it is said to them: Make obeisance to the Kind God, they say, "And what is the God of beneficence? Shall we make obeisance to what you bid us? And it adds to their aversion.

61. Blessed is He Who made the constellations in the heavens and made therein a lamp and a shining moon.

62. And He it is Who made the night and the day to follow each other for him who desires to be mindful or desires to be thankful.

63. And the servants of the Kind God are they who walk on the earth in humbleness, and when the ignorant address them, they say, "Peace.

64. And they who pass the night prostrating themselves before their Lord and standing.

65. And they who say, "Oh our Lord! turn away from us the punishment of hell, certainly the punishment thereof is a lasting

66. Certainly it is an evil home and evil place to stay.

67. And they who when they spend, are neither extravagant nor parsimonious, and keep between these the just mean.

68. And they who do not call upon another god with God and do not slay the soul, which God has forbidden except in the requirements of justice, and who do not commit fornication and he who does this shall find a requital of sin;

69. The punishment shall be doubled to him on the day of resurrection, and he shall abide therein in abasement;

70. Except him who repents and believes and does a good deed; so these are they of whom God changes the evil deeds to good ones; and God is Forgiving, Merciful.
71. And whoever repents and does good, he certainly turns to God properly.
72. And they who do not bear witness to what is false, and when they pass by what is vain, they pass by nobly.
73. And they who, when reminded of the words of their Lord, do not fall down thereat deaf and blind.
74. And they who say, "Oh our Lord! grant us in our wives and our offspring the joy of our eyes, and make us guides to those who guard against evil.
75. These shall be rewarded with high places because they were patient, and shall be met therein with greetings and salutations.
76. Abiding well therein; the home and the resting-place.
77. Say, "My Lord would not care for you were it not for your prayer; but you have indeed rejected the truth, so that which shall cleave shall come.

Chapter 26 — Al-Shu'ara — The Poets

In the name of God, the Kind, the Merciful.

¹. Ta Sin Mim.
². These are the verses of the Book that makes things clear.
³. Perhaps you will kill yourself with grief because they do not believe.
⁴. If We please, We should send down upon them a sign from the heaven so that their necks should stoop to it.
⁵. And there does not come to them a new reminder from the Kind God but they turn aside from it.
⁶. So they have indeed rejected the truth, therefore the news of that which they mock shall soon come to them.
⁷. Do they not see the earth, how many of every noble kind We have caused to grow in it?
⁸. Most certainly there is a sign in that, but most of them will not believe.
⁹. And most certainly your Lord is the Mighty, the Merciful.
¹⁰. And when your Lord called out to Moses, saying, "Go to the unjust people --
¹¹. The people of Pharoah: Will they not guard against evil?
¹². He said, "Oh my Lord! certainly I fear that they will reject me;
¹³. And by heart straightens, and my tongue is not eloquent, therefore send You to Aaron to help me;
¹⁴. And they have a crime against me, therefore I fear that they may slay me.
¹⁵. He said, "By no means, so go you both with Our signs; certainly We are with you, hearing;
¹⁶. Then come to Pharoah and say, "Certainly we are the messengers of the Lord of the worlds:
¹⁷. Then send with us the children of Israel.
¹⁸. Pharoah said, "Did we not bring you up as a child among us, and you tarried among us for many years of your life?
¹⁹. And you did that deed of yours which you did, and you are one of the ungrateful.
²⁰. He said, "I did it then while I was of those unable to see the right course;
²¹. So I fled from you when I feared you, then my Lord granted me wisdom and made me of the apostles;
²². And is it a favor of which you remind me that you have enslaved the children of Israel?
²³. Pharoah said, "And what is the Lord of the worlds?
²⁴. He said, "The Lord of the heavens and the earth and what is between them, if you would be sure.
²⁵. Pharoah said to those around him: Do you not hear?
²⁶. He said, "Your Lord and the Lord of your fathers of old.
²⁷. Said he: Most certainly your Prophet who is sent to you is mad.
²⁸. He said, "The Lord of the east and the west and what is between them, if you understand.
²⁹. Said he: If you will take a god besides me, I will most certainly make you one of the imprisoned.
³⁰. He said, "What! even if I bring to you something manifest?
³¹. Said he: Bring it then, if you are of the truthful ones.
³². So he cast down his rod, and lo! it was an obvious serpent,
³³. And he drew forth his hand, and lo! it appeared white to the onlookers.

34. Pharoah said to the chiefs around him: Most certainly this is a skillful magician,
35. Who desires to turn you out of your land with his magic; what is it then that you advise?
36. They said, "Give him and his brother respite and send heralds into the cities
37. That they should bring to you every skillful magician.
38. So the magicians were gathered together at the appointed time on the fixed day,
39. And it was said to the people: Will you gather together?
40. Haply we may follow the magicians, if they are the vanquishers.
41. And when the magicians came, they said to Pharoah: Shall we get a reward if we are the vanquishers?
42. He said, "Yes, and certainly you will then be of those who are made near.
43. Moses said to them: Cast what you are going to cast.
44. So they cast down their cords and their rods and said, "By Pharoah's power, we shall most certainly be victorious.
45. Then Moses cast down his staff and lo! it swallowed up the lies they told.
46. And the magicians were thrown down prostrate;
47. They said, "We believe in the Lord of the worlds:
48. The Lord of Moses and Aaron.
49. Said he: You believe in him before I give you permission; most certainly he is the chief of you who taught you the magic, so you shall know: certainly I will cut off your hands and your feet on opposite sides, and certainly I will crucify you all.
50. They said, "No harm; certainly to our Lord we go back;
51. Certainly we hope that our Lord will forgive us our wrongs because we are the first of the believers.
52. And We revealed to Moses, saying, "Go away with My servants travelling by night, certainly you will be pursued.
53. So Pharoah sent heralds into the cities;
54. Most certainly these are a small company;
55. And most certainly they have enraged us;
56. And most certainly we are a vigilant multitude.
57. So We turned them out of gardens and springs,
58. And treasures and fine dwellings,
59. Even so. And We gave them as a heritage to the children of Israel.
60. Then they pursued them at sunrise.
61. So when the two hosts saw each other, the companions of Moses cried out: Most certainly we are being overtaken.
62. He said, "By no means; certainly my Lord is with me: He will show me a way out.
63. Then We revealed to Moses: Strike the sea with your staff. So it had cloven asunder, and each part was like a huge mound.
64. And We brought near, there, the others.
65. And We saved Moses and those with him, all of them.
66. Then We drowned the others.
67. Most certainly there is a sign in this, but most of them do not believe.
68. And most certainly your Lord is the Mighty, the Merciful.
69. And recite to them the story of Abraham.
70. When he said to his father and his people: What do you worship?
71. They said, "We worship idols, so we shall be their votaries.
72. He said, "Do they hear you when you call?

73. Or do they profit you or cause you harm?
74. They said, "No, we found our fathers doing so.
75. He said, "Have you then considered what you have been worshiping:
76. You and your ancient sires.
77. Certainly they are enemies to me, but not so the Lord of the worlds;
78. Who created me, then He has shown me the way:
79. And He Who gives me to eat and gives me to drink:
80. And when I am sick, then He restores me to health
81. And He Who will cause me to die, then give me life;
82. And Who, I hope, will forgive me my mistakes on the day of judgment.
83. My Lord: Grant me wisdom, and join me with the good
84. And order for me a proper mention to posterity
85. And make me of the heirs of the garden of bliss
86. And forgive my father, for certainly he is among those who have gone astray;
87. And disgrace me not on the day when they are raised
88. The day on which property will not avail, nor sons
89. Except him who comes to God with a heart free from evil.
90. And the garden shall be brought near for those who guard against evil,
91. And the hell shall be made clear to the erring ones,
92. And it shall be said to them: Where are those that you used to worship;
93. Besides God? Can they help you or yet help themselves?
94. So they shall be thrown down into it, they and the erring ones,
95. And the hosts of the Satan, all.
96. They shall say while they contend therein:
97. By God! we were certainly in great error,
98. When we made you equal to the Lord of the worlds;
99. And none but the guilty led us astray;
100. So we have no advocates,
101. Nor a true friend;
102. But if we could but once return, we would be of the believers.
103. Most certainly there is a sign in this, but most of them do not believe.
104. And most certainly your Lord is the Mighty, the Merciful.
105. The people of Noah rejected the apostles.
106. When their brother Noah said to them: Will you not guard against evil?
107. Certainly I am a faithful apostle to you;
108. Therefore guard against the punishment of God and obey me.
109. And I do not ask you any reward for it; my reward is only with the Lord of the worlds:
110. So guard against the punishment of God and obey me.
111. They said, "Shall we believe in you while the meanest follow you?
112. He said, "And what knowledge have I of what they do?
113. Their account is only with my Lord, if you could perceive
114. And I am not going to drive away the believers;
115. I am nothing but a simple complainer.
116. They said, "If you desist not, Oh Noah, you shall most certainly be of those stoned to death.
117. He said, "My Lord! Certainly my people give me the lie!
118. Therefore judge You between me and them with a just judgment, and deliver me and those who are with me of the believers.

119. So We delivered him and those with him in the laden ark.
120. Then We drowned the rest afterwards
121. Most certainly there is a sign in this, but most of them do not believe.
122. And most certainly your Lord is the Mighty, the Merciful.
123. Ad gave the lie to the apostles.
124. When their brother Hud said to them: Will you not guard against evil?
125. Certainly I am a faithful apostle to you;
126. Therefore guard against the punishment of God and obey me:
127. And I do not ask you any reward for it; certainly my reward is only with the Lord of the worlds
128. Do you build on every height a monument? Vain is it that you do:
129. And you make strong fortresses that perhaps you may abide
130. And when you lay hands on men you lay hands like tyrants;
131. So guard against the punishment of God and obey me
132. And be careful of your duty to Him Who has given you abundance of what you know.
133. He has given you abundance of cattle and children
134. And gardens and fountains;
135. Certainly I fear for you the punishment of a grievous day
136. They said, "It is the same to us whether you reprimand or are not one of the those who reprimands.
137. This is nothing but a custom of the ancients;
138. And we are not going to be punished.
139. So they gave him the lie, then We destroyed them. Most certainly there is a sign in this, but most of them do not believe.
140. And most certainly your Lord is the Mighty, the Merciful.
141. Samood gave the lie to the apostles
142. When their brother Salih said to them: Will you not guard against evil?
143. Certainly I am a faithful apostle to you
144. Therefore guard against the punishment of God and obey me:
145. And I do not ask you any reward for it; my reward is only with the Lord of the worlds:
146. Will you be left secure in what is here;
147. In gardens and fountains,
148. And cornfields and palm-trees having fine spadices?
149. And you hew houses out of the mountains exultingly;
150. Therefore guard against the punishment of God and obey me;
151. And do not obey the bidding of the extravagant,
152. Who make mischief in the land and do not act aright.
153. They said, "You are only of the deluded ones;
154. You are only a mortal like ourselves; so bring a sign if you are one of the truthful.
155. He said, "This is a she-camel; she shall have her portion of water, and you have your portion of water on an appointed time;
156. And do not touch her with evil, or a grievouspunishment might come upon you.
157. But they hamstrung her, then regretted;
158. So the punishment overtook them. Most certainly there is a sign in this, but most of them do not believe.
159. And most certainly your Lord is the Mighty, the Merciful.
160. The people of Lot gave the lie to the apostles.

161. When their brother Lot said to them: Will you not guard against evil?
162. Certainly I am a faithful apostle to you;
163. Therefore guard against the punishment of God and obey me:
164. And I do not ask you any reward for it; my reward is only with the Lord of the worlds;
165. What! do you come to the males from among the creatures
166. And leave what your Lord has created for you of your wives? No, you are a people exceeding limits.
167. They said, "If you desist not, Oh Lot! you shall certainly be of those who are expelled.
168. He said, "Certainly I am of those who utterly abhor your doing:
169. My Lord ! deliver me and my followers from what they do.
170. So We delivered him and his followers all,
171. Except an old woman, among those who remained behind.
172. Then We utterly destroyed the others.
173. And We rained down upon them a rain, and evil was the rain on those warned.
174. Most certainly there is a sign in this, but most of them do not believe.
175. And most certainly your Lord is the Mighty, the Merciful.
176. The dwellers of the thicket gave the lie to the apostles.
177. When Shu'aib said to them: Will you not guard against evil?
178. Certainly I am a faithful apostle to you;
179. Therefore guard against the punishment of God and obey me:
180. And I do not ask you any reward for it, my reward is only with the Lord of the worlds;
181. Give a full measure and do not be of those who diminish;
182. And weigh things with a right balance,
183. And do not wrong men of their things, and do not act corruptly in the earth, making mischief.
184. And guard against the punishment of Him who created you and the former nations.
185. They said, "You are only of those deluded;
186. And you are only a mortal like ourselves, and we know you to be certainly of the liars.
187. Therefore cause a portion of the heaven to come down upon us, if you are one of the truthful.
188. He said, "My Lord knows best what you do.
189. But they called him a liar, so the punishment of the day of covering overtook them; certainly it was the punishment of a grievous day.
190. Most certainly there is a sign in this, but most of them do not believe.
191. And most certainly your Lord is Mighty, the Merciful.
192. And most certainly this is a revelation from the Lord of the worlds.
193. The Faithful Spirit has descended with it,
194. Upon your heart that you may be of the alarmgivers
195. In plain Arabic language.
196. And most certainly the same is in the scriptures of the ancients.
197. Is it not a sign to them that the learned men of the Israelites know it?
198. And if we had revealed it to any of the foreigners
199. So that he should have recited it to them, they would not have believed therein.
200. Thus have We caused it to enter into the hearts of the guilty.
201. They will not believe in it until they see the painful punishment.
202. And it shall come to them all of a sudden, while they shall not perceive;
203. Then they will say, "Shall we be respited?
204. What! do they still seek to hasten on Our punishment?

205. Have you then considered if We let them enjoy themselves for years,
206. Then there comes to them that with which they are threatened,
207. That which they were made to enjoy shall not avail them?
208. And We did not destroy any town but it had its alarmgivers,
209. To remind, and We are never unjust.
210. And the Satans have not come down with it.
211. And it behooves them not, and they have not the power to do it.
212. Most certainly they are far removed from the hearing of it.
213. So call not upon another god with God, or you willbe among those who are punished.
214. And warn your nearest relations,
215. And be kind to him who follows you of the believers.
216. But if they disobey you, then say, "Certainly I am clear of what you do.
217. And rely on the Mighty, the Merciful,
218. Who sees you when you stand up.
219. And your turning over and over among those who prostrate themselves before God.
220. Certainly He is the Hearing, the Knowing.
221. Shall I inform you of him upon whom the Satans descend?
222. They descend upon every lying, sinful one,
223. They incline their ears, and most of them are liars.
224. And as to the poets, those who go astray follow them.
225. Do you not see that they wander about bewildered in every valley?
226. And that they say that which they do not do,
227. Except those who believe and do good and remember God much, and defend themselves after they are oppressed; and they who act unjustly shall know to what final place of turning they shall turn back.

Chapter 27 — Al-Naml — The Ant

In the name of God, the Kind, the Merciful.

1. Ta Sin! These are the verses of the Koran and the Book that makes things clear
2. A guidance and good news for the believers,
3. Who keep up prayer and pay the poor-rate, and of the hereafter, they are sure.
4. As to those who do not believe in the hereafter, We have certainly made their deeds fair-seeming to them, but they blindly wander on.
5. These are they who shall have an evil punishment, and in the hereafter they shall be the greatest losers.
6. And most certainly you are made to receive the Koran from the Wise, the Knowing God.
7. When Moses said to his family: Certainly I see fire; I will bring to you from it some news, or I will bring to you therefrom a burning firebrand so that you may warm yourselves.
8. So when he came to it a voice was uttered saying, "Blessed is Whoever is in the fire and whatever is about it; and glory be to God, the Lord of the worlds;
9. Oh Moses! certainly I am God, the Mighty, the Wise;
10. And cast down your staff. So when he saw it in motion as if it were a serpent, he turned back retreating and did not return: Oh Moses! fear not; certainly the apostles shall not fear in My presence;
11. Neither he who has been unjust, then he does good instead after evil, for certainly I am the Forgiving, the Merciful:
12. And enter your hand into the opening of your bosom, it shall come forth white without evil; among nine signs to Pharoah and his people, certainly they are a transgressing people.
13. So when Our clear signs came to them, they said, "This is clear sorcery.
14. And they denied them unjustly and proudly while their soul had been convinced of them; consider, then how was the end of the mischief-makers.
15. And certainly We gave knowledge to David and Solomon, and they both said, "Praise be to God, Who has made us to excel many of His believing servants.
16. And Solomon was David's heir, and he said, "Oh men! we have been taught the language of birds, and we have been given all things; most certainly this is great grace.
17. And his hosts of the jinn and the men and the birds were gathered to him, and they were formed into groups.
18. Until when they came to the valley of the Naml, a Namlite said, "Oh Naml! enter your houses, that Solomon and his hosts may not crush you while they do not know.
19. So he smiled, wondering at her word, and said, "My Lord! grant me that I should be grateful for Your favor which You have bestowed on me and on my parents, and that I should do good such as You are pleased with, and make me enter, by Your mercy, into Your servants, the good ones.
20. And he reviewed the birds, then said, "How is it I see not the hoopoe or is it that he is of the absentees?
21. I will most certainly punish him with a severe punishment, or kill him, or he shall bring to me a clear plea.
22. And he tarried not long, then said, "I comprehend that which you do not comprehend and I have brought to you a sure information from Sheba.

23. Certainly I found a woman ruling over them, and she has been given abundance and she has a mighty throne:

24. I found her and her people adoring the sun instead of God, and the Satan has made their deeds fair-seeming to them and thus turned them from the way, so they do not go aright

25. That they do not make obeisance to God, Who brings forth what is hidden in the heavens and the earth and knows what you hide and what you make manifest:

26. God, there is no god but He: He is the Lord of mighty power.

27. He said, "We will see whether you have told the truth or whether you are of the liars:

28. Take this my letter and hand it over to them, then turn away from them and see what answer they return.

29. She said, "Oh chief! certainly an honorable letter has been delivered to me

30. Certainly it is from Solomon, and certainly it is in the name of God, the Kind, the Merciful;

31. Saying, "exalt not yourselves against me and come to me in submission.

32. She said, "Oh chiefs! give me advice respecting my affair: I never decide an affair until you are in my presence.

33. They said, "We are possessors of strength and possessors of mighty prowess, and the command is yours, therefore see what you will command.

34. She said, "Certainly the kings, when they enter a town, ruin it and make the noblest of its people to be low, and thus they always do;

35. And certainly I am going to send a present to them, and shall wait to see what answer do the messengers bring back.

36. So when he came to Solomon, he said, "What! will you help me with wealth? But what God has given me is better than what He has given you. No, you are exultant because of your present;

37. Go back to them, so we will most certainly come to them with hosts which they shall have no power to oppose, and we will most certainly expel them therefrom in abasement, and they shall be in a state of embarassment.

38. He said, "Oh chiefs! which of you can bring to me her throne before they come to me in submission?

39. One audacious among the jinn said, "I will bring it to you before you rise up from your place; and most certainly I am strong and trusty for it.

40. One who had the knowledge of the Book said, "I will bring it to you in the twinkling of an eye. Then when he saw it settled beside him, he said, "This is of the grace of my Lord that He may try me whether I am grateful or ungrateful; and whoever is grateful, he is grateful only for his own soul, and whoever is ungrateful, then certainly my Lord is Self-sufficient, Honored.

41. He said, "Alter her throne for her, we will see whether she follows the right way or is of those who do not go aright.

42. So when she came, it was said, "Is your throne like this? She said, "It is as it were the same, and we were given the knowledge before it, and we were submissive.

43. And what she worshiped besides God prevented her, certainly she was of an unbelieving people.

44. It was said to her: Enter the palace; but when she saw it she deemed it to be a great expanse of water, and bared her legs. He said, "Certainly it is a palace made smooth with glass. She said, "My Lord! certainly I have been unjust to myself, and I submit with Solomon to God, the Lord of the worlds.

45. And certainly We sent to Samood their brother Salih, saying, "Serve God; and lo! they became two sects quarrelling with each other.

46. He said, "Oh my people! why do you seek to hasten on the evil before the good? Why do

you not ask forgiveness of God so that you may be dealt with mercifully?

47. They said, "We have met with ill luck on account of you and on account of those with you. He said, "The cause of your evil fortune is with God; no, you are a people who are tried.

48. And there were in the city nine persons who made mischief in the land and did not act aright.

49. They said, "Swear to each other by God that we will certainly make a sudden attack on him and his family by night, then we will say to his heir: We did not witness the destruction of his family, and we are most certainly truthful.

50. And they planned a plan, and We planned a plan while they perceived not.

51. See, then, how was the end of their plan that We destroyed them and their people, all of them.

52. So those are their houses fallen down because they were unjust, most certainly there is a sign in this for a people who know.

53. . And We delivered those who believed and who guarded against evil.

54. And We sent Lot, when he said to his people: What! do you commit indecency by looking?

55. What! do you indeed approach men lustfully rather than women? No, you are a people who act ignorantly.

56. But the answer of his people was no other except that they ~s said, "Turn out Lot's followers from your town; certainly they are a people who would keep pure!

57. But We delivered him and his followers except his wife; We ordered her to be of those who remained behind.

58. And We rained on them a rain, and evil was the rain of those who had been warned.

59. Say, "Praise be to God and peace on His servants whom He has chosen: is God better, or what they associate with Him?

60. No, He Who created the heavens and the earth, and sent down for you water from the cloud; then We cause to grow thereby beautiful gardens; it is not possible for you that you should make the trees thereof to grow. Is there a god with God? No! they are people who deviate.

61. Or, Who made the earth a resting place, and made in it rivers, and raised on it mountains and placed between the two seas a barrier. Is there a god with God? No! most of them do not know!

62. Or, Who answers the distressed one when he calls upon Him and removes the evil, and He will make you successors in the earth. Is there a god with God? Little is it that you mind!

63. Or, Who guides you in utter darkness of the land and the sea, and Who sends the winds as good news before His mercy. Is there a god with God? Exalted by God above what they associate with Him.

64. Or, Who originates the creation, then reproduces it and Who gives you sustenance from the heaven and the earth. Is there a god With God? Say, "Bring your proof if you are truthful.

65. Say, "No one in the heavens and the earth knows the unseen but God; and they do not know when they shall be raised.

66. No, their knowledge respecting the hereafter is slight and hasty; no, they are in doubt about it; no, they are quite blind to

67. And those who disbelieve say, "What! when we have become dust and our fathers too, shall we certainly be brought forth?

68. We have certainly been promised this, we and our fathers before; these are nothing but stories of the ancients

69. Say, "Travel in the earth, then see how was the end of the guilty.

70. And grieve not for them and do not be distressed because of what they plan.

71. And they say, "When will this threat come to pass, if you are truthful?

72. Say, "Maybe there may have drawn near to you somewhat of that which you seek to hasten on.

73. And certainly your Lord is the Lord of grace to men, but most of them are not grateful.

74. And most certainly your Lord knows what their hearts conceal and what they manifest.
75. And there is nothing concealed in the heaven and the earth but it is in a clear book.
76. Certainly this Koran declares to the children of Israel most of what they differ in.
77. And most certainly it is a guidance and a mercy for the believers.
78. Certainly your Lord will judge between them by his judgment, and He is the Mighty, the knowing.
79. Therefore rely on God; certainly you are on the clear truth.
80. Certainly you do not make the dead to hear, and you do not make the deaf to hear the call when they go back retreating.
81. Nor can you be a guide to the blind out of their error; you cannot make to bear any one except those who believe in Our words, so they submit.
82. And when the word shall come to pass against them, We shall bring forth for them a creature from the earth that shall i wound them, because people did not believe in Our words.
83. And on the day when We will gather from every nation a party from among those who rejected Our words, then they shall be formed into groups.
84. Until when they come, He will say, "Did you reject My words while you had no comprehensive knowledge of them? Or what was it that you did?
85. And the word shall come to pass against them because they were unjust, so they shall not speak.
86. Do they not consider that We have made the night that. they may rest therein, and the day to give light? Most certainly there are signs in this for a people who believe.
87. And on the day when the trumpet shall be blown, then those who are in the heavens and those who are in the earth shall be terrified except such as God please, and all shall come to him abased.
88. And you see the mountains, you think them to be solid, and they shall pass away as the passing away of the cloud -- the handiwork of God Who has made every thing thoroughly; certainly He is Aware of what you do.
89. Whoever brings good, he shall have better than it; and they shall be secure from terror on the day.
90. And whoever brings evil, these shall be thrown down on their faces into the fire; shall you be rewarded for anything except what you did?
91. I am commanded only that I should serve the Lord of this city, Who has made it sacred, and His are all things; and I am commanded that I should be of these who submit;
92. And that I should recite the Koran. Therefore whoever goes aright, he goes aright for his own soul, and whoever goes ' astray, then say, "I am only one of the alarmgivers.
93. And say, "Praise be to God, He will show you His signs so that you shall recognize them; nor is your Lord heedless of what you do.

Chapter 28 — Al-Qasas — The Narratives

In the name of God, the Kind, the Merciful.

1. Ta Sin Mim.
2. These are the verses of the Book that makes things clear.
3. We recite to you from the account of Moses and Pharoah with truth for people who believe.
4. Certainly Pharoah exalted himself in the land and made its people into parties, weakening one party from among them; he slaughtered their sons and let their women live; certainly he was one of the mischief-makers.
5. And We desired to bestow a favor upon those who were deemed weak in the land, and to make them the Imams, and to make them the heirs,
6. And to grant them power in the land, and to make Pharoah and Haman and their hosts see from them what they feared.
7. And We revealed to Moses's mothers, saying, "Give him suck, then when you fear for him, cast him into the river and do not fear nor grieve; certainly We will bring him back to you and make him one of the apostles.
8. And Pharoah's family took him up that he might be an enemy and a grief for them; certainly Pharoah and Haman and their hosts were wrongdoers.
9. And Pharoah's wife said, "A refreshment of the eye to me and to you; do not slay him; maybe he will be useful to us, or we may take him for a son; and they did not perceive.
10. And the heart of Moses's mother was free from anxiety she would have almost disclosed it had We not strengthened her heart so that she might be of the believers.
11. And she said to his sister: Follow him up. So she watched him from a distance while they did not perceive,
12. And We ordered that he refused to suck any foster mother before, so she said, "Shall I point out to you the people of a house who will take care of him for you, and they will be benevolent to him?
13. So We gave him back to his mother that her eye might be refreshed, and that she might no grieve, and that she might know that the promise of God is true, but most of them do not know.
14. And when he attained his maturity and became full grown, We granted him wisdom and knowledge; and thus do We reward those who do good to others.
15. And he went into the city at a time of unvigilance on the part of its people, so he found therein two men fighting, one being of his party and the other

of his foes, and he who was of his party cried out to him for help against him who was of his enemies, so Moses struck him with his fist and killed him. He said, "This is on account of the Satan's doing; certainly he is an enemy, openly leading astray.

16. He said, "My Lord! certainly I have done harm to myself, so do You protect me. So He protected him; certainly He is the Forgiving, the Merciful.

17. He said, "My Lord! because You have bestowed a favor on me, I shall never be a backer of the guilty.

18. And he was in the city, fearing, awaiting, when lo! he who had asked his assistance the day before was crying out to him for aid. Moses said to him: You are most certainly one erring manifestly.

19. So when he desired to seize him who was an enemy to them both, he said, "Oh Moses! do you intend to kill me as you killed a person yesterday? You desire nothing but that you should be a tyrant in the land, and you do not desire to be of those who act aright.

20. And a man came running from the farthest part of the city. He said, "Oh Moses! certainly the chiefs are conspiring together to slay you, you should depart at once; because I am one of those who wish you well.

21. So he went forth therefrom, fearing, awaiting, and he said, "My Lord! deliver me from the unjust people.

22. And when he turned his face towards Madyan, he said, "Maybe my Lord will guide me in the right path.

23. And when he came to the water of Madyan, he found on it a group of men watering, and he found besides them two women keeping back their flocks. He said, "What is the matter with you? They said, "We cannot water until the shepherds take away their sheep from the water, and our father is a very old man.

24. So he watered their sheep for them, then went back to the shade and said, "My Lord! certainly I stand in need of whatever good You might send down to me.

25. Then one of the two women came to him walking bashfully. She said, "My father invites you that he may give you the reward of your having watered for us. So when he came to him and gave to him the account, he said, "Fear not, you are secure from the unjust people.

26. Said one of them: Oh my father! employ him, certainly the best of those that you can employ is the strong man, the faithful one.

27. He said, "I desire to marry one of these two daughters of mine to you on condition that you should serve me for eight years; but if you complete ten, it will be of your own free will, and I do not wish to be hard to you; if God please, you will find me one of the good.

²⁸. He said, "This shall be an agreement between me and you; whichever of the two terms I fulfill, there shall be no wrongdoing to me; and God is a witness of what we say.

²⁹. So when Moses had fulfilled the term, and he journeyed with his family, he perceived on this side of the mountain a fire. He said to his family: Wait, I have seen a fire, maybe I will bring to you from it some news or a brand of fire, so that you may warm yourselves.

³⁰. And when he came to it, a voice was uttered from the right side of the valley in the blessed spot of the bush, saying, "Oh Moses! certainly I am God, the Lord of the worlds.

³¹. And saying, "Cast down you staff. So when he saw it in motion as if it were a serpent, he turned back retreating, and did not return. Oh Moses! come forward and fear not; certainly you are of those who are secure;

³². Enter your hand into the opening of your bosom, it will come forth white without evil, and draw your hand to yourself to ward off fear: so these two shall be two arguments from your Lord to Pharoah and his chiefs, certainly they are a transgressing people.

³³. He said, "My Lord! certainly I killed one of them, so I fear that they might slay me;

³⁴. And my brother, Aaron, he is more eloquent of tongue than I, therefore send him with me as an aider, verifying me: certainly I fear that they would reject me.

³⁵. He said, "We will strengthen your arm with your brother, and We will give you both an authority, so that they shall not reach you; go with Our signs; you two and those who follow you shall be uppermost.

³⁶. So when Moses came to them with Our clear signs, they said, "This is nothing but created sorcery, and we never heard of it amongst our forefathers.

³⁷. And Moses said, "My Lord knows best who comes with guidance from Him, and whose shall be the good end of the home; certainly the unjust shall not be successful.

³⁸. And Pharoah said, "Oh chiefs! I do not know of any god for you besides myself; therefore kindle a fire for me, Oh Haman, for brick, then prepare for me a lofty building so that I may obtain knowledge of Moses's God, and most certainly I think him to be one of the liars.

³⁹. And he was unjustly proud in the land, he and his hosts, and they deemed that they would not be brought back to Us.

⁴⁰. So We caught hold of him and his hosts, then We cast them into the sea, and see how was the end of the unjust.

⁴¹. And We made them Imams who call to the fire, and on the day of resurrection they shall not be assisted.

⁴². And We caused a curse to follow them in this world, and on the day of resurrection they shall be of those made to appear hideous.

⁴³. And certainly We gave Moses the Book after We had destroyed the former generations, clear explanations for men and a guidance and a mercy, that they may be mindful.

⁴⁴. And you were not on the western side when We revealed to Moses the commandment, and you were not among the witnesses;

⁴⁵. But We raised up generations, then life became prolonged to them; and you were not dwelling among the people of Madyan, reciting to them Our words, but We were the senders.

⁴⁶. And you were not on this side of the mountain when We called, but a mercy from your Lord that you may warn a people to whom no alarmgiver came before you, that they may be mindful.

⁴⁷. And were it not that there should happen to them a disaster for what their hands have sent before, then they should say, "Our Lord! why did You not send to us an apostle so that we would have followed Your words and been of the believers !

⁴⁸. But now when the truth has come to them from Us, they say, "Why is he not given the like of what was given to Moses? What! did they not disbelieve in what Moses was given before? They say, "Two magicians backing up each other; and they say, "Certainly we are unbelievers in all.

⁴⁹. Say, "Then bring some other book from God which is a better guide than both of them, that I may follow it, if you are truthful. ⁵⁰. But if they do not answer you, then know that they only follow their low desires; and who is more erring than he who follows his low desires without any guidance from God? Certainly God does not guide the unjust people.

⁵¹. And certainly We have made the word to reach them so that they may be mindful.

⁵². As to those whom We gave the Book before it, they are believers in it.

⁵³. And when it is recited to them they say, "We believe in it certainly it is the truth from our Lord; certainly we were submitters before this.

⁵⁴. These shall be granted their reward twice, because they are steadfast and they repel evil with good and spend out of what We have given them.

⁵⁵. And when they hear idle talk they turn aside from it and say, "We shall have our deeds and you shall have your deeds; peace be on you, we do not desire the ignorant.

⁵⁶. Certainly you cannot guide whom you love, but God guides whom He pleases, and He knows best the followers of the right way.

⁵⁷. And they say, "If we follow the guidance with you, we shall be carried off

from our country. What! have We not settled them in a safe, sacred territory to which fruits of every kind shall be drawn? -- a sustenance from Us; but most of them do not know.

58. And how many a town have We destroyed which exulted in its means of subsistence, so these are their homes, they have not been dwelt in after them except a little, and We are the inheritors,

59. And your Lord never destroyed the towns until He raised in their metropolis an apostle, reciting to them Our words, and We never destroyed the towns except when their people were unjust.

60. And whatever things you have been given are only a provision of this world's life and its adornment, and whatever is with God is better and more lasting; do you not then understand?

61. Is he to whom We have made a good promise which he shall meet with like him whom We have provided with the provisions of this world's life, then on the day of resurrection he shall be of those who are brought up?

62. And on the day when He will call them and say, "Where are those whom you deemed to be My associates?

63. Those against whom the sentence has become confirmed will say, "Our Lord! these are they whom we caused to err; we caused them to err as we ourselves did err; to You we declare ourselves to be clear of them; they never served Us.

64. And it will be said, "Call your associate-gods. So they will call upon them, but they will not answer them, and they shall see the punishment; would that they had followed the right way!

65. And on the day when He shall call them and say, "What was the answer you gave to the apostles?

66. Then the pleas shall become obscure to them on that day, so they shall not ask each other.

67. But as to him who repents and believes and does good, maybe he will be among the successful:

68. And your Lord creates and chooses whom He pleases; to choose is not theirs; glory be to God, and exalted be He above what they associate with Him.

69. And your Lord knows what their hearts conceal and what they manifest.

70. And He is God, there is no god but He! All praise is due to Him in this life and the hereafter, and His is the judgment, and to Him you shall be brought back.

71. Say, "Tell me, if God were to make the night to continue incessantly on you till the day of resurrection, who is the god besides God that could bring you light? Do you not then hear?

72. Say, "Tell me, if God were to make the day to continue incessantly on you till the day of resurrection, who is the god besides God that could bring you

the night in which you take rest? Do you not then see?

73. And out of His mercy He has made for you the night and the day, so that you might rest therein, and that you may seek of His grace, and that you may give thanks.

74. And on the day when He shall call them and say, "Where are those whom you deemed to be My associates?

75. And We will draw forth from among every nation a witness and say, "Bring your proof; then shall they know that the truth is God's, and that which they created shall depart from them.

76. Certainly Qaroun was of the people of Moses, but he rebelled against them, and We had given him of the treasures, so much so that his hoards of wealth would certainly weigh down a company of men possessed of great strength. When his people said to him: Do not exult, certainly God does not love the exultant;

77. And seek by means of what God has given you the future home, and do not neglect your portion of this world, and do good to others as God has done good to you, and do not seek to make mischief in the land, certainly God does not love the mischief-makers.

78. He said, "I have been given this only on account of the knowledge I have. Did he not know that God had destroyed before him of the generations those who were mightier in strength than he and greater in assemblage? And the guilty shall not be asked about their faults.

79. So he went forth to his people in his finery. Those who desire this world's life said, "Oh would that we had the like of what Qaroun is given; most certainly he is possessed of mighty good fortune.

80. And those who were given the knowledge said, "Woe to you! God's reward is better for him who believes and does good, and none is made to receive this except the patient.

81. Thus We made the earth to swallow up him and his home; so he had no body of helpers to assist him against God nor was he of those who can defend themselves.

82. And those who yearned for his place only the day before began to say, "Ah! know that God amplifies and straightens the means of subsistence for whom He pleases of His servants; had not God been kind to us, He would most certainly have abased us; ah! know that the ungrateful are never successful.

83. As for that future home, We assign it to those who have no desire to exalt themselves in the earth nor to make mischief and the good end is for those who guard against evil

84. Whoever brings good, he shall have better than it, and whoever brings evil,

those who do evil shall not be rewarded for anything except for what they did.

⁸⁵. Most certainly He Who has made the Koran binding on you will bring you back to the destination. Say, "My Lord knows best him who has brought the guidance and him who is in great error.

⁸⁶. And you did not expect that the Book would be inspired to you, but it is a mercy from your Lord, therefore do not be a backer-up of the unbelievers.

⁸⁷. And let them not turn you aside from the words of God after they have been revealed to you, and call men to your Lord and do not be of the polytheists.

⁸⁸. And call not with God any other god; there is no god but He, every thing is perishable but He; His is the judgment, and to Him you shall be brought back.

Chapter 29 — Al-Ankabut — The Spider

In the name of God, the Kind, the Merciful.

1. Alif Lam Mim.
2. Do men think that they will be left alone on saying, We believe, and not be tried?
3. And certainly We tried those before them, so God will certainly know those who are true and He will certainly know the liars.
4. Or do they who work evil think that they will escape Us? Evil is it that they judge!
5. Whoever hopes to meet God, the term appointed by God will then most certainly come; and He is the Hearing, the Knowing.
6. And whoever strives hard, he strives only for his own soul; most certainly God is Self-sufficient, above need of the worlds.
7. And as for those who believe and do good, We will most certainly do away with their evil deeds and We will most certainly reward them the best of what they did.
8. And We have enjoined on man goodness to his parents, and if they contend with you that you should associate others with Me, of which you have no knowledge, do not obey them, to Me is your return, so I will inform you of what you did.
9. And as for those who believe and do good, We will most certainly cause them to enter among the good.
10. And among men is he who says: We believe in God; but when he is persecuted in the way of God he thinks the persecution of men to be as the punishment of God; and if there come assistance from your Lord, they would most certainly say, "Certainly we were with you. What! does God know best what is in the hearts of mankind.
11. And most certainly God will know those who believe and most certainly He will know the hypocrites.
12. And those who disbelieve say to those who believe: Follow our path and we will bear your wrongs. And never shall they be the bearers of any of their wrongs; most certainly they are liars.
13. And most certainly they shall carry their own burdens, and other burdens with their own burdens, and most certainly they shall be questioned on the resurrection day as to what they created.
14. And certainly We sent Noah to his people, so he remained among them a thousand years save fifty years. And the deluge overtook them, while they were unjust.
15. So We delivered him and the inmates of the ark, and made it a sign to the nations.
16. And We sent Abraham, when he said to his people: Serve God and be careful of your duty to Him; this is best for you, if you did but know:
17. You only worship idols besides God and you create a lie certainly they whom you serve besides God do not control for you any sustenance, therefore seek the sustenance from God and serve Him and be grateful to Him; to Him you shall be brought back.
18. And if you reject the truth, nations before you did indeed reject the truth; and nothing is incumbent on the apostle but a plain delivering of the message.
19. What! do they not consider how God originates the creation, then reproduces it? Certainly that is easy to God.
20. Say, "Travel in the earth and see how He makes the first creation, then God creates the latter creation; certainly God has power over all things.

²¹. He punishes whom He pleases and has mercy on whom He pleases, and to Him you shall be turned back.

²². And you shall not escape in the earth nor in the heaven, and you have n protection nor help besides God.

²³. And as to those who disbelieve in the words of God and His meeting, they have despaired of My mercy, and these it is that shall have a painful punishment.

²⁴. So nothing was the answer of his people except that they said, "Slay him or burn him; then God delivered him from the fire; most certainly there are signs in this for a people who believe.

²⁵. And he said, "You have only taken for yourselves idols besides God by way of friendship between you in this world's life, then on the resurrection day some of you shall deny others, and some of you shall curse others, and your home is the fire, and you shall not have any helpers.

²⁶. And Lot believed in Him, and he said, "I am fleeing to my Lord, certainly He is the Mighty, the Wise.

²⁷. And We granted him Isaac and Jacob, and caused the t prophethood and the book to remain in his seed, and We gave him his reward in this world, and in the hereafter he will most certainly be among the good.

²⁸. And We sent Lot when he said to his people: Most certainly you are guilty of an indecency which none of the nations has ever done before you;

²⁹. What! do you come to the males and commit robbery on the highway, and you commit evil deeds in your assemblies? But nothing was the answer of his people except that they said, "Bring on us God's punishment, if you are one of the truthful.

³⁰. He said, "My Lord! help me against the mischievous people.

³¹. And when Our messengers came to Abraham with the good news, they said, "Certainly we are going to destroy the people of this town, for its people are unjust.

³². He said, "Certainly in it is Lot. They said, "We know well who is in it; we shall certainly deliver him and his followers, except his wife; she shall be of those who remain behind.

³³. And when Our messengers came to Lot he was grieved on account of them, and he felt powerless to protect them; and they said, "Fear not, nor grieve; certainly we will deliver you and your followers, except your wife; she shall be of those who remain behind.

³⁴. Certainly We will cause to come down upon the people of this town a punishment from heaven, because they transgressed. ³⁵. And certainly We have left a clear sign of it for a people who understand.

³⁶. And to Madyan We sent their brother Shuaib, so he said, "Oh my people! serve God and fear the latter day and do not act corruptly in the land, making mischief.

³⁷. But they rejected him, so a severe earthquake overtook them, and they became motionless bodies in their home.

³⁸. And We destroyed Ad and Samood, and from their dwellings this is apparent to you indeed; and the Satan made their deeds seem good to them, so he kept them away from the right path, though they were endowed with intelligence and skill,

³⁹. And We destroyed Qaroun and Pharoah and Haman; and certainly Moses came to them with clear explanations, but they behaved arrogantly in the land; yet they could not outstrip Us.

⁴⁰. So each We punished for his sin; of them was he on whom We sent down a violent storm, and of them was he whom the rumbling overtook, and of them was he whom We made to be swallowed up by the earth, and of them was he whom We drowned; and it did not seem to God that He should be unjust to them, but they were unjust to their own souls.

⁴¹. The story of those who take guardians besides God is as the story of the spider that makes for itself a house; and most certainly the frailest of the houses is the spider's house did they

but know.

⁴². Certainly God knows whatever thing they call upon besides Him; and He is the Mighty, the Wise.

⁴³. And as for these examples, We set them forth for men, and none understand them but the learned.

⁴⁴. God created the heavens and the earth with truth; most certainly there is a sign in this for the believers.

⁴⁵. Recite that which has been revealed to you of the Book and keep up prayer; certainly prayer keeps one away from indecency and evil, and certainly the remembrance of God is the greatest, and God knows what you do.

⁴⁶. And do not dispute with the followers of the Book except by what is best, except those of them who act unjustly, and say, "We believe in that which has been revealed to us and revealed to you, and our God and your God is One, and to Him do we submit.

⁴⁷. And thus have We revealed the Book to you. So those whom We have given the Book believe in it, and of these there are those who believe in it, and none deny Our words except the unbelievers.

⁴⁸. And you did not recite before it any book, nor did you transcribe one with your right hand, for then could those who say untrue things have doubted.

⁴⁹. No! these are clear words in the hearts of those who are granted knowledge; and none deny Our words except the unjust.

⁵⁰. And they say, "Why are not signs sent down upon him from his Lord? Say, "The signs are only with God, and I am only a plain alarmgiver.

⁵¹. Is it not enough for them that We have revealed to you the Book which is recited to them? Most certainly there is mercy in this and a reminder for a people who believe.

⁵². Say, "God is sufficient as a witness between me and you; He knows what is in the heavens and the earth. And as for those who believe in the falsehood and disbelieve in God, these it is that are the losers.

⁵³. And they ask you to hasten on the punishment; and had not a term been appointed, the punishment would certainly have come to them; and most certainly it will come to them all of a sudden while they will not perceive.

⁵⁴. They ask you to hasten on the punishment, and most certainly hell encompasses the unbelievers;

⁵⁵. On the day when the punishment shall cover them from above them, and from beneath their feet; and He shall say, "Taste what you did.

⁵⁶. Oh My servants who believe! certainly My earth is vast, therefore Me alone should you serve.

⁵⁷. Every soul must taste of death, then to Us you shall be brought back.

⁵⁸. And as for those who believe and do good, We will certainly give them home in the high places in gardens beneath which rivers flow, abiding therein; how good the reward of the workers:

⁵⁹. Those who are patient, and on their Lord do they rely.

⁶⁰. And how many a living creature that does not carry its sustenance: God sustains it and yourselves; and He is the Hearing, the Knowing.

⁶¹. And if you ask them, Who created the heavens and the earth and made the sun and the moon subservient, they will certainly say, God. From where are they then turned away?

⁶². God makes abundant the means of subsistence for whom He pleases of His servants, and straightens them for whom He pleases certainly God is Aware of all things.

⁶³. And if you ask them Who is it that sends down water from the clouds, then gives life to the earth with it after its death, they will certainly say,

God. Say, "All praise is due to God. No, most of them do not understand. ⁶⁴. And this life of the world is nothing but a sport and a play; and as for the next home, that most certainly is the life -- did they but know!

⁶⁵. So when they ride in the ships they call upon God, being sincerely obedient to Him, but when He brings them safe to the land, lo! they associate others with Him;

⁶⁶. Thus they become ungrateful for what We have given them, so that they may enjoy; but they shall soon know.

⁶⁷. Do they not see that We have made a sacred territory secure, while men are carried off by force from around them? Will they still believe in the falsehood and disbelieve in the favour of God?

⁶⁸. And who is more unjust than one who forges a lie against God, or gives the lie to the truth when it has come to him? Will not in hell be the home of the unbelievers?

⁶⁹. And as for those who strive hard for Us, We will most certainly guide them in Our ways; and God is most certainly with the doers of good.

Chapter 30 — Al-Rum — The Romans

In the name of God, the Kind, the Merciful.

1. Alif Lam Mim.
2. The Romans are vanquished,
3. In a near land, and they, after being vanquished, shall overcome,
4. Within a few years. God's is the command before and after; and on that day the believers shall rejoice,
5. With the help of God; He helps whom He pleases; and He is the Mighty, the Merciful;
6. This is God's promise! God will not fail His promise, but most people do not know.
7. They know the outward of this world's life, but of the hereafter they are absolutely heedless.
8. Do they not reflect within themselves: God did not create the heavens and the earth and what is between them two but with truth, and for an appointed term? And most certainly most of the people are deniers of the meeting of their Lord.
9. Have they not travelled in the earth and seen how was the end of those before them? They were stronger than these in prowess, and dug up the earth, and built on it in greater abundance than these have built on it, and there came to them their apostles with clear explanations; so it did not seem to God that He should deal with them unjustly, but they dealt unjustly with their own souls.
10. Then evil was the end of those who did evil, because they | rejected the words of God and used to mock them.
11. God originates the creation, then reproduces it, then to Him you shall be brought back.
12. And at the time when the hour shall come the guilty shall be in despair.
13. And they shall not have any advocates from among their gods they have joined with God, and they shall be deniers of their associate-gods.
14. And at the time when the hour shall come, at that time they shall become separated one from the other.
15. Then as to those who believed and did good, they shall be made happy in a garden.
16. And as to those who disbelieved and rejected Our words and the meeting of the hereafter, these shall be brought over to the punishment.
17. Therefore glory be to God when you enter upon the time of the evening and when you enter upon the time of the morning.
18. And to Him belongs praise in the heavens and the earth, and at nightfall and when you are at midday.
19. He brings forth the living from the dead and brings forth the dead from the living, and gives life to the earth after its death, and thus shall you be brought forth.
20. And one of His signs is that He created you from dust, then lo! you are mortals who scatter.
21. And one of His signs is that He created mates for you from yourselves that you may find rest in them, and He put between you love and compassion; most certainly there are signs in this for a people who reflect.
22. And one of His signs is the creation of the heavens and the earth and the diversity of your tongues and colors; most certainly there are signs in this for the learned.
23. And one of His signs is your sleeping and your seeking of His grace by night and by day; most certainly there are signs in this for a people who would hear.

24. And one of His signs is that He shows you the lightning for fear and for hope, and sends down water from the clouds then gives life therewith to the earth after its death; most certainly there are signs in this for a people who understand

25. And one of His signs is that the heaven and the earth subsist by His command, then when He calls you with a single call from out of the earth, lo! you come forth.

26. And His is whosoever is in the heavens and the earth; all are obedient to Him.

27. And He it is Who originates the creation, then reproduces it, and it is easy to Him; and His are the most exalted attributes in the heavens and the earth, and He is the Mighty, the Wise.

28. He sets forth to you a story relating to yourselves: Have you among those whom your right hands possess partners in what We have given you for sustenance, so that with respect to it you are alike; you fear them as you fear each other? Thus do We make the words distinct for a people who understand.

29. No! those who are unjust follow their low desires without any knowledge; so who can guide him whom God makes err? And they shall have no helpers.

30. Then set your face upright for religion in the right state -- the nature made by God in which He has made men; there is no altering of God's creation; that is the right religion, but most people do not know --

31. Turning to Him, and be careful of your duty to Him and keep up prayer and do not be one of the polytheists

32. Of those who divided their religion and became seas every sect rejoicing in what they had with them

33. And when harm afflicts men, they call upon their Lord, turning to Him, then when He makes them taste of mercy from Him, lo! some of them begin to associate others with their Lord,

34. So as to be ungrateful for what We have given them; but enjoy yourselves for a while, for you shall soon come to know.

35. Or, have We sent down upon them an authority so that it speaks of that which they associate with Him?

36. And when We make people taste of mercy they rejoice in it, and if an evil happen to them for what their hands have already wrought, lo! they are in despair.

37. Do they not see that God makes ample provision for whom He pleases, or straightens? Most certainly there are signs in this for a people who believe.

38. Then give to the near of kin his due, and to the needy and the wayfarer; this is best for those who desire God's pleasure, and these it is who are successful.

39. And whatever you lay out as usury, so that it may increase in the property of men, it shall not increase with God; and whatever you give in charity, desiring God's pleasure -- it is these persons that shall get manifold.

40. God is He Who created you, then gave you sustenance, then He causes you to die, then brings you to life. Is there any of your associate-gods who does anything like this? Glory be to Him, and exalted be He above what they associate with Him.

41. Corruption has appeared in the land and the sea on account of what the hands of men have wrought, that He may make them taste a part of that which they have done, so that they may return.

42. Say, "Travel in the land, then see how was the end of those before; most of them were polytheists.

43. Then turn your face straight to the right religion before there come from God the day which cannot be averted; on that day they shall become separated.

44. Whoever disbelieves, he shall be responsible for his disbelief, and whoever does good, they

prepare good for their own souls,

45. That He may reward those who believe and do good out of His grace; certainly He does not love the unbelievers.

46. And one of His signs is that He sends forth the winds bearing good news, and that He may make your taste of His mercy, and that the ships may run by His command, and that you may seek of His grace, and that you may be grateful.

47. And certainly We sent before you apostles to their people, so they came to them with clear explanations, then We gave the punishment to those who were guilty; and helping the believers is ever incumbent on Us.

48. God is he Who sends forth the winds so they raise a cloud, then He spreads it forth in the sky as He pleases, and He breaks it up so that you see the rain coming forth from inside it; then when He causes it to fall upon whom He pleases of His servants, lo! they are joyful

49. Though they were before this, before it was sent down upon them, confounded in sure despair.

50. Look then at the signs of God's mercy, how He gives life to the earth after its death, most certainly He will raise the dead to life; and He has power over all things.

51. And if We send a wind and they see it to be yellow, they would after that certainly continue to disbelieve

52. For certainly you cannot, make the dead to hear and you cannot make the deaf to hear the call, when they turn back and

53. Nor can you lead away the blind out of their error. You cannot make to hear any but those who believe in Our words so they shall submit.

54. God is He Who created you from a state of weakness then He gave strength after weakness, then ordered weakness and hoary hair after strength; He creates what He pleases, and He is the Knowing, the Powerful.

55. And at the time when the hour shall come, the guilty shall swear that they did not tarry but an hour; thus are they ever turned away.

56. And those who are given knowledge and faith will say, "Certainly you tarried according to the ordinance of God till the day of resurrection, so this is the day of resurrection, but you did not know.

57. But on that day their excuse shall not profit those who were unjust, nor shall they be regarded with goodwill.

58. And certainly We have set forth for men every kind of example in this Koran; and if you should bring them a word, those who disbelieve would certainly say, "You are nothing but false claimants.

59. Thus does God set a seal on the hearts of those who do not know.

60. Therefore be patient; certainly the promise of God is true and let not those who have no certainty hold you in light estimation.

Chapter 31 — Luqman — Luqman

In the name of God, the Kind, the Merciful.

1. Alif Lam Mim.
2. These are verses of the Book of Wisdom
3. A guidance and a mercy for the doers of goodness,
4. Those who keep up prayer and pay the poor-rate and they are certain of the hereafter.
5. These are on a guidance from their Lord, and these are they who are successful:
6. And of men is he who takes instead frivolous discourse to lead astray from God's path without knowledge, and to take it for a mockery; these shall have an abasing punishment.
7. And when Our words are recited to him, he turns back proudly, as if he had not heard them, as though in his ears were a heaviness, therefore announce to him a painful punishment.
8. As for those who believe and do good, they shall certainly have gardens of bliss,
9. Abiding in them; the promise of God; a true promise, and He is the Mighty, the Wise.
10. He created the heavens without pillars as you see them, and He put mountains upon the earth so that it might shake you, and He spread in it animals of every kind; and We sent down water from the cloud, then caused to grow therein vegetation of every noble kind.
11. This is God's creation, but show Me what those besides Him have created. No, the unjust are in great error
12. And certainly We gave wisdom to Luqman, saying, "Be grateful to God. And whoever is grateful, he is only grateful for his own soul; and whoever is ungrateful, then certainly God is Self-sufficient, Praised.
13. And when Luqman said to his son while he reprimanded him: Oh my son! do not associate anything with God; most certainly polytheism is a grievous iniquity --
14. And We have enjoined man in respect of his parents -- his mother bears him with faintings upon faintings and his weaning takes two years -- saying, "Be grateful to Me and to both your parents; to Me is the eventual coming.
15. And if they contend with you that you should associate with Me what you have no knowledge of, do not obey them, and keep company with them in this world kindly, and follow the way of him who turns to Me, then to Me is your return, then will I inform you of what you did --
16. Oh my son! certainly if it is the very weight of the grain of a mustard-seed, even though it is in the heart of rock, or high above in the heaven or deepdown in the earth, God will bring it to light; certainly God is Knower of subtleties, Aware;
17. Oh my son! keep up prayer and enjoin the good and forbid the evil, and bear patiently that which happens to you; certainly these acts require courage;
18. And do not turn your face away from people in contempt, nor go about in the land exulting overmuch; certainly God does not love any self-conceited boaster;
19. And pursue the right course in your going about and lower your voice; certainly the most hateful of voices is braying of the asses.
20. Do you not see that God has made what is in the heavens and what is in the earth subservient to you, and made complete to you His favors outwardly and inwardly? And among men is he who disputes in respect of God though having no knowledge nor guidance, nor a book giving light.
21. And when it is said to them: Follow what God has revealed, they say, "No, we follow that

on which we found our fathers. What! though the Satan calls them to the punishment of the burning fire!

22. And whoever submits himself wholly to God and he is the doer of good to others, he indeed has taken hold of the firmest thing upon which one can lay hold; and God's is the end of affairs.

23. And whoever disbelieves, let not his disbelief grieve you; to Us is their return, then will We inform them of what they did certainly God is the Knower of what is in the hearts.

24. We give them to enjoy a little, then will We drive them to a severe punishment.

25. And if you ask them who created the heavens and the earth, they will certainly say, "God. Say, "All praise is due to God; no! most of them do not know.

26. What is in the heavens and the earth is God's; certainly God is the Self-sufficient, the Praised.

27. And were every tree that is in the earth made into pens and the sea to supply it with ink, with seven more seas to increase it, the words of God would not come to an end; certainly God is Mighty, Wise.

28. Neither your creation nor your raising is anything but as a single soul; certainly God is Hearing, Seeing.

29. Do you not see that God makes the night to enter into the day, and He makes the day to enter into the night, and He has made the sun and the moon subservient to you; each pursues its course till an appointed time; and that God is Aware of what you do?

30. This is because God is the Truth, and that which they call upon besides Him is the falsehood, and that God is the High, the Great.

31. Do you not see that the ships run on in the sea by God's favor that He may show you of His signs? Most certainly there are signs in this for every patient endurer, grateful one.

32. And when a wave like mountains covers them they call upon God, being sincere to Him in obedience, but when He brings them safe to the land, some of them follow the middle course; and none denies Our signs but every perfidious, ungrateful one.

33. Oh people! guard against the punishment of your Lord and dread the day when a father shall not make any satisfaction for his son, nor shall the child be the maker of any satisfaction for his father; certainly the promise of God is true, therefore let not this world's life deceive you, nor let the arch-deceiver deceive you with respect to God.

34. Certainly God is He with Whom is the knowledge of the hour, and He sends down the rain and He knows what is in the wombs; and no one knows what he shall earn on the morrow; and no one knows in what land he shall die; certainly God is Knowing, Aware.

Chapter 32 — Al-Sajdah — The Adoration

In the name of God, the Kind, the Merciful.

1. Alif Lam Mim.
2. The revelation of the Book, there is no doubt in it, is from the Lord of the worlds.
3. Or do they say, "He has created it? No! it is the truth from your Lord that you may warn a people to whom no alarmgiver has come before you, that they may follow the right direction.
4. God is He Who created the heavens and the earth and what is between them in six periods, and He sat upon the throne of authority; you do not have besides Him any guardian or any advocate, will you not then mind?
5. He regulates the affair from the heaven to the earth; then shall it ascend to Him in a day the measure of which is a thousand years of what you count.
6. This is the Knower of the unseen and the seen, the Mighty the Merciful,
7. Who made good everything that He has created, and He began the creation of man from dust.
8. Then He made his progeny of an extract, of water held in light estimation.
9. Then He made him complete and breathed into him of His spirit, and made for you the ears and the eyes and the hearts; little is it that you give thanks.
10. And they say, "What! when we have become lost in the earth, shall we then certainly be in a new creation? No! they are disbelievers in the meeting of their Lord.
11. Say, "The angel of death who is given charge of you shall cause you to die, then to your Lord you shall be brought back.
12. And could you but see when the guilty shall hang down their heads before their Lord: Our Lord! we have seen and we have heard, therefore send us back, we will do good; certainly now we are certain.
13. And if We had pleased We would certainly have given to every soul its guidance, but the word which had gone forth from Me was just: I will certainly fill hell with the jinn and men together.
14. So taste, because you neglected the meeting of this day of yours; certainly We abandon you; and taste the abiding punishment for what you did.
15. Only they believe in Our words who, when they are reminded of them, fall down making obeisance and celebrate the praise of their Lord, and they are not proud.
16. Their sides draw away from their beds, they call upon their Lord in fear and in hope, and they spend benevolently out of what We have given them.
17. So no soul knows what is hidden for them of that which will refresh the eyes; a reward for what they did.
18. Is he then who is a believer like him who is a transgressor? They are not equal.
19. As for those who believe and do good, the gardens are their abiding-place; an entertainment for what they did.
20. And as for those who transgress, their home is the fire; whenever they desire to go forth from it they shall be brought back into it, and it will be said to them: Taste the punishment of the fire which you called a lie.
21. And most certainly We will make them taste of the nearer punishment before the greater punishment that haply they may turn.
22. And who is more unjust than he who is reminded of the words of his Lord, then he turns away from them? Certainly We will give punishment to the guilty.

²³. And certainly We gave the Book to Moses, so do not be in doubt concerning the receiving of it, and We made it a guide for the children of Israel.

²⁴. And We made of them Imams to guide by Our command when they were patient, and they were certain of Our words.

²⁵. Certainly your Lord will judge between them on the day of resurrection concerning that wherein they differ.

²⁶. Does it not point out to them the right way, how many of the generations, in whose homes they go about, did We destroy before them? Most certainly there are signs in this; will they not then hear?

²⁷. Do they not see that We drive the water to a land having no herbage, then We bring forth thereby seed-produce of which their cattle and they themselves eat; will they not then see?

²⁸. And they say, "When will this judgment take place, If you are truthful?

²⁹. Say, "On the day of judgment the faith of those who now disbelieve will not profit them, nor will they be respited.

³⁰. Therefore turn away from them and wait, certainly they too are waiting.

Chapter 33 — Al-Ahzab — The Clans

In the name of God, the Kind, the Merciful.

¹. Oh Prophet! be careful of your duty to God and do not comply with the wishes of the unbelievers and the hypocrites; certainly God is Knowing, Wise;

². And follow what is revealed to you from your Lord; certainly God is Aware of what you do;

³. And rely on God; and God is sufficient for a Protector.

⁴. God has not made for any man two hearts within him; nor has He made your wives whose backs you liken to the backs of your mothers as your mothers, nor has He made those whom you assert to be your sons your real sons; these are the words of your mouths; and God speaks the truth and He guides to the way.

⁵. Assert their relationship to their fathers; this is more equitable with God; but if you do not know their fathers, then they are your brethren in faith and your friends; and there is no blame on you concerning that in which you made a mistake, but concerning that which your hearts do purposely blame may rest on you, and God is Forgiving, Merciful.

⁶. The Prophet has a greater claim on the faithful than they have on themselves, and his wives are as their mothers; and the possessors of relationship have the better claim in the ordinance of God to inheritance, one with respect to another, than other believers, and than those who have fled
their homes, except that you do some good to your friends; this is written in the Book.

⁷. And when We made a covenant with the prophets and with you, and with Noah and Abraham and Moses and Jesus, son of Mary, and We made with them a strong covenant

⁸. That He may question the truthful of their truth, and He has prepared for the unbelievers a painful punishment.

⁹. Oh you who believe! call to mind the favor of God to you when there came down upon you hosts, so We sent against them a strong wind and hosts, that you saw not, and God is Seeing what you do.

¹⁰. When they came upon you from above you and from below you, and when the eyes turned dull, and the hearts rose up to the throats, and you began to think diverse thoughts of God.

¹¹. There the believers were tried and they were shaken with severe shaking.

¹². And when the hypocrites and those in whose hearts was a disease began to say, "God and His Prophet did not promise us victory but only to deceive.

¹³. And when a party of them said, "Oh people of Yasrib! there IS no place to stand for you here, therefore go back; and a party of them asked permission of the prophet, saying. Certainly our houses are exposed; and they were not exposed; they only desired to fly away.

¹⁴. And if an entry were made upon them from the outlying parts of it, then they were asked to wage war, they would certainly have done it, and they would not have stayed in it but a little while.

¹⁵. And certainly they had made a covenant with God before, that they would not turn their backs; and God's covenant shall be inquired of.

¹⁶. Say, "Flight shall not do you any good if you fly from death or slaughter, and in that case you will not be allowed to enjoy yourselves but a little.

¹⁷. Say, "Who is it that can withhold you from God if He intends to do you evil, rather He intends to show you mercy? And they will not find for themselves besides God any guardian

or a helper.

¹⁸. God knows indeed those among you who hinder others and those who say to their brethren: Come to us; and they come not to the fight but a little, ¹⁹. Being wretched with respect to you; but when fear comes, you will see them looking to you, their eyes rolling like one swooning because of death; but when the fear is gone they smite you with sharp tongues, being wretched of the good things. These have not believed, therefore God has made their doing nothing; and this is easy to God.

²⁰. They think the allies are not gone, and if the allies should come again they would fain be in the deserts with the desert Arabs asking for news about you, and if they were among you they would not fight save a little. ²¹. Certainly you have in the Prophet of God an excellent exemplar for him who hopes in God and the latter day and remembers God much.

²². And when the believers saw the allies, they said, "This is what God and His Prophet promised us, and God and His Prophet spoke the truth; and it only increased them in faith and submission.

²³. Of the believers are men who are true to the covenant which they made with God: so of them is he who accomplished his vow, and of them is he who yet waits, and they have not changed in the least

²⁴. That God may reward the truthful for their truth, and punish the hypocrites if He please or turn to them mercifully; certainly God is Forgiving, Merciful.

²⁵. And God turned back the unbelievers in their rage; they did not obtain any advantage, and God sufficed the believers in fighting; and God is Strong, Mighty.

²⁶. And He drove down those of the followers of the Book who backed them from their fortresses and He cast awe into their hearts; some you killed and you took captive another part.

²⁷. And He made you heirs to their land and their dwellings and their property, and to a land which you have not yet trodden, and God has power over all things.

²⁸. Oh Prophet! say to your wives: If you desire this world's life and its adornment, then come, I will give you provisions and allow you to have a proper departure

²⁹. And if you desire God and His Prophet and the latter home, then certainly God has prepared for the doers of good among you a mighty reward.

³⁰. Oh wives of the prophet! whoever of you commits an open indecency, the punishment shall be increased to her doubly; and this IS easy to God.

³¹. And whoever of you is obedient to God and His Prophet and does good, We will give to her her reward doubly, and We have prepared for her an honorable sustenance.

³². Oh wives of the Prophet! you are not like any other of the women; If you will be on your guard, then do not be soft in your speech, or he in whose heart there is a disease mightyearn; and speak a good word.

³³. And stay in your houses and do not display your finery like the displaying of the ignorance of yore; and keep up prayer, and pay the poor-rate, and obey God and His Prophet. God only desires to keep away the uncleanness from you, Oh people of the House! and to purify you a thorough purifying.

³⁴. And keep to mind what is recited in your houses of the words of God and the wisdom; certainly God is Knower of subtleties, Aware.

³⁵. Certainly the men who submit and the women who submit, and the believing men and the believing women, and the obeying men and the obeying women, and the truthful men and the truthful women, and the patient men and the patient women and the humble men and the humble women, and the almsgiving men and the almsgiving women, and the fasting men and the fasting women, and the men who guard their private parts and the women who guard, and the men who remember God much and the women who remember -- God has

prepared for them forgiveness and a mighty reward.

36. And it behooves not a believing man and a believing woman that they should have any choice in their matter when God and His Prophet have decided a matter; and whoever disobeys God and His Prophet, he certainly strays greatly.

37. And when you said to him to whom God had shown favor and to whom you had shown a favor: Keep your wife to yourself and be careful of your duty to God; and you concealed in your soul what God would bring to light, and you feared men, and God had a greater right that you should fear Him. But when Zaid had accomplished his want of her, We gave her to you as a wife, so that there should be no difficulty for the believers in respect of the wives of their adopted sons, when they have accomplished their want of them; and God's command shall be performed.

38. There is no harm in the Prophet doing that which God has ordered for him; such has been the course of God with respect to those who have gone before; and the command of God is a decree that is made absolute:

39. Those who deliver the messages of God and fear Him, and do not fear any one but God; and God is sufficient to take account.

40. Muhammad is not the father of any of your men, but he is the Prophet of God and the Last of the prophets; and God is cognizant of all things.

41. Oh you who believe! remember God, remembering frequently,

42. And glorify Him morning and evening.

43. He it is Who sends His blessings on you, and so do His angels, that He may bring you forth out of utter darkness into the light; and He is Merciful to the believers.

44. Their salutation on the day that they meet Him shall be, Peace, and He has prepared for them an honourable reward.

45. Oh Prophet! certainly We have sent you as a witness, and as a bearer of good news and as a alarmgiver,

46. And as one inviting to God by His permission, and as a light-giving torch.

47. And give to the believers the good news that they shall have a great grace from God.

48. And do not be compliant to the unbelievers and the hypocrites, and leave unregarded their annoying talk, and rely on God; and God is sufficient as a Protector.

49. Oh you who believe! when you marry the believing women, then divorce them before you touch them, you have in their case no term which you should reckon; so make some provision for them and send them forth properly.

50. Oh Prophet! certainly We have made lawful to you your wives whom you have given their dowries, and those whom your right hand possesses out of those whom God has given to you as prisoners of war, and the daughters of your paternal uncles and the daughters of your paternal aunts, and the daughters of your maternal uncles and the daughters of your maternal aunts who fled with you; and a believing woman if she gave herself to the Prophet, if the Prophet desired to marry her -- specially for you, not for the rest of believers; We know what We have ordered for them concerning their wives and those whom their right hands possess in order that no blame may attach to you; and God is Forgiving, Merciful.

51. You may put off whom you please of them, and you may take to you whom you please, and whom you desire of those whom you had separated provisionally; no blame attaches to you; this is most proper, so that their eyes may be cool and they may not grieve, and that they should be pleased, all of them with what you give them, and God knows what is in your hearts; and God is Knowing, Forbearing.

52. It is not allowed to you to take women afterwards, nor that you should change them for

other wives, though their beauty be pleasing to you, except what your right hand possesses and God is Watchful over all things.

53. Oh you who believe! do not enter the houses of the Prophet unless permission is given to you for a meal, not waiting for its cooking being finished -- but when you are invited, enter, and when you have taken the food, then disperse -- not seeking to listen to talk; certainly this gives the Prophet trouble, but he forbears from you, and God does not forbear from the truth And when you ask of them any goods, ask of them from behind a curtain; this is purer for your hearts and for their hearts; and it does not behoove you that you should give trouble to the Prophet of God, nor that you should marry his wives after him ever; certainly this is grievous in the sight of God.

54. If you do a thing openly or do it in secret, then certainly God is Aware of all things.

55. There is no blame on them in respect of their fathers, nor their brothers, nor their brothers' sons, nor their sisters' sons nor their own women, nor of what their right hands possess; and be careful of your duty to God; certainly God is a witness of all things.

56. Certainly God and His angels bless the Prophet; Oh you who believe! call for Divine blessings on him and salute him with a becoming salutation.

57. Certainly as for those who speak evil things of God and His Prophet, God has cursed them in this world and the here after, and He has prepared for them a punishment bringing disgrace.

58. And those who speak evil things of the believing men and the believing women without their having earned it, they are guilty indeed of a false accusation and a great sin.

59. Oh Prophet! say to your wives and your daughters and the women of the believers that they let down upon them their over-garments; this will be more proper, that they may be known, and thus they will not be given trouble; and God is Forgiving, Merciful.

60. If the hypocrites and those in whose hearts is a disease and the agitators in the city do not desist, We shall most certainly set you over them, then they shall not be your neighbors in it but for a little while;

61. Cursed: wherever they are found they shall be seized and murdered, a horrible murdering

62. Such has been the course of God with respect to those who have gone before; and you shall not find any change in the course of God.

63. Men ask you about the hour; say, "The knowledge of it is only with God, and what will make you comprehend that the : hour may be near.

64. Certainly God has cursed the unbelievers and has prepared for them a burning fire,

65. To abide therein for a long time; they shall not find a protector or a helper.

66. On the day when their faces shall be turned back into the fire, they shall say, "Oh would that we had obeyed God and obeyed the Prophet!

67. And they shall say, "Oh our Lord! certainly we obeyed our leaders and our great men, so they led us astray from the path;

68. Oh our Lord! give them a double punishment and curse them with a great curse.

69. Oh you who believe! do not be like those who spoke evil things of Moses, but God cleared him of what they said, and he was worthy of regard with God.

70. Oh you who believe! be careful of your duty to God and speak the right word,

71. He will put your deeds into a right state for you, and forgive you your faults; and whoever obeys God and His Prophet, he indeed achieves a mighty success.

72. Certainly We offered the trust to the heavens and the earth and the mountains, but they refused to be unfaithful to it and feared from it, and man has turned unfaithful to it; certainly he is unjust, ignorant;

73. So God will reprimand the hypocritical men and the hypocritical women and the polytheistic

men and the polytheistic women, and God will turn mercifully to the believing women, and God is Forgiving, Merciful.

Chapter 34 — Al-Saba — Sheba

In the name of God, the Kind, the Merciful.

1. All praise is due to God, Whose is what is in the heavens and what is in the earth, and to Him is due all praise in the hereafter; and He is the Wise, the Aware.
2. He knows that which goes down into the earth and that which comes out of it, and that which comes down from the heaven and that which goes up to it; and He is the Merciful, the Forgiving.
3. And those who disbelieve say, "The hour shall not come upon us. Say, "Yea! by my Lord, the Knower of the unseen, it shall certainly come upon you; not the weight of an atom becomes absent from Him, in the heavens or in the earth, and neither less than that nor greater, but all is in a clear book
4. That He may reward those who believe and do good; these it is for whom is forgiveness and an honorable sustenance.
5. And as for those who strive hard in opposing Our words, these it is for whom is a painful punishment of an evil kind.
6. And those to whom the knowledge has been given see that which has been revealed to you from your Lord, that is the truth, and it guides into the path of the Mighty, the Praised.
7. And those who disbelieve say, "Shall we point out to you a man who informs you that when you are scattered the utmost scattering you shall then be most certainly raised in to a new creation?
8. He has created a lie against God or there is madness in him. No! those who do not believe in the hereafter are in torment and in great error.
9. Do they not then consider what is before them and what is behind them of the heaven and the earth? If We please We will make them disappear in the land or bring down upon them a portion from the heaven; most certainly there is a sign in this for every servant turning to God.
10. And certainly We gave to David excellence from Us: Oh mountains! sing praises with him, and the birds; and We made the iron pliant to him,
11. Saying, "Make ample coats of mail, and assign a time to the making of coats of mail and do good; certainly I am Seeing what you do.
12. And We made the wind subservient to Solomon, which made a month's journey in the morning and a month's journey in the evening, and We made a fountain of molten copper to flow out for him, and of the jinn there were those who worked before him by the command of his Lord; and whoever turned aside from Our command from among them, We made him taste of the punishment of burning.
13. They made for him what he pleased of fortresses and images, and bowls large as watering-troughs and cooking-pots that will not move from their place; give thanks, Oh family of David! and very few of My servants are grateful.
14. But when We decreed death for him, nothing showed them his death but a creature of the earth that ate away his staff; and when it fell down, the jinn came to know plainly that if they had known the unseen, they would not have tarried in abasing torment.
15. Certainly there was a sign for Sheba in their home; two gardens on the right and the left; eat of the sustenance of your Lord and give thanks to Him: a good land and a Forgiving Lord!
16. But they turned aside, so We sent upon them a torrent of which the rush could not be withstood, and in place of their two gardens We gave to them two gardens yielding bitter fruit

and growing tamarisk and a few lote-trees.

17. This We avenged them with because they disbelieved; and We do not punish any but the ungrateful.

18. And We made between them and the towns which We had blessed other towns to be easily seen, and We apportioned the journey therein: Travel through them nights and days, secure.

19. And they said, "Oh our Lord! make spaces to be longer between our journeys; and they were unjust to themselves so We made them stories and scattered them with an utter scattering; most certainly there are signs in this for every patient, grateful one

20. And certainly the Satan found true his conjecture concerning them, so they follow him, except a party of the believers.

21. And he has no authority over them, but that We may distinguish him who believes in the hereafter from him who is in doubt concerning it; and your Lord is the Preserver of all things

22. Say, "Call upon those whom you assert besides God; they do not control the weight of an atom in the heavens or in the earth nor have they any partnership in either, nor has He among them any one to back Him up.

23. And intercession will not avail anything with Him save of him whom He permits. Until when fear shall be removed from their hearts, They shall say, "What is it that your Lord said? They shall say, "The truth. And He is the Most High, the Great.

24. Say, "Who gives you the sustenance from the heavens and the earth? Say, "God. And most certainly we or you are on a right way or in great error

25. Say, "You will not be questioned as to what we are guilty of, nor shall we be questioned as to what you do.

26. Say, "Our Lord will gather us together, then will He judge between us with the truth; and He is the greatest Judge, the All-knowing.

27. Say, "Show me those whom you have joined with Him as associates; by no means can you do it. No! He is God, the Mighty, the Wise.

28. And We have not sent you but to all the men as a bearer of good news and as a alarmgiver, but most men do not know.

29. And they say, "When will this promise be fulfilled if you are truthful?

30. Say, "You have the appointment of a day from which you cannot hold back any while, nor can you bring it on.

31. And those who disbelieve say, "By no means will we believe in this Koran, nor in that which is before it; and could you see when the unjust shall be made to stand before their Lord, bandying words one with another! Those who were reckoned weak shall say to those who were proud: Had it not been for you we would certainly have been believers.

32. Those who were proud shall say to those who were deemed weak: Did we turn you away from the guidance after it had come to you? No, you yourselves were guilty.

33. And those who were deemed weak shall say to those who were proud. No, it was planning by night and day when you told us to disbelieve in God and to set up likes with Him. And they shall conceal regret when they shall see the punishment; and We will put shackles on the necks of those who disbelieved; they shall not be avenged but what they did.

34. And We never sent a alarmgiver to a town but those who led lives in ease in it said, "We are certainly disbelievers in what you are sent with. 35. And they say, "We have more wealth and children, and we shall not be punished.

36. Say, "Certainly my Lord amplifies the means of subsistence for whom He pleases and straightens for whom He pleases, but most men do not know.

37. And not your wealth nor your children, are the things which bring you near Us in station,

but whoever believes and does good, these it is for whom is a double reward for what they do, and they shall be secure in the highest places.

38. And as for those who strive in opposing Our words, they shall be caused to be brought to the punishment.

39. Say, "Certainly my Lord amplifies the means of subsistence for whom He pleases of His servants and straightens them for whom He pleases, and whatever thing you spend, He exceeds It in reward, and He is the best of
Sustainers.

40. And on the day when He will gather them all together, then will He say to the angels: Did these worship you?

41. They shall say, "Glory be to You! You are our Guardian, not they; no! they worshiped the jinn; most of them were believers in them.

42. So on that day one of you shall not control profit or harm for another, and We will say to those who were unjust: Taste the punishment of the fire which you called a lie.

43. And when Our clear words are recited to them, they say, "This is nothing but a man who desires to turn you away from that which your fathers worshiped. And they say, "This is nothing but a lie that is created. And those who disbelieve say of the truth when it comes to them: This is only clear sorcery.

44. And We have not given them any books which they read, nor did We send to them before you a alarmgiver.

45. And those before them rejected the truth, and these have not yet attained a tenth of what We gave them, but they gave the lie to My apostles, then how was the manifestation of My disapproval?

46. Say, "I exhort you only to one thing, that rise up for God's sake in twos and singly, then ponder: there is no madness in your fellow-citizen; he is only a alarmgiver to you before a severe punishment.

47. Say, "Whatever reward I have asked of you, that is only for yourselves; my reward is only with God, and He is a witness of all things.

48. Say, "Certainly my Lord utters the truth, the great Knower of the unseen.

49. Say, "The truth has come, and the falsehood shall vanish and shall not come back.

50. Say, "If I err, I err only against my own soul, and if I follow a right direction, it ?s because of what my Lord reveals to me; certainly He is Hearing, Nigh.

51. And could you see when they shall become terrified, but then there shall be no escape and they shall be seized upon from a near place

52. And they shall say, "We believe in it. And how shall the attaining of faith be possible to them from a distant place?

53. And they disbelieved in it before, and they utter conjectures with regard to the unseen from a distant place.

54. And a barrier shall be placed between them and that which they desire, as was done with the likes of them before: certainly they are in a disquieting doubt.

Chapter 35 — Al-Fatir — The Founder

In the name of God, the Kind, the Merciful.

1. All praise is due to God, the Originator of the heavens and the earth, the Maker of the angels, messengers flying on wings, two, and three, and four; He increases in creation what He pleases; certainly God has power over all things.

2. Whatever God grants to men of His mercy, there is none to withhold it, and what He withholds there is none to send it forth after that, and He is the Mighty, the Wise

3. Oh men! call to mind the favor of God on you; is there any creator besides God who gives you sustenance from the heaven and the earth? There is no god but Him; from where are you then turned away?

4. And if they call you a liar, truly apostles before you were called liars, and to God are all affairs returned.

5. Oh men! certainly the promise of God is true, therefore let not the life of this world deceive you, and let not the arch-deceiver deceive you respecting God.

6. Certainly the Satan is your enemy, so take him for an enemy; he only invites his party that they may be inmates of the burning.

7. As for those who disbelieve, they shall have a severe punishment, and as for those who believe and do good, they shall have forgiveness and a great reward.

8. What! is he whose evil deed is made fairseeming to him so much so that he considers it good? Now certainly God makes err whom He pleases and guides aright whom He pleases, so let not your soul waste away in grief for them; certainly God is Cognizant of what they do

9. And God is He Who sends the winds so they raise a cloud, then We drive it on to a dead country, and therewith We give life to the earth after its death; even so is the quickening.

10. Whoever desires honor, then to God belongs the honor wholly. To Him do ascend the good words; and the good deeds, lift them up, and as for those who plan evil deeds, they shall have a severe punishment; and as for their plan, it shall perish.

11. And God created you of dust, then of the life-germ, then He made you pairs; and no female bears, nor does she bring forth, except with His knowledge; and no one whose life is lengthened has his life lengthened, nor is anything diminished of one's life, but it is all in a book; certainly this is easy to God.

12. And the two seas are not alike: the one sweet, that subdues thirst by its excessive sweetness, pleasant to drink; and the other salt, that burns by its saltness; yet from each of them you eat fresh flesh and bring forth ornaments which you wear; and you see the ships cleave through it that you may seek of His bounty and that you may be grateful.

13. He causes the night to enter in upon the day, and He causes the day to enter in upon the night, and He has made subservient to you the sun and the moon; each one follows its course to an appointed time; this is God, your Lord, His is the kingdom; and those whom you call upon besides Him do not control a straw.

14. If you call on them they shall not hear your call, and even if they could hear they shall not answer you; and on the resurrection day they will deny your associating them with God; and none can inform you like the One Who is Aware.

15. Oh men! you are they who stand in need of God, and God is He Who is the Self-sufficient, the Praised One.

¹⁶. If He please, He will take you off and bring a new generation.

¹⁷. And this is not hard to God.

¹⁸. And a burdened soul cannot bear the burden of another and if one weighed down by burden should cry for another to carry its burden, nothing of it shall be carried, even though he be near of kin. You warn only those who fear their Lord in secret and keep up prayer; and whoever purifies himself, he purifies himself only for the good of his own soul; and to God is the eventual coming.

¹⁹. And the blind and the seeing are not alike

²⁰. Nor the darkness and the light,

²¹. Nor the shade and the heat,

²². Neither are the living and the dead alike. Certainly God makes whom He pleases hear, and you cannot make those hear who are in the graves.

²³. You are nothing but a complainer.

²⁴. Certainly We have sent you with the truth as a bearer of good news and a alarmgiver; and there is not a people but a alarmgiver has gone among them.

²⁵. And if they call you a liar, so did those before them indeed call their apostles liars; their apostles had come to them with clear explanations, and with scriptures, and with the illuminating book.

²⁶. Then did I punish those who disbelieved, so how was the manifestation of My disapproval?

²⁷. Do you not see that God sends down water from the cloud, then We bring forth therewith fruits of various colors; and in the mountains are streaks, white and red, of various hues and others intensely black?

²⁸. And of men and beasts and cattle are various species of it likewise; those of His servants only who are possessed of knowledge fear God; certainly God is Mighty, Forgiving.

²⁹. Certainly they who recite the Book of God and keep up prayer and spend out of what We have given them secretly and openly, hope for a gain which will not perish.

³⁰. That He may pay them back fully their rewards and give them more out of His grace: certainly He is Forgiving, Multiplier of rewards.

³¹. And that which We have revealed to you of the Book, that is the truth verifying that which is before it; most certainly with respect to His servants God is Aware, Seeing.

³². Then We gave the Book for an inheritance to those whom We chose from among Our servants; but of them is he who makes his soul to suffer a loss, and of them is he who takes a middle course, and of them is he who is foremost in deeds of goodness by God's permission; this is the great excellence.

³³. Gardens of perpetuity, they shall enter therein; they shad be made to wear therein bracelets of gold and pearls, and their dress therein shall be silk.

³⁴. And they shall say, "All praise is due to God, Who has made grief to depart from us; most certainly our Lord is Forgiving, Multiplier of rewards,

³⁵. Who has made us alight in a house abiding for ever out of . His grace; toil shall not touch us therein, nor shall fatigue therein afflict us.

³⁶. And as for those who disbelieve, for them is the fire of hell; it shall not be finished with them entirely so that they should die, nor shall the punishment thereof be lightened to them: even thus do We retribute every ungrateful one.

³⁷. And they shall cry therein for succour: Oh our Lord ! take us out, we will do good deeds other than those which we used to do. Did We not preserve you alive long enough, so that he who would be mindful in it should mind? And there came to you the alarmgiver; therefore taste; because for the unjust, there is no helper.

³⁸. Certainly God is the Knower of what is unseen in the heavens and the earth; certainly He

is Cognizant of what is in the hearts.

³⁹. He it is Who made you rulers in the land; therefore whoever disbelieves, his unbelief is against himself; and their unbelief does not increase the disbelievers with their Lord in anything except hatred; and their unbelief does not increase the disbelievers in anything except loss.

⁴⁰. Say, "Have you considered your associates which you call upon besides God? Show me what part of the earth they have created, or have they any share in the heavens; or, have We given them a book so that they follow a clear argument thereof? No, the unjust do not hold out promises one to another but only to deceive.

⁴¹. Certainly God upholds the heavens and the earth so that they will not come to nothing; and if they should come to nothing, there Is none who can uphold them after Him; certainly He is the Forbearing, the Forgiving.

⁴². And they swore by God with the strongest of their oaths that if there came to them a alarmgiver they would be better guided than any of the nations; but when there came to them a complainer it increased them in nothing but aversion.

⁴³. In behaving proudly in the land and in planning evil; and the evil plans shall not beset any save the authors of it. Should they then wait for anything except the way of the former people? For you shall not find any alteration in the course of God; and you shall not find any change in the course of God.

⁴⁴. Have they not travelled in the land and seen how was the end of those before them while they were stronger than these in power? And God is not such that any thing in the heavens or in the earth should escape Him; certainly He is Knowing, Powerful.

⁴⁵. And were God to punish men for what they earn, He would not leave on the back of it any creature, but He respites them till an appointed term; so when their doom shall come, then certainly God is Seeing with respect to His servants.

Chapter 36 — Ya Sin — Ya Sin

In the name of God, the Kind, the Merciful.

1. Ya Sin.
2. I swear by the Koran full of wisdom
3. Most certainly you are one of the apostles
4. On a right way.
5. A revelation of the Mighty, the Merciful.
6. That you may warn a people whose fathers were not warned, so they are heedless.
7. Certainly the word has proved true of most of them, so they do not believe.
8. Certainly We have placed chains on their necks, and these reach up to their chins, so they have their heads raised aloft.
9. And We have made before them a barrier and a barrier behind them, then We have covered them over so that they do not see.
10. And it is alike to them whether you warn them or warn them not: they do not believe.
11. You can only warn him who follows the reminder and fears the Kind God in secret; so announce to him forgiveness and an honorable reward.
12. Certainly We give life to the dead, and We write down what they have sent before and their footprints, and We have recorded everything in a clear writing.
13. And set out to them an example of the people of the town, when the messengers came to it.
14. When We sent to them two, they rejected both of them, then We strengthened them with a third, so they said, "Certainly we are messengers to you.
15. They said, "You are nothing but mortals like ourselves, nor has the Kind God revealed anything; you only lie.
16. They said, "Our Lord knows that we are most certainly messengers to you.
17. And nothing devolves on us but a clear deliverance of the message.
18. They said, "Certainly we augur evil from you; if you do not desist, we will certainly stone you, and there shall certainly afflict you a painful punishment from us.
19. They said, "Your evil fortune is with you; what! if you are reminded! No, you are an extravagant people.
20. And from the remote part of the city there came a man running, he said, "Oh my people! follow the messengers;
21. Follow him who does not ask you for reward, and they are the followers of the right course;
22. And what reason have I that I should not serve Him Who brought me into existence? And to Him you shall be brought back;
23. What! shall I take besides Him gods whose intercession, If the Kind God should desire to afflict me with a harm, shall not help me At all, nor shall they be able to deliver me?
24. In that case I shall most certainly be in clear error:
25. Certainly I believe in your Lord, therefore hear me.
26. It was said, "Enter the garden. He said, "Oh would that my people had known
27. Of that on account of which my Lord has forgiven me and made me of the honored ones!
28. And We did not send down upon his people after him any hosts from heaven, nor do We ever send down.
29. It was nothing but a single cry, and lo! they were still.

30. Alas for the servants! there comes not to them an apostle but they mock at him.

31. Do they not consider how many of the generations have We destroyed before them, because they do not turn to them?

32. And all of them shall certainly be brought before Us.

33. And a sign to them is the dead earth: We give life to it and bring forth from it grain so they eat of it.

34. And We make therein gardens of palms and grapevines and We make springs to flow forth in it,

35. That they may eat of the fruit thereof, and their hands did not make it; will they not then be grateful?

36. Glory be to Him Who created pairs of all things, of what the earth grows, and of their kind and of what they do not know.

37. And a sign to them is the night: We draw forth from it the day, then lo! they are in the dark;

38. And the sun runs on to a term appointed for it; that is the ordinance of the Mighty, the Knowing.

39. And as for the moon, We have ordered for it stages till it becomes again as an old dry palm branch.

40. Neither is it allowable to the sun that it should overtake the moon, nor can the night outstrip the day; and all float on in a sphere.

41. And a sign to them is that We bear their offspring in the laden ship.

42. And We have created for them the like of it, what they will ride on.

43. And if We please, We can drown them, then there shall be no succorer for them, nor shall they be rescued

44. But by mercy from Us and for enjoyment till a time.

45. And when it is said to them: Guard against what is before you and what is behind you, that mercy may be had on you.

46. And there comes not to them a word of the words of their Lord but they turn aside from it.

47. And when it is said to them: Spend out of what God has given you, those who disbelieve say to those who believe: Shall we feed him whom, if God please, He could feed? You are just in clear error.

48. And they say, "When will this threat come to pass, if you are truthful?

49. They wait not for anything but a single cry which will overtake them while they yet contend with one another.

50. So they shall not be able to make a bequest, nor shall they return to their families.

51. And the trumpet shall be blown, when lo ! from their graves they shall hasten on to their Lord.

52. They shall say, "Oh woe to us! who has raised us up from our sleeping-place? This is what the Kind God promised and the apostles told the truth.

53. There would be nothing but a single cry, when lo ! they shall all be brought before Us;

54. So this day no soul shall be dealt with unjustly in the least; and you shall not be rewarded anything but that which you did.

55. Certainly the dwellers of the garden shall on that day be in an occupation quite happy.

56. They and their wives shall be in shades, reclining on raised couches.

57. They shall have fruits therein, and they shall have whatever they desire.

58. Peace: a word from a Merciful Lord.

59. And get aside today, Oh guilty ones!

60. Did I not charge you, Oh children of Adam ! that you should not serve the Satan? Certainly he is your open enemy,

61. And that you should serve Me; this is the right way.
62. And certainly he led astray numerous people from among you. What! could you not then understand?
63. This is the hell with which you were threatened.
64. Enter into it this day because you disbelieved.
65. On that day We will set a seal upon their mouths, and their hands shall speak to Us, and their feet shall bear witness of what they earned.
66. And if We please We would certainly put out their eyes, then they would run about groping for the way, but how should they see?
67. And if We please We would certainly transform them in their place, then they would not be able to go on, nor will they return.
68. And whomsoever We cause to live long, We reduce him to an abject state in constitution; do they not then understand?
69. And We have not taught him poetry, nor is it meet for him; it is nothing but a reminder and a plain Koran,
70. That it may warn him who would have life, and that the word may prove true against the unbelievers.
71. Do they not see that We have created cattle for them, out of what Our hands have wrought, so they are their masters? 72. And We have subjected them to them, so some of them they have to ride upon, and some of them they eat.
73. And therein they have advantages and drinks; will they not then be grateful?
74. And they have taken gods besides God that they may be helped.
75. But they shall not be able to assist them, and they shall be a host brought up before them.
76. Therefore let not their speech grieve you; certainly We know what they do in secret and what they do openly.
77. Does not man see that We have created him from the small seed? Then lo! he is an open disputant.
78. And he strikes out a likeness for Us and forgets his own creation. Says he: Who will give life to the bones when they are rotten?
79. Say, "He will give life to them Who brought them into existence at first, and He is cognizant of all creation
80. He Who has made for you the fire to burn from the green tree, so that with it you kindle fire.
81. Is not He Who created the heavens and the earth able to create the like of them? Yea! and He is the Creator of all, the Knower.
82. His command, when He intends anything, is only to say to it: Be, so it is.
83. Therefore glory be to Him in Whose hand is the kingdom of all things, and to Him you shall be brought back.

Chapter 37 — Al-Saffat — The Rangers

In the name of God, the Kind, the Merciful.

1. I swear by those who draw themselves out in ranks
2. Then those who drive away with reproof,
3. Then those who recite, being mindful,
4. Most certainly your God is One:
5. The Lord of the heavens and the earth and what is between them, and Lord of the easts.
6. Certainly We have adorned the nearest heaven with an adornment, the stars,
7. And there is a safeguard against every rebellious Satan.
8. They cannot listen to the exalted assembly and they are thrown at from every side,
9. Being driven off, and for them is a perpetual punishment,
10. Except him who snatches off but once, then there follows him a brightly shining flame.
11. Then ask them whether they are stronger in creation or those others whom We have created. Certainly We created them of firm clay.
12. No! you wonder while they mock,
13. And when they are reminded, they mind not,
14. And when they see a sign they incite one another to scoff,
15. And they say, "This is nothing but clear magic:
16. What! when we are dead and have become dust and bones, shall we then certainly be raised,
17. Or our fathers of yore?
18. Say, "Aye! and you shall be abject.
19. So it shall only be a single cry, when lo! they shall see.
20. And they shall say, "Oh woe to us! this is the day of requital.
21. This is the day of the judgment which you called a lie.
22. Gather together those who were unjust and their associates, and what they used to worship
23. Besides God, then lead them to the way to hell.
24. And stop them, for they shall be questioned:
25. What is the matter with you that you do not help each other?
26. No! on that day they shall be submissive.
27. And some of them shall advance towards others, questioning each other.
28. They shall say, "Certainly you used to come to us from the right side.
29. They shall say, "No, you yourselves were not believers;
30. And we had no authority over you, but you were an inordinate people;
31. So the sentence of our Lord has come to pass against us: now we shall certainly taste;
32. So we led you astray, for we ourselves were erring.
33. So they shall on that day be sharers in the punishment one with another.
34. Certainly thus do We deal with the guilty.
35. Certainly they used to behave proudly when it was said to them: There is no god but God;
36. And to say, "What! shall we indeed give up our gods for the sake of a mad poet?
37. No: he has come with the truth and verified the apostles.
38. Most certainly you will taste the painful punishment.
39. And you shall not be rewarded except for what you did.
40. Save the servants of God, the purified ones.

41. For them is a known sustenance,
42. Fruits, and they shall be highly honored,
43. In gardens of pleasure,
44. On thrones, facing each other.
45. A bowl shall be made to go round them from water running out of springs,
46. White, delicious to those who drink.
47. There shall be no trouble in it, nor shall they be exhausted therewith.
48. And with them shall be those who restrain the eyes, having beautiful eyes;
49. As if they were eggs carefully protected.
50. Then shall some of them advance to others, questioning each other.
51. A speaker from among them shall say, "Certainly I had a comrade of mine,
52. Who said, "What! are you indeed of those who accept the truth?
53. What! when we are dead and have become dust and bones, shall we then be certainly brought to judgment?
54. He shall say, "Will you look on?
55. Then he looked down and saw him in the midst of hell.
56. He shall say, "By God! you had almost caused me to perish;
57. And had it not been for the favor of my Lord, I would certainly have been among those brought up.
58. Is it then that we are not going to die,
59. Except our previous death? And we shall not be reprimandd?
60. Most certainly this is the mighty achievement.
61. For the like of this then let the workers work.
62. Is this better as an entertainment or the tree of Zaqqum?
63. Certainly We have made it to be a trial to the unjust.
64. Certainly it is a tree that-grows in the bottom of the hell;
65. Its produce is as it were the heads of the serpents.
66. Then most certainly they shall eat of it and fill their bellies with it.
67. Then most certainly they shall have after it to drink of a mixture prepared in boiling water.
68. Then most certainly their return shall be to hell.
69. Certainly they found their fathers going astray,
70. So in their footsteps they are being hastened on.
71. And certainly most of the ancients went astray before them,
72. And certainly We sent among them alarmgivers.
73. Then see how was the end of those warned,
74. Except the servants of God, the purified ones.
75. And Noah did certainly call upon Us, and most excellent answerer of prayer are We.
76. And We delivered him and his followers from the mighty distress.
77. And We made his offspring the survivors.
78. And We perpetuated to him praise among the later generations.
79. Peace and salutation to Noah among the nations.
80. Thus do We certainly reward the doers of good.
81. Certainly he was of Our believing servants.
82. Then We drowned the others
83. And most certainly Abraham followed his way.
84. When he came to his Lord with a free heart,
85. When he said to his father and his people: What is it that you worship?

86. A lie -- gods besides God -- do you desire?
87. What is then your idea about the Lord of the worlds?
88. Then he looked at the stars, looking up once,
89. Then he said, "Certainly I am sick of your worshiping these.
90. So they went away from him, turning back.
91. Then he turned aside to their gods secretly and said, "What! do you not eat?
92. What is the matter with you that you do not speak?
93. Then he turned against them secretly, smiting them with the right hand.
94. So they people advanced towards him, hastening.
95. Said he: What! do you worship what you hew out?
96. And God has created you and what you make.
97. They said, "Build for him a furnace, then cast him into the burning fire.
98. And they desired a war against him, but We brought them low.
99. And he said, "Certainly I fly to my lord; He will guide me.
100. My Lord! grant me of the doers of good deeds.
101. So We gave him the good news of a boy, possessing forbearance.
102. And when he attained to working with him, he said, "Oh my son! certainly I have seen in a dream that I should sacrifice you; consider then what you see. He said, "Oh my father! do what you are commanded; if God please, you will find me of the patient ones.
103. So when they both submitted and he threw him down upon his forehead,
104. And We called out to him saying, "Oh Abraham!
105. You have indeed shown the truth of the vision; certainly thus do We reward the doers of good:
106. Most certainly this is a great trial.
107. And We ransomed him with a Feat sacrifice.
108. And We perpetuated praise to him among the later generations.
109. Peace be on Abraham.
110. Thus do We reward the doers of good.
111. Certainly he was one of Our believing servants.
112. And We gave him the good news of Isaac, a prophet among the good ones.
113. And We showered Our blessings on him and on Isaac; and of their offspring are the doers of good, and also those who are clearly unjust to their own souls.
114. And certainly We conferred a favor on Moses and Aaron.
115. And We delivered them both and their people from the mighty distress.
116. And We helped them, so they were the vanquishers.
117. And We gave them both the Book that made things clear.
118. And We guided them both on the right way.
119. And We perpetuated praise to them among the later generations.
120. Peace be on Moses and Aaron.
121. Even thus do We reward the doers of good.
122. Certainly they were both of Our believing servants.
123. And Elias was most certainly of the apostles.
124. When he said to his people: Do you not guard against evil?
125. What! do you call upon Ba'l and abandon the best of the creators,
126. God, your Lord and the Lord of your fathers of yore?
127. But they called him a liar, therefore they shall most certainly be brought up.
128. But not the servants of God, the purified ones.
129. And We perpetuated to him praise among the later generations.

130. Peace be on Elias.
131. Even thus do We reward the doers of good.
132. Certainly he was one of Our believing servants.
133. And Lot was most certainly of the apostles.
134. When We delivered him and his followers, all --
135. Except an old woman who was amongst those who tarried.
136. Then We destroyed the others.
137. And most certainly you pass by them in the morning,
138. And at night; do you not then understand?
139. And Yunus was most certainly of the apostles.
140. When he ran away to a ship completely laden,
141. So he shared with them, but was of those who are cast off.
142. So the fish swallowed him while he did that for which he blamed himself
143. But had it not been that he was of those who glorify Us,
144. He would certainly have tarried in its belly to the day when they are raised.
145. Then We cast him on to the vacant surface of the earth while he was sick.
146. And We caused to grow up for him a gourdplant.
147. And We sent him to a hundred thousand, rather they exceeded.
148. And they believed, so We gave them provision till a time.
149. Then ask them whether your Lord has daughters and they have sons.
150. Or did We create the angels females while they were witnesses?
151. Now certainly it is of their own lie that they say, "
152. God has begotten; and most certainly they are liars.
153. Has He chosen daughters in preference to sons?
154. What is the matter with you, how is it that you judge?
155. Will you not then mind?
156. Or have you a clear authority?
157. Then bring your book, if you are truthful.
158. And they assert a relationship between Him and the jinn; and certainly the jinn do know that they shall certainly be brought up;
159. Glory be to God for freedom from what they describe;
160. But not so the servants of God, the purified ones.
161. So certainly you and what you worship,
162. Not against Him can you cause any to fall into trial,
163. Save him who will go to hell.
164. And there is none of us but has an assigned place,
165. And most certainly we are they who draw themselves out in ranks,
166. And we are most certainly they who declare the glory of God.
167. And certainly they used to say, "
168. Had we a reminder from those of yore,
169. We would certainly have been the servants of God -- the purified ones.
170. But now they disbelieve in it, so they will come to know.
171. And certainly Our word has already gone forth in respect of Our servants, the apostles:
172. Most certainly they shall be the assisted ones
173. And most certainly Our host alone shall be the victorious ones.
174. Therefore turn away from them till a time,
175. And then see them, so they too shall see.

176. What! would they then hasten on Our punishment?
177. But when it shall descend in their court, evil shall then be the morning of the warned ones.
178. And turn away from them till a time
179. And then see, for they too shall see.
180. Glory be to your Lord, the Lord of Honor, above what they describe.
181. And peace be on the apostles.
182. And all praise is due to God, the Lord of the worlds.

Chapter 38 — Saad — Saad

In the name of God, the Kind, the Merciful.

¹. Saad, I swear by the Koran, full of admonition.

². No! those who disbelieve are in self-exaltation and opposition.

³. How many did We destroy before them of the generations, then they cried while the time of escaping had passed away.

⁴. And they wonder that there has come to them a alarmgiver from among themselves, and the disbelievers say, "This is an magician, a liar.

⁵. What! makes he the gods a single God? A strange thing is this, to be sure!

⁶. And the chief persons of them break forth, saying, "Go and steadily adhere to your gods; this is most certainly a thing sought after.

⁷. We never heard of this in the former faith; this is nothing but a forgery:

⁸. Has the reminder been revealed to him from among us? No! they are in doubt as to My reminder. No! they have not yet tasted My punishment!

⁹. Or is it that they have the treasures of the mercy of your Lord, the Mighty, the great Giver?

¹⁰. Or is it that theirs is the kingdom of the heavens and the earth and what is between them? Then let them ascend by any

¹¹. A host of deserters of the allies shall be here put to flight.

¹². The people of Noah and Ad, and Pharoah, the lord of spikes, rejected apostles before them.

¹³. And Samood and the people of Lot and the dwellers of the thicket; these were the parties.

¹⁴. There was none of them but called the apostles liars, so just was My retribution.

¹⁵. Nor do these await anything but a single cry, there being no delay in it.

¹⁶. And they say, "Oh our Lord! hasten on to us our portion before the day of judging.

¹⁷. Bear patiently what they say, and remember Our servant David, the possessor of power; certainly he was frequent in returning to God.

¹⁸. Certainly We made the mountains to sing the glory of God in unison with him at the evening and the sunrise,

¹⁹. And the birds gathered together; all joined in singing with him.

²⁰. And We strengthened his kingdom and We gave him wisdom and a clear judgment.

²¹. And has there come to you the story of the litigants, when they made an entry into the private chamber by ascending over the walls?

²². When they entered in upon David and he was frightened at them, they said, "Fear not; two litigants, of whom one has acted wrongfully towards the other, therefore decide between us with justice, and do not act unjustly, and guide us to the right way.

²³. Certainly this is my brother; he has ninety-nine ewes and I have a single ewe; but he said, "Make it over to me, and he has prevailed against me in discourse.

²⁴. He said, "Certainly he has been unjust to you in demanding your ewe to add to his own ewes; and most certainly most of the partners act wrongfully towards one another, save those who believe and do good, and very few are they; and David was sure that We had tried him, so he sought the protection of his Lord and he fell down bowing and turned time after time to Him.

²⁵. Therefore We rectified for him this, and most certainly he had a nearness to Us and an excellent resort.

²⁶. Oh David! certainly We have made you a ruler in the land; so judge between men with

justice and do not follow desire, or it might lead you to stray from the path of God; as do those who go astray from the path of God, they shall certainly have a severe punishment because they forgot the day of judgment.

27. And We did not create the heaven and the earth and what is between them in vain; that is the opinion of those who disbelieve then woe to those who disbelieve on account of the fire.

28. Shall We treat those who believe and do good like the mischief-makers in the earth? Or shall We make those who guard against evil like the wicked?

29. It is a Book We have revealed to you abounding in good that they may ponder over its verses, and that those endowed with understanding may be mindful.

30. And We gave to David Solomon, a most excellent servant! Certainly he was frequent in returning to God.

31. When there were brought to him in the evening horses still when standing, swift when running --

32. Then he said, "Certainly I preferred the good things to the remembrance of my Lord -- until the sun set and time for Asr prayer was over, he said, "

33. Bring them back to me; so he began to slash their legs and necks.

34. And certainly We tried Solomon, and We put on his throne a mere body, so he turned to God.

35. He said, "My Lord! do You forgive me and grant me a kingdom which is not fit for being inherited by anyone after me;

36. Then We made the wind subservient to him; it made his command to run gently wherever he desired,

37. And the Satans, every builder and diver,

38. And others fettered in chains.

39. This is Our free gift, therefore give freely or withhold, without judging.

40. And most certainly he had a nearness to Us and an excellent resort.

41. And remember Our servant Job, when he called upon his Lord: The Satan has afflicted me with toil and torment.

42. Urge with your foot; here is a cool washing-place and a drink.

43. And We gave him his family and the like of them with them, as a mercy from Us, and as a reminder to those possessed of understanding.

44. And take in your hand a green branch and beat her with It and do not break your oath; certainly We found him patient; most excellent the servant! Certainly he was frequent in returning to God.

45. And remember Our servants Abraham and Isaac and Jacob, men of power and insight.

46. Certainly We purified them to a pure quality, the keeping in mind of their final home.

47. And most certainly they were with Us, of the elect, the best.

48. And remember Ishmael and Al-Yasha and Zulkifl; and they were all of the best.

49. This is a reminder; and most certainly there is an excellent resort for those who guard against evil,

50. The gardens of perpetuity, the doors are opened for them.

51. Reclining therein, calling therein for many fruits and drink.

52. And with them shall be those restraining their eyes, equals in age.

53. This is what you are promised for the day of judging.

54. Most certainly this is Our sustenance; it shall never come to an end;

55. This shall be so; and most certainly there is an evil resort for the inordinate ones;

56. Hell; they shall enter it, so evil is the resting-place.

57. This shall be so; so let them taste it, boiling and intensely cold drink.
58. And other punishment of the same kind -- of various sorts.
59. This is an army plunging in without consideration along with you; no welcome for them, certainly they shall enter fire.
60. They shall say, "No! you -- no welcome to you: you did proffer it to us, so evil is the resting-place.
61. They shall say, "Our Lord! whoever prepared it first for us, add You to him a double punishment in the fire.
62. And they shall say, "What is the matter with us that we do not see men whom we used to count among the vicious?
63. Was it that we only took them in scorn, or have our eyes now turned aside from them?
64. That most certainly is the truth: the contending one with another of the inmates of the fire.
65. Say, "I am only a alarmgiver, and there is no god but God, the One, the Subduer of all:
66. The Lord of the heavens and the earth and what is between them, the Mighty, the most Forgiving.
67. Say, "It is a message of importance,
68. And you are turning aside from it:
69. [1] had no knowledge of the exalted chiefs when they contended:
70. Nothing is revealed to me save that I am a plain alarmgiver.
71. When your Lord said to the angels; Certainly I am going to create a mortal from dust:
72. So when I have made him complete and breathed into him of My spirit, then fall down making obeisance to him.
73. And the angels did obeisance, all of them,
74. But not Iblis: he was proud and he was one of the unbelievers.
75. He said, "Oh Iblis! what prevented you that you should do obeisance to him whom I created with My two hands? Are you proud or are you of the exalted ones?
76. He said, "I am better than he; You have created me of fire, and him You did create of dust.
77. He said, "Then get out of it, for certainly you are driven away:
78. And certainly My curse is on you to the day of judgment.
79. He said, "My Lord! then respite me to the day that they are raised.
80. He said, "Certainly you are of the respited ones,
81. Till the period of the time made known.
82. He said, "Then by Your Might I will certainly make them live an evil life, all,
83. Except Your servants from among them, the purified ones.
84. He said, "The truth then is and the truth do I speak:
85. That I will most certainly fill hell with you and with those among them who follow you, all.
86. Say, "I do not ask you for any reward for it; nor am I of those who affect:
87. It is nothing but a reminder to the nations;
88. And most certainly you will come to know about it after a time.

Chapter 39 — Al-Zumar — The Companions

In the name of God, the Kind, the Merciful.

¹. The revelation of the Book is from God, the Mighty, the Wise.

². Certainly We have revealed to you the Book with the truth, therefore serve God, being sincere to Him in obedience.

³. Now, certainly, sincere obedience is due to God alone and as for those who take guardians besides Him, saying, We do not serve them save that they may make us nearer to God, certainly God will judge between them in that in which they differ; certainly God does not guide him aright who is a liar, ungrateful.

⁴. If God desire to take a son to Himself, He will certainly choose those He pleases from what He has created. Glory be to Him: He is God, the One, the Subduer of all.

⁵. He has created the heavens and the earth with the truth; He makes the night cover the day and makes the day overtake the night, and He has made the sun and the moon subservient; each one runs on to an assigned term; now certainly He is the Mighty, the great Forgiver.

⁶. He has created you from a single being, then made its mate of the same kind, and He has made for you eight of the cattle in pairs. He creates you in the wombs of your mothers -- a creation after a creation -- in triple darkness; that is God your Lord, His is the kingdom; there is no god but He; from where are you then turned away?

⁷. If you are ungrateful, then certainly God is Self-sufficient above all need of you; and He does not like ungratefulness in His servants; and if you are grateful, He likes it in you; and no bearer of burden shall bear the burden of another; then to your Lord is your return, then will He inform you of what you did; certainly He is Cognizant of what is in the hearts.

⁸. And when distress afflicts a man he calls upon his Lord turning to Him frequently; then when He makes him possess a favor from Him, he forgets that for which he called upon Him before, and sets up rivals to God that he may cause men to stray off from His path. Say, "Enjoy yourself in your ungratefulness a little, certainly you are of the inmates of the fire.

⁹. What! he who is obedient during hours of the night, prostrating himself and standing, takes care of the hereafter and hopes for the mercy of his Lord! Say, "Are those who know and those who do not know alike? Only the men of understanding are mindful.

¹⁰. Say, "Oh my servants who believe! be careful of your duty to your Lord; for those who do good in this world is good, and God's earth is spacious; only the patient will be paid back their reward in full without measure.

¹¹. Say, "I am commanded that I should serve God, being sincere to Him in obedience.

¹². And I am commanded that I shall be the first of those who submit.

¹³. Say, "I fear, if I disobey my Lord, the punishment of a grievous day.

¹⁴. Say, "God it is Whom I serve, being sincere to Him in my obedience:

¹⁵. Serve then what you like besides Him. Say, "The losers certainly are those who shall have lost themselves and their families on the day of resurrection; now certainly that is the clear loss.

¹⁶. They shall have coverings of fire above them and coverings beneath them; with that God makes His servants to fear, so be careful of your duty to Me, Oh My servants!

¹⁷. And as for those who keep off from the worship of the idols and turn to God, they shall have good news, therefore give good news to My servants,

¹⁸. Those who listen to the word, then follow the best of it; those are they whom God has

guided, and those it is who are the men of understanding.

19. What! as for him then against whom the sentence of punishment is due: What! can you save him who is in the fire?

20. But as for those who are careful of their duty to their Lord, they shall have high places, above them higher places, built for them, beneath which flow rivers; this is the promise of God: God will not fail in His promise.

21. Do you not see that God sends down water from the cloud, then makes it go along in the earth in springs, then brings forth therewith herbage of various colors, then it withers so that you see it becoming yellow, then He makes it a thing crushed and broken into pieces? Most certainly there is a reminder in this for the men of understanding.

22. What! is he whose heart God has opened for Islam so that he is in a light from his Lord like the hard-hearted? No, woe to those whose hearts are hard against the remembrance of God; those are in clear error.

23. God has revealed the best announcement, a book conformable in its various parts, repeating, whereat do shudder the skins of those who fear their Lord, then their skins and their hearts become pliant to the remembrance of God; this is God's guidance, He guides with it whom He pleases; and as for him whom God makes err, there is no guide for him.

24. Is he then who has to guard himself with his own person against the evil punishment on the resurrection day? And it will be said to the unjust: Taste what you earned.

25. Those before them rejected prophets, therefore there came to them the punishment from from where they perceived not.

26. So God made them taste the disgrace in this world's life, and certainly the punishment of the hereafter is greater; did they but know!

27. And certainly We have set forth to men in this Koran similitudes of every sort that they may mind.

28. An Arabic Koran without any crookedness, that they may guard against evil.

29. God sets forth an example: There is a slave in whom are several partners differing with one another, and there is another slave wholly owned by one man. Are the two alike in condition? All praise is due to God. No! most of them do not know.

30. Certainly you shall die and they too shall certainly die.

31. Then certainly on the day of resurrection you will contend one with another before. your Lord.

32. Who is then more unjust than he who utters a lie against God and he who gives the lie to the truth when it comes to him; is there not in hell an home for the unbelievers?

33. And he who brings the truth and he who accepts it as the truth -- these are they that guard against evil.

34. They shall have with their Lord what they please; that is the reward of the doers of good;

35. So that God will do away with the worst of what they did and give them their reward for the best of what they do.

36. Is not God sufficient for His servant? And they seek to frighten you with those besides Him; and whomsoever God makes err, there is no guide for him.

37. And whom God guides, there is none that can lead him astray; is not God Mighty, the Lord of retribution?

38. And should you ask them, Who created the heavens and the earth? They would most certainly say, "God. Say, "Have you then considered that what you call upon besides God, would they, if God desire to afflict me with harm, be the removers of His harm, or would they, if God desire to show me mercy, be the withholders of His mercy? Say, "God is sufficient for me; on Him do the reliant rely.

39. Say, "Oh my people! work in your place, certainly I am a worker, so you will come to know.
40. Who it is to whom there shall come a punishment which will disgrace him and to whom will be due a lasting punishment.
41. Certainly We have revealed to you the Book with the truth for the sake of men; so whoever follows the right way, it is for his own soul and whoever errs, he errs only to its detriment; and you are not a custodian over them.
42. God takes the souls at the time of their death, and those that die not during their sleep; then He withholds those on whom He has passed the decree of death and sends the others back till an appointed term; most certainly there are signs in this for a people who reflect.
43. Or have they taken advocates besides God? Say, "what! even though they did not ever have control over anything, nor do they understand.
44. Say, "God's is the intercession altogether; His is the kingdom of the heavens and the earth, then to Him you shall be brought back.
45. And when God alone is mentioned, the hearts of those who do not believe in the hereafter shrink, and when those besides Him are mentioned, lo! they are joyful.
46. Say, "Oh God! Originator of the heavens and the earth, Knower of the unseen and the seen! You only judge between Your servants as to that wherein they differ.
47. And had those who are unjust all that is in the earth and the like of it with it, they would certainly offer it as ransom to be saved from the evil of the punishment on the day of resurrection; and what they never thought of shall become plain to them from God.
48. And the evil consequences of what they wrought shall become plain to them, and the very thing they mocked at shall beset them.
49. So when harm afflicts a man he calls upon Us; then, when We give him a favor from Us, he says: I have been given it only by means of knowledge. No, it is a trial, but most of them do not know.
50. Those before them did say it indeed, but what they earned availed them not.
51. So there befell them the evil consequences of what they earned; and as for those who are unjust from among these, there shall happen to them the evil consequences of what they earn, and they shall not escape.
52. Do they not know that God makes ample the means of subsistence to whom He pleases, and He straightens; most certainly there are signs in this for a people who believe.
53. Say, "Oh my servants! who have acted extravagantly against their own souls, do not despair of the mercy of God; certainly God forgives the faults altogether; certainly He is the Forgiving the Merciful.
54. And return to your Lord time after time and submit to Him before there comes to you the punishment, then you shall not be helped.
55. And follow the best that has been revealed to you from your Lord before there comes to you the punishment all of a sudden while you do not even perceive;
56. Perhaps a soul might say, "Oh woe to me! for I have fallen short of my duty to God, and certainly I was of those who laughed to scorn;
57. Or it should say, "Had God guided me, I would certainly have been of those who guard against evil;
58. Or it should say when it sees the punishment: Were there only a returning for me, I should be of the doers of good.
59. Aye! My words came to you, but you rejected them, and you were proud and you were one of the unbelievers.
60. And on the day of resurrection you shall see those who lied against God; their faces shall be

blackened. Is there not in hell an home for the proud?

⁶¹. And God shall deliver those who guard against evil with their achievement; evil shall not touch them, nor shall they grieve. ⁶². God is the Creator of every thing and He has charge over every thing.

⁶³. His are the treasures of the heavens and the earth; and as for those who disbelieve in the words of God, these it is that are the losers.

⁶⁴. Say, "What! Do you then bid me serve others than God, Oh ignorant men?

⁶⁵. And certainly, it has been revealed to you and to those before you: Certainly if you associate with God, your work would certainly come to nothing and you would certainly be of the losers.

⁶⁶. No! but serve God alone and be of the thankful.

⁶⁷. And they have not honored God with the honor that is due to Him; and the whole earth shall be in His grip on the day of resurrection and the heavens rolled up in His right hand; glory be to Him, and may He be exalted above what they associate with Him.

⁶⁸. And the trumpet shall be blown, so all those that are in the heavens and all those that are in the earth shall swoon, except such as God please; then it shall be blown again, then lo! they shall stand up awaiting.

⁶⁹. And the earth shall beam with the light of its Lord, and the Book shall be laid down, and the prophets and the witnesses shall be brought up, and judgment shall be given between them with justice, and they shall not be dealt with unjustly.

⁷⁰. And every soul shall be paid back fully what it has done, and He knows best what they do.

⁷¹. And those who disbelieve shall be driven to hell in companies; until, when they come to it, its doors shall be opened, and the keepers of it shall say to them: Did not there come to you apostles from among you reciting to you the words of your Lord and warning you of the meeting of this day of yours? They shall say, "Yea! But the sentence of punishment was due against the unbelievers.

⁷². It shall be said, "Enter the gates of hell to abide therein; so evil is the home of the proud.

⁷³. And those who are careful of their duty to their Lord shall be conveyed to the garden in companies; until when they come to it, and its doors shall be opened, and the keepers of it shall say to them: Peace be on you, you shall be happy; therefore enter it to abide.

⁷⁴. And they shall say, "All praise is due to God, Who has made good to us His promise, and He has made us inherit the land; we may abide in the garden where we please; so good is the reward of the workers.

⁷⁵. And you shall see the angels going round about the throne glorifying the praise of their Lord; and judgment shall be given between them with justice, and it shall be said, "All praise is due to God, the Lord of the worlds.

Chapter 40 — Al-Mu'min — The Believer

In the name of God, the Kind, the Merciful.

¹. Ha Mim.

². The revelation of the Book is from God, the Mighty, the Knowing,

³. The Forgiver of the faults and the Acceptor of repentance, Severe to punish, Lord of bounty; there is no god but He; to Him is the eventual coming.

⁴. None dispute concerning the words of God but those who disbelieve, therefore let not their going to and fro in the cities deceive you.

⁵. The people of Noah and the parties after them rejected prophets before them, and every nation purposed against their apostle to destroy him, and they disputed by means of the falsehood that they might thereby render null the truth, therefore I destroyed them; how was then My retribution!

⁶. And thus did the word of your Lord prove true against those who disbelieved that they are the inmates of the fire.

⁷. Those who bear the power and those around Him celebrate the praise of their Lord and believe in Him and ask protection for those who believe: Our Lord! You embrace all things in mercy and knowledge, therefore grant protection to those who turn to You and follow Your way, and save them from the punishment of the hell:

⁸. Our Lord! and make them enter the gardens of perpetuity which You have promised to them and those who do good of their fathers and their wives and their offspring, certainly You are the Mighty, the Wise.

⁹. And keep them from evil deeds, and those whom You keep from evil deeds even today, indeed You have will have mercy on him, and that is the mighty achievement.

¹⁰. Certainly those who disbelieve shall be warned: Certainly God's hatred of you when you were called upon to have faith and you rejected, this is much greater than your hatred of yourselves.

¹¹. They shall say, "Our Lord! twice You made us subject to death, and twice have You given us life, so we do confess our faults; is there now a way to get out?

¹². That is because when God alone was called upon, you disbelieved, and when associates were given to Him, you believed; so judgment belongs to God, the High, the Great.

¹³. He it is Who shows you His signs and sends down for you sustenance from heaven, and none minds but he who turns to Him again and again. ¹⁴. Therefore call upon God, being sincere to Him in obedience, though the unbelievers are averse:

¹⁵. Possessor of the highest rank, Lord of power: He makes the inspiration to light by His command upon whom He pleases of His servants, that he may warn men of the day of meeting.

¹⁶. Of the day when they shall come forth, nothing concerning them remains hidden to God. To whom belongs the kingdom this day? To God, the One, the Subduer of all.

¹⁷. This day every soul shall be rewarded for what it has earned; no injustice shall be done this day; certainly God is quick in judging.

¹⁸. And warn them of the day that draws near, when hearts shall rise up o the throats, grieving inwardly; the unjust shall not have any compassionate friend nor any advocate who should be obeyed.

¹⁹. He knows the stealthy looks and that which the hearts conceal.

²⁰. And God judges with the truth; and those whom they call upon besides Him cannot judge

at all; certainly God is the Hearing, the Seeing.

21. Have they not travelled in the earth and seen how was the end of those who were before them? Mightier than these were they in strength -- and in fortifications in the land, but God destroyed them for their sins; and there was not for them any defender against God.

22. That was because there came to them their apostles with clear explanations, but they rejected them, therefore God destroyed them; certainly He is Strong, Severe in retribution.

23. And certainly We sent Moses with Our words and clear authority, 24. To Pharoah and Haman and Qaroun, but they said, "A lying magician."

25. So when he brought to them the truth from Us, they said, "Slay the sons of those who believe with him and keep their women alive; and the struggle of the unbelievers will only come to a state of hell.

26. And Pharoah said, "Let me alone that I may slay Moses and let him call upon his Lord; certainly I fear that he will change your religion or that he will make mischief to appear in the land.

27. And Moses said, "Certainly I take refuge with my Lord and -- your Lord from every proud one who does not believe in the day of judging.

28. And a believing man of Pharoah's people who hid his faith said, "What! will you slay a man because he says: My Lord is God, and indeed he has brought to you clear explanations from your Lord? And if he be a liar, on him will be his lie, and if he be truthful, there will happen to you some of that which he threatens you with; certainly God does not guide him who is extravagant, a liar:

29. Oh my people! yours is the kingdom this day, being masters in the land, but who will help us against the punishment of God if it come to us? Pharoah said, "I do not show you anything but that which I see myself, and I do not make you follow any but the right way.

30. And he who believed said, "Oh my people! certainly I fear for you the like of what befell the parties:

31. The like of what befell the people of Noah and Ad and Samood and those after them, and God does not desire injustice for His servants;

32. And, Oh my people! I fear for you the day of calling out,

33. The day on which you will turn back retreating; there shall be no savior for you from God, and whomsoever God causes to err, there is no guide for him:

34. And certainly Joseph came to you before with clear explanations, but you ever remained in doubt as to what he brought; until when he died, you said, "God will never raise an apostle after him. Thus does God cause him to err who is extravagant, a doubter

35. Those who dispute concerning the words of God without any authority that He has given them; greatly hated is it by God and by-those who believe. Thus does God set a seal over the heart of every proud, haughty one.

36. And Pharoah said, "Oh Haman! build for me a tower that I may attain the means of access,

37. The means of access to the heavens, then reach the God of Moses, and I certainly think him to be a liar. And thus the evil of his deed was made fairseeming to Pharoah, and he was turned away from the way; and the struggle of Pharoah di dnot end in anything but destruction.

38. And he who believed said, "Oh my people! follow me, I will guide you to the right course;

39. Oh my people! this life of the world is only a passing enjoyment, and certainly the hereafter is the home to settle;

40. Whoever does an evil, he shall not be repaid with anything but the like of it, and whoever does good, whether male or female, and he is a believer, these shall enter the garden, in which they shall be given sustenance without measure.

41. And, Oh my people! how is it that I call you to salvation and you call me to the fire?

⁴². You call on me that I should disbelieve in God and associate with Him that of which I have no knowledge, and I call you to the Mighty, the most Forgiving;

⁴³. No doubt that what you call me to has no title to be called to in this world, nor in the hereafter, and that our turning back is to God, and that the extravagant are the inmates of the fire;

⁴⁴. So you shall remember what I say to you, and I entrust my affair to God, Certainly God sees the servants.

⁴⁵. So God protected him from the evil consequences of what they planned, and the most evil punishment overtook Pharoah's people:

⁴⁶. The fire; they shall be brought before it every morning and evening and on the day when the hour shall come to pass: Let the Pharoah's people be given the severest punishment.

⁴⁷. And when they shall contend one with another in the fire, then the weak shall say to those who were proud: Certainly we were your followers; will you now protect us from some of this fire?

⁴⁸. Those who were proud shall say, "Certainly we are all in it: certainly God has judged between the servants.

⁴⁹. And those who are in the fire shall say to the keepers of hell: Call upon your Lord that He may lighten to us one day of the punishment.

⁵⁰. They shall say, "Did not your apostles come to you with clear explanations? They shall say, "Yea. They shall say, "Then call. And the call of the unbelievers is only in error.

⁵¹. Most certainly We help Our apostles, and those who believe, in this world's life and on the day when the witnesses shall stand

⁵². The day on which their excuse shall not benefit the unjust, and for them is curse and for them is the evil home.

⁵³. And certainly We gave Moses the guidance, and We made the children of Israel inherit the Book,

⁵⁴. A guidance and a reminder to the men of understanding.

⁵⁵. Therefore be patient; certainly the promise of God is true; and ask protection for your fault and sing the praise of your Lord in the evening and the morning.

⁵⁶. Certainly as for those who dispute about the words of God without any authority that has come to them, there is nothing in their hearts but a desire to become great which they shall never attain to; Therefore seek refuge in God, certainly He is the Hearing, the Seeing.

⁵⁷. Certainly the creation of the heavens and the earth is greater than the creation of the men, but most people do not know

⁵⁸. And the blind and the seeing are not alike, nor those who believe and do good and the evil-doer; little is it that you are mindful.

⁵⁹. Most certainly the hour is coming, there is no doubt therein, but most people do not believe.

⁶⁰. And your Lord says: Call upon Me, I will answer you; certainly those who are too proud for My service shall soon enter hell abased.

⁶¹. God is He Who made for you the night that you may rest therein and the day to see; most certainly God is kind to men, but most men do not give thanks.

⁶². That is God, your Lord, the Creator of everything; there is no God but He; from where are you then turned away?

⁶³. Thus were turned away those who denied the words of God.

⁶⁴. God is He Who made the earth a resting-place for you and the heaven a canopy, and He formed you, and made your forms well, and He provided you with worthwhile things; that is God, your Lord; blessed then is God, the Lord of the worlds.

⁶⁵. He is the Living, there is no god but He, therefore call on Him, being sincere to Him in obedience; all praise is due to God, the Lord of the

worlds.

66. Say, "I am forbidden to serve those whom you call upon besides God when clear explanations have come to me from my Lord, and I am commanded that I should submit to the Lord of the worlds.

67. He it is Who created you from dust, then from a small lifegerm, then from a clot, then He brings you forth as a child, then that you may attain your maturity, then that you may be old -- and of you there are some who are caused to die before -- and that you may reach an appointed term, and that you may understand.

68. He it is Who gives life and brings death, so when He decrees an affair, He only says to it: Be, and it is.

69. Have you not seen those who dispute with respect to the words of God: how are they turned away?

70. Those who reject the Book and that with which We have sent Our Prophet; but they shall soon come to know,

71. When the fetters and the chains shall be on their necks; they shall be dragged

72. Into boiling water, then in the fire shall they be burned;

73. Then shall it be said to them: Where is that which you used to set up

74. Besides God? They shall say, "They are gone away from us, no, we used not to call upon anything before. Thus does God confound the unbelievers.

75. That is because you exulted in the land unjustly and because you behaved insolently.

76. Enter the gates of hell to abide therein, evil then is the home of the proud.

77. So be patient, certainly the promise of God is true. So should We make you see part of what We threaten them with, or should We cause you to die, to Us shall they be returned.

78. And certainly We sent apostles before you: there are some of them that We have mentioned to you and there are others whom We have not mentioned to you, and it was not meet for an apostle that he should bring a sign except with God's permission, but when the command of God came, judgment was given with truth, and those who treated it as a lie were lost.

79. God is He Who made the cattle for you that you may ride on some of them, and some of them you eat.

80. And there are advantages for you in them, and that you may attain thereon a want which is in your hearts, and upon them and upon the ships you are borne.

81. And He shows you His signs: which then of God's signs will you deny?

82. Have they not then journeyed in the land and seen how was the end of those before them? They were more in numbers than these and greater in strength and in fortifications in the land, but what they earned did not avail them.

83. Then when their apostles came to them with clear explanations, they exulted in what they had with them of knowledge, and there beset them that which they used to mock.

84. But when they saw Our punishment, they said, "We believe in God alone and we deny what we used to associate with Him.

85. But their belief was not going to profit them when they had seen Our punishment; this is God's law, which has indeed obtained in the matter of His servants, and there the unbelievers are lost.

Chapter 41 — Ha Mim Sajda/Fusilaat — Distinct Verses

In the name of God, the Kind, the Merciful.

1. Ha Mim!
2. A revelation from the Kind, the Merciful God:
3. A Book of which the verses are made plain, an Arabic Koran for a people who know:
4. A herald of good news and a warning, but most of them turn aside so they hear not.
5. And they say, "Our hearts are under coverings from that to which you call us, and there is a heaviness in our ears, and a veil hangs between us and you, so work, we too are working."
6. Say, "I am only a mortal like you; it is revealed to me that your God is one God, therefore follow the right way to Him and ask His forgiveness; and woe to the polytheists;
7. To those who do not give poor-rate and they are unbelievers in the hereafter.
8. As for those who believe and do good, they shall certainly have a reward never to be cut off.
9. Say, "What! do you indeed disbelieve in Him Who created the earth in two periods, and do you set up equals with Him? That is the Lord of the Worlds.
10. And He made in it mountains above its surface, and He blessed therein and made therein its foods, in four periods: alike for the seekers.
11. Then He directed Himself to the heaven and it is a vapor, so He said to it and to the earth: Come both, willingly or unwillingly. They both said, "We come willingly.
12. So He ordered them seven heavens in two periods, and revealed in every heaven its affair; and We adorned the lower heaven with brilliant stars and made it to guard; that is the decree of the Mighty, the Knowing.
13. But if they turn aside, then say, "I have warned you of a scourge like the scourge of Ad and Samood.
14. When their apostles came to them from before them and from behind them, saying, Serve nothing but God, they said, "If our Lord had pleased He would certainly have sent down angels, so we are certainly unbelievers in that with which you are sent.
15. Then as to Ad, they were unjustly proud in the land, and they said, "Who is mightier in strength than we? Did they not see that God Who created them was mightier than they in strength, and they denied Our words?
16. So We sent on them a furious wind in unlucky days, that We may make them taste the punishment of abasement in this world's life; and certainly the punishment of the hereafter is much more abasing, and they shall not be helped.
17. And as to Samood, We showed them the right way, but they chose error above guidance, so there overtook them the scourge of an abasing punishment for what they earned.
18. And We delivered those who believed and guarded against evil.
19. And on the day that the enemies of God shall be brought together to the fire, then they shall be formed into groups.
20. Until when they come to it, their ears and their eyes and their skins shall bear witness against them as to what they did.
21. And they shall say to their skins: Why have you borne witness against us? They shall say, "God Who makes everything speak has made us speak, and He created you at first, and to Him you shall be brought back.
22. And you did not veil yourselves or your ears and your eyes and your skins might bear witness

against you, but you thought that God did not know much of what you did.

23. And that was your evil thought which you entertained about your Lord that has tumbled you down into hell, so are you become of the lost ones.

24. Then if they will endure, still the fire is their home, and if they ask for goodwill, then are they not of those who shall be granted goodwill.

25. And We have appointed for them comrades so they have made fair-seeming to them what is before them and what is behind them, and the word proved true against them -- among the nations of the jinn and the men that have passed away before them -- that they shall certainly be losers.

26. And those who disbelieve say, "Do not listen to this Koran and make noise therein, perhaps you may overcome.

27. Therefore We will most certainly make those who disbelieve taste a severe punishment, and We will most certainly reward them for the evil deeds they used to do.

28. That is the reward of the enemies of God -- the fire; for them therein shall be the house of long abiding; a reward for their denying Our words.

29. And those who disbelieve will say, "Our Lord! show us those who led us astray from among the jinn and the men that we may trample them under our feet so that they may be of the lowest.

30. As for those who say, "Our Lord is God, then continue in the right way, the angels descend upon them, saying, "Fear not, nor be grieved, and receive good news of the garden which you were promised.

31. We are your guardians in this world's life and in the hereafter, and you shall have therein what your souls desire and you shall have therein what you ask for:

32. A provision from the Forgiving, the Merciful.

33. And who speaks better than he who calls to God while he himself does good, and says: I am certainly of those who submit?

34. And not alike are the good and the evil. Repel evil with what is best, when lo! he between whom and you was enmity would be as if he were a warm friend.

35. And none are made to receive it but those who are patient, and none are made to receive it but those who have a mighty good fortune.

36. And if an interference of the Satan should cause you mischief, seek refuge in God; certainly He is the Hearing, the Knowing.

37. And among His signs are the night and the day and the sun and the moon; do not make obeisance to the sun nor to the moon; and make obeisance to God Who created them, if Him it is that you serve.

38. But if they are proud, yet those with your Lord glorify Him during the night and the day, and they are not tired.

39. And among His signs is this, that you see the earth still, but when We send down on it the water, it stirs and swells: most certainly He Who gives it life is the Giver of life to the dead; certainly He has power over all things.

40. Certainly they who deviate from the right way concerning Our words are not hidden from Us. What! is he then who is cast into the fire better, or he who comes safe on the day of resurrection? Do what you like, certainly He sees what you do.

41. Certainly those who disbelieve in the reminder when it comes to them, and most certainly it is a Mighty Book:

42. Falsehood shall not come to it from before it nor from behind it; a revelation from the Wise, the Praised One.

43. Nothing is said to you but what was said indeed to the apostles before you; certainly your

Lord is the Lord of forgiveness and the Lord of painful retribution.

⁴⁴. And if We had made it a Koran in a foreign tongue, they would certainly have said, "Why have not its words been made clear? What! a foreign tongue and an Arabian! Say, "It is to those who believe a guidance and a healing; and as for those who do not believe, there is a heaviness in their ears and it is obscure to them; these shall be called to from a far-off place.

⁴⁵. And certainly We gave the Book to Moses, but it has been argued about, and had not a word already gone forth from your Lord, judgment would certainly have been given between them; and most certainly they are in a disquieting doubt about it.

⁴⁶. Whoever does good, it is for his own soul, and whoever does evil, it is against it; and your Lord is not in the least unjust to the servants.

⁴⁷. To Him is referred the knowledge of the hour, and there come not forth any of the fruits from their coverings, nor does a female bear, nor does she give birth, but with His knowledge; and on the day when He shall call out to them, Where are those whom you called My associates? They shall say, "We declare to You, none of us is a witness.

⁴⁸. And away from them shall go what they called upon before, and they shall know for certain that there is no escape for them.

⁴⁹. Man is never tired of praying for good, and if evil touch him, then he is despairing, hopeless.

⁵⁰. And if We make him taste mercy from Us after distress that has touched him, he would most certainly say, "This is of me, and I do not think the hour will come to pass, and if I am sent back to my Lord, I shall have with Him sure good; but We will most certainly inform those who disbelieved of what they did, and We will most certainly make them taste of hard punishment.

⁵¹. And when We show favor to man, he turns aside and withdraws himself; and when evil touches him, he makes lengthy supplications.

⁵². Say, "Tell me if it is from God; then you disbelieve in it, who is in greater error than he who is in a prolonged opposition?

⁵³. We will soon show them Our signs in the Universe and in their own souls, until it will become quite clear to them that it is the truth. Is it not sufficient as regards your Lord that He is a witness over all things?

⁵⁴. Now certainly they are in doubt as to the meeting of their Lord; now certainly He encompasses all things.

Chapter 42 — Al-Shura — The Consultation

In the name of God, the Kind, the Merciful.

1. Ha Mim. 2. Ain Sin Qaf.
3. Thus does God, the Mighty, the Wise, reveal to you, and thus He revealed to those before you.
4. His is what is in the heavens and what is in the earth, and He is the High, the Great.
5. The heavens may almost rend asunder from above them and the angels sing the praise of their Lord and ask forgiveness for those on earth; now certainly God is the Forgiving, the Merciful.
6. And as for those who take guardians besides Him, God watches over them, and you have not charge over them.
7. And thus have We revealed to you an Arabic Koran, that you may warn the mother city and those around it, and that you may give warning of the day of gathering together wherein is no doubt; a party shall be in the garden and another party in the burning fire.
8. And if God had pleased He would certainly have made them a single comunity, but He makes whom He pleases enter into His mercy, and the unjust it is that shall have no guardian or helper.
9. Or have they taken guardians besides Him? But God is the Guardian, and He gives life to the dead, and He has power over all things.
10. And in whatever thing you disagree, the judgment thereof is in God's hand; that is God, my Lord, on Him do I rely and to Him do I turn time after time.
11. The Originator of the heavens and the earth; He made mates for you from among yourselves, and mates of the cattle too, multiplying you thereby; nothing like a likeness of Him; and He is the Hearing, the Seeing.
12. His are the treasures of the heavens and the earth; He makes ample and straightens the means of subsistence for whom He pleases; certainly He is Cognizant of all things.
13. He has made plain to you of the religion what He enjoined upon Noah and that which We have revealed to you and that which We enjoined upon Abraham and Moses and Jesus that keep to obedience and do not be divided therein; hard to the unbelievers is that which you call them to; God chooses for Himself whom He pleases, and guides to Himself him who turns to Him, frequently.
14. And they did not become divided until after knowledge had come to them out of envy among themselves; and had not a word gone forth from your Lord till an appointed term, certainly judgment would have been given between them; and those who were made to inherit the Book after them are most certainly in disquieting doubt concerning it.
15. To this then go on inviting, and go on steadfastly on the right way as you are commanded, and do not follow their low desires, and say, "I believe in what God has revealed of the Book, and I am commanded to do justice between you: God is our Lord and your Lord; we shall have our deeds and you shall have your deeds; no plea need there be now between us and you: God will gather us together, and to Him is the return.
16. And as for those who dispute about God after that obedience has been rendered to Him, their plea is null with their Lord, and upon them is wrath, and for them is severe punishment.
17. God it is Who revealed the Book with truth, and the balance, and what shall make you know that haply the hour be near?
18. Those who do not believe in it would hasten it on, and those who believe are in fear from it, and they know that it is the truth. Now most certainly those who dispute obstinately con-

cerning the hour are in a great error.

19. God is Benignant to His servants; He gives sustenance to whom He pleases, and He is the Strong, the Mighty.

20. Whoever desires the gain of the hereafter, We will give him more of that again; and whoever desires -- the gain of this world, We give him of it, and in the hereafter he has no portion.

21. Or have they associates who have prescribed for them any religion that God does not sanction? And were it not for the word of judgment, decision would have certainly been given between them; and certainly the unjust shall have a painful punish^ment.

22. You will see the unjust fearing on account of what they have earned, and it must happen to them; and those who believe and do good shall be in the meadows of the gardens; they shall have what they please with their Lord: that is the great grace.

23. That is of which God gives the good news to His servants, to those who believe and do good deeds. Say, "I do not ask of you any reward for it but love for my near relatives; and whoever earns good, We give him more of good therein; certainly God is Forgiving, Grateful.

24. Or do they say, "He has created a lie against God? But if God pleased, He would seal your heart; and God will blot out the falsehood and confirm the truth with His words; certainly He is Cognizant of what is in the hearts.

25. And He it is Who accepts repentance from His servants and pardons the evil deeds and He knows what you do;

26. And He answers those who believe and do good deeds, and gives them more out of His grace; and as for the unbelievers, they shall have a severe punishment.

27. And if God should amplify the provision for His servants they would certainly revolt in the earth; but He sends it down according to a measure as He pleases; certainly He is Aware of, Seeing, His servants.

28. And He it is Who sends down the rain after they have despaired, and He unfolds His mercy; and He is the Guardian, the Praised One.

29. And one of His signs is the creation of the heavens and the earth and what He has spread forth in both of them of living beings; and when He pleases He is all-powerful to gather them together.

30. And whatever sickness happens to you, it is on account of what your hands have wrought, and yet He pardons most of your faults.

31. And you cannot escape in the earth, and you shall not have a guardian or a helper besides God.

32. And among His signs are the ships in the sea like mountains.

33. If He pleases, He causes the wind to become still so that they lie motionless on its back; most certainly there are signs in this for every patient, grateful one,

34. Or He may make them founder for what they have earned, and even then pardon most;

35. And that those who dispute about Our words may know; there is no place of refuge for them.

36. So whatever thing you are given, that is only a provision of this world's life, and what is with God is better and more lasting for those who believe and rely on their Lord.

37. And those who. shun the great sins and indecencies, and whenever they are angry they forgive.

38. And those who respond to their Lord and keep up prayer, and their rule is to take counsel among themselves, and who spend out of what We have given them.

39. And those who, when great wrong afflicts them, defend themselves.

40. And the payment for evil is punishment like it, but whoever forgives and amends, he shall have his reward from God; certainly He does not love the unjust.

41. And whoever defends himself after his being oppressed, these it is against whom there is no way to blame.

⁴². The way to blame is only against those who oppress men and revolt in the earth unjustly; these shall have a painful punishment.

⁴³. And whoever is patient and forgiving, these most certainly are actions due to courage.

⁴⁴. And whomsoever God makes err, he has no guardian after Him; and you shall see the unjust, when they see the punishment, saying, "Is there any way to return?

⁴⁵. And you shall see them brought before it humbling themselves because of the abasements, looking with a faint glance. And those who believe shall say, "Certainly the losers are they who have lost themselves and their followers on the resurrection day. Now certainly the iniquitous shall remain in lasting punishment.

⁴⁶. And they shall have no friends to help them besides God; and -- whomsoever God makes err, he shall have no way.

⁴⁷. Hearken to your Lord before there comes the day from God for which there shall be no averting; you shall have no refuge on that day, nor shall it be yours to make a denial.

⁴⁸. But if they turn aside, We have not sent you as a watcher over them; on you is only to deliver the message; and certainly when We make man taste mercy from Us, he rejoices thereat; and if an evil afflicts them on account of what their hands have already done, then-certainly man is ungrateful.

⁴⁹. God's is the kingdom of the heavens and the earth; He creates what He pleases; He grants to whom He pleases daughters and grants to whom He pleases sons.

⁵⁰. Or He makes them of both sorts, male and female; and He makes whom He pleases barren; certainly He is the Knowing, the Powerful.

⁵¹. And it is not for any mortal that God should speak to them, they could not bear to hear and they did not see.

⁵². And thus did We reveal to you an inspired book by Our command. You did not know what the Book was, nor what the faith was, but We made it a light, guiding thereby whom We please of Our servants; and most certainly you show the way to the right path:

⁵³. The path of God, Whose is whatsoever is in the heavens and whatsoever is in the earth; now certainly to God do all affairs eventually come.

Chapter 43 — Al-Zhukruf — Ornaments of Gold

In the name of God, the Kind, the Merciful.

¹. Ha Mim.

². I swear by the Book that makes things clear:

³. Certainly We have made it an Arabic Koran that you may understand.

⁴. And certainly it is in the original of the Book with Us, truly elevated, full of wisdom.

⁵. What! shall We then turn away the reminder from you altogether because you are an extravagant people?

⁶. And how many a prophet have We sent among the ancients.

⁷. And there came not to them a prophet but they mocked at him.

⁸. Then We destroyed those who were stronger than these in prowess, and the case of the ancients has gone before,

⁹. And if you should ask them, Who created the heavens and the earth? they would most certainly say, "The Mighty, the Knowing One, has created them;

¹⁰. He Who made the earth a resting-place for you, and made in it ways for you that you may go aright;

¹¹. And He Who sends down water from the cloud according to a measure, then We raise to life thereby a dead country, even thus shall you be brought forth;

¹². And He Who created pairs of all things, and made for you of the ships and the cattle what you ride on,

¹³. That you may firmly sit on their backs, then remember the favor of your Lord when you are firmly seated thereon, and say, "Glory be to Him Who made this subservient to us and we were not able to do it

¹⁴. And certainly to our Lord we must return.

¹⁵. And they assign to Him a part of His servants; man, to be sure, is clearly ungrateful.

¹⁶. What! has He taken daughters to Himself of what He Himself creates and chosen you to have sons?

¹⁷. And when one of them is given news of that of which he sets up as a likeness for the Kind God, his face becomes black and he is full of rage. ¹⁸. What! that which is made in ornaments and which in contention is unable to make plain speech!

¹⁹. And they make the angels -- them who are the servants of the Kind God -- female divinities. What! did they witness their creation? Their evidence shall be written down and they shall be questioned.

²⁰. And they say, "If the Kind God had pleased, we should never have worshiped them. They have no knowledge of this; they only lie.

²¹. Or have We given them a book before it so that they hold fast to it?

²². No! they say, "We found our fathers on a course, and certainly we are guided by their footsteps.

²³. And thus, We did not send before you any alarmgiver in a town, but those who led easy lives in it said, "Certainly we found our fathers on a course, and certainly we are followers of their footsteps.

²⁴. The alarmgiver said, "What! even if I bring to you a better guide than that on which you found your fathers? They said, "Certainly we are unbelievers in that with which you are sent.

²⁵. So We inflicted retribution on them, then see how was the end of the rejecters.

26. And when Abraham said to his father and his people: Certainly I am clear of what you worship,
27. Save Him Who created me, for certainly He will guide me.
28. And he made it a word to continue in his posterity that they may return.
29. No! I gave them and their fathers to enjoy until there came to them the truth and a Prophet making clear the truth.
30. And when there came to them the truth they said, "This is magic, and certainly we are disbelievers in it.
31. And they say, "Why was not this Koran revealed to a man of importance in the two towns?
32. Will they distribute the mercy of your Lord? We distribute among them their livelihood in the life of this world, and We have exalted some of them above others in degrees, that some of them may take others in subjection; and the mercy of your Lord is better than what they amass.
33. And were it not that all people had been a single nation, We would certainly have assigned to those who disbelieve in the Kind God to make of silver the roofs of their houses and the stairs by which they ascend.
34. And the doors of their houses and the couches on which they recline,
35. And other embellishments of gold; and all this is nothing but provision of this world's life, and the hereafter is with your Lord only for those who guard against evil.
36. And whoever turns himself away from the remembrance of the Kind God, We appoint for him a Satan, so he becomes his associate.
37. And most certainly they turn them away from the path, and they think that they are guided aright:
38. Until when he comes to Us, he says: Oh would that between me and you there were the distance of the East and the West; so evil is the associate!
39. And since you were unjust, it will not profit you this day that you are sharers in the punishment.
40. What! can you then make the deaf to hear or guide the blind and him who is in clear error?
41. But if We should take you away, still We shall inflict retribution on them;
42. Rather We will certainly show you that which We have promised them; for certainly We are the possessors of full power over them.
43. Therefore hold fast to that which has been revealed to you; certainly you are on the right path.
44. And most certainly it is a reminder for you and your people, and you shall soon be questioned.
45. And ask those of Our apostles whom We sent before you: Did We ever appoint gods to be worshiped besides the Kind God?
46. And certainly We sent Moses with Our words to Pharoah and his chiefs, so he said, "Certainly I am the apostle of the Lord of the worlds.
47. But when he came to them with Our signs, lo! they laughed at them. 48. And We did not show them a sign but it was greater than its like, and We overtook them with punishment that they may turn.
49. And they said, "Oh magician! call on your Lord for our sake, as He has made the covenant with you; we shall certainly be the followers of the right way.
50. But when We removed from them the punishment, lo! they broke the pledge.
51. And Pharoah proclaimed amongst his people: Oh my people! is not the kingdom of Egypt mine? And these rivers flow beneath me; do you not then see?
52. No! I am better than this fellow, who is contemptible, and who can hardly speak distinctly:
53. But why have not bracelets of gold been put upon him, or why have there not come with him angels as companions?

⁵⁴. So he incited his people to levity and they obeyed him: certainly they were a transgressing people.

⁵⁵. Then when they displeased Us, We inflicted a retribution on them, so We drowned them all together,

⁵⁶. And We made them a precedent and example to the later generations.

⁵⁷. And when a description of the son of Mary is given, lo! your people raise a clamor thereat.

⁵⁸. And they say, "Are our gods better, or is he? They do not set it forth to you save by way of disputation; no, they are a contentious people.

⁵⁹. He was nothing but a servant on whom We bestowed favor, and We made him an example for the children of Israel.

⁶⁰. And if We please, We could make among you angels to be successors in the land.

⁶¹. And most certainly it is a knowledge of the hour, therefore have no doubt about it and follow me: this is the right path.

⁶². And let not the Satan prevent you; certainly he is your open enemy.

⁶³. And when Jesus came with clear explanations he said, "I have come to you indeed with wisdom, and that I may make clear to you part of what you differ in; so be careful of your duty to God and obey me:

⁶⁴. Certainly God is my Lord and your Lord, therefore serve Him; this is the right path:

⁶⁵. But parties from among them differed, so woe to those who were unjust because of the punishment of a painful day.

⁶⁶. Do they wait for anything but the hour, that it should come ! upon them all of a sudden while they do not perceive?

⁶⁷. The friends shall on that day be enemies one to another, except those who guard against evil.

⁶⁸. Oh My servants! there is no fear for you this day, nor shall you grieve.

⁶⁹. Those who believed in Our words and were submissive:

⁷⁰. Enter the garden, you and your wives; you shall be made happy.

⁷¹. There shall be sent round to them golden bowls and drinking-cups and therein shall be what their souls yearn after and wherein the eyes shall delight, and you shall abide therein.

⁷². And this is the garden which you are given as an inheritance on account of what you did.

⁷³. For you therein are many fruits of which you shall eat.

⁷⁴. Certainly the guilty shall abide in the punishment of hell.

⁷⁵. It shall not be abated from them and they shall therein be despairing.

⁷⁶. And We are not unjust to them, but they themselves were unjust.

⁷⁷. And they shall call out: Oh Malik! let your Lord make an end of us. He shall say, "Certainly you shall tarry.

⁷⁸. Certainly We have brought you the truth, but most of you are averse to the truth.

⁷⁹. Or have they settled an affair? Then certainly We are the settlers.

⁸⁰. Or do they think that We do not hear what they conceal and their secret discourses? Aye! and Our messengers with them write down.

⁸¹. Say, "If the Kind God has a son, I am the foremost of those who serve.

⁸². Glory to the Lord of the heavens and the earth, the Lord of power, from what they describe.

⁸³. So leave them plunging into false discourses and sporting until they meet their day which they are threatened with.

⁸⁴. And He it is Who is God in the heavens and God in the earth; and He is the Wise, the Knowing.

⁸⁵. And blessed is He Whose is the kingdom of the heavens and the earth and what is between them, and with Him is the knowledge of the hour, and to Him shall you be brought back.

86. And those whom they call upon besides Him have no authority for intercession, but he who bears witness of the truth and they know him.
87. And if you should ask them who created them, they would certainly say, "God. From where are they then turned back?
88. Consider his cry: Oh my Lord! certainly they are a people who do not believe.
89. So turn away from them and say, Peace, for they shall soon come to know.

Chapter 44 — Al-Dukhan — The Smoke

In the name of God, the Kind, the Merciful.

1. Ha Mim!
2. I swear by the Book that makes clear the truth.
3. Certainly We revealed it on a blessed night certainly We are forever warning --
4. Therein every wise affair is made distinct,
5. A command from Us; certainly We are the senders of apostles,
6. A mercy from your Lord, certainly He is the Hearing, the Knowing,
7. The Lord of the heavens and the earth and what is between them, if you would be sure.
8. There is no god but He; He gives life and causes death, your Lord and the Lord of your fathers of yore.
9. No, they are in doubt, they sport.
10. Therefore keep waiting for the day when the heaven shall bring an evident smoke,
11. That shall overtake men; this is a painful punishment.
12. Our Lord! remove from us the punishment; certainly we are believers.
13. How shall they be reminded, and there came to them a Prophet making clear the truth,
14. Yet they turned their backs on him and said, "One taught by others, a madman.
15. Certainly We will remove the punishment a little, but you will certainly return to evil.
16. On the day when We will seize them with the most violent seizing; certainly We will inflict retribution.
17. And certainly We tried before them the people of Pharoah, and there came to them a noble apostle,
18. Saying, "Deliver to me the servants of God, certainly I am a faithful apostle to you,
19. And that do not exalt yourselves against God, certainly I will bring to you a clear authority:
20. And certainly I take refuge with my Lord and your Lord that you should stone me to death:
21. And if you do not believe in me, then leave me alone.
22. Then he called upon his Lord: These are a guilty people.
23. So go forth with My servants by night; certainly you will be pursued:
24. And leave the sea intervening; certainly they are a host that shall be drowned.
25. How many of the gardens and fountains have they left!
26. And cornfields and noble places!
27. And good things wherein they rejoiced;
28. Thus it was, and We gave them as a heritage to another people.
29. So the heaven and the earth did not weep for them, nor were they respited.
30. And certainly We delivered the children of Israel from the abasing punishment,
31. From Pharoah; certainly he was haughty, and one of the extravagant.
32. And certainly We chose them, having knowledge, above the nations.
33. And We gave them of the words wherein was clear blessing.
34. Most certainly these do say, "
35. There is nothing but our first death and we shall not be raised again.
36. So bring our fathers back, if you are truthful.
37. Are they better or the people of Tubba and those before them? We destroyed them, for certainly they were guilty.

38. And We did not create the heavens and the earth and what is between them in sport.
39. We did not create them both but with the truth, but most of them do not know.
40. Certainly the day of separation is their appointed term, of all of them

41. The day on which a friend shall not help his friend at all, nor shall they be helped,
42. Save those on whom God shall have mercy; certainly He is the Mighty the Merciful.
43. Certainly the tree of the Zaqqum,
44. Is the food of the sinful
45. Like dregs of oil; it shall boil in their bellies,
46. Like the boiling of hot water.
47. Seize him, then drag him down into the middle of the hell;
48. Then pour above his head of the torment of the boiling water:
49. Taste; you forsooth are the mighty, the honorable:
50. Certainly this is what you disputed about.
51. Certainly those who guard against evil are in a secure place,
52. In gardens and springs;
53. They shall wear of fine and thick silk, sitting face to face;
54. Thus shall it be, and We will wed them with Houris pure, beautiful ones.
55. They shall call therein for every fruit in security;
56. They shall not taste therein death except the first death, and He will save them from the punishment of the hell,
57. A grace from your Lord; this is the great achievement.
58. So have We made it easy in your tongue that they may be mindful.
59. Therefore wait; certainly they are waiting.

Chapter 45 — Al-Jathiyah — The Kneeling

In the name of God, the Kind, the Merciful.

¹. Ha Mim.

². The revelation of the Book is from God, the Mighty, the Wise. ³. Most certainly in the heavens and the earth there are signs for the believers.

⁴. And in your own creation and in what He spreads abroad of animals there are signs for a people that are sure;

⁵. And in the variation of the night and the day, and in what God sends down of sustenance from the cloud, then gives life thereby to the earth after its death, and in the changing of the winds, there are signs for a people who understand.

⁶. These are the words of God which We recite to you with truth; then in what announcement would they believe after God and His words?

⁷. Woe to every sinful liar,

⁸. Who hears the words of God recited to him, then persists proudly as though he had not heard them; so award him a painful punishment.

⁹. And when he comes to know of any of Our words, he takes it for a joke; these it is that shall have degrading punishment.

¹⁰. Before them is hell, and there shall not help them at all of what they earned, nor those whom they took for guardians besides God, and they shall have a grievous punishment.

¹¹. This is guidance; and as for those who disbelieve in the words of their Lord, they shall have a painful punishment on account of uncleanness.

¹². God is He Who made subservient to you the sea that the ships may run therein by His command, and that you may seek of His kindness, so that you may give thanks.

¹³. And He has made subservient to you whatsoever is in the heavens and whatsoever is in the earth, all, from Himself; most certainly there are signs in this for a people who acknowledge it.

¹⁴. Say to those who believe that they forgive those who do not fear the days of God that He may reward a people for what they earn.

¹⁵. Whoever does good, it is for his own soul, and whoever does evil, it is against himself; then you shall be brought back to your -- Lord.

¹⁶. And certainly We gave the Book and the wisdom and the prophecy to the children of Israel, and We gave them fine things, and We made them excel the nations.

¹⁷. And We gave them clear explanations in the affair, but they did not differ until after knowledge had come to them out of envy among themselves; certainly your-Lord will judge between them on the day of resurrection concerning that wherein they differed.

¹⁸. Then We have made you follow a course in the affair, therefore follow it, and do not follow the low desires of those who do not know.

¹⁹. Certainly they shall not avail you in the least against God; and certainly the unjust are friends of each other, and God is the guardian of those who guard against evil.

²⁰. These are clear proofs for men, and a guidance and a mercy for a people who are sure.

²¹. No! do those who have wrought evil deeds think that We will make them like those who believe and do good -- that their life and their death shall be equal? Evil it is that they judge.

²². And God created the heavens and the earth with truth and that every soul may be rewarded for what it has earned and they shall not be wronged.

23. Have you then considered him who takes his low desire for his god, and God has made him err having knowledge and has set a seal upon his ear and his heart and put a covering upon his eye. Who can then guide him after God? Will you not then be mindful?

24. And they say, "There is nothing but our life in this world; we live and die and nothing destroys us but time, and they have no knowledge of that; they only conjecture.

25. And when Our clear words are recited to them, their argument is no other than that they say, "Bring our fathers back if you are truthful.

26. Say, "God gives you life, then He makes you die, then will He gather you to the day of resurrection wherein is no doubt, but most people do not know.

27. And God's is the kingdom of the heavens and the earth; and on the day when the hour shall come to pass, on that day shall they perish who say false things.

28. And you shall see every nation kneeling down; every nation shall be called to its book: today you shall be rewarded for what you did.

29. This is Our book that speaks against you with justice; certainly We wrote what you did,

30. Then as to those who believed and did good, their Lord will make them enter into His mercy; that is the great achievement.

31. As to those who disbelieved: What! were not My words recited to you? But you were proud and you were a guilty people.

32. And when it was said, Certainly the promise of God is true and as for the hour, there is no doubt about it, you said, "We do not know what the hour is; we do not think that it will come to pass save a passing thought, and we are not at all sure.

33. And the evil consequences of what they did shall become clear to them and that which they mocked shall encompass them.

34. And it shall be said, "Today We abandon you as you neglected the meeting of this day of yours and your home is the fire, and there are not for you any helpers:

35. That is because you took the words of God for a joke and This worldly life deceived you. So on that day they shall not be protected from it, nor shall they be granted goodwill.

36. Therefore to God is due all praise, the Lord of the heavens and the Lord of the earth, the Lord of the worlds.

37. And to Him belongs greatness in the heavens and the earth, and He is the Mighty, the Wise.

Chapter 46 — Al-Ahqaf — The Sand Dunes

In the name of God, the Kind, the Merciful.

1. Ha Mim.
2. The revelation of the Book is from God, the Mighty, the Wise.
3. We did not create the heavens and the earth and what is between them two save with truth and for an appointed term; and those who disbelieve turn aside from what they are warned of.
4. Say, "Have you considered what you call upon besides God? Show me what they have created of the earth, or have they a share in the heavens? Bring me a book before this or traces of knowledge, if you are truthful.
5. And who is in greater error than he who calls besides God upon those that will not answer him till the day of resurrection and they are heedless of their call?
6. And when men are gathered together they shall be their enemies, and shall be deniers of their worshiping them.
7. And when Our clear words are recited to them, those who disbelieve say with regard to the truth when it comes to them: This is truly magic.
8. No! they say, "He has created it. Say, "If I have created it, you do not control anything for me from God; He knows best what you utter concerning it; He is enough as a witness between me and you, and He is the Forgiving, the Merciful.
9. Say, "I am not the first of the apostles, and I do not know what will be done with me or with you: I do not follow anything but that which is revealed to me, and I am nothing but a plain alarmgiver.
10. Say, "Have you considered if it is from God, and you disbelieve in it, and a witness from among the children of Israel has borne witness of one like it, so he believed, while you are big with pride; certainly God does not guide the unjust people.
11. And those who disbelieve say concerning those who believe: If it had been a good, they would not have gone ahead of us therein. And as they do not seek to be rightly directed thereby, they say, "It is an old lie.
12. And before it the Book of Moses was a guide and a mercy: and this is a Book verifying it in the Arabic language that it may warn those who are unjust and as good news for the doers of good.
13. Certainly those who say, Our Lord is God, then they continue on the right way, they shall have no fear nor shall they grieve.
14. These are the dwellers of the garden, abiding therein: a reward for what they did.
15. And We have enjoined on man doing of good to his parents; with trouble did his mother bear him and with trouble did she bring him forth; and the bearing of him and the weaning of him was thirty months; until when he attains his maturity and reaches forty years, he says: My Lord! grant me that I may give thanks for Your favor which You have bestowed on me and on my parents, and that I may do good which pleases You and do good to me in respect of my offspring; certainly I turn to You, and certainly I am of those who submit.
16. These are they from whom We accept the best of what they have done and pass over their evil deeds, among the dwellers of the garden; the promise of truth which they were promised.
17. And he who says to his parents: Fie on you! do you threaten me that I shall be brought forth when generations have already passed away before me? And they both call for God's aid: Woe to you! believe, certainly the promise of God is true. But he says: This is nothing but stories

of the ancients.

18. These are they against whom the word has proved true among nations of the jinn and the men that have already passed away before them; certainly they are losers.

19. And for all are degrees according to what they did, and that He may pay them back fully their deeds and they shall not be wronged.

20. And on the day when those who disbelieve shall be brought before the fire: You did away with your good things in your life of the world and you enjoyed them for a while, so today you shall be rewarded with the punishment of abasement because you were unjustly proud in the land and because you transgressed.

21. And mention the brother of Ad; when he warned his people in the sandy plains, -- and indeed alarmgivers came before him and after him -- saying "Serve none but God; certainly I fear for you the punishment of a grievous day."

22. They said, "Have you come to us to turn us away from our gods; then bring us what you threaten us with, if you are of the truthful ones.

23. He said, "The knowledge is only with God, and I deliver to you the message with which I am sent, but I see you are a people who are ignorant.

24. So when they saw it as a cloud appearing in the sky advancing towards their valleys, they said, "This is a cloud which will give us rain. No! it is what you sought to hasten on, a blast of wind in which is a painful punishment,

25. Destroying everything by the command of its Lord, so they became such that nothing could be seen except their dwellings. Thus do We reward the guilty people.

26. And certainly We had established them in what We have not established you in, and We had given -- them ears and eyes and hearts, but neither their ears, nor their eyes, nor did their hearts help them at all, since they denied the words of God, and that which they mocked encompassed them.

27. And certainly We destroyed the towns which are around you, and We repeat the words that they might turn.

28. Why did not then those help them whom they took for gods besides God to draw them near to Him? No! they were lost to them; and this was
their lie and what they created.

29. And when We turned towards you a party of the jinn who listened to the Koran; so when they came to it, they said, "Be silent; then when it was finished, they turned back to their people warning them.

30. They said, "Oh our people! we have listened to a Book revealed after Moses verifying that which is before it, guiding to the truth and to a right path:

31. Oh our people! accept the Divine caller and believe in Him, He will forgive you of your faults and protect you from a painful punishment.

32. And whoever does not accept the-Divine caller, he shall not escape in the earth and he shall not have guardians besides Him, these are in great error.

33. Have they not considered that God, Who created the heavens and the earth and was not tired by their creation, is able to give life to the dead? Aye! He has certainly power over all things.

34. And on the day when those who disbelieve shall be brought before the fire: Is it not true? They shall say, "Aye! by our Lord! He will say, "Then taste the punishment, because you disbelieved.

35. Therefore bear up patiently as did the apostles endowed with constancy bear up with patience and do not seek to hasten for them their doom. On the day that they shall see what they are promised they shall be as if they had not tarried save an hour of the day. A sufficient exposition! Shall then any be destroyed save the transgressing people?

Chapter 47 — Muhammad — Mohammed

In the name of God, the Kind, the Merciful.

1. As for those who disbelieve and turn away from God's way, He shall render their works ineffective.
2. And as for those who believe and do good, and believe in what has been revealed to Muhammad, and it is the very truth from their Lord, He will remove their evil from them and improve their condition.
3. That is because those who disbelieve follow falsehood, and those who believe follow the truth from their Lord; thus does God set forth to men their examples.
4. So when you meet in battle those who disbelieve, then smite the necks until when you have overcome them, then make them prisoners, and afterwards either set them free as a favor or let them ransom themselves until the war terminates. That shall be so; and if God had pleased He would certainly have exacted what is due from them, but that He may try some of you by means of others; and as for those who are slain in the way of God, He will by no means allow their deeds to perish.
5. He will guide them and improve their condition.
6. And cause them to enter the garden which He has made known to them.
7. Oh you who believe! if you help the cause of God, He will help you and make firm your feet.
8. And as for those who disbelieve, for them is destruction and He has made their deeds ineffective.
9. That is because they hated what God revealed, so He rendered their deeds null.
10. Have they not then journeyed in the land and seen how was the end of those before them: God brought down destruction upon them, and the unbelievers shall have the like of it.
11. That is because God is the Protector of those who believe, and because the unbelievers shall have no protector for them.
12. Certainly God will make those who believe and do good enter gardens beneath which rivers flow; and those who disbelieve enjoy themselves and eat as the beasts eat, and the fire is their home.
13. And how many a town which was far more powerful than the town of yours which has driven you out: We destroyed them so there was no helper for them.
14. What! is he who has a clear argument from his Lord like him to whom the evil of his work is made fairseeming: and they follow their low desires.
15. A story of the garden which those guarding against evil are promised: Therein are rivers of water that does not alter, and rivers of milk the taste whereof does not change, and rivers of drink delicious to those who drink, and rivers of honey clarified and for them therein are all fruits and protection from their Lord. Are these like those who abide in the fire and who are made to drink boiling water so it rends their bowels asunder.
16. And there are those of them who seek to listen to you, until when they go forth from you, they say to those who have been given the knowledge: What was it that he said just now? These are they upon whose hearts God has set a seal and they follow their low desires.
17. And as for those who follow the right direction, He increases them in guidance and gives them their guarding against evil.
18. Do they then wait for anything but the hour that it should come to them all of a sudden?

Now indeed the tokens of it have already come, but how shall they have their reminder when it comes on them?

19. So know that there is no god but God, and, ask protection for your fault and for the believing men and the believing women; and God knows the place of your returning and the place of your abiding.

20. And those who believe say, "Why has not a chapter been revealed? But when a decisive chapter is revealed, and fighting is mentioned therein you see those in whose hearts is a disease look to you with the look of one fainting because of death. Woe to them then!

21. Obedience and a gentle word was proper; but when the affair becomes settled, then if they remain true to God it would certainly be better for them.

22. But if you held command, you were sure to make mischief in the land and cut off the ties of kinship!

23. Those it is whom God has cursed so He has made them deaf and blinded their eyes.

24. Do they not then reflect on the Koran? No, on the hearts there are locks.

25. Certainly as for those who return on their backs after that guidance has become obvious to them, the Satan has made it a light matter to them; and He gives them respite.

26. That is because they say to those who hate what God has revealed: We will obey you in some of the affairs; and God knows their secrets.

27. But how will it be when the angels cause them to die smiting their backs.

28. That is because they follow what is displeasing to God and are averse to His pleasure, therefore He has made null their deeds.

29. Or do those in whose hearts is a disease think that God will not bring forth their spite?

30. And if We please We would have made you know them so that you would certainly have recognized them by their marks and most certainly you can recognize them by the intent of their speech; and God knows your deeds.

31. And most certainly We will try you until We have known those among you who exert themselves hard, and the patient, and made your case manifest.

32. Certainly those who disbelieve and turn away from God's way and oppose the Prophet after that guidance has become clear to them cannot harm God in any way, and He will make null their deeds.

33. Oh you who believe! obey God and obey the Prophet, and do not make your deeds have no effect.

34. Certainly those who disbelieve and turn away from God's way, then they die while they are unbelievers, God will by no means forgive them.

35. And do not be slack so as to cry for peace and you have the upper hand, and God is with you, and He will not bring your deeds to nothing.

36. The life of this world is only idle sport and play, and if you believe and guard against evil He will give you your rewards, and will not ask of you your possessions.

37. If He should ask you for it and urge you, you will be wretched, and He will bring forth your malice.

38. Behold! you are those who are called upon to spend in God's way, but among you are those who are wretched, and whoever is wretched is wretched against his own soul; and God is Self-sufficient and you have need of Him, and if you turn back He will bring in your place another people, then they will not be like you.

Chapter 48 — Al-Fath — The Victory/Triumph

In the name of God, the Kind, the Merciful.

¹. Certainly We have given to you a clear victory

². That God may forgive your community their past faults and those to follow and complete His favor to you and keep you on a right way,

³. And that God might help you with a mighty help.

⁴. He it is Who sent down tranquillity into the hearts of the believers that they might have more of faith added to their faith -- and God's are the hosts of the heavens and the earth, and God is Knowing, Wise --

⁵. That He may cause the believing men and the believing women to enter gardens beneath which rivers flow to abide therein and remove from them their evil; and that is a grand achievement with God

⁶. And that He may punish the hypocritical men and the hypocritical women, and the polytheistic men and the polytheistic women, the entertainers of evil thoughts about God. On them is the evil turn, and God is wroth with them and has cursed them and prepared hell for them, and evil is the resort.

⁷. And God's are the hosts of the heavens and the earth; and God is Mighty, Wise.

⁸. Certainly We have sent you as a witness and as a bearer of good news and as an alarmgiver,

⁹. That you may believe in God and His Prophet and may aid him and revere him; and that you may declare His glory, morning and evening.

¹⁰. Certainly those who swear allegiance to you do but swear allegiance to God; the hand of God is above their hands. Therefore whoever breaks his faith, he breaks it only to the injury of his own soul, and whoever fulfills what he has covenanted with God, He will grant him a mighty reward.

¹¹. Those of the dwellers of the desert who were left behind will say to you: Our property and our families kept us busy, so ask forgiveness for us. They say with their tongues what is not in their hearts. Say, "Then who can control anything for you from God if He intends to do you harm or if He intends to do you good; no, God is Aware of what you do:

¹². No! you rather thought that the Prophet and the believers would not return to their families ever, and that was made fairseeming to your hearts and you thought an evil thought and you were a people doomed to perish.

¹³. And whoever does not believe in God and His Prophet, then certainly We have prepared burning fire for the unbelievers.

¹⁴. And God's is the kingdom. of the heavens and the earth; He forgives whom He pleases and punishes whom He pleases, and God is Forgiving, Merciful.

¹⁵. Those who are left behind will say when you set forth for the gaining of acquisitions: Allow us that we may follow you. They desire to change the world of God. Say, "By no means shall you follow us; thus did God say before. But they will say, "No! you are jealous of us. No! they do not understand but a little.

¹⁶. Say to those of the dwellers of the desert who were left behind: You shall soon be invited to fight against a people possessing mighty prowess; you will fight against them until they submit; then if you obey, God will grant you a good reward; and if you turn back as you turned back before, He will punish you with a painful punishment.

17. There is no harm in the blind, nor is there any harm in the lame, nor is there any harm in the sick if they do not go forth; and whoever obeys God and His Prophet, He will cause him to enter gardens beneath which rivers flow, and whoever turns back, He will punish him with a painful punishment.

18. Certainly God was well pleased with the believers when they swore allegiance to you under the tree, and He knew what was in their hearts, so He sent down tranquillity on them and rewarded them with a near victory,

19. And many acquisitions which they will take; and God is Mighty, Wise.

20. God promised you many acquisitions which you will take, then He hastened on this one for you and held back the hands of men from you, and that it may be a sign for the believers and that He may guide you on a right path.

21. And others which you have not yet been able to achieve God has certainly encompassed them, and God has power over all things.

22. And if those who disbelieve fight with you, they would certainly turn their backs, then they would not find any protector or a helper.

23. Such has been the course of God that has indeed run before, and you shall not find a change in God's course.

24. And He it is Who held back their hands from you and your hands from them in the valley of Mecca after He had given you victory over them; and God is Seeing what you do.

25. It is they who disbelieved and turned you away from the Sacred Mosque and turned off the offering withheld from arriving at its destined place; and were it not for the believing men and the believing women, whom, not having known, you might have trodden down, and thus something hateful might have afflicted you on their account without knowledge -- so that God may cause to enter into His mercy whomsoever He pleases; had they been widely separated one from another, We would certainly have punished those who disbelieved from among them with a painful punishment.

26. When those who disbelieved harbored in their hearts feelings of disdain, the disdain of the days of ignorance, but God sent down His tranquillity on His Prophet and on the believers, and made them keep the word of guarding against evil, and they were entitled to it and worthy of it; and God is Cognizant of all things.

27. Certainly God had shown to His Prophet the vision with truth: you shall most certainly enter the Sacred Mosque, if God pleases, in security, some having their heads shaved and others having their hair cut, you shall not fear, but He knows what you do not know, so He brought about a near victory before that.

28. He it is Who sent His Prophet with the guidance and the true religion that He may make it prevail over all the religions; and God is enough for a witness.

29. Mohammed is the Prophet of God, and those with him are firm of heart against the unbelievers, compassionate among themselves; you will see them bowing down, prostrating themselves, seeking grace from God and pleasure; their marks are in their faces because of the effect of prostration; that is their description in the Torah and their description in the Gospel; like as seed-produce that puts forth its sprout, then strengthens it, so it becomes stout and stands firmly on its stem, delighting the sowers that He may enrage the unbelievers on account of them; God has promised those among them who believe and do good, forgiveness and a great reward.

Chapter 49 — Al-Hujurat — The Chambers/Rooms

In the name of God, the Kind, the Merciful.

1. Oh you who believe! do not be forward in the presence of God and His Prophet, and be careful of your duty to God; certainly God is Hearing, Knowing.
2. Oh you who believe! do not raise your voices above the voice of the Prophet, and do not speak loud to him as you speak loud to one another, or your actions might become nothing while you do not perceive.
3. Certainly those who lower their voices before God's Prophet are they whose hearts God has proved for guarding against evil; they shall have forgiveness and a great reward.
4. As for those who call out to you from behind the private chambers, certainly most of them do not understand.
5. And if they wait patiently until you come out to them, it would certainly be better for them, and God is Forgiving, Merciful.
6. Oh you who believe! if an evil-doer comes to you with a claim, look carefully into it, because you might harm people with ignorance, and then you would be sorry for what you have done.
7. And know that among you is God's Prophet; should he obey you in many a matter, you would certainly fall into distress, but God has endeared the faith to you and has made it seemly in your hearts, and He has made hateful to you unbelief and transgression and disobedience; these it is that are the followers of a right way.
8. By grace from God and as a favor; and God is Knowing, Wise.
9. And if two parties of the believers quarrel, make peace between them; but if one of them acts wrongfully towards the other, fight that which acts wrongfully until it returns to God's command; then if it returns, make peace between them with justice and act equitably; certainly God loves those who act equitably.
10. The believers are but brethren, therefore make peace between your brethren and be careful of your duty to God that mercy may be had on you.
11. Oh you who believe! let not one people laugh at another people perchance they may be better than they, nor let women laugh at other women, perchance they may be better than they; and do not find fault with your own people nor call one another by nicknames; evil is a bad name after faith, and whoever does not turn, these it is that are the unjust.
12. Oh you who believe! avoid most of suspicion, for certainly suspicion in some cases is a sin, and do not spy nor let some of you backbite others. Does one of you like to eat the flesh of his dead brother? But you abhor it; and be careful of your duty to God, certainly God is Oft-returning to mercy, Merciful.
13. Oh you men! certainly We have created you of a male and a female, and made you tribes and families that you may know each other; certainly the most honorable of you with God is the one among you most careful of his duty; certainly God is Knowing, Aware.
14. The dwellers of the desert say, "We believe. Say, "You do not believe but say, We submit; and faith has not yet entered into your hearts; and if you obey God and His Prophet, He will not diminish any of your deeds; certainly God is Forgiving, Merciful.
15. The believers are only those who believe in God and His Prophet then they doubt not and struggle hard with their wealth and their lives in the way of God; they are the truthful ones.
16. Say, "Do you apprise God of your religion, and God knows what is in the heavens and what

is in the earth; and God is Cognizant of all things.

17. They think that they lay you under an obligation by becoming Muslims. Say, "Lay me not under obligation by your Islam: rather God lays you under an obligation by guiding you to the faith if you are truthful. 18. Certainly God knows the unseen things of the heavens and the earth; and God sees what you do.

Chapter 50 — Al-Qaf — Qaf

In the name of God, the Kind, the Merciful.

1. Qaf. I swear by the glorious Koran that Muhammad is the Prophet of God.
2. No! they wonder that there has come to them a alarmgiver from among themselves, so the unbelievers say, "This is a wonderful thing:
3. What! when we are dead and have become dust? That is afar from probable return.
4. We know indeed what the earth diminishes of them, and with Us is a writing that preserves.
5. No, they rejected the truth when it came to them, so they are now in a state of confusion.
6. Do they not then look up to heaven above them how We have made it and adorned it and it has no gaps?
7. And the earth, We have made it plain and cast in it mountains and We have made to grow therein of all beautiful kinds,
8. To give sight and as a reminder to every servant who turns frequently to God.
9. And We send down from the cloud water abounding in good, then We cause to grow thereby gardens and the grain that is reaped,
10. And the tall palm-trees having spadices closely set one above another,
11. A sustenance for the servants, and We give life thereby to a dead land; thus is the rising.
12. Others before them rejected prophets: the people of Noah and the dwellers of Ar-Rass and Samood,
13. And Ad and Pharoah and Lot's brethren,
14. And the dwellers of the grove and the people of Tuba; all rejected the apostles, so My threat came to pass.
15. Were We then fatigued with the first creation? Yet are they in doubt with regard to a new creation.
16. And certainly We created man, and We know what his mind suggests to him, and We are nearer to him than his life-vein.
17. When the two receivers receive, sitting on the right and on the left.
18. He utters not a word but there is by him a watcher at hand.
19. And the stupor of death will come in truth; that is what you were trying to escape.
20. And the trumpet shall be blown; that is the day of the threatening.
21. And every soul shall come, with it a driver and a witness.
22. Certainly you were heedless of it, but now We have removed from you your veil, so your sight today is sharp.
23. And his companions shall say, "This is what is ready with me.
24. Do cast into hell every ungrateful, rebellious one,
25. Forbidder of good, exceeder of limits, doubter,
26. Who sets up another god with God, so do cast him into severe punishment.
27. His companion will say, "Our Lord! I did not lead him into inordinacy but he himself was in a great error.
28. He will say, "Do not quarrel in My presence, and indeed I gave you the threatening beforehand:
29. My word shall not be changed, nor am I in the least unjust to the servants.
30. On the day that We will say to hell: Are you filled up? And it will say, "Are there any more?

³¹. And the garden shall be brought near to those who guard against evil, not far off:
³². This is what you were promised, it is for every one who turns frequently to God, keeps His limits;
³³. Who fears the Kind God in secret and comes with a penitent heart:
³⁴. Enter it in peace, that is the day of abiding.
³⁵. They have therein what they wish and with Us is more yet.
³⁶. And how many a generation did We destroy before them who were mightier in prowess than they, so they went about and about in the lands. Is there a place of refuge?
³⁷. Most certainly there is a reminder in this for him who has a heart or he gives ear and is a witness.
³⁸. And certainly We created the heavens and the earth and what is between them in six periods and there touched Us not any fatigue.
³⁹. Therefore be patient of what they say, and sing the praise of your Lord before the rising of the sun and before the setting.
⁴⁰. And glorify Him in the night and after the prayers.
⁴¹. And listen on the day when the crier shall cry from a near place
⁴². The day when they shall hear the cry in truth; that is the day of coming forth.
⁴³. Certainly We give life and cause to die, and to Us is the eventual coming;
⁴⁴. The day on which the earth shall cleave asunder under them, they will make haste; that is a gathering together easy to Us.
⁴⁵. We know best what they say, and you are not one to compel them; therefore remind him by means of the Koran who fears My threat.

Chapter 51 — Al-Dhariyat — The Scatterering Winds

In the name of God, the Kind, the Merciful.
1. I swear by the wind that scatters far and wide,
2. Then those clouds bearing the load of minute things in space.
3. Then those ships that glide easily,
4. Then those angels who distribute blessings by Our command;
5. What you are threatened with is most certainly true,
6. And the judgment must most certainly come about.
7. I swear by the heaven full of ways.
8. Most certainly you are at variance with each other in what you say,
9. He is turned away from it who would be turned away.
10. Cursed be the liars,
11. Who are in a gulf of ignorance neglectful;
12. They ask: When is the day of judgment?
13. It is the day on which they shall be tried at the fire.
14. Taste your persecution! this is what you would hasten on.
15. Certainly those who guard against evil shall be in gardens and fountains.
16. Taking what their Lord gives them; certainly they were before that, the doers of good.
17. They used to sleep but little in the night.
18. And in the morning they asked forgiveness.
19. And in their property was a portion due to him who begs and to him who is denied good.
20. And in the earth there are signs for those who are sure,
21. And in your own souls too; will you not then see?
22. And in the heaven is your sustenance and what you are threatened with.
23. And by the Lord of the heavens and the earth! it is most certainly the truth, just as you do speak.
24. Has there come to you information about the honored guests of Abraham?
25. When they entered upon him, they said, "Peace. Peace, said he, a strange people.
26. Then he turned aside to his family secretly and brought a fat roasted calf,
27. So he brought it near them. He said, "What! will you not eat?
28. So he conceived in his mind a fear on account of them. They said, "Fear not. And they gave him the good news of a boy possessing knowledge.
29. Then his wife came up in great grief, and she struck her face and said, "An old barren woman!
30. They said, "Thus says your Lord: Certainly He is the Wise, the Knowing.
31. He said, "What is your affair then, Oh messengers!
32. They said, "Certainly we are sent to a guilty people,
33. That we may send down upon them stone of clay,
34. Sent forth from your Lord for the extravagant.
35. Then We brought forth such as were therein of the believers.
36. But We did not find therein save a single house of those who submitted the Muslims.
37. And We left therein a sign for those who fear the painful punishment.
38. And in Moses: When We sent him to Pharoah with clear authority.

39. But he turned away with his forces and said, "A magician or a mad man."
40. So We seized him and his hosts and hurled them into the sea and he was blamable.
41. And in Ad: When We sent upon them the destructive wind.
42. It did not leave anything on which it blew, but it made it like ashes.
43. And in Samood: When it was said to them: Enjoy yourselves for a while.
44. But they revolted against the commandment of their Lord, so the rumbling overtook them while they saw.
45. So they were not able to rise up, nor could they defend themselves --
46. And the people of Noah before, certainly they were a transgressing people.
47. And the heaven, We raised it high with power, and most certainly We are the makers of things ample.
48. And the earth, We have made it a wide extent; how well have We then spread it out.
49. And of everything We have created pairs that you may be mindful.
50. Therefore fly to God, certainly I am a plain alarmgiver to you from Him.
51. And do not set up with God another god: certainly I am a plain alarmgiver to you from Him.
52. Thus there did not come to those before them an apostle but they said, "A magician or a mad man."
53. Have they charged each other with this? No! they are an inordinate people.
54. Then turn your back upon them for you are not to blame;
55. And continue to remind, for certainly the reminder profits the believers.
56. And I have not created the jinn and the men except that they should serve Me.
57. I do not desire from them any sustenance and I do not desire that they should feed Me.
58. Certainly God is the Bestower of sustenance, the Lord of Power, the Strong.
59. So certainly those who are unjust shall have a portion like the portion of their companions, therefore let them not ask Me to hasten on.
60. Therefore woe to those who disbelieve because of their day which they are threatened with.

Chapter 52 — Al-Tur — The Mountain

In the name of God, the Kind, the Merciful.

1. I swear by the Mountain,
2. And the Book written
3. In an outstretched fine parchment,
4. And the House Kaaba that is visited,
5. And the elevated canopy
6. And the swollen sea
7. Most certainly the punishment of your Lord will come to pass;
8. There shall be none to avert it;
9. On the day when the heaven shall move from side to side
10. And the mountains shall pass away passing away altogether.
11. So woe on that day to those who reject the truth,
12. Those who sport entering into vain discourses.
13. The day on which they shall be driven away to the fire of hell with violence.
14. This is the fire which you used to give the lie to.
15. Is it magic then or do you not see?
16. Enter into it, then bear it patiently, or do not bear it patiently, it is the same to you; you shall be avenged only for what you did.
17. Certainly those who guard against evil shall be in gardens and bliss
18. Rejoicing because of what their Lord gave them, and their Lord saved them from the punishment of the burning fire.
19. Eat and drink pleasantly for what you did,
20. Reclining on thrones set in lines, and We will unite them to large-eyed beautiful ones.
21. And as for those who believe and their offspring follow them in faith, We will unite with them their offspring and We will not reduce any of their work; every man is responsible for what he shall have wrought.
22. And We will aid them with fruit and flesh such as they desire.
23. They shall pass therein from one to another a cup wherein there shall be nothing vain nor any sin.
24. And round them shall go boys of theirs as if they were hidden pearls.
25. And some of them shall advance towards others questioning each other.
26. Saying, "Certainly we feared before on account of our families:
27. But God has been kind to us and He has saved us from the punishment of the hot wind:
28. Certainly we called upon Him before: Certainly He is the Benign, the Merciful.
29. Therefore continue to remind, for by the grace of your Lord, you are not a soothsayer, or a madman.
30. Or do they say, "A poet, we wait for him the evil accidents of time.
31. Say, "Wait, for certainly I too with you am of those who wait.
32. No! do their understandings bid them this? Or are they an inordinate people?
33. Or do they say, "He has created it. No! they do not believe.
34. Then let them bring an announcement like it, if they are truthful.
35. Or were they created without there being anything, or are they the creators?

36. Or did they create the heavens and the earth? No! they have no assurance.
37. Or have they the treasures of your Lord with them? Or have they been set in absolute authority?
38. Or have they the means by which they listen? Then let their listener bring a clear authority.
39. Or has He daughters while you have sons?
40. Or do you ask them for a reward, so that they are overburdened by a debt?
41. Or have they the unseen so that they write it down?
42. Or do they desire a war? But those who disbelieve shall be the vanquished ones in war.
43. Or have they a god other than God? Glory be to God from what they set up with Him.
44. And if they should see a portion of the heaven coming down, they would say, "Piled up clouds.
45. Leave them then till they meet that day of theirs wherein they shall be made to swoon with terror:
46. The day on which their struggle shall not assist them at all, nor shall they be helped.
47. And certainly those who are unjust shall have a punishment besides that in the world, but most of them do not know.
48. And wait patiently for the judgment of your Lord, for certainly you are before Our eyes, and sing the praise of your Lord when you rise;
49. And in the night, give Him glory too, and at the setting of the stars.

Chapter 53 — Al-Najm — The Star

In the name of God, the Kind, the Merciful.
¹. I swear by the star when it goes down.
². Your companion does not err, nor does he go astray;
³. Nor does he speak out of desire.
⁴. It is nothing but revelation that is revealed,
⁵. The Lord of Mighty Power has taught him,
⁶. The Lord of Strength; so he attained completion,
⁷. And he is in the highest part of the horizon.
⁸. Then he drew near, then he bowed
⁹. So he was the measure of two bows or closer still.
¹⁰. And He revealed to His servant what He revealed.
¹¹. The heart was not untrue in making him see what he saw.
¹². What! do you then dispute with him as to what he saw?
¹³. And certainly he saw him in another descent,
¹⁴. At the farthest lote-tree;
¹⁵. Near which is the garden, the place to be resorted to.
¹⁶. When that which covers covered the lote-tree;
¹⁷. The eye did not turn aside, nor did it exceed the limit.
¹⁸. Certainly he saw of the greatest signs of his Lord.
¹⁹. Have you then considered the Lat and the Uzza,
²⁰. And Manat, the third, the last?
²¹. What! for you the males and for Him the females!
²². This indeed is an unjust division!
²³. They are nothing but names which you have named, you and your fathers; God has not sent for them any authority. They follow nothing but conjecture and the low desires which their souls incline to; and certainly the guidance has come to them from their Lord.
²⁴. Or shall man have what he wishes?
²⁵. No! for God is the hereafter and the former life.
²⁶. And how many an angel is there in the heavens whose intercession does not avail at all except after God has given permission to whom He pleases and chooses.
²⁷. Most certainly they who do not believe in the hereafter name the angels with female names.
²⁸. And they have no knowledge of it; they do not follow anything but conjecture, and certainly conjecture does not avail against the truth at all.
²⁹. Therefore turn aside from him who turns his back upon Our reminder and does not desire anything but this world's life.
³⁰. That is their goal of knowledge; certainly your Lord knows best him who goes astray from His path and He knows best him who follows the right direction.
³¹. And God's is what is in the heavens and what is in the earth, that He may reward those who do evil according to what they do, and that He may reward those who do good with goodness.
³². Those who keep aloof from the great sins and the indecencies but the passing idea; certainly your Lord is liberal in forgiving. He knows you best when He brings you forth from the earth and when you are embryos in the wombs of your mothers; therefore do not attribute purity

to your souls; He knows him best who guards against evil.

33. Have you then seen him who turns his back?
34. And gives a little and then withholds.
35. Has he the knowledge of the unseen so that he can see?
36. Or, has he not been informed of what is in the scriptures of Moses?
37. And of Abraham who fulfilled the commandments:
38. That no bearer of burden shall bear the burden of another-
39. And that man shall have nothing but what he strives for-
40. And that his striving shall soon be seen-
41. Then shall he be rewarded for it with the greatest reward-
42. And that to your Lord is the goal-
43. And that He it is Who makes men laugh and makes them weep;
44. And that He it is Who causes death and gives life-
45. And that He created pairs, the male and the female
46. From the small seed when it is adapted
47. And that on Him is the bringing forth a second time;
48. And that He it is Who enriches and gives to hold;
49. And that He is the Lord of the Sirius;
50. And that He did destroy the Ad of old
51. And Samood, so He spared not
52. And the people of Noah before; certainly they were most unjust and inordinate;
53. And the overthrown cities did He overthrow,
54. So there covered them that which covered.
55. Which of your Lord's benefits will you then dispute about?
56. This is a alarmgiver of the alarmgivers of old.
57. The near event will be soon.
58. There shall be none besides God to remove it.
59. Do you then wonder at this announcement?
60. And will you laugh and not weep?
61. While you are indulging in varieties.
62. So make obeisance to God and serve Him.

Chapter 54 — Al-Qamar — The Moon

In the name of God, the Kind the Merciful.

1. The hour drew near and the moon did rend asunder.
2. And if they see a miracle they turn aside and say, "Transient magic."
3. And they call it a lie, and follow their low desires; and every affair has its appointed term.
4. And certainly some narratives have come to them wherein is prevention --
5. Consummate wisdom -- but warnings do not avail;
6. So turn your back on them for the day when the inviter shall invite them to a hard task,
7. Their eyes cast down, going forth from their graves as if they were scattered locusts,
8. Hastening to the inviter. The unbelievers shall say, "This is a hard day."
9. Before them the people of Noah rejected, so they rejected Our servant and called him mad, and he was driven away.
10. Therefore he called upon his Lord: I am overcome, come You then to help.
11. So We opened the gates of the cloud with water pouring
12. And We made water to flow forth in the land in springs, so the water gathered together according to a measure already ordered.
13. And We bore him on that which was made of planks and nails
14. Sailing, before Our eyes, a reward for him who was denied.
15. And certainly We left it as a sign, but is there anyone who
16. How great was then My punishment and My warning!
17. And certainly We have made the Koran easy for remembrance, but is there anyone who will mind?
18. Ad treated the truth as a lie, so how great was My punishment and My warning!
19. Certainly We sent on them a tornado in a day of bitter ill-luck
20. Tearing men away as if they were the trunks of palm-trees torn up.
21. How great was then My punishment and My warning!
22. And certainly We have made the Koran easy for remembrance, but is there anyone who will mind?
23. Samood rejected the warning.
24. So they said, "What! a single mortal from among us! Shall we follow him? Most certainly we shall in that case be in sure error and distress:
25. Has the reminder been made to light upon him from among us? No! he is an insolent liar!
26. Tomorrow shall they know who is the liar, the insolent one.
27. Certainly We are going to send the she-camel as a trial for them; therefore watch them and have patience.
28. And inform them that the water is shared between them; every share of the water shall be regulated.
29. But they called their companion, so he took the sword and killed her.
30. How great was then My punishment and My warning!
31. Certainly We sent upon them a single cry, so they were like the dry fragments of trees which the maker of an enclosure collects.
32. And certainly We have made the Koran easy for remembrance, but is there anyone who will mind?

33. The people of Lot treated the warning. as a lie.
34. Certainly We sent upon them a stonestorm, except Lot's followers; We saved them a little before daybreak,
35. A favor from Us; thus do We reward him who gives thanks.
36. And certainly he warned them of Our violent seizure, but they obstinately disputed the warning.
37. And certainly they endeavored to turn him from his guests, but We blinded their eyes; so taste My punishment and My warning.
38. And certainly a lasting punishment overtook them in the morning.
39. So taste My punishment and My warning.
40. And certainly We have made the Koran easy for remembrance, but is there anyone who will mind?
41. And certainly the warning came to Pharoah's people.
42. They rejected all Our words, so We overtook them after the manner of a Mighty, Powerful One.
43. Are the unbelievers of yours better than these, or is there an exemption for you in the scriptures?
44. Or do they say, "We are a host allied together to help each other?
45. Soon shall the hosts be routed, and they shall turn their backs.
46. No, the hour is their promised time, and the hour shall be most grievous and bitter.
47. Certainly the guilty are in error and distress.
48. On the day when they shall be dragged upon their faces into the fire; taste the touch of hell.
49. Certainly We have created everything according to a measure.
50. And Our command is but one, as the twinkling of an eye.
51. And certainly We have already destroyed the likes of you, but is there anyone who will mind?
52. And everything they have done is in the writings.
53. And everything small and great is written down.
54. Certainly those who guard against evil shall be in gardens and rivers,
55. In the seat of honor with a most Powerful King.

Chapter 55 — Al-Rahman — The Kind

In the name of God, the Kind, the Merciful.
1. The Kind God,
2. Taught the Koran.
3. He created man,
4. Taught him the mode of expression.
5. The sun and the moon follow a judging.
6. And the herbs and the trees do adore Him.
7. And the heaven, He raised it high, and He made the balance
8. That you may not be inordinate in respect of the measure.
9. And keep up the balance with equity and do not make the measure deficient.
10. And the earth, He has set it for living creatures;
11. Therein is fruit and palms having sheathed clusters,
12. And the grain with its husk and fragrance.
13. Which then of the bounties of your Lord will you deny?
14. He created man from dry clay like earthen vessels,
15. And He created the jinn of a flame of fire.
16. Which then of the bounties of your Lord will you deny?
17. Lord of the East and Lord of the West.
18. Which then of the bounties of your Lord will you deny?
19. . He has made the two seas to flow freely so that they meet together:
20. Between them is a barrier which they cannot pass.
21. Which then of the bounties of your Lord will you deny?
22. There come forth from them pearls, both large and small.
23. Which then of the bounties of your Lord will you deny?
24. And His are the ships reared aloft in the sea like mountains.
25. Which then of the bounties of your Lord will you deny?
26. Everyone on it must pass away.
27. And there will endure for ever the person of your Lord, the Lord of glory and honor.
28. Which then of the bounties of your Lord will you deny?
29. All those who are in the heavens and the earth ask of Him; every moment He is in a state of glory.
30. Which then of the bounties of your Lord will you deny?
31. Soon will We apply Ourselves to you, Oh you two armies.
32. Which then of the bounties of your Lord will you deny?
33. Oh assembly of the jinn and the men! If you are able to pass through the regions of the heavens and the earth, then pass through; you cannot pass through but with authority.
34. Which then of the bounties of your Lord will you deny?
35. The flames of fire and smoke will be sent on you two, then you will not be able to defend yourselves.
36. Which then of the bounties of your Lord will you deny?
37. And when the heaven is rent asunder, and then becomes red like red hide.
38. Which then of the bounties of your Lord will you deny?

39. So on that day neither man nor jinni shall be asked about his sin.
40. Which then of the bounties of your Lord will you deny?
41. The guilty shall be recognized by their marks, so they shall be seized by the forelocks and the feet.
42. Which then of the bounties of your Lord will you deny?
43. This is the hell which the guilty called a lie.
44. Round about shall they go between it and hot, boiling water.
45. Which then of the bounties of your Lord will you deny?
46. And for him who fears to stand before his Lord are two gardens.
47. Which then of the bounties of your Lord will you deny?
48. Having in them various kinds.
49. Which then of the bounties of your Lord will you deny?
50. In both of them are two fountains flowing.
51. Which then of the bounties of your Lord will you deny?
52. In both of them are two pairs of every fruit.
53. Which then of the bounties of your Lord will you deny?
54. Reclining on beds, the inner coverings of which are of silk brocade; and the fruits of the two gardens shall be within reach.
55. Which then of the bounties of your Lord will you deny?
56. In them shall be those who restrained their eyes; before them neither man nor jinni shall have touched them.
57. Which then of the bounties of your Lord will you deny?
58. As though they were rubies and pearls.
59. Which then of the bounties of your Lord will you deny?
60. Is the reward of goodness anything but goodness?
61. Which then of the bounties of your Lord will you deny?
62. And besides these two are two other gardens;
63. Which then of the bounties of your Lord will you deny?
64. Both inclining to blackness.
65. Which then of the bounties of your Lord will you deny?
66. In both of them are two springs gushing forth.
67. Which then of the bounties of your Lord will you deny?
68. In both are fruits and palms and pomegranates.
69. Which then of the bounties of your Lord will you deny?
70. In them are fine things, beautiful ones.
71. Which then of the bounties of your Lord will you deny?
72. Pure ones confined to the pavilions.
73. Which then of the bounties of your Lord will you deny?
74. Man has not touched them before them nor jinni.
75. Which then of the bounties of your Lord will you deny?
76. Reclining on green cushions and beautiful carpets.
77. Which then of the bounties of your Lord will you deny?
78. Blessed be the name of your Lord, the Lord of Glory and Honor!

Chapter 56 — Al-Waqi'ah — The Event

In the name of God, the Kind, the Merciful.
1. When the great event comes to pass,
2. There is no belying its coming to pass –
3. Abasing one party, exalting the other,
4. When the earth shall be shaken with a severe shaking,
5. And the mountains shall be made to crumble with an awful crumbling,
6. So that they shall be as scattered dust.
7. And you shall be three sorts.
8. Then as to the companions of the right hand; how happy are the companions of the right hand!
9. And as to the companions of the left hand; how wretched are the companions of the left hand!
10. And the foremost are the foremost,
11. These are they who are drawn near to God,
12. In the gardens of bliss.
13. A numerous company from among the first,
14. And a few from among the latter.
15. On thrones decorated,
16. Reclining on them, facing one another.
17. Round about them shall go youths never altering in age,
18. With goblets and ewers and a cup of pure drink;
19. They shall not be affected with headache thereby, nor shall they get exhausted,
20. And fruits such as they choose,
21. And the flesh of fowl such as they desire.
22. And pure, beautiful ones,
23. The like of the hidden pearls:
24. A reward for what they used to do.
25. They shall not hear therein vain or sinful discourse,
26. Except the word peace, peace.
27. And the companions of the right hand; how happy are the companions of the right hand!
28. Amid thornless lote-trees,
29. And banana-trees with fruits, one above another.
30. And extended shade,
31. And water flowing constantly,
32. And abundant fruit,
33. Neither intercepted nor forbidden,
34. And exalted thrones.
35. Certainly We have made them to grow into a new growth,
36. Then We have made them virgins,
37. Loving, equals in age,
38. For the sake of the companions of the right hand.
39. A numerous company from among the first,
40. And a numerous company from among the last.
41. And those of the left hand, how wretched are those of the left hand!

42. In hot wind and boiling water,
43. And the shade of black smoke,
44. Neither cool nor honorable.
45. Certainly they were before that made to live in ease and plenty.
46. And they persisted in the great violation.
47. And they used to say, "What! when we die and have become dust and bones, shall we then indeed be raised?
48. Or our fathers of yore?
49. Say, "The first and the last,
50. Shall most certainly be gathered together for the appointed hour of a known day.
51. Then shall you, Oh you who err and call it a lie!
52. Most certainly eat of a tree of Zaqqoom,
53. And fill your bellies with it;
54. Then drink over it of boiling water;
55. And drink as drinks the thirsty camel.
56. This is their entertainment on the day of requital.
57. We have created you, why do you not then assent?
58. Have you considered the seed?
59. Is it you that create it or are We the creators?
60. We have ordered death among you and We are not to be overcome,
61. In order that We may bring in your place the likes of you and make you grow into what you know not.
62. And certainly you know the first growth, why do you not then mind?
63. Have you considered what you sow?
64. Is it you that cause it to grow, or are We the causers of growth?
65. If We pleased, We should have certainly made it broken down into pieces, then would you begin to lament:
66. Certainly we are burdened with debt:
67. No! we are deprived.
68. Have you considered the water which you drink?
69. Is it you that send it down from the clouds, or are We the senders?
70. If We pleased, We would have made it salty; why do you not then give thanks?
71. Have you considered the fire which you strike?
72. Is it you that produce the trees for it, or are We the producers?
73. We have made it a reminder and an advantage for the wayfarers of the desert.
74. Therefore glorify the name of your Lord, the Great.
75. But no! I swear by the falling of stars;
76. And most certainly it is a very great oath if you only knew;
77. Most certainly it is an honored Koran,
78. In a book that is protected
79. None shall touch it save the purified ones.
80. A revelation by the Lord of the worlds.
81. Do you then hold this announcement in contempt?
82. And to give it the lie you make your means of subsistence.
83. Why is it not then that when it soul comes up to the throat,
84. And you at that time look on --
85. And We are nearer to it than you, but you do not see --

86. Then why is it not -- if you are not held under authority --
87. That you send it not back -- if you are truthful?
88. Then if he is one of those drawn near to God,
89. Then happiness and bounty and a garden of bliss.
90. And if he is one of those on the right hand,
91. Then peace to you from those on the right hand.
92. And if he is one of the rejecters, the erring ones,
93. He shall have an entertainment of boiling water,
94. And burning in hell.
95. Most certainly this is a certain truth.
96. Therefore glorify the name of your Lord, the Great.

Chapter 57 — Al-Hadid — The Iron

In the name of God, the Kind, the Merciful.

1. Whatever is in the heavens and the earth declares the glory of God, and He is the Mighty, the Wise.
2. His is the kingdom of the heavens and the earth; He gives life and causes death; and He has power over all things.
3. He is the First and the Last and the Ascendant over all and the Knower of hidden things, and He is Cognizant of all things.
4. He it is who created the heavens and the earth in six periods, and He is firm in power; He knows that which goes deep down into the earth and that which comes forth out of it, and that which comes down from the heaven and that which goes up into it, and He is with you wherever you are; and God sees what you do.
5. His is the kingdom of the heavens and the earth; and to God are all affairs returned.
6. He causes the night to enter in upon the day, and causes the day to enter in upon the night, and He is Cognizant of what is in the hearts.
7. Believe in God and His Prophet, and spend out of what He has made you to be successors of; for those of you who believe and spend shall have a great reward.
8. And what reason have you that you should not believe in God? And the Prophet calls on you that you may believe in your Lord, and indeed He has made a covenant with you if you are believers.
9. He it is who sends down clear words upon His servant, that he may bring you forth from utter darkness into light; and most certainly God is Kind, Merciful to you.
10. And what reason have you that you should not spend in God's way? And God's is the inheritance of the heavens and the earth, not alike among you are those who spent before the victory and fought and those who did not: they are more exalted in rank than those who spent and fought afterwards; and God has promised good to all; and God is Aware of what you do.
11. Who is there that will offer to God a good gift so He will double it for him, and he shall have an excellent reward.
12. On that day you will see the faithful men and the faithful women -- their light running before them and on their right hand -- good news for you today: gardens beneath which rivers flow, to abide therein, that is the grand achievement.
13. On the day when the hypocritical men and the hypocritical women will say to those who believe: Wait for us, that we may have light from your light; it shall be said, "Turn back and seek a light. Then separation would be brought about between them, with a wall having a door in it; as for the inside of it, there shall be mercy in it, and as for the outside of it, before it there shall be punishment.
14. They will cry out to them: Were we not with you? They shall say, "Yea! but you caused yourselves to fall into temptation, and you waited and doubted, and vain desires deceived you till the threatened punishment of God came, while the arch-deceiver deceived you about God.
15. So today ransom shall not be accepted from you nor from those who disbelieved; your home is the fire; it is your friend and evil is the resort.
16. Has not the time yet come for those who believe that their hearts should be humble for the remembrance of God and what has come down of the truth? And -that they should not be

like those who were given the Book before, but the time became prolonged to them, so their hearts hardened, and most of them are transgressors.

17. Know that God gives life to the earth after its death; indeed, We have made the words clear to you that you may understand.

18. Certainly as for the charitable men and the charitable women and those who set apart for God a proper portion, it shall be doubled for them and they shall have a noble reward.

19. And as for those who believe in God and His apostles, these it is that are the truthful and the faithful ones in the sight of their Lord: they shall have their reward and their light, and as for those who disbelieve and reject Our words, these are the inmates of the hell.

20. Know that this world's life is only sport and play and gaiety and boasting among yourselves, and a vying in the multiplication of wealth and children, like the rain, whose causing the vegetation to grow, pleases the husbandmen, then it withers away so that you will see it become yellow, then it becomes dried up and broken down; and in the hereafter is a severe punishment and also forgiveness from God and His pleasure; and this world's life is nothing but means of deception.

21. Hasten to forgiveness from your Lord and to a garden the extensiveness of which is as the extensiveness of the heaven and the earth; it is prepared for those who believe in God and His apostles; that is the grace of God: He gives it to whom He pleases, and God is the Lord of mighty grace.

22. No evil happen tos on the earth nor in your own souls, but it is in a book before We bring it into existence; certainly that is easy to God:

23. So that you may not grieve for what has escaped you, nor be exultant at what He has given you; and God does not love any arrogant boaster:

24. Those who are wretched and enjoin niggardliness on men; and whoever turns back, then certainly God is He Who is the Self sufficient, the Praised.

25. Certainly We sent Our apostles with clear explanations, and sent down with them the Book and the balance that men may conduct themselves with equity; and We have made the iron, wherein is great violence and advantages to men, and that God may know who helps Him and His apostles in the secret; certainly God is Strong, Mighty.

26. And certainly We sent Noah and Abraham and We gave to their offspring the gift of prophecy and the Book; so there are among them those who go aright, and most of them are transgressors.

27. Then We made Our apostles to follow in their footsteps, and We sent Jesus son of Mary afterwards, and We gave him the Gospel, and We put in the hearts of those who followed him kindness and mercy; and as for monkery, they innovated it -- We did not prescribe it to them -- only to seek God's

pleasure, but they did not observe it with its due observance; so We gave to those of them who believed their reward, and most of them are transgressors.

28. Oh you who believe! be careful of your duty to God and believe in His Prophet: He will give you two portions of His mercy, and make for you a light with which you will walk, and forgive you, and God is Forgiving, Merciful;

29. So that the followers of the Book may know that they do not control anything of the grace of God, and that grace is in God's hand, He gives it to whom He pleases; and God is the Lord of mighty grace.

Chapter 58 — Al-Mujadilah — She Who Pleaded

In the name of God, the Kind, the Merciful.

¹. God indeed knows the plea of her who pleads with you about her husband and complains to God, and God knows the contentions of both of you; certainly God is Hearing, Seeing.

². As for those of you who put away their wives by likening their backs to the backs of their mothers, they are not their mothers; their mothers are no others than those who gave them birth; and most certainly they utter a hateful word and a falsehood and most certainly God is Pardoning, Forgiving. ³. And as for those who put away their wives by likening their backs to the backs of their mothers then would recall what they said, they should free a captive before they touch each other; to that you are reprimanded to conform; and God is Aware of what you do.

⁴. But whoever has not the means, let him fast for two months successively before they touch each other; then as for him who is not able, let him feed sixty needy ones; that is in order that you may have faith in God and His Prophet, and these are God's limits, and the unbelievers shall have a painful punishment.

⁵. Certainly those who act in opposition to God and His Prophet shall be laid down prostrate as those before them were laid down prostrate; and indeed We have revealed clear words, and the unbelievers shall have an abasing punishment.

⁶. On the day when God will raise them up all together, then inform them of what they did: God has recorded it while they have forgotten it; and God is a witness of all things.

⁷. Do you not see that God knows whatever is in the heavens and whatever is in the earth? Nowhere is there a secret counsel between three persons but He is the fourth of them, nor between five but He is the sixth of them, nor less than that nor more but He is with them wheresoever they are; then He will inform them of what they did on the day of resurrection: certainly God is Cognizant of all things.

⁸. Have you not seen those who are forbidden secret counsels, then they return to what they are forbidden, and they hold secret counsels for sin and revolt and disobedience to the Prophet, and when they come to you they greet you with a greeting with which God does not greet you, and they say in themselves: Why does not God punish us for what we say? Hell is enough for them; they shall enter it, and evil is the resort.

⁹. Oh you who believe! when you confer together in private, do not give to each other counsel of sin and revolt and disobedience to the Prophet, and give to each other counsel of goodness and guarding against evil; and be careful of your duty to God, to Whom you shall be gathered together.

¹⁰. Secret counsels are only the work of the Satan that he may cause to grieve those who believe, and he cannot hurt them in the least except with God's permission, and on God let the believers rely.

¹¹. Oh you who believe! when it is said to you, Make room in your assemblies, then make ample room, God will give you ample, and when it is said, "Rise up, then rise up. God will exalt those of you who believe, and those who are given knowledge, in high degrees; and God is Aware of what you do.

¹². Oh you who believe! when you consult the Prophet, then offer something in charity before your consultation; that is better for you and purer; but if you do not find, then certainly God is Forgiving, Merciful.

13. Do you fear that you will not be able to give in charity before your consultation? So when you do not do it and God has turned to you mercifully, then keep up prayer and pay the poor-rate and obey God and His Prophet; and God is Aware of what you do.

14. Have you not seen those who befriend a people with whom God is wroth? They are neither of you nor of them, and they swear falsely while they know.

15. God has prepared for them a severe punishment; certainly what they do is evil.

16. They make their oaths to serve as a cover so they turn away from God's way; therefore they shall have an abasing punishment.

17. Neither their wealth nor their children shall assist them at all against God; they are the inmates of the fire, therein they shall abide.

18. On the day that God will raise them up all, then they will swear to Him as they swear to you, and they think that they have something; now certainly they are the liars.

19. The Satan has gained the mastery over them, so he has made them forget the remembrance of God; they are the Satan's party; now certainly the Satan's party are the losers.

20. Certainly as for those who are in opposition to God and His Prophet; they shall be among the most abased.

21. God has written down: I will most certainly prevail, I and My apostles; certainly God is Strong, Mighty.

22. You shall not find a people who believe in God and the latter day befriending those who act in opposition to God and His Prophet, even though they were their own fathers, or their sons, or their brothers, or their kinsfolk; these are they into whose hearts He has impressed faith, and whom He has strengthened with an inspiration from Him: and He will cause them to enter gardens beneath which rivers flow, abiding therein; God is well-pleased with them and they are well-pleased with Him these are God's party: now certainly the party of God are the successful ones.

Chapter 59 — Al-Hashr — The Banishment

In the name of God, the Kind the Merciful.

1. Whatever is in the heavens and whatever is in the earth declares the glory of God, and He is the Mighty, the Wise.
2. He it is Who caused those who disbelieved of the followers of the Book to go forth from their homes at the first banishment you did not think that they would go forth, while they were certain that their fortresses would defend them against God; but God came to them from where they did not expect, and cast terror into their hearts; they demolished their houses with their own hands and the hands of the believers; therefore take a lesson, Oh you who have eyes!
3. And had it not been that God had decreed for them the exile, He would certainly have punished them in this world, and in the hereafter they shall have punishment of the fire.
4. That is because they acted in opposition to God and His Prophet, and whoever acts in opposition to God, then certainly God is severe in retributing evil.
5. Whatever palm-tree you cut down or leave standing upon its roots, It is by God's command, and that He may abase the transgressors.
6. And whatever God restored to His Prophet from them you did not press forward against it any horse or a riding camel but God gives authority to His apostles against whom He pleases, and God has power over all things.
7. Whatever God has restored to His Prophet from the people of the towns, it is for God and for the Prophet, and for the near of kin and the orphans and the needy and the wayfarer, so that it may not be a thing taken by turns among the rich of you, and whatever the Prophet gives you, accept it, and from whatever he forbids you, keep back, and be careful of your duty to God; certainly God is severe in retributing evil:
8. It is for the poor who fled their homes and their possessions, seeking grace of God and His pleasure, and assisting God and His Prophet: these it is that are the truthful.
9. And those who made their home in the city and in the faith before them love those who have fled to them, and do not find in their hearts a need of what they are given, and prefer them before themselves though poverty may afflict them, and whoever is preserved from the niggardliness of his soul, these it is that are the successful ones.
10. And those who come after them say, "Our Lord! forgive us and those of our brethren who had precedence of us in faith, and do not allow any spite to remain in our hearts towards those who believe, our Lord! certainly You are Kind, Merciful.
11. Have you not seen those who have become hypocrites? They say to those of their brethren who disbelieve from among the followers of the Book: If you are driven forth, we shall certainly go forth with you, and we will never obey any one concerning you, and if you are fought against, we will certainly help you, and God bears witness that they are most certainly liars.
12. Certainly if these are driven forth, they will not go forth with them, and if they are fought against, they will not help them, and even if they help-them, they will certainly turn their backs, then they shall not be helped.
13. You are certainly greater in being feared in their hearts than God; that is because they are a people who do not understand
14. They will not fight against you in a body save in fortified towns or from behind walls; their fighting between them is severe, you may think them as one body, and their hearts are disunited;

that is because they are a people who have no sense.

¹⁵. Like those before them shortly; they tasted the evil result of their affair, and they shall have a painful punishment.

¹⁶. Like the Satan when he says to man: Disbelieve, but when he disbelieves, he says: I am certainly clear of you; certainly I fear God, the Lord of the worlds.

¹⁷. Therefore the end of both of them is that they are both in the fire to abide therein, and that is the reward of the unjust.

¹⁸. Oh you who believe! be careful of your duty to God, and let every soul consider what it has sent on for the morrow, and be careful of your duty to God; certainly God is Aware of what you do.

¹⁹. And do not be like those who abandoned God, so He made them abandon their own souls: these it is that are the transgressors.

²⁰. Not alike are the inmates of the fire and the dwellers of the garden: the dwellers of the garden are they that are the achievers.

²¹. Had We sent down this Koran on a mountain, you would certainly have seen it falling down, splitting asunder because of the fear of God, and We set

forth these parables to men that they may reflect.

²². He is God besides Whom there is no god; the Knower of the unseen and the seen; He is the Kind, the Merciful

²³. He is God, besides Whom there is no god; the King, the Holy, the Giver of peace, the Granter of security, Guardian over all, the Mighty, the

Supreme, the Possessor of every greatness Glory be to God from what they set up with Him.

²⁴. He is God the Creator, the Maker, the Fashioner; His are the most excellent names; whatever is in the heavens and the earth declares His glory; and He is the Mighty, the Wise.

Chapter 60 — Al-Mumtahhanah — She Who is Examined

In the name of God, the Kind, the Merciful.

1. Oh you who believe! do not take My enemy and your enemy for friends: would you offer them love while they deny what has come to you of the truth, driving out the Prophet and yourselves because you believe in God, your Lord? If you go forth struggling hard in My path and seeking My pleasure, would you great love to them? And I know what you conceal and what you manifest; and whoever of you does this, he indeed has gone astray from the straight path.

2. If they find you, they will be your enemies, and will stretch forth towards you their hands and their tongues with evil, and they ardently desire that you may disbelieve.

3. Your relationship would not profit you, nor your children on the day of resurrection; He will decide between you; and God sees what you do.

4. Indeed, there is for you a good example in Abraham and those with him when they said to their people: Certainly we are clear of you and of what you serve besides God; we declare ourselves to be clear of you, and enmity and hatred have appeared between us and you forever until you believe in God alone -- but not in what Abraham said to his father: I would certainly ask forgiveness for you, and I do not control for you anything from God -- Our Lord! on You do we rely, and to You do we turn, and to You is the eventual coming:

5. Our Lord! do not make us a trial for those who disbelieve, and forgive us, our Lord! certainly You are the Mighty, the Wise.

6. Certainly there is for you in them a good example, for him who fears God and the last day; and whoever turns back, then certainly God is the Self-sufficient, the Praised.

7. It may be that God will bring about friendship between you and those whom you hold to be your enemies among them; and God is Powerful; and God is Forgiving, Merciful.

8. God does not forbid you respecting those who have not made war against you on account of your religion, and have not driven you forth from your homes, that you show them kindness and deal with them justly; certainly God loves the doers of justice.

9. God only forbids you respecting those who made war upon you on account of your religion, and drove you forth from your homes and backed up others in your expulsion, that you make friends with them, and whoever makes friends with them, these are the unjust.

10. Oh you who believe! when believing women come to you fleeing, then examine them; God knows best their faith; then if you find them to be believing women, do not send them back to the unbelievers, neither are these women lawful for them, nor are those men lawful for them, and give them what they have spent; and no blame attaches to you in marrying them when you give them their dowries; and hold not to the ties of marriage of unbelieving women, and ask for what you have spent, and let them ask for what they have spent. That is God's judgment; He judges between you, and God is Knowing, Wise.

11. And if anything out of the dowries of your wives has passed away from you to the unbelievers, then your turn comes, give to those whose wives have gone away the like of what they have spent, and be careful of your duty to God in Whom you believe.

12. Oh Prophet! when believing women come to you giving you a pledge that they will not compare any with God, and will not steal, and will not commit fornication, and will not kill their children, and will not bring a defamation which they have created of themselves, and will not disobey you in what is good, accept their pledge, and ask forgiveness for them from

God; certainly God is Forgiving, Merciful.

13. Oh you who believe! do not make friends with a people with whom God is wroth; indeed they despair of the hereafter as the unbelievers despair of those in tombs.

Chapter 61 — Al-Saff — The Ranks

In the name of God, the Kind, the Merciful.

1. Whatever is in the heavens and whatever is in the earth declares the glory of God; and He is the Mighty, the Wise.
2. Oh you who believe! why do you say that which you do not do?
3. It is most hateful to God that you should say that which you do not do.
4. Certainly God loves those who fight in His way in ranks as if they were a firm and compact wall.
5. And when Moses said to his people: Oh my people! why do you give me trouble? And you know indeed that I am God's apostle to you; but when they turned aside, God made their hearts turn aside, and God does not guide the transgressing people.
6. And when Jesus son of Mary said, "Oh children of Israel! certainly I am the apostle of God to you, verifying that which is before me of the Torah and giving the good news of a Prophet who will come after me, his name being Ahmad, but when he came to them with clear explanations they said, "This is clear magic.
7. And who is more unjust than he who forges a lie against God and he is invited to Islam, and God does not guide the unjust people.
8. They desire to put out the light of God with their mouths but God will perfect His light, though the unbelievers may be averse.
9. He it is Who sent His Prophet with the guidance and the true religion, that He may make it overcome the religions, all of them, though the polytheists may be averse.
10. Oh you who believe! shall I lead you to a merchandise which may deliver you from a painful punishment?
11. You shall believe in God and His Prophet, and struggle hard in God's way with your property and your lives; that is better for you, did you but know!
12. He will forgive you your faults and cause you to enter into gardens, beneath which rivers flow, and fine dwellings in gardens of perpetuity; that is the mighty achievement;
13. And yet another blessing that you love: help from God and a victory near at hand; and give good news to the believers.
14. Oh you who believe! be helpers in the cause of God, as~ Jesus son of Mary said to his disciples: Who are my helpers in the cause of God? The disciples said, "We are helpers in the cause of God. So a party of the children of Israel believed and another party disbelieved; then We aided those who believed against their enemy, and they became uppermost.

Chapter 62 — Al-Jumu'ah — The Congregation

In the name of God, the Kind, the Merciful.

1. Whatever is in the heavens and whatever is in the earth declares the glory of God, the King, the Holy, the Mighty, the Wise.
2. He it is Who raised among the inhabitants of Mecca a Prophet from among themselves, who recites to them His words and purifies them, and teaches them the Book and the Wisdom, although they were before certainly in clear error,
3. And others from among them who have not yet joined them; and He is the Mighty, the Wise.
4. That is God's grace; He grants it to whom He pleases, and God is the Lord of mighty grace.
5. The likeness of those who were charged with the Torah, then they did not observe it, is as the likeness of the ass bearing books, evil is the likeness of the people who reject the words of God; and God does not guide the unjust people.
6. Say, "Oh you who are Jews, if you think that you are the favorites of God to the exclusion of other people, then invoke death If you are truthful.
7. And they will never invoke it because of what their hands have sent before; and God is Cognizant of the unjust.
8. Say, "As for the death from which you flee, that will certainly overtake you, then you shall be sent back to the Knower of the unseen and the seen, and He will inform you of that which you did.
9. Oh you who believe! when the call is made for prayer on Friday, then hasten to the remembrance of God and leave off trading; that is better for you, if you know.
10. But when the prayer is ended, then disperse abroad in the land and seek of God's grace, and remember God much, that you may be successful.
11. And when they see merchandise or sport they break up for It, and leave you standing. Say, "What is with God is better than sport and better than merchandise, and God is the best of Sustainers.

Chapter 63 — Al-Munafiqun — The Hypocrites

In the name of God, the Kind, the Merciful.

1. When the hypocrites come to you, they say, "We bear witness that you are most certainly God's Prophet; and God knows that you are most certainly His Prophet, and God bears witness that the hypocrites are certainly liars.
2. They make their oaths a shelter, and thus turn away from God's way; certainly evil is that which they do.
3. That is because they believe, then disbelieve, so a seal is set upon their hearts so that they do not understand.
4. And when you see them, their persons will please you, and If they speak, you will listen to their speech; they are as if they were big pieces of wood clad with garments; they think every cry to be against them. They are the enemy, therefore beware of them; may God destroy them, from where are they turned back?
5. And when it is said to them: Come, the Prophet of God will ask forgiveness for you, they turn back their heads and you may see them turning away while they are big with pride.
6. It is alike to them whether you beg forgiveness for them or do not beg forgiveness for them; God will never forgive them; certainly God does not guide the transgressing people.
7. They it is who say, "Do not spend upon those who are with the Prophet of God until they break up. And God's are the treasures of the heavens and the earth, but the hypocrites do not understand.
8. They say, "If we return to Medina, the mighty will certainly drive out the meaner therefrom; and to God belongs the might and to His Prophet and to the believers, but the hypocrites do not know.
9. Oh you who believe! let not your wealth, or your children, divert you from the remembrance of God; and whoever does that, these are the losers.
10. And spend out of what We have given you before death comes to one of you, so that he should say, "My Lord! why did You not lull me to a near term, so that I should have given alms and been of the doers of good deeds?
11. And God does not respite a soul when its appointed term has come, and God is Aware of what you do.

Chapter 64 — Al-Taghabun — The Mutual Deceit

In the name of God, the Kind, the Merciful.

1. Whatever is in the heavens and whatever is in the earth declares the glory of God; to Him belongs the kingdom, and to Him is due all praise, and He has power over all things.
2. He it is Who created you, but one of you is an unbeliever and another of you is a believer; and God sees what you do.
3. He created the heavens and the earth with truth, and He formed you, and then made your forms well, and He is the ultimate destination.
4. He knows what is in the heavens and the earth, and He knows what you hide and what you manifest; and God is Cognizant of what is in the hearts.
5. Has there not come to you the story of those who disbelieved before, then tasted the evil result of their conduct, and they had a painful punishment?
6. That is because there came to them their apostles with clear explanations, but they said, "Shall mortals guide us? So they disbelieved and turned back, and God does not stand in need of anything, and God is Self-sufficient, Praised.
7. Those who disbelieve think that they shall never be raised. Say, "Aye! by my Lord! you shall most certainly be raised, then you shall most certainly be informed of what you did; and that is easy to God.
8. Therefore believe in God and His Prophet and the Light which We have revealed; and God is Aware of what you do.
9. On the day that He will gather you for the day of gathering, that is the day of loss and gain; and whoever believes in God and does good, He will remove from him his evil and cause him to enter gardens beneath which rivers flow, to abide therein forever; that is the great achievement.
10. And as for those who disbelieve and reject Our words, they are the inmates of the fire, to abide therein and evil is the resort.
11. No harm comes about but by God's permission; and whoever believes in God, He guides aright his heart; and God is Cognizant of all things.
12. And obey God and obey the Prophet, but if you turn back, then upon Our Prophet devolves only the clear delivery of the message. 13. God, there is no god but He; and upon God, then, let the believers rely.
14. Oh you who believe! certainly from among your wives and your children there is an enemy to you; therefore beware of them; and if you pardon and forbear and forgive, then certainly God is Forgiving, Merciful.
15. Your possessions and your children are only a trial, and God it is with Whom is a great reward.
16. Therefore be careful of your duty to God as much as you can, and hear and obey and spend, it is better for your souls; and whoever is saved from the greediness of his soul, these it is that are the successful.
17. If you set apart for God a proper portion, He will double it for you and forgive you; and God is the Multiplier of rewards, Forbearing,
18. The Knower of the unseen and the seen, the Mighty, the Wise.

Chapter 65 — Al-Talaq — The Divorce

In the name of God, the Kind, the Merciful.

1. Oh Prophet! when you divorce women, divorce them for- their prescribed time, and calculate the number of the days prescribed, and be careful of your duty to God, your Lord. Do not drive them out of their houses, nor should they themselves go forth, unless they commit an open indecency; and these are the limits of God, and whoever goes beyond the limits of God, he indeed does injustice to his own soul. You do not know that God may after that bring about reunion.

2. So when they have reached their prescribed time, then retain them with kindness or separate them with kindness, and call to witness two men of justice from among you, and give upright testimony for God. With that is reprimanded he who believes in God and the latter day; and whoever is careful
of his duty to God, He will make for him an outlet,

3. And give him sustenance from from where he thinks not; and whoever trusts in God, He is sufficient for him; certainly God attains His purpose; God indeed has appointed a measure for everything.

4. And as for those of your women who have despaired of menstruation, if you have a doubt, their prescribed time shall be three months, and of those too who have not had their courses; and as for the pregnant women, their prescribed time is that they lay down their burden; and whoever is careful of
his duty to God He will make easy for him his affair.

5. That is the command of God which He has revealed to you, and whoever is careful of his duty to God, He will remove from him his evil and give him a big reward.

6. Lodge them where you lodge according to your means, and do not injure them in order that you may straighten them; and it they are pregnant, spend on them until they lay down their burden; then if they suckle for you, give them their repayment and enjoin one another among you to do good; and if you
disagree, another woman shall suckle for him.

7. Let him who has abundance spend out of his abundance and whoever has his means of subsistence straightened to him, let him spend out of that which God has given him; God does not lay on any soul a burden except to the extent to which He has granted it; God brings about ease after difficulty.

8. And how many a town which rebelled against the commandment of its Lord and His apostles, so We called it to account severely and We reprimandd it with a stern punishment.

9. So it tasted the evil result of its conduct, and the end of its affair was hell.

10. God has prepared for them severe punishment, therefore be careful of your duty to God, Oh men of understanding who believe! God has indeed revealed to you a reminder,

11. An Prophet who recites to you the clear words of God so that he may bring forth those who believe and do good deeds from darkness into light; and whoever believes in God and does good deeds, He will cause him to enter gardens beneath which rivers now, to abide therein forever, God has indeed given him proper sustenance.

12. God is He Who created seven heavens, and of the earth the like of them; the decree continues to descend among them, that you may know that God has power over all things and that God indeed encompasses all things in His knowledge.

Chapter 66 — Al- Tahrim — The Prohibition

In the name of God, the Kind, the Merciful.

1. Oh Prophet! why do you forbid yourself that which God has made lawful for you; you seek to please your wives; and God is Forgiving, Merciful.

2. God indeed has sanctioned for you the expiation of your oaths and God is your Protector, and He is the Knowing the Wise.

3. And when the prophet secretly communicated a piece of information to one of his wives -- but when she informed others of it, and God made him to know it, he made known part of it and avoided part; so when he informed her of it, she said, "Who informed you of this? He said, "The Knowing, the one Aware,
informed me.

4. If you both turn to God, then indeed your hearts are already inclined to this; and if you back up each other against him, then certainly God it is Who is his Guardian, and Gabriel and-the believers that do good, and the angels after that are the aiders.

5. Maybe, his Lord, if he divorce you, will give him in your place wives better than you, submissive, faithful, obedient, penitent, adorers, fasters, widows and virgins.

6. Oh you who believe! save yourselves and your families from a fire whose fuel is men and stones; over it are angels stern and strong, they do not disobey God in what He commands them, and do as they are commanded.

7. Oh you who disbelieve! do not urge excuses today; you shall be rewarded only according to what you did.

8. Oh you who believe! turn to God a sincere turning; maybe your Lord will remove from you your evil and cause you to enter gardens beneath which rivers flow, on the day on which God will not abase the Prophet and those who believe with him; their light shall run on before them and on their right hands; they shall say, "Our Lord! make perfect for us our light, and grant us protection, certainly You have power over all things.

9. Oh Prophet! strive hard against the unbelievers and the hypocrites, and be hard against them; and their home is hell; and evil is the resort.

10. God sets forth an example to those who disbelieve the wife of Noah and the wife of Lot: they were both under two of Our righteous servants, but they acted treacherously towards them so they availed them nothing against God, and it was said, "Enter both the fire with those who enter.

11. And God sets forth an example to those who believe the wife of Pharoah when she said, "My Lord! build for me a house with You in the garden and deliver me from Pharoah and his doing, and deliver me from the unjust people:

12. And Mary, the daughter of Imran, who guarded her chastity, so We breathed into her of Our inspiration and she accepted the truth of the words of her Lord and His books, and she was of, the obedient ones.

Chapter 67 — Al-Mulak — The Kingdom

In the name of God, the Kind, the Merciful.
1. Blessed is He in Whose hand is the kingdom, and He has power over all things,
2. Who created death and life that He may try you -- which of you is best in deeds; and He is the Mighty, the Forgiving,
3. Who created the seven heavens one above another; you see no incongruity in the creation of the Kind God; then look again, can you see any disorder?
4. Then turn back the eye again and again; your look shall '~ come back to you confused while it is fatigued.
5. And certainly We have adorned this lower heaven with lamps and We have made these missiles for the Satans, and We have prepared for them the punishment of burning.
6. And for those who disbelieve in their Lord is the punishment of hell, and evil is the resort.
7. When they shall be cast therein, they shall hear a loud moaning of it as it heaves,
8. Almost bursting for fury. Whenever a group is cast into it, its keeper shall ask them: Did there not come to you a alarmgiver?
9. They shall say, "Yea! indeed there came to us a alarmgiver, but we rejected him and said, "God has not revealed anything, you are only in a great error.
10. And they shall say, "Had we but listened or pondered, we should not have been among the inmates of the burning fire.
11. So they shall acknowledge their sins, but far will be forgiveness from the inmates of the burning fire.
12. As for those who fear their Lord in secret, they shall certainly have forgiveness and a great reward.
13. And conceal your word or emphasize it; certainly He is Cognizant of what is in the hearts.
14. Does He not know, Who created? And He is the Knower of the subtleties, the Aware.
15. He it is Who made the earth smooth for you, therefore go about in the spacious sides thereof, and eat of His sustenance, and to Him is the return after death.
16. Are you secure of those in the heaven that He should not make the earth to swallow you up? Then lo! it shall be in a state of commotion.
17. Or are you secure of those in the heaven that He should not send down upon you a punishment? Then shall you know how was My warning.
18. And certainly those before them rejected the truth, then how was My disapproval.
19. Have they not seen the birds above them expanding their wings and contracting them? What is it that withholds them save the Kind God? Certainly He sees everything.
20. Or who is it that will be a host for you to assist you besides the Kind God? The unbelievers are only in deception.
21. Or who is it that will give you sustenance if He should withhold His sustenance? No! they persist in disdain and aversion.
22. What! is he who goes prone upon his face better guided or he who walks upright upon a straight path?
23. Say, "He it is Who brought you into being and made for you the ears and the eyes and the hearts: little is it that you give thanks.
24. Say, "He it is Who multiplied you in the earth and to Him you shall be gathered.

²⁵. And they say, "When shall this threat be executed if you are truthful?

²⁶. Say, "The knowledge thereof is only with God and I am only a simple messenger.

²⁷. But when they shall see it nearby, the faces of those who disbelieve shall be sorry, and it shall be said; This is that which you used to call for.

²⁸. Say, "Have you considered if God should destroy me and those with me -- rather He will have mercy on us; yet who will protect the unbelievers from a painful punishment?

²⁹. Say, "He is the Kind God, we believe in Him and on Him do we rely, so you shall come to know who it is that is in clear error.

³⁰. Say, "Have you considered if your water should go down, who is it then that will bring you flowing water?

Chapter 68 — Al-Qalam — The Pen

In the name of God, the Kind, the Merciful.
1. Noon. I swear by the pen and what the angels write,
2. By the grace of your Lord you are not mad.
3. And most certainly you shall have a reward never to be cut off.
4. And most certainly you conform yourself to sublime morality.
5. So you shall see, and they too shall see,
6. Which of you is afflicted with madness.
7. Certainly your Lord knows best him who errs from His way, and He knows best the followers of the right course.
8. So do not yield to the rejecters.
9. They wish that you should be pliant so they too would be pliant.
10. And yield not to any mean swearer
11. Defamer, going about with slander
12. Forbidder of good, outstepping the limits, sinful,
13. Ignoble, besides all that, base-born;
14. Because he possesses wealth and sons.
15. When Our words are recited to him, he says: Stories of those of yore.
16. We will brand him on the nose.
17. Certainly We will try them as We tried the owners of the garden, when they swore that they would certainly cut off the produce in the morning,
18. And were not willing to set aside a portion for the poor.
19. Then there encompassed it a visitation from your Lord while they were sleeping.
20. So it became as black, barren land.
21. And they called out to each other in the morning,
22. Saying, "Go early to your tilled soil if you would cut the produce.
23. So they went, while they consulted together secretly,
24. Saying, "No poor man shall enter it today upon you.
25. And in the morning they went, having the power to prevent.
26. But when they saw it, they said, "Most certainly we have gone astray
27. No! we are made to suffer privation.
28. The best of them said, "Did I not say to you, Why do you not glorify God?
29. They said, "Glory be to our Lord, certainly we were unjust.
30. Then some of them advanced against others, blaming each other.
31. Said they: Oh woe to us! certainly we were inordinate:
32. Maybe, our Lord will give us instead one better than it; certainly to our Lord do we make our humble petition.
33. Such is the punishment, and certainly the punishment of the hereafter is greater, did they but know!
34. Certainly those who guard against evil shall have with their Lord gardens of bliss.
35. What! shall We then make i. e. treat those who submit as the guilty?
36. What has happened to you? How do you judge?
37. Or have you a book wherein you read,

38. That you have certainly therein what you choose?
39. Or have you received from Us an agreement confirmed by an oath extending to the day of resurrection that you shall certainly have what you demand?
40. Ask them which of them will vouch for that,
41. Or have they associates if they are truthful.
42. On the day when there shall be a severe sickness, and they shall be called upon to make obeisance, but they shall not be able,
43. Their looks cast down, abasement shall overtake them; and they were called upon to make obeisance indeed while yet they were safe.
44. So leave Me and him who rejects this announcement; We will overtake them by degrees, from where they perceive not:
45. And I do bear with them, certainly My plan is firm.
46. Or do you ask from them a reward, so that they are burdened with debt?
47. Or have they the knowledge of the unseen, so that they write it down?
48. So wait patiently for the judgment of your Lord, and do not be like the companion of the fish, when he cried while he was in distress.
49. Were it not that favor from his Lord had overtaken him, he would certainly have been cast down upon the naked Found while he was blamed.
50. Then his Lord chose him, and He made him of the good.
51. And those who disbelieve would almost smite you with their eyes when they hear the reminder, and they say, "Most certainly he is mad.
52. And it is nothing but a reminder to the nations.

Chapter 69 — Al-Haqqah — The Inevitable

In the name of God, the Kind, the Merciful.

1. The sure calamity!
2. What is the sure calamity!
3. And what would make you realize what the sure calamity is!
4. Samood and Ad called the striking calamity a lie.
5. Then as to Samood, they were destroyed by an excessively severe punishment.
6. And as to Ad, they were destroyed by a roaring, violent blast.
7. Which He made to prevail against them for seven nights and eight days unremittingly, so that you might have seen the people therein prostrate as if they were the trunks of hollow palms.
8. Do you then see of them one remaining?
9. And Pharoah and those before him and the overthrown cities continuously committed sins.
10. And they disobeyed the Prophet of their Lord, so He punished them with a vehement punishment.
11. Certainly We bore you up in the ship when the water rose high,
12. So that We may make it a reminder to you, and that the retaining ear might retain it.
13. And when the trumpet is blown with a single blast,
14. And the earth and the mountains are borne away and crushed with a single crushing.
15. On that day shall the great event come to pass,
16. And the heaven shall cleave asunder, so that on that day it shall be frail,
17. And the angels shall be on the sides thereof; and above I them eight shall bear on that day your Lord's power.
18. On that day you shall be exposed to view -- no secret of yours shall remain hidden.
19. Then as for him who is given his book in his right hand, he will say, "Lo! read my book:
20. Certainly I knew that I shall meet my account.
21. So he shall be in a life of pleasure,
22. In a lofty garden,
23. The fruits of which are near at hand:
24. Eat and drink pleasantly for what you did beforehand in the days gone by.
25. And as for him who is given his book in his left hand he shall say, "Oh would that my book had never been given me:
26. And I had not known what my account was:
27. Oh would that it had made an end of me:
28. My wealth has availed me nothing:
29. My authority is gone away from me.
30. Lay hold on him, then put a chain on him,
31. Then cast him into the burning fire,
32. Then thrust him into a chain the length of which is seventy cubits.
33. Certainly he did not believe in God, the Great,
34. Nor did he urge the feeding of the poor.
35. Therefore he has not here today a true friend,
36. Nor any food except refuse,
37. Which none but the wrongdoers eat.

38. But no! I swear by that which you see,
39. And that which you do not see.
40. Most certainly, it is the Word brought by an honored Prophet,
41. And it is not the word of a poet; little is it that you believe;
42. Nor the word of a soothsayer; little is it that you mind.
43. It is a revelation from the Lord of the worlds.
44. And if he had fabricated against Us some of the sayings,
45. We would certainly have seized him by the right hand,
46. Then We would certainly have cut off his aorta.
47. And not one of you could have withheld Us from him.
48. And most certainly it is a reminder for those who guard against evil.
49. And most certainly We know that some of you are rejecters.
50. And most certainly it is a great grief to the unbelievers.
51. And most certainly it is the true certainty
52. Therefore-glorify the name of your Lord, the Great.

Chapter 70 — Al-Mu'arij — The Ways of Ascent

In the name of God, the Kind, the Merciful.
1. One demanding, demanded the punishment which must happen to
2. The unbelievers -- there is none to avert it --
3. From God, the Lord of the ways of Ascent.
4. To Him ascend the angels and the Spirit in a day the measure of which is fifty thousand years.
5. Therefore endure with worthy patience.
6. Certainly they think it to be far off,
7. And We see it nearby.
8. On the day when the heaven shall be as molten copper
9. And the mountains shall be as tufts of wool
10. And friend shall not ask of friend
11. Though they shall be made to see each other. The guilty one would fain redeem himself from the punishment of that day by sacrificing his children,
12. And his wife and his brother
13. And the nearest of his kinsfolk who gave him shelter,
14. And all those that are in the earth, wishing then that this might deliver him.
15. By no means! Certainly it is a flaming fire
16. Dragging by the head,
17. It shall claim him who turned and fled from truth,
18. And amasses wealth then shuts it up.
19. Certainly man is created of a hasty temperament
20. Being greatly grieved when evil afflicts him
21. And wretched when good happens to him
22. Except those who pray,
23. Those who are constant at their prayer
24. And those in whose wealth there is a fixed portion.
25. For him who begs and for him who is denied good
26. And those who accept the truth of the judgment day
27. And those who are fearful of the punishment of their Lord --
28. Certainly the punishment of their Lord is a thing not to be felt secure of --
29. And those who guard their private parts,
30. Except in the case of their wives or those whom their right hands possess -- for these certainly are not to be blamed,
31. But he who seeks to go beyond this, these it is that go beyond the limits --
32. And those who are faithful to their trusts and their covenant
33. And those who are upright in their testimonies,
34. And those who keep a guard on their prayer,
35. Those shall be in gardens, honored.
36. But what is the matter with those who disbelieve that they hasten on around you,
37. On the right hand and on the left, in sundry parties?
38. Does every man of them desire that he should be made to enter the garden of bliss?

³⁹. By no means! Certainly We have created them of what they know.
⁴⁰. But no! I swear by the Lord of the Easts and the Wests that We are certainly able
⁴¹. To bring instead others better than them, and We shall not be overcome.
⁴². Therefore leave them alone to go on with the false discourses and to sport until they come face to face with that day of theirs with which they are threatened;
⁴³. The day on which they shall come forth from their graves in haste,
as if they were hastening on to a goal,
⁴⁴. Their eyes cast down; disgrace shall overtake them; that is the day which they were threatened with.

Chapter 71 — Nuh — Noah

In the name of God, the Kind, the Merciful.

1. Certainly We sent Noah to his people, saying, "Warn your people before there come upon them a painful punishment.
2. He said, "Oh my people! Certainly I am a plain alarmgiver to you:
3. That you should serve God and be careful of your duty to Him and obey me:
4. He will forgive you some of your faults and grant you a delay to an appointed term; certainly the term of God when it comes is not postponed; did you but know!
5. He said, "Oh my Lord! certainly I have called my people by night and by day!
6. But my call has only made them flee the more:
7. And whenever I have called them that You might forgive them, they put their fingers in their ears, cover themselves with their garments, and persist and are puffed up with pride:
8. Then certainly I called to them aloud:
9. Then certainly I spoke to them in public and I spoke to them in secret:
10. Then I said, Ask forgiveness of your Lord, certainly He is the most Forgiving:
11. He will send down upon you the cloud, pouring down abundance of rain:
12. And help you with wealth and sons, and make for you gardens, and make for you rivers.
13. What is the matter with you that you fear not the greatness of God?
14. And indeed He has created you through various grades:
15. Do you not see how God has created the seven heavens ,- one above another,
16. And made the moon therein a light, and made the sun a lamp?
17. And God has made you grow out of the earth as a growth:
18. Then He returns you to it, then will He bring you forth a new bringing forth:
19. And God has made for you the earth a wide expanse,
20. That you may go along therein in wide paths.
21. Noah said, "My Lord! certainly they have disobeyed me and followed him whose wealth and children have added to him nothing but loss.
22. And they have planned a very great plan.
23. And they say, "By no means leave your gods, nor leave Wadd, nor Suwa; nor Yaghus, and Yauq and Nasr.
24. And indeed they have led astray many, and do not increase the unjust in at all but in error.
25. Because of their wrongs they were drowned, then made to enter fire, so they did not find any helpers besides God.
26. And Noah said, "My Lord! leave not upon the land any dweller from among the unbelievers:
27. For certainly if You leave them they will lead astray Your servants, and will not beget any but immoral, ungrateful children
28. My Lord! forgive me and my parents and him who enters my house believing, and the believing men and the believing women; and do not increase the unjust in anyting but destruction!

Chapter 72 — Al-Jinn — The Jinn

In the name of God, the Kind, the Merciful.

1. Say, "It has been revealed to me that a party of the jinn listened, and they said, "Certainly we have heard a wonderful Koran,
2. Guiding to the right way, so we believe in it, and we will not set up any one with our Lord:
3. And that He -- exalted be the majesty of our Lord -- has not taken a consort, nor a son:
4. And that the foolish amongst us used to forge extravagant things against God:
5. And that we thought that men and jinn did not utter a lie against God:
6. And that persons from among men used to seek refuge with persons from among jinn, so they increased them in wrongdoing:
7. And that they thought as you think, that God would not raise anyone:
8. And that we sought to reach heaven, but we found it filled with strong guards and flaming stars.
9. And that we used to sit in some of the sitting-places thereof to steal a hearing, but he who would try to listen now would find a flame lying in wait for him:
10. And that we know not whether evil is meant for those who are on earth or whether their Lord means to bring them good:
11. And that some of us are good and others of us are below that: we are sects following different ways:
12. And that we know that we cannot escape God in the earth, nor can we escape Him by flight:
13. And that when we heard the guidance, we believed in it; so whoever believes in his Lord, he should neither fear loss nor being overtaken by disgrace:
14. And that some of us are those who submit, and some of us are the deviators; so whoever submits, these aim at the right way:
15. And as to the deviators, they are fuel of hell:
16. And that if they should keep to the right way, We would certainly give them to drink of abundant water,
17. So that We might try them with respect to it; and whoever turns aside from the reminder of his Lord, He will make him enter into an afflicting punishment:
18. And that the mosques are God's, therefore call not upon any one with God:
19. And that when the servant of God stood up calling upon Him, they nearly crowded him to death.
20. Say, "I only call upon my Lord, and I do not associate any one with Him.
21. Say, "I do not control for you evil or good.
22. Say, "Certainly no one can protect me against God, nor can I find besides Him any place of refuge:
23. It is only a delivering of words from God and His messages; and whoever disobeys God and His Prophet certainly he shall have the fire of hell to abide therein for a long time.
24. Until when they see what they are threatened with, then shall they know who is weaker in helpers and fewer in number.
25. Say, "I do not know whether that with which you are threatened be nearby or whether my Lord will appoint for it a term:
26. The Knower of the unseen! so He does not reveal His secrets to any,
27. Except to him whom He chooses as an apostle; for certainly He makes a guard to march

before him and after him,

²⁸. So that He may know that they have truly delivered the messages of their Lord, and He encompasses what is with them and He records the number of all things.

Chapter 73 — Al-Muzzammil — The Wrapped Up

In the name of God, the Kind, the Merciful.

1. Oh you who have wrapped up in your garments!
2. Rise to pray in the night except a little,
3. Half of it, or lessen it a little,
4. Or add to it, and recite the Koran as it ought to be recited.
5. Certainly We will make to light upon you a weighty Word.
6. Certainly the rising by night is the firmest way to tread and the best corrective of speech.
7. Certainly you have in the day time a long occupation.
8. And remember the name of your Lord and devote yourself to Him with exclusive devotion.
9. The Lord of the East and the West -- there is no god but He -- therefore take Him for a protector.
10. And bear patiently what they say and avoid them with a becoming avoidance.
11. And leave Me and the rejecters, the possessors of ease and plenty, and respite them a little.
12. Certainly with Us are heavy fetters and a flaming fire,
13. And food that chokes and a painful punishment,
14. On the day when the earth and the mountains shall quake and the mountains shall become as heaps of sand let loose.
15. Certainly We have sent to you a Prophet, a witness against you, as We sent an apostle to Pharoah.
16. But Pharoah disobeyed the apostle, so We laid on him a violent hold.
17. How, then, will you guard yourselves, if you disbelieve, on the day which shall make children grey-headed?
18. The heaven shall rend asunder thereby; His promise is ever brought to fulfillment.
19. Certainly this is a reminder, then let him, who will take the way to his Lord.
20. Certainly your Lord knows that you pass in prayer nearly two-thirds of the night, and sometimes half of it, and sometimes a third of it, and also a party of those with you; and God measures the night and the day. He knows that you are not able to do it, so He has turned to you mercifully, therefore read what is easy of the Koran. He knows that there must be among you sick, and others who travel in the land seeking of the bounty of God, and others who fight in God's way, therefore read as much of it as is easy to you, and keep up prayer and pay the poor-rate and offer to God a fine gift, and whatever of good you send on beforehand for yourselves, you will find it with God; that is best and greatest in reward; and ask forgiveness of God; certainly God is Forgiving, Merciful.

Chapter 74 — Al-Mudathir — The Covered One

In the name of God, the Kind, the Merciful.

1. Oh you who are clothed!
2. Arise and warn,
3. And your Lord do magnify,
4. And your garments do purify,
5. And uncleanness do shun,
6. And bestow not favors that you may receive again with increase,
7. And for the sake of your Lord, be patient.
8. For when the trumpet is sounded,
9. That, at that time, shall be a difficult day,
10. For the unbelievers, anything but easy.
11. Leave Me and him whom I created alone,
12. And give him vast riches,
13. And sons dwelling in his presence,
14. And I adjusted affairs for him adjustably;
15. And yet he desires that I should add more!
16. By no means! certainly he offers opposition to Our words.
17. I will make a distressing punishment overtake him.
18. Certainly he reflected and guessed,
19. But may he be cursed how he plotted;
20. Again, may he be cursed how he plotted;
21. Then he looked,
22. Then he frowned and scowled,
23. Then he turned back and was big with pride,
24. ~Then he said, "This is nothing but sorcery, narrated from others;"
25. This is nothing but the word of a mortal.
26. I will cast him into hell.
27. And what will make you realize what hell is?
28. It leaves nothing nor does it spare anything.
29. It scorches the mortal.
30. Over it are nineteen.
31. And We have not made the wardens of the fire others than angels, and We have not made their number but as a trial for those who disbelieve, that those who have been given the book may be certain and those who believe may increase in faith, and those who have been given the book and the believers may not doubt, and that those in whose hearts is a disease and the unbelievers may say, "What does God mean by this story? Thus does God make err whom He pleases, and He guides whom He pleases, and none knows the hosts of your Lord but He Himself; and this is nothing but a reminder to the mortals.
32. No; I swear by the moon,
33. And the night when it departs,
34. And the daybreak when it shines;
35. Certainly it hell is one of the gravest misfortunes,

36. A warning to mortals,
37. To him among you who wishes to go forward or remain behind.
38. Every soul is held in pledge for what it earns,
39. Except the people of the right hand,
40. In gardens, they shall ask each other
41. About the guilty:
42. What has brought you into hell?
43. They shall say, "We were not of those who prayed;
44. And we used not to feed the poor;
45. And we used to enter into vain discourse with those who entered into vain discourses.
46. And we used to call the day of judgment a lie;
47. Till death overtook us.
48. So the intercession of advocates shall not avail them.
49. What is then the matter with them, that they turn away from the admonition
50. As if they were asses taking fright
51. That had fled from a lion?
52. No; every one of them desires that he may be given pages spread out;
53. No! but they do not fear the hereafter.
54. No! it is certainly an admonition.
55. So whoever pleases may mind it.
56. And they will not mind unless God please. He is worthy to be feared and worthy to forgive.

Chapter 75 — Al-Qiyamah — The Resurrection

In the name of God, the Kind, the Merciful.
1. No! I swear by the day of resurrection.
2. No! I swear by the self-accusing soul.
3. Does man think that We shall not gather his bones?
4. Yea! We are able to make complete his very fingertips
5. No! man desires to give the lie to what is before him.
6. He asks: When is the day of resurrection?
7. So when the sight becomes dazed,
8. And the moon becomes dark,
9. And the sun and the moon are brought together,
10. Man shall say on that day: Whither to fly to?
11. By no means! there shall be no place of refuge!
12. With your Lord alone shall on that day be the place of rest.
13. Man shall on that day be informed of what he sent before and what he put off.
14. No! man is evidence against himself,
15. Though he puts forth his excuses.
16. Do not move your tongue with it to make haste with it,
17. Certainly on Us devolves the collecting of it and the reciting of it.
18. Therefore when We have recited it, follow its recitation.
19. Again on Us devolves the explaining of it.
20. No! But you love the present life,
21. And neglect the hereafter.
22. Some faces on that day shall be bright,
23. Looking to their Lord.
24. And other faces on that day shall be gloomy,
25. Knowing that there will be made to happen to them some great calamity.
26. No! When it comes up to the throat,
27. And it is said, "Who will be a magician?
28. And he is sure that it is the hour of parting
29. And sickness is combined with sickness;
30. To your Lord on that day shall be the driving.
31. So he did not accept the truth, nor did he pray,
32. But called the truth a lie and turned back,
33. Then he went to his followers, walking away in haughtiness.
34. Nearer to you is destruction and nearer,
35. Again consider how nearer to you and nearer.
36. Does man think that he is to be left to wander without an aim?
37. Was he not a small seed in the seminal elements,
38. Then he was a clot of blood, so He created him then made him perfect.
39. Then He made of him two kinds, the male and the female.
40. Is not He able to give life to the dead?

Chapter 76 — Al-Dahr — Time

In the name of God, the Kind, the Merciful.

1. There certainly came over man a period of time when he was a thing not worth mentioning.
2. Certainly We have created man from a small life-germ uniting itself: We mean to try him, so We have made him hearing, seeing.
3. Certainly We have shown him the way: he may be thankful or unthankful.
4. Certainly We have prepared for the unbelievers chains and shackles and a burning fire.
5. Certainly the righteous shall drink of a cup the admixture of which is camphor
6. A fountain from which the servants of God shall drink; they make it to flow forth well.
7. They fulfill vows and fear a day the evil of which shall be spreading far and wide.
8. And they give food out of love for Him to the poor and the orphan and the captive:
9. We only feed you for God's sake; we desire from you neither reward nor thanks:
10. Certainly we fear from our Lord a stern, distressful day.
11. Therefore God win guard them from the evil of that day and cause them to meet with ease and happiness;
12. And reward them, because they were patient, with garden and silk,
13. Reclining therein on raised couches, they shall find therein neither the severe heat of the sun nor intense cold.
14. And close down upon them shall be its shadows, and its fruits shall be made near to them, being easy to reach.
15. And there shall be made to go round about them vessels of silver and goblets which are of glass,
16. Transparent as glass, made of silver; they have measured them according to a measure.
17. And they shall be made to drink therein a cup the admixture of which shall be ginger,
18. Of a fountain therein which is named Salsabil.
19. And round about them shall go youths never altering in age; when you see them you will think them to be scattered pearls.
20. And when you see there, you shall see blessings and a great kingdom.
21. Upon them shall be garments of fine green silk and thick silk interwoven with gold, and they shall be adorned with bracelets of silver, and their Lord shall make them drink a pure drink.
22. Certainly this is a reward for you, and your striving shall be repaid.
23. Certainly We Ourselves have revealed the Koran to you revealing it in portions.
24. Therefore wait patiently for the command of your Lord, and obey not from among them a sinner or an ungrateful one.
25. And glorify the name of your Lord morning and evening.
26. And during part of the night adore Him, and give glory to Him a long part of the night.
27. Certainly these love the transitory and neglect a grievous day before them.
28. We created them and made firm their make, and when We please We will bring in their place the likes of them by a change.
29. Certainly this is a reminder, so whoever pleases takes to his Lord a way.
30. And you do not please except that God please, certainly God is Knowing, Wise;
31. He makes whom He pleases to enter into His mercy; and as for the unjust, He has prepared for them a painful punishment.

Chapter 77 — Al-Mursulat — Those Sent Forth

In the name of God, the Kind, the Merciful.
1. I swear by the emissary winds, sent one after another for men's benefit,
2. By the raging hurricanes,
3. Which scatter clouds to their destined places,
4. Then separate them one from another,
5. Then I swear by the angels who bring down the revelation,
6. To clear or to warn.
7. Most certainly what you are threatened with must come to pass.
8. So when the stars are made to lose their light,
9. And when the heaven is rent asunder,
10. And when the mountains are carried away as dust,
11. And when the apostles are gathered at their appointed time.
12. To what day is the doom fixed?
13. To the day of decision.
14. And what will make you comprehend what the day of decision is?
15. Woe on that day to the rejecters.
16. Did We not destroy the former generations?
17. Then did We follow them up with later ones.
18. Even thus shall We deal with the guilty.
19. Woe on that day to the rejecters.
20. Did We not create you from contemptible water?
21. Then We placed it in a secure resting-place,
22. Till an appointed term,
23. So We proportion it -- how well are We at proportioning things.
24. Woe on that day to the rejecters.
25. Have We not made the earth to draw together to itself,
26. The living and the dead,
27. And made therein lofty mountains, and given you to drink of sweet water?
28. Woe on that day to the rejecters.
29. Walk on to that which you called a lie.
30. Walk on to the covering having three branches,
31. Neither having the coolness of the shade nor availing against the flame.
32. Certainly it sends up sparks like palaces,
33. As if they were tawny camels.
34. Woe on that day to the rejecters.
35. This is the day on which they shall not speak,
36. And permission shall not be given to them so that they should offer excuses.
37. Woe on that day to the rejecters.
38. This is the day of decision: We have gathered you and those of yore.
39. So if you have a plan, plan against Me now.
40. Woe on that day to the rejecters.
41. Certainly those who guard against evil shall be amid shades and fountains,

42. And fruits such as they desire.
43. Eat and drink pleasantly because of what you did.
44. Certainly thus do We reward the doers of good.
45. Woe on that day to the rejecters.
46. Eat and enjoy yourselves for a little; certainly you are guilty.
47. Woe on that day to the rejecters.
48. And where it is said to them: Bow down, they do not bow down.
49. Woe on that day to the rejecters.
50. In what announcement, then, after it, will they believe?

Chapter 78 — Al-Naba' — The Great Event

In the name of God, the Kind, the Merciful.
1. Of what do they ask one another?
2. About the great event,
3. About which they differ?
4. No! they shall soon come to know
5. No! No! they shall soon know.
6. Have We not made the earth an even expanse?
7. And the mountains as projections thereon?
8. And We created you in pairs,
9. And We made your sleep to be restful to you,
10. And We made the night to be a covering,
11. And We made the day for seeking livelihood.
12. And We made above you seven strong ones,
13. And We made a shining lamp,
14. And We send down from the clouds water pouring forth abundantly,
15. That We may bring forth thereby corn and herbs,
16. And gardens dense and luxuriant.
17. Certainly the day of decision is a day appointed:
18. The day on which the trumpet shall be blown so you shall come forth in hosts,
19. And the heaven shall be opened so that it shall be all openings,
20. And the mountains shall be moved off so that they shall remain a mere semblance.
21. Certainly hell lies in wait,
22. A place of resort for the inordinate,
23. Living therein for ages.
24. They shall not taste therein cool nor drink
25. But boiling and intensely cold water,
26. Requital corresponding.
27. Certainly they feared not the account,
28. And called Our words a lie, giving the lie to the truth.
29. And We have recorded everything in a book,
30. So taste! for We will not add to you anything but punishment.
31. Certainly for those who guard against evil is achievement,
32. Gardens and vineyards,
33. And those showing freshness of youth, equals in age,
34. And a pure cup.
35. They shall not hear therein any vain words nor lying.
36. A reward from your Lord, a gift according to a judging:
37. The Lord of the heavens and the earth and what is between them, the Kind God, they shall not be able to address Him.
38. The day on which the spirit and the angels shall stand in ranks; they shall not speak except he whom the Kind God permits and who speaks the right thing.

³⁹. That is the sure day, so whoever desires may take refuge with his Lord.
⁴⁰. Certainly We have warned you of a punishment near at hand: the day when man shall see what his two hands have sent before, and the unbeliever shall say, "O! would that I were dust!

Chapter 79 — Al-Nazi'at — The Draggers

In the name of God, the Kind, the Merciful.
1. I swear by the angels who violently pull out the souls of the wicked,
2. And by those who gently draw out the souls of the blessed,
3. And by those who float in space,
4. Then those who are foremost going ahead,
5. Then those who regulate the affair.
6. The day on which the quaking one shall quake,
7. What must happen afterwards shall follow it.
8. Hearts on that day shall palpitate,
9. Their eyes cast down.
10. They say, "Shall we indeed be restored to our first state?
11. What! when we are rotten bones?
12. They said, "That then would be a return occasioning loss.
13. But it shall be only a single cry,
14. When lo! they shall be wakeful.
15. Has not there come to you the story of Moses?
16. When his Lord called upon him in the holy valley, twice,
17. Go to Pharoah, certainly he has become inordinate.
18. Then say, "Have you a desire to purify yourself:
19. And I will guide you to your Lord so that you should fear.
20. So he showed him the mighty sign.
21. But he rejected the truth and disobeyed.
22. Then he went back hastily.
23. Then he gathered men and called out.
24. Then he said, "I am your lord, the most high.
25. So God seized him with the punishment of the hereafter and the former life.
26. Most certainly there is in this a lesson to him who fears.
27. Are you the harder to create or the heaven? He made it.
28. He raised high its height, then put it into a right good state.
29. And He made dark its night and brought out its light.
30. And the earth, He expanded it after that.
31. He brought forth from it its water and its pasturage.
32. And the mountains, He made them firm,
33. A provision for you and for your cattle.
34. But when the great predominating calamity comes;
35. The day on which man shall recollect what he strove after,
36. And the hell shall be made obvious to him who sees
37. Then as for him who is inordinate,
38. And prefers the life of this world,
39. Then certainly the hell, that is the home.
40. And as for him who fears to stand in the presence of his Lord and forbids the soul from low desires,

41. Then certainly the garden -- that is the home.
42. They ask you about the hour, when it will come.
43. About what! You are one to remind of it.
44. To your Lord is the goal of it.
45. You are only a alarmgiver to him who would fear it.
46. On the day that they see it, it will be as though they had not tarried but the latter part of a day or the early part of it.

Chapter 80 — 'Abasa — He Frowned

In the name of God, the Kind, the Merciful.
1. He frowned and turned his back,
2. Because there came to him the blind man.
3. And what would make you know that he would purify himself,
4. Or become reminded so that the reminder should profit him?
5. As for him who considers himself free from need of you,
6. To him do you address yourself.
7. And no blame is on you if he would not purify himself
8. And as to him who comes to you striving hard,
9. And he fears,
10. From him will you divert yourself.
11. No! certainly it is an admonishment.
12. So let him who pleases mind it.
13. In honored books,
14. Exalted, purified,
15. In the hands of scribes
16. Noble, virtuous.
17. Cursed be man! how ungrateful is he!
18. Of what thing did He create him?
19. Of a small seed; He created him, then He made him according to a measure,
20. Then as for the way -- He has made it easy for him
21. Then He causes him to die, then assigns to him a grave,
22. Then when He pleases, He will raise him to life again.
23. No; but he has not done what He bade him.
24. Then let man look to his food,
25. That We pour down the water, pouring it down in abundance,
26. Then We cleave the earth, cleaving it asunder,
27. Then We cause to grow therein the grain,
28. And grapes and clover,
29. And the olive and the palm,
30. And thick gardens,
31. And fruits and herbage
32. A provision for you and for your cattle.
33. But when the deafening cry comes,
34. The day on which a man shall fly from his brother,
35. And his mother and his father,
36. And his spouse and his son --
37. Every man of them shall on that day have an affair which will occupy him.
38. Many faces on that day shall be bright,
39. Laughing, joyous.
40. And many faces on that day, on them shall be dust,
41. Darkness shall cover them.
42. These are they who are unbelievers, the wicked.

Chapter 81 — Al-Takwir — The Folded Up

In the name of God, the Kind, the Merciful.

1. When the sun is covered,
2. And when the stars darken,
3. And when the mountains are made to pass away,
4. And when the camels are left untended,
5. And when the wild animals are made to go forth,
6. And when the seas are set on fire,
7. And when souls are united,
8. And when the female infant buried alive is asked
9. For what sin she was killed,
10. And when the books are spread,
11. And when the heaven has its covering removed,
12. And when the hell is kindled up,
13. And when the garden is brought nearby,
14. Every soul shall then know what it has prepared.
15. But no! I swear by the stars,
16. That run their course and hide themselves,
17. And the night when it departs,
18. And the morning when it brightens,
19. Most certainly it is the Word of an honored messenger,
20. The processor of strength, having an honorable place with the Lord of the Dominion,
21. One to be obeyed, and faithful in trust.
22. And your companion is not gone mad.
23. And of a truth he saw himself on the clear horizon.
24. Nor of the unseen is he a tenacious concealer.
25. Nor is it the word of the cursed Satan,
26. Whither then will you go?
27. It is nothing but a reminder for the nations,
28. For him among you who pleases to go straight.
29. And you do not please except that God please, the Lord of the worlds.

Chapter 82 — Al-Infitar — The Rending

In the name of God, the Kind, the Merciful.
1. When the heaven becomes torn apart,
2. And when the stars become dispersed,
3. And when the seas are made to flow forth,
4. And when the graves are laid open,
5. Every soul shall know what it has sent before and held back.
6. Oh man ! what has beguiled you from your Lord, the Kind one,
7. Who created you, then made you complete, then made you symmetrical?
8. Into whatever form He pleased He constituted you.
9. No! but you give the lie to the judgment day,
10. And most certainly there are keepers over you
11. Honorable recorders,
12. They know what you do.
13. Most certainly the righteous are in bliss,
14. And most certainly the wicked are in burning fire,
15. They shall enter it on the day of judgment.
16. And they shall by no means be absent from it.
17. And what will make you realize what the day of judgement is?
18. Again, what will make you realize what the day of judgment is?
19. The day on which no soul shall control anything for another soul; and the command on that day shall be entirely God's.

Chapter 83 — Al-Tatfif — The Measruement Cheaters

In the name of God, the Kind, the Merciful.

1. Woe to the defrauders,
2. Who, when they take the measure of their dues from men take it fully,
3. But when they measure out to others or weigh out for them, they are deficient.
4. Do not these think that they shall be raised again
5. For a mighty day,
6. The day on which men shall stand before the Lord of the worlds?
7. No! most certainly the record of the wicked is in the Sijjin.
8. And what will make you know what the Sijjin is?
9. It is a written book.
10. Woe on that day to the rejecters,
11. Who give the lie to the day of judgment.
12. And none gives the lie to it but every exceeder of limits, sinful one
13. When Our words are recited to him, he says: Stories of those of yore.
14. No! rather, what they used to do has become like rust . upon their hearts.
15. No! most certainly they shall on that day be debarred from their Lord.
16. Then most certainly they shall enter the burning fire.
17. Then shall it be said, "This is what you gave the lie to.
18. No! Most certainly the record of the righteous shall be in the Iliyin.
19. And what will make you know what the highest Iliyin is?
20. It is a written book,
21. Those who are drawn near to God shall witness it.
22. Most certainly the righteous shall be in bliss,
23. On thrones, they shall gaze;
24. You will recognize in their faces the brightness of bliss.
25. They are made to quaff of a pure drink that is sealed to others.
26. The sealing of it is with musk; and for that let the aspirers aspire.
27. And the admixture of it is a water of Tasnim,
28. A fountain from which drink they who are drawn near to God.
29. Certainly they who are guilty used to laugh at those who believe.
30. And when they passed by them, they winked at one another.
31. And when they returned to their own followers they returned exulting.
32. And when they saw them, they said, "Most certainly these are in error;
33. And they were not sent to be keepers over them.
34. So today those who believe shall laugh at the unbelievers;
35. On thrones, they will look.
36. Certainly the disbelievers are rewarded as they did.

Chapter 84 — Al-Inshiqaq — The Tearing Apart

In the name of God, the Kind, the Merciful.
1. When Heaven bursts apart,
2. And obeys its Lord and it must.
3. And when the earth is stretched,
4. And casts forth what is in it and becomes empty,
5. And obeys its Lord and it must.
6. Oh man! certainly you must strive to attain to your Lord, a hard striving until you meet Him.
7. Then as to him who is given his book in his right hand,
8. He shall be reckoned with by an easy judging,
9. And he shall go back to his people joyful.
10. And as to him who is given his book behind his back,
11. He shall call for hell,
12. And enter into burning fire.
13. Certainly he was erstwhile joyful among his followers.
14. Certainly he thought that he would never return.
15. Yea! certainly his Lord does ever see him.
16. But no! I swear by the sunset redness,
17. And the night and that which it drives on,
18. And the moon when it grows full,
19. That you shall most certainly enter one state after another.
20. But what is the matter with them that they do not believe,
21. And when the Koran is recited to them they do not make obeisance?
22. No! those who disbelieve give the lie to the truth.
23. And God knows best what they hide,
24. So announce to them a painful punishment~
25. Except those who believe and do good; for them is a reward that shall never be cut off.

Chapter 85 — Al-Buruj — The Celestial Stations

In the name of God, the Kind, the Merciful.

1. I swear by the mansions of the stars,
2. And the promised day,
3. And the bearer of witness and those against whom the witness is borne.
4. Cursed be the makers of the pit,
5. Of the fire kept burning with fuel,
6. When they sat by it,
7. And they were witnesses of what they did with the believers.
8. And they did not take vengeance on them for anything except that they believed in God, the Mighty, the Praised,
9. Whose is the kingdom of the heavens and the earth; and God is a Witness of all things.
10. Certainly as for those who persecute the believing men and the believing women, then do not repent, they shall have the punishment of hell, and they shall have the punishment of burning.
11. Certainly as for those who believe and do good, they shall have gardens beneath which rivers flow, that is the great achievement.
12. Certainly the might of your Lord is great.
13. Certainly He it is Who originates and reproduces,
14. And He is the Forgiving, the Loving,
15. Lord of the Arsh, the Glorious,
16. The great doer of what He will.
17. Has not there come to you the story of the hosts,
18. Of Pharoah and Samood?
19. No! those who disbelieve are in the act of giving the lie to the truth.
20. And God encompasses them on every side.
21. No! it is a glorious Koran,
22. In a guarded tablet.

Chapter 86 — Al-Tariq — The Nightly Visitor

In the name of God, the Kind, the Merciful.
1. I swear by the heaven and the comer by night;
2. And what will make you know what the comer by night is?
3. The star of piercing brightness;
4. There is not a soul but over it is a keeper.
5. So let man consider of what he is created:
6. He is created of water pouring forth,
7. Coming from between the back and the ribs.
8. Most certainly He is able to return him to life.
9. On the day when hidden things shall be made manifest,
10. He shall have neither strength nor helper.
11. I swear by the rain-giving heavens,
12. And the earth splitting with plants;
13. Most certainly it is a decisive word,
14. And it is no joke.
15. Certainly they will make a scheme,
16. And I too will make a scheme.
17. So grant the unbelievers a respite: let them alone for a

Chapter 87 — Al-A'la — The Most High

In the name of God, the Kind, the Merciful.

1. Glorify the name of your Lord, the Most High,
2. Who creates, then makes complete,
3. And Who makes things according to a measure, then guides them to their goal,
4. And Who brings forth herbage,
5. Then makes it dried up, dust-colored.
6. We will make you recite so you shall not forget,
7. Except what God pleases, certainly He knows the manifest, and what is hidden.
8. And We will make your way smooth to a state of ease.
9. Therefore do remind, certainly reminding does profit.
10. He who fears will mind,
11. And the most unfortunate one will avoid it,
12. Who shall enter the great fire;
13. Then therein he shall neither live nor die.
14. He indeed shall be successful who purifies himself,
15. And magnifies the name of his Lord and prays.
16. No! you prefer the life of this world,
17. While the hereafter is better and more lasting.
18. Most certainly this is in the earlier scriptures,
19. The scriptures of Abraham and Moses.

Chapter 88 — Al-Ghashiyah — The Calamity

In the name of God, the Kind, the Merciful.
1. Has not there come to you the news of the calamity?
2. Some faces on that day shall be downcast,
3. Laboring, toiling,
4. Entering into burning fire,
5. Made to drink from a boiling spring.
6. They shall have no food but of thorns,
7. Which will neither fatten nor avail against hunger.
8. Other faces on that day shall be happy,
9. Well-pleased because of their striving,
10. In a lofty garden,
11. Wherein you shall not hear vain talk.
12. Therein is a fountain flowing,
13. Therein are thrones raised high,
14. And drinking-cups ready placed,
15. And cushions set in a row,
16. And carpets spread out.
17. Will they not then consider the camels, how they are created?
18. And the heaven, how it is reared aloft,
19. And the mountains, how they are firmly fixed,
20. And the earth, how it is made a vast expanse?
21. Therefore do remind, for you are only a reminder.
22. You are not a watcher over them;
23. But whoever turns back and disbelieves,
24. God will punish him with the greatest punishment.
25. Certainly to Us is their turning back,
26. Then certainly upon Us is the taking of their account.

Chapter 89 — Al-Fajr — The Daybreak

In the name of God, the Kind, the Merciful.

1. I swear by the daybreak,
2. And the ten nights,
3. And the even and the odd,
4. And the night when it departs.
5. Truly in that there is an oath for those who possess understanding.
6. Have you not considered how your Lord dealt with Ad,
7. The people of Aram, possessors of lofty buildings,
8. The like of which were not created in the other cities;
9. And with Samood, who hewed out the rocks in the valley,
10. And with Pharoah, the lord of hosts,
11. Who committed inordinacy in the cities,
12. So they made great mischief therein?
13. Therefore your Lord let down upon them a portion of the punishment.
14. Most surely your Lord is watching.
15. And as for man, when his Lord tries him, then treats him with honor and makes him lead an easy life, he says: My Lord honors me.
16. But when He tries him differently, then straightens to him his means of subsistence, he says: My Lord has disgraced me.
17. No! but you do not honor the orphan,
18. Nor do you urge one another to feed the poor,
19. And you eat away the heritage, devouring everything indiscriminately,
20. And you love wealth with exceeding love.
21. No! when the earth is made to crumble to pieces,
22. And your Lord comes and also the angels in ranks,
23. And hell is made to appear on that day. On that day shall man be mindful, and what shall being mindful then avail him?
24. He shall say, "O! would that I had sent before for this my life!
25. But on that day shall no one punish with anything like His punishment,
26. And no one shall bind with anything like His binding.
27. Oh soul that are at rest!
28. Return to your Lord, well-pleased with him, well-pleasing Him,
29. So enter among My servants,
30. And enter into My garden.

Chapter 90 — Al-Balad — The City

In the name of God, the Kind, the Merciful.
1. No! I swear by this city.
2. And you shall be made free from obligation in this city --
3. And the begetter and whom he begot.
4. Certainly We have created man to be in distress.
5. Does he think that no one has power over him?
6. He shall say, "I have wasted much wealth.
7. Does he think that no one sees him?
8. Have We not given him two eyes,
9. And a tongue and two lips,
10. And pointed out to him the two conspicuous ways?
11. But he would not attempt the uphill road,
12. And what will make you comprehend what the uphill road is?
13. It is the setting free of a slave,
14. Or the giving of food in a day of hunger
15. To an orphan, having relationship,
16. Or to the poor man lying in the dust.
17. Then he is of those who believe and charge one another to show patience, and charge one another to show compassion.
18. These are the people of the right hand.
19. And as for those who disbelieve in our words, they are the people of the left hand.
20. On them is fire closed over.

Chapter 91 — Al-Shams — The Sun

In the name of God, the Kind, the Merciful.
1. I swear by the sun and its brilliance,
2. And the moon when it follows the sun,
3. And the day when it shows it,
4. And the night when it draws a veil over it,
5. And the heaven and Him Who made it,
6. And the earth and Him Who extended it,
7. And the soul and Him Who made it perfect,
8. Then He inspired it to understand what is right and wrong for it;
9. He will indeed be successful who purifies it,
10. And he will indeed fail who corrupts it.
11. Samood gave the lie to the truth in their inordinacy,
12. When the most unfortunate of them broke forth with
13. So God's apostle said to them Leave alone God's she-camel, and give her to drink.
14. But they called him a liar and slaughtered her, therefore their Lord crushed them for their sin and leveled them with the ground.
15. And He fears not its consequence.

Chapter 92 — Al-Lail — The Night

In the name of God, the Kind, the Merciful.
1. I swear by the night when it draws a veil,
2. And the day when it shines in brightness,
3. And the creating of the male and the female,
4. Your striving is most certainly directed to various ends.
5. Then as for him who gives away and guards against evil,
6. And accepts the best,
7. We will facilitate for him the easy end.
8. And as for him who is wretched and considers himself free from need of God,
9. And rejects the best,
10. We will facilitate for him the difficult end.
11. And his wealth will not avail him when he perishes.
12. Certainly Ours is it to show the way,
13. And most certainly Ours is the hereafter and the former.
14. Therefore I warn you of the fire that flames:
15. None shall enter it but the most unhappy,
16. Who gives the lie to the truth and turns his back.
17. And away from it shall be kept the one who guards most against evil,
18. Who gives away his wealth, purifying himself
19. And no one has with him any boon for which he should be rewarded,
20. Except the seeking of the pleasure of his Lord, the Most High.
21. And he shall soon be well-pleased.

Chapter 93 — Al-Duha — The Brightness

In the name of God, the Kind, the Merciful.

1. I swear by the early hours of the day,
2. And the night when it covers with darkness.
3. Your Lord has not abandoned you, nor has He become displeased,
4. And certainly what comes after is better for you than that which has gone before.
5. And soon will your Lord give you so that you shall be well pleased.
6. Did He not find you an orphan and give you shelter?
7. And find you lost i. e. unrecognized by men and guide them to you?
8. And find you in want and make you to be free from want?
9. Therefore, as for the orphan, do not oppress him.
10. And as for him who asks, do not chide him,
11. And as for the favor of your Lord, do announce it.

Chapter 94 — Al-Inshirah — The Expansion

In the name of God, the Kind, the Merciful.
1. Have We not expanded for you your heart,
2. And taken off from you your burden,
3. Which pressed heavily upon your back,
4. And exalted for you your esteem?
5. Certainly with difficulty is ease.
6. With difficulty is certainly ease.
7. So when you are free, nominate.
8. And make your Lord your exclusive object.

Chapter 95 — Al-Tin — The Fig

In the name of God, the Kind, the Merciful.
1. I swear by the fig and the olive,
2. And mount Sinai,
3. And this city made secure,
4. Certainly We created man in the best make.
5. Then We render him the lowest of the low.
6. Except those who believe and do good, so they shall have a reward never to be cut off.
7. Then who can give you the lie after this about the judgment?
8. Is not God the best of the Judges?

Chapter 96 — Al-'Alaq — The Clot

In the name of God, the Kind, the Merciful.
1. Read in the name of your Lord Who created.
2. He created man from a clot.
3. Read and your Lord is Most Honorable,
4. Who taught to write with the pen
5. Taught man what he knew not.
6. No! man is most certainly inordinate,
7. Because he sees himself free from want.
8. Certainly to your Lord is the return.
9. Have you seen him who forbids
10. A servant when he prays?
11. Have you considered if he were on the right way,
12. Or enjoined guarding against evil?
13. Have you considered if he gives the lie to the truth and turns his back?
14. Does he not know that God does see?
15. No! if he desist not, We would certainly smite his forehead,
16. A lying, sinful forehead. 17. Then let him summon his council,
18. We too would summon the braves of the army.
19. No! obey him not, and make obeisance and draw near to God.

Chapter 97 — Al-Qadr — The Grandeur

In the name of God, the Kind, the Merciful.
1. Certainly We revealed it on the grand night.
2. And what will make you comprehend what the grand night
3. The grand night is better than a thousand months.
4. The angels and Gibreel descend in it by the permission of their Lord for every affair,
5. Peace! it is till the break of the morning.

Chapter 98 — Al-Bayyinah — The Clear Evidence

In the name of God, the Kind, the Merciful.

1. Those who disbelieved from among the followers of the Book and the polytheists could not have separated from the faithful until there had come to them the clear evidence:
2. An apostle from God, reciting pure pages,
3. Wherein are all the right ordinances.
4. And those who were given the Book did not become divided except after clear evidence had come to them.
5. And they were not enjoined anything except that they should serve God, being sincere to Him in obedience, upright, and keep up prayer and pay the poor-rate, and that is the right religion.
6. Certainly those who disbelieve from among the followers of the Book and the polytheists shall be in the fire of hell, abiding therein; they are the worst of men.
7. As for those who believe and do good, certainly they are the-best of men.
8. Their reward with their Lord is gardens of perpetuity beneath which rivers flow, abiding therein for ever; God is well pleased with them and they are well pleased with Him; that is for him who fears his Lord.

Chapter 99 — Al-Zilzal — The Quaking

In the name of God, the Kind, the Merciful.
1. When the earth is shaken with her violent shaking,
2. And the earth brings forth her burdens,
3. And man says: What has happened tp her?
4. On that day she shall tell her news,
5. Because your Lord had inspired her.
6. On that day men shall come forth in sundry bodies that they may be shown their works.
7. So. he who has done an atom's weight of good shall see it
8. And he who has done an atom's weight of evil shall see it.

Chapter 100 — Al-'Adiyat — The Chargers

In the name of God, the Kind, the Merciful.
1. I swear by the runners breathing pantingly,
2. Then those that produce fire striking,
3. Then those that make raids at morn,
4. Then thereby raise dust,
5. Then rush thereby upon an assembly:
6. Most certainly man is ungrateful to his Lord.
7. And most certainly he is a witness of that.
8. And most certainly he is tenacious in the love of wealth.
9. Does he not then know when what is in the graves is raised,
10. And what is in the hearts is made apparent?
11. Most certainly their Lord that day shall be fully aware of them.

Chapter 101 — Al-Qari'ah — The Calamity

In the name of God, the Kind, the Merciful.
1. The terrible calamity!
2. What is the terrible calamity?
3. And what will make you comprehend what the terrible calamity is?
4. The day on which men shall be as scattered moths,
5. And the mountains shall be as loosened wool.
6. Then as for him whose measure of good deeds is heavy,
7. He shall live a pleasant life.
8. And as for him whose measure of good deeds is light,
His home shall be the abyss.
And what will make you know what it is?
11. A burning fire.

Chapter 102 — Al-Takathur — Striving in Abundance

In the name of God, the Kind, the Merciful.
1. Abundance diverts you,
2. Until you come to the graves.
3. No! you shall soon know,
4. No! No! you shall soon know.
5. No! if you had known with a certain knowledge,
6. You should most certainly have seen the hell;
7. Then you shall most certainly see it with the eye of certainty;
8. Then on that day you shall most certainly be questioned about the bounty.

Chapter 103 — Al-'Asr — The Age

In the name of God, the Kind, the Merciful.

[1]. I swear by the time,

[2]. Most certainly man is in loss,

[3]. Except those who believe and do good, and urge on each other truth, and urge on each other patience.

Chapter 104 — Al-Humazah — The Slanderer

In the name of God, the Kind, the Merciful.
1. Woe to every slanderer, defamer,
2. Who amasses wealth and considers it a provision against mishap;
3. He thinks that his wealth will make him immortal.
4. No! he shall most certainly be hurled into the crushing disaster,
5. And what will make you realize what the crushing disaster is?
6. It is the fire kindled by God,
7. Which rises above the hearts.
8. Certainly it shall be closed over upon them,
9. In extended columns.

Chapter 105 — Al-Fil — The Elephant

In the name of God, the Kind, the Merciful.
1. Have you not considered how your Lord dealt with the possessors of the elephant?
2. Did He not cause their war to end in confusion,
3. And send down to prey upon them birds in flocks,
4. Casting against them stones of baked clay,
5. So He rendered them like straw eaten up?

Chapter 106 — Al-Quraish — The Quraish Clan

In the name of God, the Kind, the Merciful.
[1]. For the protection of the Quraish --
[2]. Their protection during their trading caravans in the winter and the summer –
[3]. So let them serve the Lord of this House
[4] Who feeds them against hunger and gives them security against fear.

Chapter 107 — l-Ma'un — Alms

In the name of God, the Kind, the Merciful.
1. Have you considered him who calls the judgment a lie?
2. That is the one who treats the orphan with harshness,
3. And does not urge others to feed the poor.
4. So woe to the praying ones,
5. Who are unmindful of their prayers,
6. Who do good to be seen,
7. And withhold the necessaries of life.

Chapter 108 — Al-Kauthar — The Abundance of Good

In the name of God, the Kind, the Merciful.
1. Certainly We have given you the fountain of abundance,
2. Therefore pray to your Lord and make a sacrifice.
3. Certainly your enemy is the one who shall be without a future.

Chapter 109 — Al-Kafirun — The Unbelievers

In the name of God, the Kind, the Merciful.
1. Say, "Oh unbelievers!
2. I do not serve that which you serve,
3. Nor do you serve Him Whom I serve:
4. Nor am I going to serve that which you serve,
5. Nor are you going to serve Him Whom I serve:
6. You shall have your religion and I shall have my religion.

Chapter 110 — Al-Nasr — The Aid

In the name of God, the Kind, the Merciful.
1. When there comes the aid of God and the victory,
2. And you see men entering the religion of God in companies,
3. Then celebrate the praise of your Lord, and ask His forgiveness; certainly He will often show mercy.

Chapter 111 — Al-Lahab — The Flame

In the name of God, the Kind, the Merciful.
1. Hell overtake both hands of Abu Lahab, and he will perish.
2. His wealth and what he earns will not benefit him.
3. He shall soon burn in fire that flames,
4. And his wife, the bearer of fuel,
5. Upon her neck a halter of strongly twisted rope.

Chapter 112 — Al-Ikhlas — The Unity

In the name of God, the Kind, the Merciful.
1. Say, "He, God, is One.
2. God is He on Whom all depend.
3. He begets not, nor is He begotten.
4. And none is like Him.

Chapter 113 — Al-Falaq —The Dawn

In the name of God, the Kind, the Merciful.
1. Say, "I seek refuge in the Lord of the dawn,
2. From the evil of what He has created,
3. And from the evil of the utterly dark night when it comes,
4. And from the evil of those who blow on knots,
5. And from the evil of the envious when he envies

Chapter 114 — Al-Nas — The People

In the name of God, the Kind, the Merciful.
1. Say, "I seek refuge in the Lord of men,
2. The King of men,
3. The God of men,
4. From the evil of the whisperings of the slinking Satan,
5. Who whispers into the hearts of men,
6. From among the demons (jinns) and the men.

NOTES

NOTES

NOTES

NOTES

THE KORAN

SAINT GAUDENS MODERN ENGLISH VERSION

Edited by
Kevin E. Ready

www.ingramcontent.com/pod-product-compliance
Lightning Source LLC
Chambersburg PA
CBHW020055020526
44112CB00031B/174